NATURAL ACTS

CLASS : CULTURE

NATURAL ACTS

GENDER, RACE, AND RUSTICITY IN COUNTRY MUSIC

Pamela Fox

THE UNIVERSITY OF MICHIGAN PRESS

Ann Arbor

2012   2011   2010   2009   4   3   2   1

A CIP catalog record for this book is available from the British Library.

Library of Congress Cataloging-in-Publication Data

Fox, Pamela, 1958–
Natural acts : gender, race, and rusticity in country music /
Pamela Fox.
p. cm. — (Class: culture)
Includes bibliographical references and index.
ISBN 978-0-472-07068-8 (cloth : alk. paper)
ISBN 978-0-472-05068-0 (pbk. : alk. paper)
1. Country music—History and criticism.   2. Women country
musicians—United States.   3. Blackface entertainers—United States.
4. Sex role in music.   I. Title.
ML3524.F73   2009
781.64209—dc22   2009018641

FOR MARK AND ANA

ACKNOWLEDGMENTS

Although completion of this book has been a long time coming, it gives me pleasure to remember, and to thank, all who helped to sustain me *and* my work through these years of research and writing.

I am deeply indebted to the support of other scholars in the fields of country and popular music studies, as well as working-class studies, whose own work has inspired and energized me. Their generous offers of time and astute advice on grant proposals, chapter drafts, or conference papers—all of the myriad stages that nudge a book project along—have been invaluable. Sincere thanks to George Lipsitz, Barry Shank, Aaron Fox, and Gayle Wald; Amy Lang and Bill Mullen—the editors of the Class : Culture series; and especially Barbara Ching, who has encouraged my efforts from the outset and developed into both a good friend and a trenchant collaborator. I am also grateful to the anonymous reviewers of the manuscript, whose rigorous yet good-natured feedback helped greatly improve the final version.

Equal appreciation goes to other colleagues and friends who have cheered me on over the long haul and in some cases also commented on parts of the book: Caren Kaplan; Lindsay Kaplan; Michael Ragussis; Elizabeth Velez; Samantha Pinto; You-Me Park; Leona Fisher; Gay Cima; Lucy Maddox; Lori Merish; Steve Wurtzler; Barbara, Sam, and Ethan Dyer; Peggy Shaker and Holmes Brown; and Sheila and Peter Rowny. My family in Illinois—mother, sisters, nieces, and nephews—have also patiently put up with truncated or distracted visits over the years as I have put time on task. I thank them for their understanding and interest.

I have received significant institutional support as well. Georgetown University's Graduate School and English Department have awarded me numerous grants and research fellowships that guaranteed precious writing/research time. The English Department's administrative assistant, Donna Even-Kesef, cheerfully and oh-so-skillfully helped me assemble the manuscript; Pema Levy served as my indefatigable student research assistant, insisting that no request was too small or too large; and English Department graduate students Jennifer Goff, Kathryn Jett, and Robyn Russo expressed unflagging enthusiasm for both country music itself and my approach to its study.

I also want to acknowledge the tremendous support I received from the research staff at the Country Music Hall of Fame and Museum, particularly senior historian John Rumble, who was exceptionally generous with his time and expertise; Tim Davis, the photo collection manager; and Lauren Bufferd, who guided my initial archival work. This book would not have been possible without their knowledge and assistance.

My editor at the University of Michigan Press, LeAnn Fields, deserves special recognition. I cannot thank her enough for both her faith in this project and her patience as we saw it through to fruition. It was a pleasure and a privilege to work with someone so astute about the complex intersections of working-class and country music culture. I prized not only her keen vision but her extraordinary kindness: both inform every facet of this book.

But without a doubt, I am most indebted to Mark Popovich and our daughter, Ana, who bore the brunt of my cumulative hours away writing, thinking, and listening with characteristic good humor and resilience. I am grateful for your unfailing support, which ranged from emotional and intellectual sustenance to daily partnership on the nitty-gritty details of family life (not to mention more immersion in country music than you had ever bargained for . . . but you've come to love it as much as I always have, right? Right?). This book is lovingly dedicated to you both.

Portions of this book have appeared elsewhere in slightly different forms. An abbreviated version of chapter 4 was first published as "Recycled 'Trash': Gender and Authenticity in Country Music Autobiography" in *American Quarterly* 50, no. 2 (June 1998): 234–66, and a selection from chapter 5 first appeared as "Time as 'Revelator': Alt.Country Women's Performance of the Past," in *Old Roots, New Routes: The Cultural Politics of Alt.Country Music*, ed. Pamela Fox and Barbara Ching (Ann Arbor: University of Michigan Press, 2008): 134–53.

CONTENTS

CHAPTER 1

Blacking Up and Dressing Down: Unmasking Country Music Authenticity

> The peculiarity of Southern experience didn't end when the boll weevil ate up the cotton crop. We didn't cease to be a separate country when Burger King came to Meridian. We're as peculiar a people now as we ever were, and the fact that our culture is under assault has forced us to become even more peculiar than we were before.
>
> —Dennis Covington, *Salvation on Sand Mountain: Snake Handling and Redemption in Southern Appalachia*

> "Authenticity" . . . is a quality not of the music as such (how it is actually made), but of the story it is heard to tell, the narrative of musical interaction in which the listeners place themselves.
>
> —Simon Frith, *Performing Rites: On the Value of Popular Music*

One winter night in 1950, the Grand Ole Opry featured its immensely popular, if waning, blackface comic duo Jamup and Honey, alongside current hit-maker Red Foley, perennial favorite "Cousin" Minnie Pearl, and newly rising star Hank Williams. While a typically haphazard mélange of barn dance acts, this program also brought together a particular collection of texts—skit, song, and introductory patter—highlighting country music's persistent roots in racial and class masquerade.[1] With great visual and verbal flare, the stage comedians predictably performed an exaggerated calculus of "country" identity, but the musical artists also invoked the history of vaudeville and minstrelsy: Williams sang his early smash hit "Lovesick Blues," which was first recorded by ex–Al Field's minstrel performer Emmett "Nigger" Miller, and Foley's novelty tune "Aunt Jemima's Plaster" introduced another suggestive icon from that tradition.[2] Rather than the domestic trademark for foodstuffs, however, Jemima here transforms into an entrepreneur selling the concoction called "oven plaster." A bizarre blend of sheepskin, beeswax, flax seed, buttermilk, and horse glue, the pastelike substance stops up holes and "cures anything from a chill to a cough." Though obscured somewhat by the song's crowd-pleasing comic refrain, this homemade appliqué or coating in fact functions as both healing and masking device with long-lasting effects: "you'll have trouble," Foley warns, "when you try to take it off."[3]

Referencing both the burnt-cork makeup of the blackface stage and the suspect remedies hawked by earlier medicine show "doctors," as well as barn dance sponsors (such as "Crazy Water Crystals"), Jemima's "plaster" can be read as just one kind of recurrent trope throughout country music history: the stylized mimicry of "white" and "black" rusticity that proves to be at once curative, constitutive, and concealing by simultaneously granting presence *and* absence.[4] It reappears in the post–civil rights era in only slightly less vulgar modes—of the *Hee Haw* variety—as well as subtler forms. Two up-to-the-moment examples culled from alternative and mainstream country demonstrate the resilience of both blackface and hillbilly posturing:

In 1992, folk/alt.country artist Michelle Shocked recorded *Arkansas Traveler,* a collection of nineteenth-century minstrel and fiddle tunes paired with original lyrics.[5] The album's liner notes reveal that Shocked initially sought to include a cover image of herself in blackface to "provide a genuine focus on the real 'roots'" of the music and to emphasize that the "blackface tradition is alive and well hidden behind a modern mask." Such masquerade offers Shocked an ostensibly "respectful" form of *transformation* accomplished through *identification,* yet it functions distinctly outside the parameters of realism and authenticity. The album-cover images playfully enact this dynamic within an equivalent visual economy of difference focused on white rusticity: on the front cover, Shocked poses as a postmodern version of the title song's slick "traveler" transposed onto a stereotypic barn dance stage set, while on the back of the album insert she conjures a respectable farm girl touting an old-fashioned microphone.

In 2005, mega–country star Faith Hill released to much fanfare the single and music video "Mississippi Girl," a carefully crafted tribute to her small-town Southern roots. This glamorous performer, who over time had followed Shania Twain into the lucrative crossover pop music market, suddenly engaged in a drastic image makeover, substituting mousy brown curls and broken-in jeans for her trademark platinum blond locks and designer gowns. More significantly, the song lyrics exploited another time-tested version of rusticity in this music—autobiographical claims to country authenticity—by reassuring her fans, "they might know me all around the world / But y'all I'm still a Mississippi girl."[6] Hill's down-home persona emerged at a strategic moment in the country industry. The maverick movement known as "alternative country," dedicated to restoring and revaluing country's traditions and authentic sound, had begun to influence (rather than simply critique) the mainstream, as evidenced by newcomer Gretchen Wilson: her eponymous "Redneck Woman" single, which soared to the top spot on the country singles charts in spring 2004, revived an older paradigm for country female performers by reaching back to the irrepressible hillbilly spirit of Loretta Lynn. One year later, Wilson's collaborator John Rich penned "Mississippi Girl" expressly for Hill, who watched it become the highest chart debut of *her* career.[7]

This book offers a new way of understanding these shifting renditions of rusticity by illuminating gender's role in the production of more explicitly classed and racialized performative practices. The Opry's Jemima, Shocked's tongue-in-cheek Arkansan rube, and Hill's Mississippi ingenue (a more innocent counterpart to Wilson's brassy "woman") serve as just three distinctly gendered inflections of "country" identity in need of fresh critical attention. *Natural Acts: Gender, Race, and Rusticity in Country Music* draws on the interdisciplinary fields of feminist cultural studies, working-class studies, popular music studies, and critical race studies to reexamine the relationship among three constructs: rusticity, authenticity, and country music history.

Authenticity has quite a storied history itself within both the country music industry and decades of evolving scholarship. While academia has for the most part abandoned the authentic as any kind of meaningful analytic category, country music discourse (in all arenas) has tended to preserve it, in hopes, perhaps, of underscoring this cultural form's very visibility and viability as an object of study. As John Hartigan Jr. has suggested generally about "white trash" representation, country music is one form of popular culture that until quite recently has proven singularly "unpopular" as both a consumer item for upscale audiences and a legitimate research area for cultural critics.[8] Whether associated with sound, a specific cultural, regional, or class identity, visual image, or audience, country authenticity has ensured the sheer *presence* of what Dennis Covington calls a "peculiar" and embattled people, even as its shifting construction has satirized, as well as idealized, country or folk culture. Despite its diverse iconography and uses, the definition of "country" has been traditionally grounded in rusticity, a class-based concept rooted in unspoiled rural life and values, as well as humble class origins. When extended to musical culture, it connotes plain, unpretentious arrangements; old-time instruments such as the banjo and fiddle; and performers who not only inspire audience identification but themselves identify with the songs they sing.[9]

Popular music critics since the 1970s have successfully framed the question of authenticity as a battle over country music's rustic "roots" and (hence) "soul." Lamenting country's increasing commercialization and crossover appeal, they argue that its earlier artistic integrity has been compromised, if not lost entirely, and that the music's connection to the American "common man" has been severed.[10] Until recently, country music historians have typically recast this notion of authenticity as a subcultural mode of opposition, examining the ways in which the country music performer can give voice to a specific, often overlooked experience and culture of class disenfranchisement.[11] This book aligns itself with an alternative wing of scholarship problematizing both of these assumptions by establishing that country music has been a commercial enterprise since its very inception. Richard Peterson, for instance, directly argues that the music's heralded "tradition" has always functioned as a marketable and ideological "resource," while Barbara Ching has convincingly approached "hard country" as self-conscious or performative "burlesque" rather than sincere or natural essence.[12] This book similarly investigates and in many ways deconstructs the notion of authenticity associated with country music's esteemed legacy of musical texts but argues that gender and race are equally important to its construction—indeed, are crucial to its very materialization. *Natural Acts* reveals how the uneven *coalescence* of gender, class, and race positionalities fuels country's claims to authenticity and its concomitant performative practices.

FEMINIST COUNTRY MUSIC SCHOLARSHIP

Popular feminist histories such as Mary Bufwack and Robert Oermann's *Finding Her Voice* have performed an invaluable service in documenting the "saga of women in country music."[13] Charting female performers' contributions to the genre from its earliest beginnings to its recent trends, *Finding Her Voice* set a new standard for country music historiography, restoring, as its title suggests, "'silenced' voices" to the conventional narrative and an exhaustive supply of materials to the collective archive. Its outlook and methodology, however, clearly grew out of 1970s-style second-wave feminism concentrated on identity politics and goals of "equal" representation. Although Bufwack and Oermann's study usefully presents itself as a "view of American society through the songs and styles of the working class," its intersectional approach tends to operate with a reductive conception of gender. Such historical surveys reproduce standard notions of authenticity, extending the category to include certain neglected women artists but stopping short of considering how unstable models of femininity and masculinity, working in conjunction with other markers of identity, shape the very definition of country identity.[14]

Joli Jensen and Barbara Ching have undoubtedly expanded this terrain in their respective examinations of the Nashville Sound and hard country. Both, for example, valuably critique gender codes governing the honky-tonk persona. Deeming the tavern and its musical culture "a man's world," Jensen notes that "the songs are usually sung by men, the majority of the customers are men, and the songs describe life from a man's point of view. Women appear in the honky-tonk world as fallen angels, corrupted by city life." Ching proposes a more complex rationale for white male dominance of this genre: although its "abjection is constantly portrayed by an absurdly unregenerate white man who jokes and suffers while women and conventionally successful men brandish . . . normative values," it "now seems a virtual monopoly of white males" because "a truly effective burlesque of the American dream must be enacted by those who in theory should stoically enjoy the privileges of power." Yet I think it's fair to say that gender remains a marginal concern to their projects as a whole, often too wedded to the literal (i.e., female vs. male performers).[15]

The 2004 essay collection *A Boy Named Sue: Gender and Country Music* has most recently advanced the discussion not only by positioning gender as "one of the central dynamics of country music history and culture" but by acknowledging that its "remarkably flexible" coding has been "far less predictable than the somewhat rigid dichotomy between male and female cultural domains that has characterized past scholarship on the subject would suggest."[16] Gender similarly constitutes the (tenuous) center of this study but only in its conjunction with race as well as class, to produce shifting models of authenticity at particular moments in country music history.[17] Since the mid-1980s, feminist theory has grappled with ways to move beyond standard identity politics and has variously envisioned the interconnections of these three conceptual categories within the arenas of social relations, identity formation, and cultural representation as "interlocking" structures or systems of oppression (such as capitalism and patriarchy); "intersectionality" of subordinate/dominant positionalities within women's daily lives; and "scattered hegemonies" of transnational power relations, to name but a few.[18] As Joan Acker writes, "scholars working on the interweaving of race, class, gender, and other axes, dimensions, or forms of inequality or exploitation agree that these are simultaneous processes, socially constructed, historically and geographically specific, and involving material, ideological, and psychological elements which create and recreate unequal economic and power distributions."[19] Yet those feminists explicitly focused on the relationship between gender and class—encompassing groups as variable as earlier Marxists and later materialists—struggle with articulating a structural model that actively accounts for racism, misogyny, and homophobia yet still retains class exploitation as the principal animating force of a capitalist social formation.[20]

Sociologists such as Acker and Beverly Skeggs offer particularly helpful frameworks. Acker begins with a model of class "practices" that become "racialized and gendered," so that "gender and racial/ethnic divisions, subordinations, and meanings are created as part of the material and ideological creation and recreation of class practices and relations," whether "pursuing material interests" in the workplace or constructing racialized images of femininity and masculinity to construct markets and particular workforce populations. Skeggs is more concerned with white British working-class women's attempts to reconfigure their class identities through access to cultural capital.[21] This book takes cues from both theorists as I explore the racialized and gendered class practices of a music industry clearly embedded in dominant class structures governed by white middle-to-upper-class men yet almost exclusively associated with Southern white rustic or working-class imagery, lowbrow cultural taste, and artists who convincingly represent both in their personal histories. To elucidate this music's periodic reinvention of authenticity, I attend to various texts, practices, and locations that figure shifting intersections of whiteness and blackness, femininity and masculinity, and low and "respectable" classes.

THEORIZING RUSTICITY

Natural Acts thus reads a wide array of country music texts as a series of gendering practices that alternately de- and *renaturalize* the white and largely working-class male and female performers of country music stages and recording studios from the 1930s through the present. Informed by the work of contemporary minstrelsy theorists such as Eric Lott and W. T. Lhamon Jr., as well as feminist theorists such as Acker, Skeggs, and Judith Butler, it analyzes the visual images, scripts, lyrics, publicity materials, published memoirs, and signature sounds of iconic artists such as Hank Williams, Kitty Wells, and Dolly Parton, critically neglected earlier performers such as Jamup and Honey and Jean Shepard, and very recent figures such as Gillian Welch in order to demonstrate how the performance of rusticity engages with myriad power dynamics in the construction of an authentic country subject. While poor or working-class white men serve as the normative model for authenticity in representational figures such as the country hillbilly and the more urban honky-tonk loner, white rusticity itself undergoes an initial feminization process that spurs subsequent efforts by modern and contemporary artists to reclaim masculinity.

To chart these discursive and representational transformations, I introduce a conception of rustic identity that certainly draws on nineteenth-century visions of the noble savage but also articulates a much more self-conscious and fraught understanding of its underside—a sudden, perilous slide into the distinctly *un*natural. As Sylvia Jenkins Cook and Anthony Harkins have established, "poor white" imagery found in both popular and highbrow magazines and novels from the eighteenth through the twentieth centuries frequently accentuated grotesque forms "quite out of the order of nature." This "unnatural" (non)subject also sported an ambiguous racial identity, as Harkins notes of the ubiquitous "hillbilly" archetype: "Middle-class white Americans could see these people as a fascinating and exotic 'other' akin to Native Americans or Blacks, while at the same time sympathize with them as poorer and less modern versions of themselves."[22] In the fledgling country music industry of the late 1920s and 1930s, this deformed and suspiciously "nonwhite" body, at times made startlingly real during the lean Depression years, became one notable backdrop for barn dance performers asked to fashion their own representations of "hillbilly" experience. Some rejected it outright, such as those who adopted the more respectable "mountaineer" pose, while others, especially comedians, further accentuated its excessive qualities. The specter continued to haunt country music, however, as it encountered various renditions of modernity in the postwar period and beyond.

Butler's larger theory of identity formation serves as a useful template for reading these performative images crafted in response to dominant prototypes—but with a twist. For Butler, every "act" of "assuming" an identity (be it sexed or raced—class doesn't merit explicit mention) requires the exclusion or repudiation of others. First, we identify with an abject position, then disavow it. In being compelled to adopt a heterosexual identity, for instance, we initially identify with homosexuality, then reject it for fear of being designated as "inhuman,"[23] occupying "those 'unlivable' and 'uninhabitable' zones of social life which are nevertheless densely populated by those who do not enjoy the status of the subject."[24] Country music, however, typically requires an identification *with* abjection: low Others marked off from the professional/intellectual middle-class arena who often express a measure of class consciousness. Performers and audiences must thus finally refuse the refusal, as it were, in order to claim an authentically rustic identity. The initial identification with class abjection never gets entirely disavowed.[25] Yet clearly, such identity comes at a price, prompting for some a complex, mediated strategy in its performance.

As Butler has handily demonstrated over the course of her career, gender is perhaps the key "site" for the articulation of naturalization discourses. Like racial performance, it functions as a mechanism for illustrating the mediated relationship between an "original" already signifying "the natural" and its stylized imitation. My approach, however, demands that such discourses and images be approached as racialized *and* gendered class practices—and further, not just in the quotidian and unconscious "assumption" of identity but in an explicitly theatrical mode of performance. Since Butler makes clear that her model of performative identity unequivocally involves "*not . . .* taking on a mask,"[26] minstrelsy theory is equally crucial to articulating the literal production of country authenticity in its early formulation on the barn dance stage. Eric Lott's 1993 pronouncement that "blackface, in a real if partial sense, figured class" reimagined the mask trope as a double-edged kind of "love" and "theft" of African American cultural identity, registering both identification and disavowal among its "low" white nineteenth-century audiences.[27]

While it remains a provocative and contested theory, Lott's model has allowed other scholars to similarly conceive of potential alliances among multiple subjugated communities within the fragile dynamic of blackface performance—to elucidate its *contradictory* amalgam of desires, fears, and tensions.[28] W. T. Lhamon, for instance, views blackface as one continually redeployed facet of an Atlantic "lore cycle" spanning the nineteenth and twentieth centuries. Its minstrel mask signals a fundamentally "compounded identity" rather than simple "replacement" of one racial marker for another, wherein white performers could "see themselves in the hounded image of the free/escaped black . . . on the lam" but could also "construct their own whiteness as the polar opposite of what they were rehearsing as blackness."[29]

These reconsiderations of racial performance inform this study of country music's construction of rusticity as it originates in barn dance programming and subsequently shapes later iconography. In the following pages, I argue that despite its contemporary coding as a retrograde practice, the exaggerated mimicry of "white" and/or "black" country identity can ironically register a desire to appear respectable—to be, in fact, "modern." Racialized and gendered class minstrelsy provides the poor Southern white performer a different means of deflecting the sense of being at once primitive and "un"-natural. Whether he/she adopts a pronounced Southern drawl and hick costume like the rube comic or applies a burnt-cork "mask" and imitates an outlandish version of "black" speech like the blackface artist, both forms of mimicry offer the opportunity to in some senses reify, rather than actually "live," class and racial Otherness by self-consciously performing it. When ritualized or formalized, that Otherness appears distanced or removed even if not altogether negated, permitting a simultaneous identification *and* disavowal. Borne of anxiety over one's status as a legitimate subject, this strategy blurs the line dividing class cultural visibility and "misrecognition." At the same time, the gendering of these theatrical types has racialized effects: the feminization of white rusticity, for instance, may also lead to—but is never entirely offset by—the appropriation of a mythic black masculinity in minstrel performance. Female "rube" characters are correspondingly masculinized and thus similarly risk the threat of censure, but women performers also momentarily escape restrictive feminine conventions by taking on such illicit roles.

My approach is highly indebted to Barbara Ching's and Aaron Fox's nuanced theories of country performativity yet seeks to make room for even more complicated structures of feeling by acknowledging less celebratory sensibilities such as shame. As I have argued elsewhere, cultural studies has long engaged in its own image "makeover" of working-class cultures, understandably seeking to replace the stock portrait of a passive, reactionary, bigoted white male with an equally static vision of a progressive, resistant subject defiantly producing an onslaught of counterhegemonic texts.[30] While both scholars certainly steer clear of the most reductive tendencies in this approach, they also become limited by their own respective missions to reclaim dignity for the practitioners of country music. For Ching, a cultural critic, that means viewing hard country almost always as a highly self-conscious critique of, rather than simultaneous longing for, cultural distinction and an ever-present disregard for the authentic.[31] For Fox, an ethnomusicologist, it means reclaiming "authenticity" for local Texan working-class musicians by reading their speech and song as reflexive, "poetic" discourse that "resist[s] the alienation and objectification that is at the heart of a class-based political economy."[32] Class shame remains buried, a seemingly obsolete (or merely retrograde) condition in the mid-to-late twentieth century. This book is equally concerned with the effects of cultural distinction, alienation, and objectification, yet it is trying to understand, perhaps more fully, how country performers and listeners might have sought refuge in such excessive and demeaning renditions of rusticity while at other moments successfully recasting them. Its focus on artist and audience engagement with such performative rubrics works in tandem with an investigation of how corporate and cultural institutions such as Music Row and earlier barn dance programming, as well as popular culture industries overall, have authorized and altered such constructions of authentic country identity to retain power in the hands of a class cultural elite.

RECONSTRUCTIVE HISTORY

While at times challenging the standard narrative of country's evolution as a cultural form, *Natural Acts* does proceed more or less chronologically as it conducts a historicized exploration of the interwoven relationships among class abjection, gender norms, constructions of whiteness, and markers of modernity. The text focuses on the deeply imbricated ideological ties among five modes and moments of performance seldom brought together: blackface and "rube" comedy during the barn dance era; postwar honky-tonk music and culture; country star memoirs of the 1980s and '90s; and the recent revivalist phenomenon known as alternative country. I link two familiar and often privileged foundational phases in country music history—the barn dance and honky-tonk eras—with two performative modes that tend to be minimized, if not entirely neglected, in more traditional studies: minstrelsy, a recurring staple of country music programming from the 1920s through the early 1950s, and the lowbrow genre of the celebrity memoir/autobiography, launched by Loretta Lynn's *Coal Miner's Daughter* in 1976 and since joined by a host of successors. I argue that while barn dance and honky-tonk have both been frequently marshaled to represent the very definition of country "essence," their representations are indebted to, work in concert with, and propel others that have yet to receive their scholarly due. Earlier blackface performance and modern autobiographical texts, equally concerned with delineating notions of "natural" identity, complicate and comment on the better-known performative and musical styles of barn dance and honky-tonk. And as an arguably postmodern cultural movement, today's alt.country music explicitly works to recover all four as signifiers of traditional authenticity abandoned by Top 40 country radio.

Together, they comprise an alternative history of country authenticity as a gendered and racialized class construction. As the following capsule chapter descriptions will detail, these five performative modes reveal a shift from rustic to urban sensibilities and locales as the Southern white working class migrated to the industrial North during the Depression and postwar eras. But embedded in this progression is another, equally significant shift from feminine to masculine models of country identity as country music entered into a distinctly uneasy relationship with modernity. Signaled by the advent of certain kinds of technology (affecting song production and arrangement, for example) and the music's more advanced commercialization, modernity is typically deemed the primary culprit of country's demise as an authentic cultural form. But modern culture also clearly helped to offset the stigma of rusticity, which for male performers came to be associated with a shameful, feminized obsolescence, while for female performers it continued, at least through the immediate postwar period, to epitomize women's role as the guardians of both conventional domesticity and rural "folk" culture.

This study builds to demonstrate that as "proper" repositories of country femininity, women have served as contradictory and ultimately marginalized signifiers of country authenticity: initially figured as the composite private and public ideal of "home" during the Depression era, yet dismissed as the autonomous and desiring honky-tonk "angel"—the antithetical "cold" quintessence of postwar and 1950s modernity—when rejecting or reconfiguring that earlier rustic archetype, and similarly critiqued once again in the mid-1960s and later by "hard country" enthusiasts of the 1980s and '90s as the *corruption* of that rustic past due to later female performers' ostensible embodiment of country's "sell-out" pop sensibility (beginning with the "Nashville Sound" of the 1950s and early '60s). At the same time, male performers' and listeners' lingering anxieties about their very claims to a respectable masculine whiteness in Northern urban spaces produced a new performative strategy in the honky-tonk era, jettisoning prior and more theatrical class and racial modes of masquerade in favor of a modern, newly gendered "mask": "strong" white working-class manhood reflected in ostensibly autobiographical songs of sincere emotion. More recent cultural forms such as the memoir and subgenres such as alt.country continue to confront and reinscribe these patterns. Female country autobiographers and alt.country artists routinely contend with both entrenched perspectives on women's contributions to country music history, while alt.country male performers, in particular, have enthusiastically championed the honky-tonk persona.

Chapter 2 lays the text's foundation by investigating how blackface and hillbilly performative modes informed each other during country music's "Golden Age" of pre-1945 radio and stage programming to produce an influential standard of authenticity grounded in rusticity. Almost every barn dance act featured some version of the naive "hayseed" caricature now synonymous with Opry legend Minnie Pearl yet also embodied by a host of lesser-known musicians/singers/comics who often did "double-duty," from banjoist "Cousin Emmy" to Homer and Jethro to longtime bass player Speck Rhodes, who carried the tradition into the 1990s. But while most published histories of this era at least liberally document the rube's presence, few, with several notable exceptions,[33] acknowledge the existence on stage of his or her minstrel counterpart, though the latter certainly made frequent appearances—most dramatically at the Opry itself, where, as mentioned earlier, blackface duo Lasses/Jamup and Honey entertained audiences on radio and in traveling tent shows from the early 1930s into the early 1950s.

This chapter briefly traces historical connections among these minstrel and rube figures to emphasize locational similarities based in class/racial Otherness but also incorporates new primary material to unsettle any static reading of hillbilly and racial masquerade as both are deployed on the barn dance stage. The discussion includes the heroic figure of Davy Crockett; white minstrel and country performer Emmett Miller; Jamup and Honey minstrel skits (stage and radio); and *National Barn Dance*'s comic hillbilly "queen" Myrtle "Lulu Belle" Wiseman, along with early architects of barn dance programming and imagery such as George Hay and John Lair, who crafted rustic representations targeting both educated urban listeners and rural or working-class spectators. Working to negotiate such complex divisions in the production and reception of its images, barn dance alternately endorsed and overturned racism, misogyny, and classism.

Chapter 3 illuminates honky-tonk music's pivotal role in reconfiguring this ideology and iconography of rusticity in the context of postwar and Cold War urban culture. As Barry Shank has established, the honky-tonk bar itself—literally situated on the border dividing urban and rural experience—figured the contradictions of country music's encounter with modernity, conveying a competing nostalgia for and rejection of its mythic "natural" past.[34] Lyrics expressed profound feelings of displacement, as well as a newfound explicit interest in the "adult" attractions of urban life (sexual infidelity, alcoholism, workplace alienation), while musicians introduced electronic instruments into live and recorded country performance. These twin arenas of social and cultural change also produced new gendered and racialized notions of authenticity that served as an antidote to the barn dance era's emasculating rustic pose. The postwar crisis in gender relations converted the representation of "home" into a public and masculine space—the honky-tonk—rather than a private domestic one. Male honky-tonk artists mourned not the loss of the past itself, which signified their ties to an earlier Southern rural culture as well as personal family history, but the loss of women as the *embodiment* of that mythologized "home" place as they succumbed to modernity's freedoms and pleasures. At the same time, these singers and songwriters converted the earlier hillbilly's stigmatized primitiveness into the authentic, hard-hitting emotion of transplanted white Southern working-class masculinity. Racial mimicry no longer served as the bedrock for this modern, seemingly more transparent, persona. And at the level of the music itself, technology's modern "intrusion" into an ostensible folk art became salvaged as a sonically loud, intense, and distinctly masculine performance model boasting a truthful connection to the artist's life.

This chapter as a whole analyzes the connections underlying what I call "first-wave" and "second-wave" honky-tonk: its first section focuses on two male icons of the postwar period, Ernest Tubb and Hank Williams, while the second section, concentrating on the 1950s, explores female artists' response to this music's construction of gender and class relations in the "answer song" form—a convention at once enabling and limiting their agency. Discussion of two quite different figures, "Queen of Country Music" Kitty Wells and Jean Shepard, reveals that women had a particularly vexed relationship to honky-tonk as aesthetic and subculture. Their authenticity was located in the perpetual *division* between a personal "traditional" or domestic identity and a performative "modern" one, unlike that of their male counterparts.

Chapters 2 and 3 work in tandem to demonstrate that honky-tonk music, though typically prized by hard-core country enthusiasts as well as many historians for ushering country performance into the modern era, was also beset by persistent anxieties about its own respectability. Although songs by male artists claimed to deliver an unvarnished presentation of new emotional and often autobiographical "truths," other ancillary texts, such as album covers, liner notes, and fan magazines of the period, told a more complicated story that accentuated (while simultaneously glossing over) the divide between stars' down-home stage personas and their more sophisticated personal lifestyles.

This coupling of authenticity and respectability became all the more intensive—and challenging—during the next decade as the swooning Nashville Sound, crafted by record producers Owen Bradley and Billy Sherrill, dominated country's airwaves. Now a centralized and recognizable market force, the country music industry continued to appeal to its listeners as a blue-collar constituency yet sold them to advertisers as middle-class consumers with suburban, rather than rustic, tastes. The music's new lush sound—the antithesis of honky-tonk arrangements and vocals—thus introduced another, feminized variation of modernity into country's self-image. While transforming country music into a competitive, profitable force in the era of format radio, this rebranding eventually precipitated a backlash by artists and fans perceiving an "identity crisis" in the industry.[35]

Chapter 4 takes this study in an admittedly unorthodox direction by turning to the country star memoir as the next truly significant mode of authenticity discourse generated during this latter period. Emerging during the mid-1970s, a time when Hank Williams and subsequent honky-tonk stylists such as Merle Haggard and George Jones were eclipsed by pop vocalists such as Crystal Gayle and John Denver (Country Music Association award winners in 1977 and 1975), the star memoir became Nashville's new tool of authentication. It capitalized on the autobiographical strain ostensibly running through honky-tonk's and later "hard" country's most authentic ensemble of musical texts to reaffirm class identification between audience and artist while also accentuating the latter's respectability. The Austin-based Outlaws movement (fronted by Waylon Jennings, Willie Nelson, David Allan Coe, and Tompall Glaser) certainly launched a more threatening opposition to country's merger with pop music during this era—and did so, at least in part, by exploiting now deeply ensconced icons of authenticity (e.g., Jennings' "Are You Sure Hank Done It This Way?"). But this study positions the memoir as an underexamined yet equally important vehicle of cultural identity, a form both anomalous and analogous to the music itself. And while male performers have undoubtedly turned to the published memoir to validate their authenticity credentials, I argue that female artists have been pushed to appropriate its form much more strategically. Much like the honky-tonk answer song, autobiography constituted a similarly conflicted vehicle for "talking back" to this music's gendered scripts and, in the process, allowed women to verify their own authenticity as country performers.

The chapter thus examines published autobiographies by Naomi Judd,

Loretta Lynn, Reba McEntire, Dolly Parton, Minnie Pearl, and Tammy Wynette as representational life histories both emblematic of and resistant to country music "tradition." In some ways reminiscent of earlier fan magazines, these narratives, coauthored with professional writers, function as composites of both low *and* high life story, tracing the trajectory of artistic/material success yet often insisting upon a static and "natural" country identity. In content, form, and narrative voice, the country memoir indeed attempts to represent itself as an updated *version* of such authenticity. Yet as a "literary" text typically mediated by a collaborative or ghost writer, it also participates in a formal publishing arena whose conventions reflect dominant cultural tastes. This contradictory position proves particularly challenging for female star-authors who are already caught in a gendered "double bind" determining the authenticity of their private and public personas. As writers, they need to meet more elite cultural standards, but as country artists, they must burnish their rustic credentials. Finally, as working women themselves, they ironically risk losing their claims to authenticity altogether as they veer between the barriers of masculinized authenticity and a feminized version founded in domestic motherhood. The memoir thus functions overall as a highly unstable form, both shoring up the industry's investment in autobiographical claims and revealing its myriad fault lines during several decades desperate for an authenticity infusion.

Chapter 5 brings this study to a close by exploring alt.country music as the most recent and increasingly influential emblem of authenticity within the country genre. While mainstream country continued to employ its own predictable rhetoric of "tradition" in the 1980s and 1990s, it could not escape the shadow of critique that has loomed over Music Row since it married country narrative to a feminized pop aesthetic. Initially an underground "movement" championed by its premiere publication, *No Depression,* alt.country has seized the mantle of authenticity, exploiting while also altering country music's prior representations and formulas to impact the look and sound of Top 40 country artists, as well as attract a new generation of listeners.[36] Its postmodern approach, however, results in a politically problematic as well as musically innovative reclamation of country tradition. While paying tribute to country's long-neglected musical heroes, it frequently adopts a hip ironic posture and rhetoric of cultural distinction targeting an elite, upper-middle-class audience.[37] Too often, its emphasis on music as homespun art rather than commercial product transforms its fans' appreciation of rusticity into purely aestheticized consumption.

Alt.country also quite deliberately positions itself as the de facto heir to honky-tonk's raw masculinity and bravado. Although *No Depression* has demonstrated a keen interest in country music's now-taboo history of blackface performance, at least a sizeable contingent of male musicians prefer to ally themselves with hard country's "dirty white boy" legacy.[38] Alt.country female artists, somewhat akin to their predecessors who confronted masculinist master narratives of authenticity, appropriate and challenge such gendered strictures yet often replicate their ironized nostalgia for earlier expressions of class authenticity.

Approaching this music and discourse as an alternately "revivalist" and "survivalist" body of texts, the chapter focuses on a handful of representative artists—including Michelle Shocked, Hank Williams III, the Drive-By Truckers, Gillian Welch, and Iris DeMent—to uncover examples of both a new mode of hillbilly masquerade and a genuinely resistant realism. Raymond Williams' and Evan Watkins' work on alternative cultures provides a critical framework for the discussion, as both scholars are concerned with demonstrating how dominant ideologies and institutions define the "past" in order to secure their own hegemony: Williams theorizes vestiges of "residual" cultures, while Watkins studies the discourse surrounding representations of "obsolescent" or "throwaway" populations. Although some alt.country artists' revivalist sensibility subscribes to such hegemonic tendencies, other artists conceive of their music as a surviving residual "trace" of ostensibly "extinct" economically depressed communities in the late capitalist era. Alt.country thus functions as a crucial endpoint for this study, not simply extending its scrutiny of authenticity into the present moment but also illustrating modernity's lingering and perhaps surprising effects on contemporary country performance.

CHAPTER 2

Reluctant Hillbillies: Rube and Blackface Performance in the Barn Dance Era

> Given that the minstrel show has seeped well beyond its masked variants into vaudeville, thence into sitcoms, into jazz and rhythm'n'blues quartets, thence into rock-'n'-roll and hip hop dance into the musical and the novel, thence into radio and film, into the Grand Ole Opry, thence into every roadhouse and the cab of every longhaul truck beyond the Appalachians—why, then, is the minstrel show said to be over?
>
> —W. T. Lhamon Jr., *Raising Cain: Blackface Performance from Jim Crow to Hip Hop*

> A lady wrote me a nasty letter asking why do you play them silly old tunes? On the air, I replied to her: I notice in my 35 years of show business that there's 500 pairs of overalls sold to every one tuxedo suit. That's why I stick to swamp opera.
>
> —Clayton McMichen, "Clayton McMichen: Reluctant Hillbilly"

As the "hillbilly" fiddler of the 1920s–40s and the late-twentieth-century cultural critic both suggest, minstrelsy proved to be a surprisingly resilient mode of performance central to country music's rise as a commercial medium, encompassing and forever entangling the performance of "black" and "white" rustic identities. Two random issues of *Billboard* published within one month of each other in 1940 begin to illustrate this persistent coupling, one carrying an ad for minstrel products, the other a brief barn dance program review that insists, "packed houses for the WESX Cowboy Jamboree at the Empire Theater disprove claims that hillbillies are on the way out."[1] But far more formal mechanisms were also at work to insure their long-standing relationship as the barn dance program evolved into country's premiere entertainment genre in the 1930s and '40s.

Blackface appeared on a variety of country music stages from the 1910s through the early 1950s, marking the careers of now long-forgotten figures as well as some of country's most beloved stars, such as Jimmie Rodgers, Roy Acuff, and Bob Wills. Its intimate role in the music's development as a commercial enterprise is seemingly self-evident yet often obfuscated if not eradicated entirely from contemporary histories produced by both the country music industry and independent scholars. A few photos of blackface comedians or musicians may work their way into such publications, but little, if any, contextualization or analysis appears to deepen our understanding of this performative mode's relationship to modern country music culture. Several important critics have paved the way by conducting more substantive research and nuanced discussions of country's adaptations of minstrel show practices: veteran country music historian Charles K. Wolfe, who has documented blackface duo Lasses/Jamup and Honey's lasting presence on the Grand Ole Opry from the 1930s to the 1950s; Nick Tosches, who has long reveled in the "dark" nexus between "Cowboys and Niggers" in country's past and who has more recently written into history early blackface and vaudeville country singer Emmett Miller; and Robert Cantwell, whose extended meditation on Bill Monroe in his book *Bluegrass Breakdown* has created a new mythic history for "hillbilly" music that in many ways hinges upon blackface tradition.[2] With the exception of these latter two, however, few have been willing to grapple with the genuine complexities of this topic—particularly minstrelsy's implications for models of authentic country identity that have carried into the present.

Links between the minstrel and the rube personas have in some ways become a kind of truism, part and parcel of American "lore" established in the 1930s by Constance Rourke in her now-classic *American Humor.* Rourke's yoking together of the "backwoodsman" and minstrel figures at a crisis moment in the antebellum nation helps to provide one model for structuring a similar comparison between hillbilly and blackface modes reemerging in the early to mid-twentieth century. I am most interested, however, in examining the ideological connections between these two as they appeared not only disparately but together in country music and comedy acts. Just as Eric Lott's groundbreaking study of minstrelsy sought to understand "how precariously *nineteenth-century* white working people lived their whiteness," I am utilizing this now-taboo arena of country performance to illuminate comparable modes of identity formation in the context of modernity.[3]

The barn dance genre marked a crucial turning point in the development of the hillbilly/rube archetype, in part because it created a mass, explicitly national audience for its folksy images. In its inception, barn dance was an *urban* radio genre patterned on Saturday-night country dances and broadcast in major industrial cities attracting migrating Southerners.[4] As such, its regionally specific programming was crafted to appeal to Northern as well as Southern, urban as well as rural, listeners. The audience in turn constituted a mass market for the music, as well as its advertised products, which divided show segments according to specific commercial sponsors. A glance at any typical roster of barn dance acts—from the oldest and most influential, such as Chicago's *National Barn Dance* and Nashville's Grand Ole Opry, to later ventures such as Wheeling, West Virginia's WWVA *Jamboree*—reveals a bizarre panoply of musical styles and comic acts, including old-time string bands, cowboy singers, Hawaiian music, sentimental songs, hillbilly and blackface comedians, and popular crooners. As Richard Peterson outlines: "The radio barn dance was a kind of rustic variety show designed not for dancing but to be listened to. . . . In form it had much more in common with vaudeville because of the fast-paced sequence of diverse acts." Initially launched against a "jazz age" backdrop of racial intermixing, all of this "variety" masked a complex cultural agenda premised on intersecting class, race, and gender ideologies that promoted antimodern notions of authenticity in the service of a new, profoundly commercial medium.[5]

The confluence of Depression-era economic woes, Southern migration to the industrial North, and an expanded audience encompassing both middle- and working-class listeners produced an amalgam of representations depicting "authentic" country or folk culture. Charting the shift from "hillbilly" to "mountaineer" imagery in a variety of twentieth-century U.S. cultural forms, Anthony Harkins argues that the distorted depiction of poor white rural Southerners overall "served the dual and seemingly contradictory purposes of allowing the . . . generally nonrural, middle-class white, American audience to imagine a romanticized past, while simultaneously enabling that same audience to recommit itself to modernity by caricaturing the negative aspects of premodern, uncivilized society." The term *hillbilly* signified "degradation, violence, animalism, and carnality, as well as . . . romantic rurality, cultural and ethnic independence and self-sufficiency." Focusing on barn dance, historian Kristine McCusker similarly suggests that "performers utilized popular images of a supposedly traditional past rooted in the Appalachian mountains," a past that held double-edged significance: a "counterpoint to the sterility and artifice of . . . modern industrial culture"*and* a symptom of an isolated primitiveness out of step with contemporary urbanity. Writing in the early 1970s about his years as the program director of WLS' *National Barn Dance,* George C. Biggar still clings to the former perspective, recalling that "traditional country dances and toe-tickling harmonica-guitar medleys were interspersed with heart songs and popular sweet and novelty numbers which brought nostalgic memories of hayrides and country 'sociables' to thousands."[6] Others in the industry, however, resented this construct's negative counterpart, the backward yokel, and eventually came to embrace the cowboy as a preferable alternative in barn dance iconography.[7]

This chapter aims to expand the critical frame surrounding our current understanding of barn dance–era rusticity by drawing out racialized and gendered dimensions that for the most part continue to hover in the margins. Harkins' study certainly contributes to the overall conversation establishing parallels between the minstrel and the rube as it incisively probes the meaning of whiteness in the hillbilly archetype, and McCusker's impressive archival work on women in barn dance performance has begun to launch a new history of the genre, uncovering gender and class implications of its nostalgic vision of Appalachian culture. What remains missing, however, is a broader approach that tracks the shifting relations among all three constructs—class, gender, and race—as they help produce notions of authentic or "natural" country identity via increasingly modern technology and mores. We need to examine white male and female rubes and blackfaced tricksters alongside middle-class sentimental "mothers" and mountaineer-cum-cowboys as they appeared on the same stage, within a single program. When we do, we can glimpse the development of a white rusticity stigmatized at least in part because it is *feminized* by long-standing cultural images of poor Southern whites, as well as particular material circumstances of mass male unemployment during the Depression years that produced "a wide-spread crisis of masculinity."[8] This gendered effect was never entirely offset by either the appropriation of black masculinity in minstrel skits *or* the middle-class trappings of other, more "properly" gendered performative roles. At the same time, I attempt to read such racialized and gendered class performances as models of a complex kind of agency available to poor or working-class white Southerners both creating and consuming these images. To begin, I concentrate on one particular component of minstrelsy studies—the notion of a performative "mask"—to explore the possibility of casting the country rube and blackface roles as modes of "insurgent culture."[9]

I. THEORIZING THE MASK

Though typically attributed to Ralph Ellison's landmark 1958 essay "Change the Joke and Slip the Yoke," notions of masquerade and masking prevalent in contemporary minstrelsy scholarship originated in Constance Rourke's 1931 study of American folk humor, which sought to establish racial mimicry as a performance of national identity—what Rourke termed a "new national mythology."[10] Ever since, cultural critics have struggled to grasp the myriad psychoanalytic and ideological dimensions of "blacking up," primarily in the context of pre– and post–Civil War America. Both Rourke and Ellison envisioned blackface as the donning of a disguise for the purpose of concealment or repression, but others have imagined quite different uses for the device, such as parody/burlesque of racist ideologies (Mahar and Cantwell) or "ventriloquism" for transgressive values and desires, permitting some identification with the black subject (Lott and, to some degree, Lhamon). And finally, several see the static black mask not simply as a disguise or cover but as a "metaphor" for commodification itself, functioning as either dehistoricized corporate/national "trademark" (Berlant) or liberatory "nexus of struggle."[11] I propose a composite conceptual model to explain the function of minstrel/rube roles for barn dance performers and audiences.

Rourke's and Ellison's highly influential mask metaphors may lead to quite different interpretations of minstrelsy's impulses and effects—in their own work as well as in subsequent followers'—but both depend upon a notion of inherent fixity or stasis. For Rourke, the Yankee, backwoods, or blackface mask was an "unchanging, unaverted countenance"—a kind of blank that served as a "safeguard, preventing revelations of surprise, anger, or dismay." She later elaborates, "The mask might be worn as an inheritance or for amusement or as a front against the world in any of these impersonations, concealing a childish and unformed countenance: but it was part of a highly self-conscious projection."[12] Twenty-seven years later, Ellison writes of a "stylized and iconic" minstrel mask that reduces its black subject "to a negative sign": "This mask, this willful stylization and modification of the natural face and hands, was imperative for the evocation of that atmosphere in which the fascination of blackness could be enjoyed, the comic catharsis achieved.

The racial identity of the performer was unimportant, the mask was the thing (the 'thing' in more ways than one) and its function was to veil the humanity of Negroes." Significantly, its frozen smile served "to repress the white audience's awareness of its moral identification with its own acts and with the human ambiguities behind the mask."[13]

Here, Ellison articulates a complex reception theory premised on (non)identification—in other words, a model of cultural consumption that cannot conceive of white identification *with* the black position. Instead, the white spectator *represses* identification with his or her own immoral racism. The mask must remain a kind of blank for white performers and audiences alike to experience a "cathartic" effect, Othering the very notion of blackness. Ellison, however, acknowledges the slipperiness of this maneuver: "When the white man steps behind the mask of the trickster his freedom is circumscribed by the fear that he is not simply miming a personification of his disorder and chaos but that he will become in fact that which he intends only to symbolize." Invoking Rourke, he concludes that "the early minstrel show . . . constituted a ritual of exorcism" that evolved into a "national art"—"the mask was an inseparable part of the national iconography."[14]

As recent critics have noted, Ellison's sophisticated analysis of blackface performance entirely transformed minstrelsy studies. His mask metaphor refuted any lingering claims to authentic or true "impersonation" of black identity and launched "the reigning view of minstrelsy as racial domination."[15] Yet as Lott's *Love and Theft* sought to establish, such a reading was beset by its own limitations, at once perceiving and overlooking the true "doubleness" of this performative mode.[16] Lott and his successors have been especially interested in broadening the scope of minstrelsy studies to incorporate classed and gendered forms of identity formation at work. The mask concept, then, has subsequently gained flexibility to accommodate theories of audience and performer transgression, as well as repression, and the exercising of protest and parody, as well as racist power.

Lott's cultural studies approach has become a kind of benchmark in this field in part because it interrogated the very notion of measuring representational authenticity. The goal, Lott claimed, was not to delineate the "false" from the "true" or to sever minstrelsy from any "genuine" African or African American cultural tradition but to understand it as a performance founded in the "simultaneous drawing up and crossing of racial boundaries." His study demonstrates the importance of documenting blackface minstrelsy's origins in actual black practices but reminds us as well that the end result is a "cultural invention, not some precious essence installed in black bodies."[17] Yet it is specifically his interest in the relationship between this charged dynamic and the development of nineteenth-century white working-class culture that has revitalized minstrelsy scholarship and certainly proven instrumental here.

Lott's radical formulation conceives of potential alliances or identifications between two subjugated groups of subjects. White culturally disenfranchised audiences recognized in minstrelsy "the racial ritual that defined their cultural position," so that the burnt-cork disguise offered "ventriloquial self-expression": "Working-class values and desires were aired and secured in the minstrel show. . . . Blackface provided a convenient mask through which to voice class resentments of all kinds." Its effects, however, were constantly double-edged, for those "resentments" were "directed as readily toward black people as toward upper-class enemies." Lott plots the shifting and ultimately threatening equation of race and class produced by "antebellum America's capitalist crisis," which created in turn a need to reinscribe racial differences among members of the working class. "Blackface minstrelsy," he concludes, "was founded on this antinomy, reinstituting with ridicule the gap between black and white working class even as it reveled in their (sometimes liberatory) identification."[18]

Other more recent contributors to this critical dialogue amplify, refine, and in some cases entirely recast Lott's ventriloquism analogy. William Mahar, for instance, identifies four varying yet related uses for burnt-cork makeup in early minstrelsy. At the most superficial level, it functions as (contested) "racial marker" of difference; as "disguise" permitting both satire and reinforcement of dominant cultural norms; as "vehicle" for a distinctly American "commercialized popular culture"; and, echoing Ellison, as "masking device" allowing performers "to shield themselves from any direct personal and psychological identification with the material."[19] As with Lott, masking serves multiple, often conflicting purposes. Yet Mahar primarily argues against any simple mask metaphor by helpfully pointing to a whole host of performative gestures critical to (even putative) "impersonation":

> The minstrel's task of "putting on a character" and the structure of racial depiction involved more than blackface makeup. When the minstrels "put on" blackface or whiteface, they assumed other traits to *dis*identify themselves. . . . Depiction or "delineation" required that the minstrel show personalities had to work with dialect; perform in costume; assume various serious and comic poses; sing, dance, or play an instrument.[20]

In conjunction—and providing a music historian's perspective—Mahar accentuates European as well as African American sources of early minstrel material in order to foreground its class-based dimensions. Exploring ethnic immigrant varieties of blackface, he charges that "racial specificity was not as essential to the overall comic effect as was the use of perceived racial and cultural differences as devices for ridiculing the cruel contradictions between the dreams and realities that lower- or middle-class Americans found in their daily lives."[21] Even when the comedy hinges upon racist ideologies, its core formulation "is often one of class masquerading as race or ethnicity."[22]

Perhaps the most dramatic and thought-provoking reconceptualization of the minstrel mask, however, appears in W. T. Lhamon's *Raising Cain.* In direct opposition to both Ellison's and Rourke's "blank countenance," Lhamon believes the "mask is itself an excellent signifier of overlap as principle"—a tool for "multivalent slashing."[23] Aiming to view blackface as one overlooked example of a broader Atlantic "insurgent" "lore cycle" spanning the nineteenth and twentieth centuries, he refocuses our attention on how such performance "can work also and simultaneously *against* racial stereotyping." Similar to Lott and Mahar, Lhamon envisions minstrelsy as a cultural form of and for the disenfranchised, especially the "lumpen" and working classes. He writes, "I want to bring out the broad interracial refusal of middle-class channeling that working men and women of all hues mounted using the corrupt tools bequeathed them by the marketplaces and other locations where they could make spectacles of themselves." Blackface is thus at once a "disguise" for white working-class youth evading hegemonic "surveillance" at particular historical moments at particular regional locations; a vehicle of self-expression for those "who had no access to presses or boardrooms"; a defiant form of self-marking ("one we are still learning to *see,* rather than look through") as a response to enforced, punitive marking of the lumpen proletariat (shaved eyebrows, iron collars); and finally, a uniform version of "abstraction" that allowed "the heterogeneous parts of the newly moiling young workers all access to the same identity tags"—"immigrants" and "rustics" alike could "identify" the "most" with Jim Crow's "raggedy black figure."[24]

But it is his particularly nuanced understanding of this performance's "slippery" nature that makes his work so valuable. For Lhamon, the minstrel mask signals a composite that holds "all the identities together without freezing them in a singular relationship or replacing the parts."[25] He goes so far as to argue that blackface, in fact, "*enact[s]* miscegenation," exposing bits of whiteness beneath the "black" layer. Ultimately, Lhamon develops a "doubling cover" theory of masking, arguing that white performers could "see themselves in the hounded image of the free/escaped black . . . on the lam" but could also "construct their own whiteness as the polar opposite of what they were rehearsing as blackness."[26] This is a "both/and" theory of practice that seems particularly well-suited to country music's embracing of both blackface and hillbilly masquerade.

It is a theory that can also be seen to complement another rendition of the minstrel mask, the commodity and/or trademark. This latter analogy seems especially pertinent to barn dance programming, which so explicitly foregrounded its own commercial foundations in its advertising logos (visible on stage and in breaks between acts) that it entirely conflated its artistic and commercial products. Cultural critic Susan Willis recasts both the minstrel mask and the commodity form itself when she conceives of blackface as *both* "the overt embodiment of the southern racist stereotyping of blacks" and, as theatrical mode, a metaphor for the commodity: in other words, "the sign of what people paid to see. It is the image consumed . . . and as such it can be either full or empty of meaning."[27] Recounting the complexity of traditional minstrelsy performance (men costumed as women; whites imitating blacks, allowing the latter to "appear" on stage), she argues that racial impersonation is at once "heavily laden with" and "hollowed of" cultural codes. For Willis, then, it is finally a potential metaphor for "transformation," rather than reification, wherein traditional meanings are given the "freedom" to be over-turned when they are exposed in the most artificial of forms.[28]

I want to suggest, however, that under particular performative conditions, reification can itself serve as another kind of tranformation. Much like the *African American* blackface performer, the poor Southern white posing as a rube may utilize the artifice of the act to deflect, rather than reconstitute, his own sense of being an "un"-natural primitive. The hick's "mask"—pronounced Southern drawl, cornpone humor, patched-up overalls—functions, much like burnt cork, as the vehicle for distancing or refusing the reality of class/racial Otherness.[29] The boundaries between identifying with and re-jecting such Otherness ironically become blurred in a performative practice initially intended to cement, rather than unsettle, country identity.

And while that same white performer's motivation to adopt a *minstrel* mask cannot be equated entirely with that of his African American counter-part—indeed, one goal of this study is to delineate the distinctions, as well as similarities, between the two—they both originate, I am arguing, out of a shared anxiety about legitimacy. At key moments in the last two centuries, rusticity came to be associated not only with a feminized class abjection and

obsolescence but also with a degraded form of whiteness. Country performers' and audiences' suspect claims to an ostensibly civilized national/racial
identity, then, contributed greatly to the tensions over embracing or eschew-
ing modern practices, symbols, and sounds.

II. HISTORICIZED COMPARISONS

Examining blackface through the lens of country music history provides a
unique vantage point in the sense that most recent critical studies remain
centered on the nineteenth century and thus highlight minstrelsy's ties to
Northern and urban, rather than Southern and rural, class cultures. Following its trajectory into the twentieth century, while enlarging the focus to include small farming communities alongside those in large urban metropoli-
tan areas and more isolated factory towns, allows us to glimpse more clearly
the overlap between black and rustic masquerade and expands conventional
interpretations of their shared appeal. Similarly, looking back to the prior
century's network of cultural representations and its links to larger economic
and ideological currents helps us to detect greater forces at work shaping
modern iconography within the country music industry, particularly the material as well as emotional losses and struggles that played out during the
1930s Depression.

Davy Crockett

As several cultural historians have hinted, the heroic figure of Davy Crockett—nineteenth-century backwoodsman extraordinaire—proves a fruitful
place to begin tracing the convergence of these two performative modes.
Created by educated urban whites in the Northeast, the Crockett myth rose
to prominence in ubiquitous pamphlets or "almanacs" published during
roughly the same period as minstrelsy, the 1830s–50s.[30] And in his most extreme depictions, he emerged a similarly comic figure of linguistic and
physical excess: "leaping, crowing, flapping his wings, he indulged in dances
resembling beast-dances among savages."[31] Supreme emblem of primeval
violence, Crockett "crossed the line between human and animal, between
civilization and chaotic nature." When battling nonwhite foes such as Indians, he actually became a cannibal and, like his minstrel counterpart,
boasted a voracious sexuality at once "oral, exhibitionistic, violent, and non-
reproductive."[32]

The Crockett stories' entertainment value also derives from similar features. Echoing the minstrel's malapropisms, his language was, as Rourke puts it, "full of free inventions": "'absquatulate,' 'slantendiclur,' 'cahoot,' 'catawampus.'" The backwoodsman and the minstrel additionally shared musical tastes and instrumentation. Rourke notes that the Crockett figure "played the flute, the fiddle, the flageolet; Negro slaves taught him the bones. . . . Both . . . were lively dancers, mixing Negro breakdowns with Irish reels and jigs."[33] (The two even converge in the term *coon* itself: as David Roediger establishes, before 1848, *coon* referred to whites, rather than blacks; Crockett's coonskin cap proves one genuine source of the term, a symbol of white rural people.[34])

Crockett clearly codes as a more heroic masculine character than minstrelsy's "Mose" or "Jim Crow." Nevertheless, he can be seen to function in similar ways, equating poor white country culture with the bestial, the scatological, the abject. One can read this positioning as a provocative "liminality" associated with the lower classes. Carroll Smith-Rosenberg, for instance, envisions Crockett as a "signifier" that "absorbs the personnel of the backwoodsmen of Appalachia never to be fully integrated by canals and railroads into a capitalist world market; the boatmen of the Western rivers, furiously autonomous yet ultimately to be submerged by Eastern transportation corporations—even the newly emergent and much feared young men of the urban working classes, without skills, often organized in gangs." But while imbued with potential threatening power, he is ultimately reigned in, she argues, by the conservative ideologies of the myth's creators. Seeming to champion change, Crockett's rugged individualism finally masks, rather than reveals, the material conditions of the "new" industrial world of the mid-nineteenth century and thus the origins of its attendant class, the bourgeoisie.[35] Lott views Crockett as another vexed example of cultural "ventriloquism" explicitly linked to the minstrel show—both created to voice traditional values yet susceptible to other agendas, illustrating the nonhegemonic currents of popular cultural forms.[36] Others interpret his excessive gestures as a cathartic disguise for the repressed white middle-class male, akin to burnt cork: "Onto the persons of Crockett and the Indians, as caricatured in the almanacs, writers and readers could project sides of themselves they chose not openly to own. They could articulate their fears of losing the civilization they had so painfully acquired over centuries and, in the meantime, could identify ambiguously with the wildness they repudiated."[37]

Yet as Catherine Albanese argues, the Crockett almanacs were not aimed solely at Eastern educated urbanites but, like the barn dance radio programs later broadcast nationally, also targeted rural audiences. What forms of identification, then, might have developed in relation to this savage white persona, and how might that identification in turn be linked to rural responses to blackface performance? Rourke suggests that both the backwoodsman and the minstrel types were popular among all kinds of antebellum audiences because they imposed a new, unifying spirit of nationhood. Both

> had been a wanderer over the land, the Negro a forced and unwilling wanderer. Each in a fashion of his own had broken bonds . . . [and] embodied a deep-lying mood of disseverance. . . . Their comedy, their irreverent wisdom, their sudden changes and adroit adaptations, provided emblems for a pioneer people who required resilience as a prime trait. . . . Laughter created ease, and even more, a sense of unity, among a people who were not yet a nation and who were seldom joined in stable communities.[38]

Commonalities were founded in a shared alienation and marginalization, yet any transgressive implications are glossed over in Rourke's model, diluted in an emerging homogenous national identity.

Lhamon's analysis yields a very different engagement with the Crockett myth. While calling attention to the early Jim Crow's "Crockettian" features—and, in a fascinating aside, noting that T. D. Rice actually sang about Crockett while performing as Crow—Lhamon focuses on Crockett's fundamental "antisociability," posing Jim Crow as the much more radical, appealing, and appropriate choice for white urban lower-class spectators. Crow is "devious" rather than outwardly "aggressive" like Crockett and "enacts *identification* with women and others." Lhamon concludes, "Crockett fought against difference in the natural world (he'll swallow lightning, wrestle bears); Jim Crow countered disdain and exclusion in the social world."[39] This theory helps to illustrate the complexities of cultural reception in urban communities during this period, but it does little to address the conflicted affiliations of white rural audiences faced with two similar caricatures, one representing white culture, one black.

If Crockett's significance is to be fully appreciated, he must be considered alongside an additional cultural legacy: imagery of poor Southern whites that was pervasive in U.S. popular culture and literature in the eighteenth and nineteenth centuries and that carried into the next. Such imagery recalls certain key features of stock minstrel types, such as "the alliance of extreme material deprivation with slyness, sloth, absurd folly, and random violence" and humor derived from "comic folklore, extravagant vulgarity, obsessive (and frequently self-serving) illogicality."[40] The poor white body appeared similarly spectacular and deformed. William Byrd's 1728 journal established the prototype of a "freakish appearance"—"yellow-skinned and nearly noseless," "idiotic, immoral, and—above all—inert."[41] Yet as cultural historians have noted, such exaggerated portraits were often cruelly brought to life by actual poverty and working conditions. Early twentieth-century mill workers, as well as the unemployed, suffered "stunted bodies," while the practice of clay-eating led to "sickly, sallow, unnatural" visages.[42] Crockett clearly resonates with this "body" of representation, but he may also have provided a way to shift its meaning—vulgar yet virile, oddly beautiful in his bestiality. He proffers a voice of agency to the white, rural, economically disenfranchised of the mid-nineteenth century who needed a means of distinguishing themselves from both slaves and free blacks, reinscribing their own whiteness. Literally blacking up was perhaps too threatening for some, the lines too blurred. Infamously stigmatized as "the melancholy spectacle of a people who have acquired civilization and then lost it,"[43] this audience may have harnessed the backwoodsman myth to reassert, as Rourke otherwise proposed, its distinctly American identity.

Crockett mania faded by the late 1840s, and as I will detail shortly, other rustic types took his place on the theater stage into the new century. The minstrel show itself also declined as a performative genre, hanging on by fits and starts in the successive wake of vaudeville, film, and radio.

Emmett Miller: The "Trick Voice" Linking Nineteenth- and Twentieth-Century Modes of Minstrelsy

One now largely forgotten figure who epitomized the extensive scope of intersections between "black" and "white" music and subcultures in the early twentieth century was "yodeling blues singer" and white minstrel performer Emmett Miller, who worked with the celebrated Al G. Field Minstrels troupe and in his time was a noted Okeh recording artist. Rescuing Miller from obscurity in the 1990s,[44] Nick Tosches calls his music an "alchemy" of genres and types, "definable neither as country nor as blues, as jazz nor as pop, as black nor as white, but as a summation and a transcendence of these bloodlines and more"—finally, a "Rosetta Stone" allowing our comprehension of the "mongrel" mix of "American music."[45] Through his ongoing research, Tosches directly links this performer from Macon, Georgia—"a white man in blackface, a hillbilly singer and a jazz singer both, a son of the South and a roue of Broadway"—to such celebrated stars of country music as Jimmie Rodgers and Bob Wills, who are now well-known for early if brief indulgences in blackface performance as they launched their careers in traveling medicine shows during the mid-to-late 1920s and early 1930s.[46] (Tosches also reaches as far forward as Hank Williams, who was a fan of Miller's *earlier* version of "Lovesick Blues.") However, they also emulated Miller's "trick voice," combining "wry, bizarre yodeling, . . . eccentric timing, . . . startling falsetto flights in the middle of vowels, . . . uncanny swoons of timbre and pitch."[47]

That voice also made for a paradoxical form of stage success: at once a unique presence and, when performing in blackface, an ostensibly skillful impersonation. Known to his friends and neighbors as "'Nigger' Miller," he was praised by reviewers for "play[ing] the part of a negro as few have done. . . . His slow, easy-going antics portray the negro as Georgians can best appreciate him."[48] Like many white minstrel men, Miller "inhabited" the role of racial other both on and off stage, conflating the two identities. His voice could be mesmerizing, but for all his performative flair, he invited comparisons between white Southern working-class "good ole boy" and rural black male.[49] As Tosches has suggested about Miller's music specifically and W. T. Lhamon has argued about minstrel performance generally, Miller's blacked-up presence in itself may have evoked a kind of miscegenation echoed in his artistic "alchemy" despite the racist ideologies fueling the highly traditional—and, by the 1920s, anachronistic—roles of his minstrel shows.[50] But those "falsetto flights" in his haunting voice also suggest another form of forbidden "amalgamation," marking a slide into the feminine analogous to the transvestism commonplace in minstrel shows.

Miller would never go on to adopt the hillbilly mask, like several of his more famous counterparts, and as a result, Tosches charges, was eventually eclipsed by this similar form of caricature. Puzzling through the relationship between minstrel and rustic stage personas, Tosches argues, "It is interesting to note that as the quaint fantasy of the happy antebellum coon, the figment on which minstrelsy was predicated, lost its currency, the parallel fantasy of the whimsical and picturesque hillbilly simultaneously rose to take its place in the subculture of southern show business."[51] However, this notion of evolutionary progression doesn't acknowledge or explain the persistent presence of both types as barn dance transformed the trappings of the medicine show and vaudeville. As such, it also fails to address the class dimensions of Miller's performance, which can hardly be reduced to the "sham" of white sophisticate passing for black rube. As we've seen, not all nineteenth-century minstrels nor twentieth-century blackface and/or hillbilly country music performers were urbane middle-class individuals acting out racist and classist hostilities on stage. Miller indeed surfaces as one key figure in the entangled history of white and black popular music and theater, but I think he registers connections that are denser—murkier—than even Tosches imagines in his impressive recovery mission.

Economically and culturally disenfranchised whites in the rural South, as well as the urban North, clearly recognized in the minstrel persona, no matter how exaggerated and ostensibly "comical," certain familiar traits and conditions that were mirrored, in turn, by the evolving rube character. Robert Cantwell recognizes this:

> The blackface minstrel's characterization of nineteenth-century black experience, a characterization which oscillated between sentimentality and ridicule, had supplied the images by which the Appalachian white, himself expelled from the rural South into the urban North, himself sentimentalized in the popular imagination and at the same time despised and caricatured, himself socially and culturally set apart, might interpret his own experiences a century later.[52]

The blackened mask potentially promotes, as well as forbids or contaminates, a basic form of identification between two groups encouraged by dominant culture to damage and fear one another.

This fragile process of identification does more than allow the poor white spectator/performer a mode of "escape" from his own marginal position—to make him or her, as Cantwell aptly puts it, "*socially* 'white'"—for such a reading suggests that minstrelsy can at best be *spurred* by identification but ultimately expressed (and resolved) as disassociation from blackness.[53] I'm trying to understand blackface *alongside* the rustic mask on the national barn dance stage: why both were needed, what both provided to a mass yet class-differentiated audience. In writing about the nineteenth-century minstrel show, Bert Ostendorf has argued that "the search for the primitive goes hand in hand with the search for the pastoral which is . . . an upper or middle class self-indulgence."[54] Twentieth-century barn dance conducts a similar kind of doubled search and thus would seem to produce a performative model that operates for its audience on myriad levels (communal, institutional, and individual; both stratified and blurred): exploiting racist ideologies and employment practices to unite white spectators across classes "under the cultural sign and sound of whiteness"; exploiting misogyny to unite male spectators of all races and classes but also promoting elitist ideas about poor rural cultures to retain hegemonic control over what still threatened to survive as a "lumpen theater" for disenfranchised black and white working-class audiences.[55]

Rural poor or working-class whites who performed as rubes, like *blacks* performing in burnt cork, may then have achieved a "type of shame management through hyperbolic self-presentation" when they imagined their more sophisticated listeners tuning in to or actually viewing their antics.[56] Like their black counterparts, they may have resorted to "the theatrical grotesques as ways of marking distance between themselves and their horror," in order to "mark" themselves in turn as modern civilized subjects.[57] Or did some take advantage of the opportunity to have their marginalized cultural identity recognized and preserved, albeit in a buffoonish commodified form? The unstable gendering of both the male and female rustic contributes to these larger structural as well as individual ideological aims, I contend, by simultaneously shoring up and dismantling white working-class/poor masculinity. Additionally, emphasis on the artifice of both the rube and black masks—what Lott designates as the "seeming counterfeit"— seems crucial to explaining why both types persisted, even as Western costuming and mythology took hold in country music during the 1930s and '40s and provided a relatively safer means of performing American middle-class whiteness.[58]

III. CLASS AND RACIAL MASQUERADE:
THE BARN DANCE SCENE

As one hybrid distillation of entertainment genres and musical styles, Emmett Miller fleshes out this neglected aspect of country music history not only by influencing later prominent performers but by crossing paths with rising WSM blackface star Lasses White as his own career was waning. Both had worked with Al Field's show, and in 1932, White publicly attested to Miller's talents in the pages of *Billboard* magazine.[59] Such intersections further establish minstrelsy as a foundation for the evolving country music industry, particularly providing radio barn dance programming with structure, pacing, and imagery. Along with its more sanitized successor, vaudeville, the minstrel show served as the skeletal support system for this increasingly popular manifestation of homespun music and culture.

Of the myriad renditions of barn dance programming to develop in this period, including Chicago's early and widely broadcast *National Barn Dance,* the Grand Ole Opry can claim an unusually direct lineage back to minstrelsy through its very name, as well as its celebrated announcer and architect George D. Hay. In the following section, I thus focus on the WSM program because of its explicit promotion of rustic imagery and sustained support of blackface comedy up through the early 1950s.[60] Discussion of class and racial masquerade will subsequently turn to less "grand" examples of barn dance programming that flourished throughout the nation during the Depression era.

WSM/Grand Ole Opry

Though now often dismissed as a kind of "grotesque" circus—a "gaseous expanding star in the concluding stages of its existence"—the Opry, much like minstrelsy itself, was originally christened as a folk alternative to highbrow opera.[61] As many minstrelsy scholars have noted, both Mark Twain and Walt Whitman professed great enthusiasm for blackface performance by casting it as the "native" equivalent of opera. Twain wrote in his autobiography, "If I could have the nigger show back . . . I should have but little further use for opera . . . it burst upon us as a glad and stunning surprise." Constance Rourke cites Whitman's infatuation with "Negro dialect," which he believed formed the foundations of "a native grand opera in America."[62] In its own fascinating set of circumstances, the Opry's name emerged as a neologism derived from the term "opera" but proudly cast as its antithesis. Charles Wolfe draws on Hay's autobiographical narrative to document this complicated moment in the fall of 1927:

> Hay and the Opry cast were waiting for a network show to end, the *NBC Music Appreciation Hour* with noted conductor Walter Damrosch, so they could come on the locally produced show. As he concluded, Damrosch lamented that there was little or "no place in the classics for realism" and conducted a short classical piece depicting a train ride. Hay, coming on seconds later, proclaimed: ". . . from here on out for the next three hours we will present nothing but realism. It will be down to earth for the 'earthy.'" He then introduced [African-American harmonicist] DeFord Bailey, who did *his* depiction of a train ride, "Pan American Blues." Afterwards, Hay said, "For the past hour we have been listening to the music taken largely from the Grand Opera, but from now on we will present the Grand Ole Opry."[63]

This early representation of barn dance programming thus officially came into being as a discursive entity via a black male performer's "earthy" imitation of a quintessential symbol of Americana that both defiantly opposed and invoked its elite counterpart. Not exactly blackface burlesque, then, but as with blacks in blackface, a curiously meta performance of racial identity and an equally evocative amalgam of gestures both exposing and reimposing class-based aesthetics.

Important studies by Wolfe and Peterson have immeasurably enriched our understanding of Hay's role as mastermind of this program's evolving "rustification," pointing primarily to his faith in its money-making potential. On an early scouting mission for WLS after World War I, Hay witnessed a modest country "hoedown" in Arkansas and "saw this same spirit being successfully fitted to the new mass medium of radio." Shortly thereafter, he moved to WSM and formulated the idea of a barn dance similar to Chicago's version but with the potential to truly expand the market premised on the performers' authenticity, noting that its "people were real and genuine and . . . really were playing what they were raised on."[64] Yet Hay encountered unanticipated formidable resistance from Nashville's "proper citizens" and thereby launched a marketing campaign attesting to "old-time" music's popularity and commercial viability while softening its image. In a 1926 article for *The Tennessean,* he wrote, "There is some delightful little folk strain that brings us all back to the soil, which runs through each of the numbers." Hay increasingly drew upon hillbilly stereotypes for his musicians' stage presence, dressing them in overalls and straw hats, despite the fact that few after 1930 fit the bill: they remained unprofessional performers but were hardly "naïve hill folk preserving an exclusive and rare heritage." As Wolfe demonstrates in contrasting photos of the Opry cast, in 1928, most were dressed in business suits and stylish dresses; in 1933, they posed before a cornfield backdrop in farm clothing.[65] Such data becomes especially useful when examining the hillbilly persona alongside the vestiges of blackface emerging on the barn dance stage during the 1930s and '40s. And Hay, like Emmett Miller, is in his own way a striking emblem and engine of their convergence.

Wolfe's mid-1970s work on the early Opry adopted long before it was fashionable a nascent cultural studies approach, rightly arguing that the Opry's "form" constituted "the complex of geographical, political, commercial, and historical factors that caused a Nashville insurance company to found and sustain a controversial radio show," including "the public relations genius of a young announcer named George Hay, who established and defined the scope of the show."[66] As seen earlier, Hay indeed functions as one nexus of the various conditions producing this relatively new cultural text, a sharp, Midwestern, middle-class journalist who developed his radio announcer skills first in Memphis, then at WLS in Chicago on the *National Barn Dance,* before landing the job at WSM in Nashville in 1926. This prior experience certainly contributed to the development of his own now-classic Opry persona as the "Solemn Old Judge," to the source of "auditory gimmicks" such as his trademark steamboat whistle (named "Hushpuckiny"), and to his overall professionalization. Still, the moniker itself, along with Hay's "genius" for producing and marketing various types of masquerade, derives from his earliest work as a court reporter for the (aptly named) *Memphis Commercial Appeal,* writing a weekly column in black dialect called "Howdy, Judge." The columns, collected and published in book form in 1926, served as the template for Hay's own blackface sketches performed with Ed McConnell in the Opry's formative years and in themselves help to illuminate his later ideas about white folk culture.[67]

Hay's foreword to the collection casts his writing as standard police court reporting, claiming "the following stories were written very much as the cases occurred. Perhaps the imagination was called upon at times, but it was very seldom necessary."[68] Yet he begins the book proper with "A Mississippi River Baptism"—an extended dramatic portrait of one Easter Sunday baptism conducted by a local black Baptist preacher that reads as a kind of shadow minstrel show, complete with stump sermon and a frequently interrupting congregation/audience. And Hay, enacting blackface performance in print, can be seen as undergoing his own ironic baptism by becoming "born again" as "de man whut totes two faces undah his hat."[69]

While this opening vignette is hardly the setting his readers anticipate, it eventually becomes clear as one works through the collection that Hay seeks to establish an equivalence between the moral authority figure of Memphis' "colored" community, the Reverend H. C. Toombs, and the city's legal authority figure meting out "justice" to whites and blacks alike, Judge L. T. Fitzhugh. Like the latter, who appears in virtually all subsequent pieces, the preacher dresses "in the conventional black robes of office" and insists upon "de barefooted truth": "Yo' haht mus' be true an' no lies mus'n 'scape f'm yo' lips." Similarly, Hay's penchant for racial dialect initially appears to respect superficial forms of cultural difference while denying any essential and significant distinctions arising from such difference: it attempts to capture all vocal and visual nuance but insists upon a general sense of humanity. His

Reverend Toombs intones: "Jesus says yo' mus' love eve'body; da's whut he says. Yo' mus' love de white man, yallah man, red man, gray man; . . . ca'se dey ain't no white an' black heavens. . . . We may sit in de back o' de street cahs an' trains, but we all sits togethah when we gits to heaven, ca'se dey ain't no back seats up deah." The text as a whole, however, undercuts such sentiment in its depiction of predominantly "cullud" defendants and white representatives of the judicial/police system. We discover that Judge Fitzhugh refers to such male defendants as "boy," repeatedly impugning their masculinity with the command to "brace up and be a man," because they appear naturally infantile, irresponsible, "shifty."[70]

One early ensemble of vignettes, titled "Three Nips of Golden Corn," offers glimpses of four court proceedings contrasting white and black defendants. The first two concern alcohol abuse and juxtapose one J. H. Barnett, who according to the arresting officer "seems to be a pretty good fellow" who happened to drink "just a little too much white mule," with Slim Young and his "negress" girl, Savannah Lamb, who make their own blackberry wine. The judge declares Barnett to be "a good, hard-working man" and fines him ten dollars, though the reader has no evidence on which to base such assessment, while Slim's character is revealed through bodily evidence: "so constructed physically that it is difficult for him to cease locomotion on an instant's notice, and so constituted mentally that, upon hearing the law's stern voice, speed is the natural course adopted by his ample and understanding feet, after word is transmitted from his curly head."[71] Slim hardly seems dangerous as the stock lazy "Negro," but the other black defendant, Helen Chatman, is sullen and menacing, a razor-wielding "brute." Here is Hay's full rendition:

"She lak to cut me t' pieces, jedge," related Lulu McAlester, negress, who exhibited a long wound on her neck.
Helen Chatman was standing behind the railing, trying to defend Herself in the face of damaging odds.
"What did you do to her first?" the court asked.
"Nothin'."
"What have you got to say for yourself, girl?"
"Not guilty!"
"Hold her to the State. Looks to me like you cut her half in two. Been in the hospital three weeks. Ought to take a few razors Away from you negroes."
"Dis heah wuz a butchah knife, jedge," added Lulu, rather carelessly. "She's de fastes' wukin' niggah wid a butchah knife I evah did see in mah whole life."

"I tole huh to leave mah man alone," commented Helen, as she walked back with Sergeant Cole.[72]

These two basic caricatures recur throughout. Fitzhugh either paternalistically dismisses their cases—"Well, you negroes go on home now, and forget this little affair. No harm was meant"—or makes judgmental pronouncements—"I thought so. . . . Negroes fight like a bunch of hyenas and never show up in court."[73]

Howdy Judge concludes with the case of a black preacher charged with gambling, bringing the collection full circle. Sam Blow, appearing in court in his own "ministerial robes," protests: "Dis heah is de mos' awful mistake what has been made in mah whole lifetime. De ve'y idea of a pastah bein' arrested is strange to behold, an I put mah right hand up to high heaven and sweah by all da's holy dat I sho' nevah did have nothin' to do wid dem policy slips. . . . As a preachah o' de gospel, I ax yo' to let me out o' dis heah foul place, ca'se I jes' nach'ly don't belong heah." Although Fitzhugh decides to "give him the benefit of the doubt in view of his calling," the court clerk brings him low, having the final word: "Here you are, Sam . . . Stick to your name and 'blow,' do you get me?"[74] Despite Reverend Toombs' protests against segregation in the opening pages, Blow's greatest offense clearly lies in his resistance to "nach'l" moral spheres dividing blacks and whites.

As Hay's announcer role on the Opry evolved, it was "the Solemn Old Judge" who emerged as Fitzhugh's true double, rather than his fictive black preachers. In his originally self-published *A Story of the Grand Ole Opry,* for instance, Hay's discussion of black Opry performer and "mascot" DeFord Bailey seems an uncanny mimicry of this earlier authoritative voice.[75] Introducing Bailey as a "wizard with the harmonica" as he recalls the program's celebrated first moments on the air, Hay suddenly switches gears to explain the performer's eventual firing in 1941:

That brings us to Deford [*sic*] Bailey, a little crippled colored boy who was a bright feature of our show for about fifteen years. Like some members of his race and other races, Deford was lazy. He knew about a dozen numbers, . . . but he refused to learn any more, even though his reward was great. He was our mascot and is still loved by the entire company. We gave him a whole year's notice to learn some more tunes, but he would not. When we were forced to give him his final notice, Deford said, without malice: "I knowed it waz comin', Judge, I knowed it wuz comin'."[76]

Bailey himself relayed quite a different version of his professional demise, insisting that he in fact desired and attempted to play different songs but was forced to offer up the same familiar handful. There was initially such an "outcry" from Opry audiences over his dismissal that he was, interestingly enough, paid to "make himself visible" on the grounds of the Ryman Auditorium.[77]

Hay clearly felt more comfortable with the stylized version of "black" "visibility" that he found in Lee Roy "Lasses" White. A fan of White's shows while still in Memphis, he brought this "dean of minstrelsy" to WSM in 1932 to launch a Friday-night minstrel show.[78] White soon paired up with Lee Davis "Honey" Wilds to form the Opry's first formal blackface comic team, Lasses and Honey, in 1934. Billed as "Dixie's Sweetest Combination," they performed regularly at the Opry for the next three years until White was replaced with "Jamup" partner David Biggs.[79]

In *A Story of the Grand Ole Opry,* Hay highlights the prior duo's success both on and off the road—each show "had 'em hangin' on the rafters in the schoolhouses throughout the territory served immediately by our station." More significantly, in hindsight, Hay makes a point of highlighting the artifice of White's performance, drawing keen distinctions between the mask and the man behind it: "Since that time Lasses White has become one of our very best friends. He is a gentleman of excellent character and a very fine artist, who has a beautiful home in West Los Angeles, California, which he and Mrs. White designed." He concludes, "Off stage, Leroy 'Lasses' White is a very quiet and dignified man, very much a gentleman." In Hay's hands, White ultimately becomes the quintessential Horatio Alger figure, for his "life story . . . is an American success story, made possible by native intelligence and hard work." In keeping with the World War II–era backdrop for the writing of this Opry "story," White's identity finally encompasses a conflation of race, class, and nationalist fervor, a twist on Hay's earlier "two faces under one hat" motif: "We understand from mutual friends that he is doing a great deal of entertaining for the service men and women stationed on the West Coast. . . . True artists are known for their generosity in times of trouble, so it follows naturally that Lasses White would give his best to his native land, which he loves so much, because Lasses is a fine American."[80] Given Hay's anxiety here to facilitate white middle-class identification with his prior minstrel star, it seems fitting that White eventually abandoned blackface (and WSM) to pursue an acting career in Western films, perhaps the only other route for achieving this putative position as a white American "gentleman."

Lasses/Jamup and Honey

Such commentary begins to tell us something about Hay's vision of blackface in relation to the Opry's folk programming even if it's only an obvious and rather late construction produced for publicity purposes. Lott argues that "a continual acknowledgment of minstrelsy's counterfeit obviously accompanied the illusion of 'blackness' onstage" and was in fact "politically necessitated by it" in order to maintain white "control" over black culture. Yet as with all mimicry, "the power disguised by the counterfeit was also invoked by it," perennially destabilizing the hegemonic effects of the performance.[81] In Hay's recounting of White's history, that instability haunts Opry minstrelsy on several levels. Its denigration of blackness is continually called into question as it both showcases and fetishizes its referent, and its concomitant faith in the superiority of whiteness equally falters. The ostensible unification of working-class and middle-class white audiences through racism thus never quite holds, though it clearly flares up at nodal points in the act. White's low-class identity exacerbates this dynamic, further blurring the lines between the minstrel and his black persona.

As noted earlier, however, Hay insisted upon a quite different fiction for his white rube performers, establishing via costuming an authentically rustic personal history whether or not they actually hailed from the hills. As marketer of such images, Hay clearly believed that he could salvage white rusticity by repackaging it as a folk heritage palatable to white consumers of all classes—another route, perhaps, to racial solidarity, as well as a way to defuse working-class oppositionality during a period of widespread poverty and unrest. Hiroko Tsuchiya has shown that industrial recreation programs sponsored by large American corporations from the turn of the century up to the early 1920s produced their own versions of working-class theater, drawing on vaudeville and minstrelsy to appease their dissatisfied workers; these programs' "messages of mindless gaiety and childlike innocence . . . appealed to management fearful of the radicalization of their employees and of impending strikes."[82]

I'm not suggesting that the Opry had such deliberately formulated political motivations. But by broadcasting from a city dubbed "the Athens of the South" and hoping to capture more highbrow as well as lowbrow listeners, the program necessarily played into dominant class ideologies—a practice later mandated by company sponsors and radio network executives.[83] Transforming potentially transgressive white lower-class performative roles into harmless "folk" facilitated such ideologies, exerting the same control over class culture that minstrelsy wielded over black culture. Yet while Hay attempted to insure that this counterfeit was a seamless performance, with no gaps displayed between on-stage and off-stage existence, the exaggeration of the mask, as in minstrelsy, surely strained credulity and thus similarly couldn't help but expose the rube *as* a construct. I'd thus like to examine this minstrelsy material on its own terms to understand other forces involved in its production and consumption.

Standard thumbnail sketches of the Lasses/Jamup and Honey duo can be found in a number of historical studies, meriting a paragraph to several pages in Charles Wolfe's numerous Opry histories or in a handful of material devoted to country comedy.[84] Wolfe's 1999 study offers the most detail on Lasses White himself and briefly situates his version of minstrelsy in relation to stage and radio work of the 1920s. A successor to legendary minstrel troupe leader William George "Honeyboy" Evans, as well as lead performer in other famous shows, this Texan farm boy eventually formed his own minstrel troupe and achieved success as a "jazz age" songwriter. Yet by the end of the decade, he realized that he needed to update the content of his programs, as well as recognize "a newer format" in order to satisfy a larger and more modern audience.[85]

That format, of course, was radio, which in 1929 converted minstrel show trappings into the hugely successful *Amos 'n' Andy*—a program that routinely interrupted Opry broadcasts on NBC stations. Since no scripts or recordings of White's own WSM Friday-night show are available, it is difficult to assess the exact changes he might have made to accommodate this new medium and new age. Wolfe draws on the material published in White's annual songbooks (1934–36)—various types of song parodies, as well as sentimental tunes—to conclude, "Just as the Vagabonds had adapted their earlier pop song styles to the Opry and moved toward a folk and old-time repertoire, so did White, another experienced professional, adapt his style and repertoire to the Opry image."[86] But unlike the Vagabonds' popular music, blackface comedy had an older, deeper relationship to the notion of "folk" or "old-time" culture and thus faced another kind of challenge. To shake associations with an anachronistic form of entertainment and its crudest set of ideas about racial difference, it had to become a bit more sanitized and appear updated.

In White's 1936 *Book of Humor and Song*, for instance, the subject matter and referents are much more contemporary than stock minstrel show bits. As Wolfe also notes, some "are relatively free of the ethnic overtones that marked many of the earlier 'coon' songs" and employ current political or news topics, particularly concerning President Roosevelt, to be both fun and timely.[87] Yet much of minstrelsy's old-time appeal lay precisely in its ties to a rural, "premodern" past. In the fledgling country music industry of the late 1920s and '30s—and particularly in the context of barn dance radio programming—minstrelsy tropes had to do double duty, as it were, teetering on the edge between two modes of rusticity: one ostensibly primitive and excessively inflected by race, class, and gender markings; one more stylized and national, approaching modernity but free of jazz age "immorality."[88]

We can certainly see such a balance being struck in the Lasses/Honey songbooks. Both performers appear on the 1936 cover sans makeup and dressed in smart suits, hats, and ties, accentuating their "natural" affiliation with white modernity. Yet the frontispiece features at the top a photo of White's All-Star Minstrel troupe, with White and Wilds in blackface, and at the bottom the duo in full costume posed as gambling "dicemen." The combination and positioning of both images suggest a kind of progression from old-style to modern racial masquerade. The accompanying page sports a mixture of standard and minstrel dialect marketing both the book and the duo's Bluebird recordings to their fans. Lastly, however, in the copy I examined, stanzas of a lengthy anonymous poem titled "The Drinking House Over the Way" had been inserted into the binding and laid over these frontispiece pages, partially obscuring them. Told from the perspective of a dying wife and mother periodically abandoned by her husband, the treacly narrative on first glance trades on the stuff of tragic folk ballads and Dickensian plots to condemn the crimes of alcoholism, concluding with the bromide, "If only it were not so handy to drink—/ The men that make laws . . . sure didn't think / Of the hearts they would break, of the souls they / would slay, / When they licensed the DRINKING-HOUSE over the way." Yet it also functions as a commentary on the vulnerability and hopelessness that accompanies poverty, which drives a "kindhearted" man to numb himself with drink and leave his wife (and baby) to die of "want, of hunger and cold." This opening mélange of conflicting images and text in itself speaks to the strange and strained network of meanings presented to WSM audiences during the Depression era, commingling poor white tragedy, feminine morality, and illicit "black" rebelliousness.

Several other components of the songbook underscore this modernized version of minstrelsy. Recent clever song parodies are juxtaposed with ads for minstrel guides, wigs, and burnt cork, as well as music and lyrics for White's original composition "Honey Bee," which could have been drawn from Hay's "Howdy, Judge" column (or vice versa): Jimmie Snead, "built just like a jimpson weed," had a wife he called "his sweet little honey bee"; when "she began to sass, / Jimmy [*sic*] hauled off and hit her . . . And he hit her with / an awful crash, / Boys, he hit her with a bottle . . . And he knocked her / through a looking glass / And he thought that he'd killed his little Honey Bee." Later in the collection, a page of jokes titled "Gentlemen Be Seated!" includes the full text of several standard minstrel routines involving an interlocutor figure speaking in standard English and Lasses and Honey getting the best of him with dialect patter and wordplay ("Naw, suh, Mr. Taylor, I just can't seem to think a thunk").[89] While readers can only begin to hear the different voice inflections in such reproduced material, they can connect the sound and flavor of blackface comedy to its visual power via an imposed image of White in standard-issue makeup and ill-fitting dress, perched on a barrel, at the top right corner of the page. I later found this same "photo" replicated on a piece of WSM stationery tucked away in the Country Music Foundation's archival file on White—a rather stunning affirmation of minstrelsy's once-central place in this station's roster of authentic images.

If the Lasses and Honey team have virtually no surviving audiotapes or scripts to represent their work for WSM and the Opry, Jamup and Honey, which paired "Honey" Wilds with several subsequent veteran partners (Tom Woods, David "Bunny" Biggs, Harold LeVan), have only quite recently begun to fare better. The 1999 Mercury Records two-CD compilation *Hank Williams Live at the Grand Ole Opry* (produced by Williams biographer Colin Escott and Kira Florita) makes available a Jamup and Honey skit from February 1950—the waning of their career but a fascinating glimpse of blackface comedy's positioning in a typical Opry program of the period, in terms of both its featured musical acts and other popular rube comedians such as Minnie Pearl and Rod Brasfield. In the course of my research, I also uncovered several important examples of their work that to my knowledge have never been discussed in print: two audiotapes of Opry programs dated 8 February 1941 and 16 February 1946 and, perhaps more significant, hundreds of Jamup and Honey radio scripts issuing primarily from the late 1940s and early 1950s (these literally buried in the original Country Music Foundation library's basement, left yellowing in a musty ledger). With editing marks and comments still intact, these scripts are invaluable, illuminating the construction of race, gender, and class at the most literal as well as hermeneutic levels. More particularly, they document a shift in country blackface representation, accentuating much more notably the grotesque and erotic, as well as reviving the formal trappings of the full-scale minstrel show itself.[90]

Jamup and Honey in Grand Ole Opry performance. (Courtesy of Country Music Hall of Fame and Museum.)

In the earlier audio skit of 1941, Jamup and Honey share the same Opry stage with Roy Acuff, the Possum Hunters, and Ford Rush (at the least: Part I of this thirty-minute aired program is missing). Sponsored by Prince Albert tobacco, the program opens with Judge Hay's trademark steamboat whistle, then features a popular vaudeville-era "heart" song performed by Acuff, "Letter Edged in Black," which earns an encore ("mighty pretty . . . give us another verse"). The program thus begins on a note of both nostalgia and sentimentality, invoking not only prior theatrical roots and traditions but also sacrosanct images of home and hearth. "Letter Edged in Black" recounts the narrative of an estranged family that reunites after the father writes a letter to the son breaking the news of his mother's death.[91] Letters "edged in black" also, of course, remind the audience of World War II, which the United States was on the brink of entering—a death notice that singularly conflates the domestic and the national spheres. As the Opry's headlining rustic performer of the moment, Acuff is a fitting choice to deliver this stirring message of family and patriotism. His signature brand of emotional vocals complements the sentimental material as well, straying toward yet avoiding a collapse into feminine territory. Additionally, his own early if brief ventures in blackface make him equally suited to introduce the next act.[92]

For after a commercial break, "Prince Albert's two minstrel boys" take the stage to treat those who want their "funny bone tickled proper." As in almost all of their routines, Jamup plays the prankster role and Honey the straight man. Here, the humor hinges primarily on malapropism rather than racialized dialect as Jamup, coached by his partner, prepares to give a speech for the town mayor: "we extend our sincere thanks" becomes, in Jamup's rendition, "we skin our shanks"; similarly, "we hope and trust" is converted to "we hope they rust," and "our efforts to amuse you" to "our efforts to abuse you." Yet the wordplay also clearly comments on politicians' deceptive and exploitative language. The skit works to decode such pat public speeches and was revived a decade later in their transgressive parody of radio programming. (It is also quite similar to a skit performed on Knoxville's WNOX in the early 1950s, with some interesting additions. These variations will be discussed later in the chapter.) Theatrical malapropism is historically associated with white working-class women and black men, whose linguistic inventiveness signals, at least in part, unlicensed sexuality.[93] Here, Jamup and Honey brilliantly manage to convey such unruly class, gender, and race associations by "speaking" the comically distorted language themselves and attributing its more malevolent qualities, when in the wrong hands, to those in power.

This night's Opry program concludes with three musical numbers: "Greenwood" (the Possum Hunters), "You Are My Sunshine" (Ford Rush), and Acuff's version of "Liza Jane." In keeping with the "earthiness" of the prior blackface act, the first is performed by a true mainstay of the Opry, originally dubbed "Dr. Humphry Bate and his Possum Hunters" by George Hay—one of his first artistic groups to undergo a rustic makeover. The second song, however, shifts the program back to the soft pop sound increasingly incorporated to retain middle-class listeners uncomfortable with pure hillbilly fare. "You Are My Sunshine" had first been recorded just one year earlier by Jimmie Davis, who would later make it the state song of Louisiana, but it was also sung by crooners such as Bing Crosby. Rush, who had worked with Hay during his brief early stint with WLS, had gone on to perform as one half of the duo Ford 'N' Glen, known for Tin Pan Alley material, and as a solo act recorded cover versions of popular hits. Yet the third number, performed again by Acuff, invokes another tie to minstrelsy in one fifteen-minute segment of the show: "Liza Jane" is a traditional tune originally published by Daniel Emmett, a member of the Virginia Minstrels, in 1843, and a variant, "Goodbye Liza Jane," was recorded twice in the 1920s, once by The Hillbillies (released under the title "Mountaineers Love Song") and once by the Tenneva Ramblers (as "Miss Liza, Poor Gal"). Acuff's own black-face roots thus reemerge as a fitting coda to this half-hour program, underscoring the connections between white and black rusticity.

The Purina-sponsored program of February 1946 is a bit more noteworthy as it marks the debut of future star hillbilly comic team Lonzo and Oscar; incorporates several bits by fellow rube comedian Rod Brasfield; and positions as guest emcee "down-home crooner" Eddy Arnold, who a year later would claim thirteen of the top twenty songs on the country charts.[94] Jamup and Honey appear somewhat late in the show, packaged between vaudeville and medicine show veteran Uncle Dave Macon and a relatively new bluegrass duo from West Virginia, the Bailes Brothers. Banjoist Macon, coding as a "natural" man from the hills with earthy predilections,[95] punctuates his performance of the instrumental tune "Grey Cat on a Tennessee Farm" with frequent bluesy shouts, the mainstay of both minstrel and unsanitized old-time music. Blackface comedy immediately follows, receiving a more suggestive introduction than in the earlier program: "To add a little more spice to these Grand Ole Opry cookins, those two sons of confusion you've always liked so well, Purina's Pranksters, Jamup and Honey!" Their lengthier skit centers on Honey's singing voice and again relies on verbal punning, though here the straight man is himself the butt of the joke. A "bass" voice becomes "base" or "vile," an affecting "cry," "tear," or "rip." The performers' give-and-take banter hinges on the struggle over silencing that voice as an artistic instrument: "I went to a professional and had my voice brought out" / "You should have had it shoved back"; "I had my voice cultivated" / "You should have had it plowed under." Finally, voice and visage become one: "My voice is so powerful I could crack a mirror" / "You could look at it as well." While played strictly for laughs, the bit also seems to address the tension inherent in Opry programming between the raw vocalizing of unprofessional "hillfolk" such as Macon and the more polished sound of mainstream popular music. Intriguingly, then, after Jamup and Honey's performance, host Eddy Arnold implores the mirthful crowd to "quiet down now, children," with "an old-time number" by the Bailes Brothers. Their "Building on the Sands," a close-harmony bluegrass gospel tune, perhaps more accurately represents a modernized version of old-time music—one that melodically and lyrically calms rather than incites its audience and discourages identification along transgressive class and racial lines.

By the early 1950s, a hint of desperateness emerges in Jamup and Honey's material that is reminiscent of minstrelsy's waning years in the prior century. Wilds and his partner adopt more exaggerated dialects to match routines preoccupied with the licentiousness of African American life. The overarching conservatism of the era certainly provides one explanation for this shift, as the war years' relaxing of previous boundaries—women flooding the workforce, African Americans serving in the military and in some cases more freely commingling with whites—had unleashed desires and discontent that needed to be contained. *Amos 'n' Andy* migrated to television between 1951 and 1953 with black actors occupying the title roles, yet protests would soon be launched as the civil rights movement began to gain ground. Hegemonic culture faced a more obvious looming crisis in its representation of race, yet class and gender were equally unstable performative categories that often achieved presence *through* racial mimicry. Barn dance's response to this postwar challenge remains more complicated than it might first appear and again proves most revealing when examined in the context of an entire Opry show, such as the one airing on 18 February 1950. Jamup and Honey are now billed as a "guest attraction" (along with Hank Williams, who was just achieving stardom), and their act dovetails with two others in fascinating ways: the previously discussed nineteenth-century tune performed by Red Foley, "Aunt Jemima's Plaster"; and a comedy routine by Minnie Pearl. Whether constructing white or black experience, all three comic texts concern aggressive women operating outside the bounds of propriety and require some mode of masquerade.

In keeping with minstrelsy's earlier mammy figure, Foley's Jemima is "old" and "clever," with the notion "that she would marry never." However, this enterprising version seeks to "live in peace" even as "none could be her master." A paean to her homemade curative, the song's breakneck pace and tongue-twisting refrain (cataloging plaster ingredients) prompt audience cheers, whistles, and laughter on the live recording, but clearly, more is at work here. Her resourceful product, like the minstrel mask it evokes, has both a reifying and a potentially liberating power. When slathered on, it "cures anything" but stubbornly remains affixed to the skin. The plaster concoction significantly allows Jemima to help those she chooses to become their own "master" yet prevents others (such as thieving cats in this rendition) from resisting bondage.

Minnie Pearl's act, interspersed between musical performances by Williams and Foley (respectively honky-tonk and spiritual numbers), introduces another unorthodox woman—one as familiar to her fans as Aunt Jemima but who might be claimed, at least by her white rural fans, as a "true" family member. "Cousin" Minnie was a fictitious character invented by a performer from a cultured Southern family, Sarah Ophelia Colley Cannon, who thus embodied the practice, if not Hay's initial vision, of Opry rusticity: the actual antithesis of country authenticity. As is typical of the rube/wench role inherited from minstrelsy and vaudeville, which accentuates the "unattractive" female comic's desperation for a mate, Minnie here immediately codes as a "man-hungry" country girl "tickled to see so many men" in the audience. But the joke itself—"sometimes I wish the lord had made me a man—he made 'em for other girls"—cuts both ways, establishing her character as an erotic being who flirts with masculinity itself (as well as lesbian sexuality, if the line is pursued all the way through).[96] Cannon follows this up with a silly bit about the wrestling club in her hometown of Grinders Switch, initially inviting audience members to "wrestle" with her, then admitting that she tackles the wrestlers themselves ("as soon as they get thrown out of the ring, the girls grab 'em up . . . I got a bruise on my elbow"). The routine manages to convey bawdiness without the explicitly cruder trappings of blackface tradition, though in this instance Minnie hardly seems the "innocent country girl" that Cannon professed was her model.[97] Finally, the performer's own well-known opposition to progressive racial politics in this period creates an additional layer of meaning for her audience to negotiate in the program as a whole.[98]

On several fronts, then, Minnie expertly paves the way for Jamup and Honey, whose skit focuses on the duo's checkered love lives. It begins with a description of Jamup's "gal":

"She's got class, good buddy."
"Oh, yeah. Is she a well-reared gal?"
"Let me have that again—"
"I said, is she a well-reared gal?"
"Yeah, and she don't do so bad in front, either!"

A few lines later, her bodily charms are clarified, to much hooting and hollering from the auditorium: "She's got the purtiest indiana figure . . . such a large southbend, man!" When Jamup inquires, "How come you ain't got you no sweetheart, Honey," he replies, "I ain't never found a gal that suits me . . . [one] who can keep the house, cook, sew, and never want to go out at night." His partner jokes, "Well, I'll dig you up one next night when I'm out at the graveyard!"[99] Eric Lott has convincingly shown that the excessive behavior and appearance of black women characters on the minstrel stage reflected antebellum racist misogyny—specifically a "horror of engulfing female bodies"—expressing white men's fear of emasculation.[100] The references here, similar to men actually performing as women in cross-dressing roles, at once dramatize and combat that anxiety by mocking women's power (and, by extension, dilute the impact of Cousin Minnie's brazenness in the prior act). Additionally, whites in blackface could tap into black men's ostensibly excessive sexuality, equally on display in this scene, and thus enhance their own masculinity, which was constantly imperiled in popular representations, including barn dance's own white rube personas. Finally, such sexuality could serve as a protest of the 1950s' renewed commitment to "workplace discipline and abstemiousness,"[101] recapturing, for just a moment, a kind of working-class solidarity alongside a broader bourgeois escape from suburban and capitalist propriety.

How, then, to read this particular program's succession of rustic personas? Jemima, Minnie, and Honey's "gal" all playfully overturn normative concepts of gender, race, and class, so that one female slave figure becomes a business tycoon, a white country girl aggressively pursues potential suitors, and another "black" woman's proper upbringing translates into an exaggerated body part. Yet by doing so, these performers also paradoxically reinforce ruling ideologies. Minnie's masculine as well as poor white traits ensure her romantic/erotic demise, while the blackface female figures are, like George Hay's Sam Blow character, shown up and finally punished for their crossing of class borders. Jemima may seem to escape such pointed ridicule, but the very absurdity of her product, accentuated by the song's increasingly nonsensical lyrics and exhausting tempo, undermines any possible social critique embedded in her novel positioning. (In fact, in an undated Jamup and Honey script, Jamup poses as an "Herb Doctor" whose "medicine" is comprised of equally ridiculous elements.) This program's subsequent acts thus unwittingly demonstrate the *necessity* of Jemima's masklike "plaster," which conceals as much as it heals.

In 1953, Jamup and Honey left the Opry entirely and began performing their blackface material on Knoxville station WNOX as part of the long-running *Midday Merry Go-Round and Tennessee Barn Dance* program emceed by Lowell Blanchard, another pivotal figure in the construction of hillbilly imagery.[102] Scripts issuing from this last phase of their career, previously deemed "lost" or irretrievable, reveal minstrelsy's dying gasp in country music culture. As such, they are at once predictable and surprising—recycling one-hundred-year-old gags in a postwar world confronting cataclysmic shifts in gender, class, and race relations. While we don't have access to transcripts or recordings of the entire WNOX barn dance program, which would presumably incorporate its own version of rube/hillbilly masquerade, these scripts at the very least give us a sustained glimpse of blackface country's twilight years.

Its potential *oppositionality* may be most evident in an undated skit (11 March, year unknown) satirizing commercial radio programming itself. Typed on a standard-issue WNOX production form bearing the skit title "RADIO CONTINUITY," this piece targets radio's formal conventions, complete with station "philosopher" and corporate sponsor. It begins as Blanchard, in minstrelsy's traditional interlocutor role, proclaims, "This is station . . . JOKE, owned and Mismanaged by Jamup and Honey." The duo immediately interrupt to announce that they've changed the call letters to "BURP" and seek to begin "Booze-casting . . . I mean . . . Broad-chasing . . . or broadcasting" in order to equate the industry with their own act's illicit proclivities. They follow with "a word from our Sponsor . . . who has made this program impossible": "Nu-Gold" cigarettes, whose "real gold" filter allows you to "inhale and fill your cavities at the same time." An attack on radio's increasingly popular soap opera narrative, aimed at female listeners, follows with the story of "Selma Fizz, girl seltzer bottle," which "asks the question: 'Should a girl turn her back on love, just because she's ten feet tall and has two heads?'" Jamup continues: "In our last episode Selma got a note from a tall dark stranger asking her to marry him. After hours of torment she still couldn't decide if he was sincere or not . . . you see the note was mimeographed." After several other advertising parodies, such as "Sipton Tea Bags," the skit concludes with a send-up of radio's trite patter that can be read further as a chilling commentary on the unchanging countenance of the blackface mask: "The Trouble with people today is . . . they don't smile enough. Why if you made up your mind for one complete day . . . and I mean with everybody . . . smile at your friends . . . at your enemies . . . at relatives . . . at strangers . . . you'd be surprised how many people will come up to you and say . . . 'All right Wise guy . . . .. Whats [*sic*] so funny?'" At this late date,

Jamup and Honey indulge in a more biting and self-conscious critique of an entire industry, which had initially provided their livelihood but eventually left their outdated performative tradition behind.

In this period, they also turn the tables on the stock judge-courthouse routine epitomized by Hay's newspaper columns and blackface performances in the 1920s. In this script (also undated, its first page missing), the program announcer has become "Judge Blanchard," presiding over a case in which Honey has been accused of stealing a watch and is being represented by his "attorney," Jamup. In "the State versus Honey B. Comb," the defendant continually undermines courtroom logic and procedure, clearly besting its authority figure. He initially pleads "not guilty" and "waives de Hearin"—"I jes don't want to heah no mo about it, dats all"; when commanded to "tell the truth" and "kiss the Bible," Honey replies, "I'm sorry your Honery, but your Pet Billy Goat is done et up de Bible." After being "sworn in," he pleads "not guilty . . . for reasons of Insanity." When Blanchard asks, "Does your Family suffer from Insanity, Honey?" he responds, "Aw Nawsuh, we enjoys every minute of it." After a series of similar outlandish rejoinders, one of which claims that he is nothing less than a "Mother," Honey is ruled to be in "contempt of court" and fined either thirty dollars or thirty days' incarceration. When asked to choose, he concludes, "Well den, Judge, your Majesty, if it's all de same wid you, we'll jes take de $30.00." (This skit is referred to in another, dated 25 April 1953, where Jamup is the defendant in a divorce case.)

This same sort of antihero appeal appears even more pronounced in a 1953 script concerning schooling. Its particular routine doesn't simply rely on malapropisms for laughs but calls attention to ungrammatical language, a highly sensitive subject with which many audience members as well as program performers could identify, and the foundation for much minstrel and rube comedy:

HONEY: How is your little ole boy, Oremus, doin in his school work dis year?

JAMUP: Mighty bad, Honey . . . Every time he say somethin de Teacher up and correcks him. . . .

HONEY: Well dat's what he's goin to school for, so's he can learn to talk proper. . . .

JAMUP: Yestiddy, de teacher asked him why he was'nt studdin, and he [sic] tole her, he say "Cause, I aint got no books." . . .

HONEY: Dat was a good reason alright. . . .

JAMUP: Den de teacher say "Oremus, don't say you aint got no books," hits proper to say "I doesn't has any books." . . .

HONEY: What did little ole Oremus tell de good woman?

JAMUP: He say "Well Teach, if dey aint nobody got no books, es jes close dis joint up and go fishin." . . . I think I'll jes take him outta school and let him grow up in ignorance wid de rest of us. . . .

HONEY: You ain't takin de proper appitude in dis thing, Jamup. If you take him outta school he'll be actin like you, and you so dumb till you acks jes like a child. . . .

JAMUP: Don't call me no child. I'm a full growed man and when anybody messes wid me, I proves it too. . . .

HONEY: Jes cause you gits out and fights, aint no sign you is a man. You got to learn how to be a gentman and be chiverous to de fair sex. . . .

As we discover in a number of their routines, however, such rules governing both gender and class behavior fail to apply in Jamup and Honey's world, since representatives of the "fair sex" have been replaced by "balloon dancers" and "big mamas" even more sexually aggressive, violent, and unschooled than men. The potential social critique embedded within unruly modes of rusticity once again becomes compromised by racist and misogynistic impulses targeting specific audience sectors.

Conditions become even more explicit in a related script from July 1954:

HONEY: Did you got to school?

JAMUP: Course I went to school. . . . I went to a very exclusive school. . . . It had bars on de windows so nobody could slip in.

HONEY: I bet dat was some school.

JAMUP: It was. . . . I had lots of fun shootin craps, while de teacher called de roll.

And in another knowing reference to blacking up, a few lines earlier, Jamup notes that his family was so poor, "my pappy couldn't afford to buy me shoes," so he "painted my feets black and braided my toes." Judith Butler's identification-disavowal dialectic once again comes to mind here as emasculation, racist humiliation, and defiance mark these final minstrel texts. The skits invite and in some ways demand a degree of identification with Jamup and Honey's abjection, yet the "seeming counterfeit" of the performance helps engineer and ultimately marks the audience's rejection of that positionality.

As I have attempted to argue, this material needs an ideological as well as a historicized analysis that attempts to take into account the deep-seated views, pleasures, and desires of both blackface fans and performers. Is George Hay's valuing of minstrelsy—and his intentions for incorporating it into barn dance programming/mythology—*necessarily* compatible with, say, Honey Wilds's twenty-five-year commitment to its performance?

We can begin to answer that question by turning to the reminiscences and reflections of Wilds's son, David, who has served as an enormously generous, if also personally invested, source on his father's career. In a 1996 interview, he first attempted to elucidate the nuances underlying the controversial race and class politics of blackface comedy by commenting on his father's relationship to blacks, and black culture, in the early twentieth-century South: "Daddy grew up just dirt poor in Southeastern Texas. When the subject of race, bigotry, or segregation would come up, he would say . . . 'Well, why not let 'em go to school together? Why not let 'em play together? I did. I was so poor I couldn't look down on a Mexican or (he would have said) a colored kid.'" Wilds continued, "He didn't really like uptight pretentious white people very much. He would spend time with black people because he had more fun with them."[103] He confirmed that this particular white minstrel had close contact, specifically, with black entertainers—"in Dallas, he hung out at one all-black theater"—and concluded, "There's no question that he gravitated toward that culture, and that's why I've always been reasonably comfortable saying that the act was in part a tribute and an homage, it was not him looking down his nose. . . . He was nobody's racist."[104]

His father himself has attested to the act's appeal to both black and white audiences during the Opry's traveling tent shows of the 1940s:

> We didn't think we were making fun of them, . . . and evidently they didn't think we were making fun of them. Half of the people we drew . . . were Negro. They filled the balconies up at almost every show. And we didn't get along too well with some of the managers of theaters we played because . . . they didn't care too much for the fact that Jamup and Honey were as popular with blacks and whites.[105]

Additionally, unlike his first partner Lee Roy White and eerily similar to Emmett Miller, Lee Davis Wilds typically referred to himself by his stage name, "Honey," even when out of makeup and frequently used his performance voice so that the two identities became fused. David Wilds offered, "He used to take it as a great compliment when people thought he actually was black from hearing his voice on the radio."[106]

Having established his father's own implicit sense of identification between poor whites and blacks, it seems curious that Wilds fails to grasp a broader tie between hillbilly musical/comedic performance and blackface on the barn dance stage. He averred, "The connection to country music was not obvious at all, as far as I'm concerned. . . . 'Oh, well, we've got Uncle Dave Macon, we've got the Fruitjar [sic] Drinkers, the next obvious step is blackface comedy.'" Almost immediately, however, when shifting the discussion to Hank Williams, he recognized that "almost every country band during that time had some guy who dressed funny, wore a goofy hat, and typically played slide guitar" in order to "offset the incredible connection to what humanity puts up with that Hank could demonstrate."[107] It is precisely that "connection"—to loss, pain, a sense of Otherness or abjection—that blackface and rube performance had the potential to embody (as well as counteract). Unquestionably, both contributed to and benefited from early radio's status as a "zone of white racial privilege."[108] But it is in this sense, I would argue, that Wild's work can be seen as a deeply troubled "tribute" to country music's audience of disenfranchised people searching for a way to be *seen* in the arena of popular culture, while simultaneously fueling the racist and classist outlooks of the Opry's middle- and working-class listeners alike.[109]

Jamup and Honey fan letters hardly articulate the duo's appeal in precisely these terms, but particularly during the Depression years, they express a keen appreciation for the performers' unique brand of comic relief. One sixty-four-year-old man wrote from Alabama in 1939 that he and his wife, braving all kinds of weather, walked "1½ tenth mile" three nights a week to hear Jamup and Honey on their neighbor's radio. A housewife and mother from Gracey, Kentucky, wrote in 1938, "You have taken my house by storm. . . . If for any reason your little show should be discontinued, it would be [nothing] short of a tragedy here," adding, "Here's hoping you continue giving us a bit of comedy at the close of a long dreary day—it brightens the evening for the whole family." Interestingly, she notes that her six sons especially love the program and while listening "put on a pantomime" of the material, actually performing in sync with Jamup and Honey. There couldn't be more dramatic evidence of blackface's power to reproduce its own jumbled set of excessive identities.[110]

Proliferating the Model: Barn Dance across the Country

The Grand Ole Opry may have perfected barn dance's hybrid representation of rusticity in its commingling of hillbilly and blackface performance, but other more modest radio and stage programs that now remain mostly a footnote in barn dance history replicated its formula during the 1930s and '40s. While few, if any, audio or film clips remain of these smaller ventures, most issued fan "souvenir" books or "family albums" that helped to perpetuate barn dance's complex discourse of country authenticity. As with the Opry's publicity materials, these texts both accentuate and deny the artifice of their programs' black and white rube performances, while capitalizing on romanticized portraits of the past.[111]

The 1937 WHO *Iowa Barn Dance Frolic Picture Book* exemplifies this trend as it describes the aims of its "mythical, typical small town" named Sunset Corners. The book's opening statement concentrates on positioning its performers as simultaneously salt-of-the-earth and urbane Midwestern individuals capable of appealing to both working- and middle-class audiences. Sunset Corners' "citizens," we learn, "glorify American Folk Music. They know the tunes our fathers and mothers sang—the same tunes that delighted their fathers and mothers as they rolled into Iowa's fertile plains and valleys in covered wagon days—for most of them were born and raised in small towns or on farms." Affiliated with the decent "folk" who pioneered the West rather than "hillbillies," they function as amalgams that prompt nostalgic "memories" of childhood but also keep their fans current with "the best offerings of modern musicians."[112] In a similar vein that sets the standard for later country music fan magazines, this introductory statement reassures its readers that *Sunset Corners Frolic* performers are "real people with normal home lives. Many of them are home owners. Most of them are college graduates. Their interests are the same as yours."

Subsequent pages proceed to introduce us to barn dance cast members in a series of photos depicting rube performers in and out of their costumes. Thus, the comic duo Lem and Martha, favorites for their "clever bantering, . . . rollicking comedy, . . . [and] musical versatility," are "in private life . . . Mr. and Mrs. Tom Lewis, home owners and substantial Iowa citizens" who knit and "dabble in real estate." Although the copy mentions that Lewis also performs regularly as half of the blackface team "Rabbit and Nappy," the photos exclusively advertise his role as white rustic and "gentleman." The opposite page displays a similar pairing, "Tillie and the Sheriff," whose act is premised on the "man-hungry" spinster conceit. "Out of character," Tillie's creator "is an attractive brunet [*sic*] with a taste for serious music"; the sheriff is "a serious young man, maestro of his own string orchestra"; and both are graduates of a well-respected Iowa university. This emphasis on highbrow interests and education links both sets of performers to the program's announcers, who pages later boast an "ability to think quickly in emergencies, appreciation of music, speaking acquaintance with at least one language other than English, precise punctuation, and a large capacity for accepting responsibility"—the precise traits that their stage personas lack.

LEM AND MARTHA

Their antics have tickled WHO listeners for more than three years. Lem was born in Lucas, Iowa; Martha in Waldron, Ill. Both were in musical comedy, vaudeville and dramatic stock before coming to radio. Their clever bantering, their rollicking comedy, their musical versatility maintains them as Barn Dance Frolic headliners.

(Center) Lem calls his musical neighbors for the Oshkosh Chore Gang program. He is also "Rabbit" of the blackface team, Rabbit and Nappy.

In private life the funsters are Mr. and Mrs. Tom Lewis, home owners and substantial Iowa citizens. Their work is your fun. Ann (Martha) knits between broadcasts. Tom dabbles in real estate. Their dog, Lucky, adopted them several years ago. Just a dog, but they're very fond of him.

"Lem and Martha," in and out of costume, 1937 *WHO Iowa Barn Dance Frolic Picture Book*. (Courtesy of Country Music Hall of Fame and Museum.)

PETER MacARTHUR

Producer of the Iowa Barn Dance Frolic, born in Port Glasgow, Scotland, his father wanted him to become a shipbuilder. To United States at age 18, he worked in Groton shipyards six months. A tuneful voice and flair for the stage sent him to New York for start of a notable career in light opera, musical comedy and vaudeville, including two years as understudy for Sir Harry Lauder. He came to radio in 1921 via Palmer School. Eminently qualified to create beautiful production numbers, as well as direct entire Barn Dance show. Beloved by all who know him, Peter is happily married.

NATIONAL
CHAMP

1936 corn husking champion Carl Carlson of Audubon, Iowa, and brother Elmer, 1935 champion, husked their way down double rows of Iowa corn before a theatre audience of 4,000 on November 21, 1936, as Barn Dance guest artists.

Minstrels

Page spread from 1937 *WHO Iowa Barn Dance Frolic Picture Book*.
Lower left: Sunset Corners Minstrels;
upper right: Southern Garden Party;
lower right: Southern Singers. (Courtesy of Country Music Hall of Fame and Museum.)

The WHO souvenir book continues to call attention to its barn dance program's fictionality in the dual-page spread showcasing four sample program numbers: a full-scale minstrel show, an "old-fashioned garden" party

OLD FASHIONED GARDEN

One of many beautiful production sets, built especially for a single Barn Dance broadcast, added eye appeal to lovely music. Featured in this setting were the Songfellows, the Calico Maids and other accomplished musicians, all appropriately costumed.

COTTON PICKERS

Norman Moon as plantation foreman, assisted by the Southern Singers, mixed chorus of negro songsters, presented a colorful musical treat in the setting shown below as production feature of an Iowa Barn Dance Frolic.

with nineteenth-century costumes, a plantation "cotton-picking" scene, and a live corn-husking championship before four thousand spectators. The tuxedo-clad Sunset Corners Minstrels, many of whom "frolic" in blackface in their formal portrait, prove a curious double to the plantation slaves, played by a "mixed chorus of negro songsters" known as the "Southern Singers": both are equally stylized acts, the former billed as one iconic image of "bygone days," the latter as "a colorful musical treat" and "production feature."

Although the white minstrel performers wear formal attire and the black performers don plantation-worker costuming, both numbers clearly code as "productions"—the latter doesn't supplant the former as a more realistic, updated panorama. As such, these acts may also reframe the extravagant Southern garden party as yet another construction for its own bygone white belles and gents. Additionally, the prior acts' *simultaneous* "staging" on the page overturns one traditional ideological effect of the nineteenth-century minstrel show, which served either as a "narrative substitute for slavery, a comfortable alternative to the idea of free black labor," or more typically as a "denial" of such labor.[113] In the souvenir book, both are disarmingly present, disrupting any such sleight of hand. At the same time, the minstrel show and the plantation chorus clearly participate in romanticizing the history of Southern racism, while the corn-husking contest—representing not white labor as much as its antithesis, a "game" of work—ironically aims to affirm the authenticity of present Midwestern country culture.

A 1941 West Virginia barn dance booklet, however, takes a slightly different approach to audience appeal, while offering a similar array of performers' photos. WMMN's *Family Album* primarily casts itself as a "valuable" employer for its region's very real "citizens," providing work for performers, office clerks, and printers, as well as entertainment and current events for its listeners, concluding, "We're mighty proud of WMMN and hope that you are too, because between the station and their listeners we can continue to be a power for good in all walks of life."[114] In the space directly above this address to readers, the page features two photos of rube comedians, one a male in blackface, the other a female dressed as "eccentric character" Petunia. The performers turn out to be a married couple with roots in vaudeville, and they appear on the next page in quite different garb: "Uncle Rufe" is dressed as a country rube, head of the "Coon Hunters," but "Petunia" is revealed to be Norma Francis Armstrong, posed in a glamour shot with her dog. Unlike other materials examined earlier, however, their biographical information *underscores* their own low-class origins, especially Norma, who "quit school in the 11th grade to join the WSM 'Grand Ole Opry' road show" before she became an "eccentric" impersonator. Here, the station discourse encourages identification between its barn dance performers and local working-class listeners. Yet the emphasis remains on clearly stylized rather than realist notions of authenticity, as another photo illustrates the strange mixture of types within a single musical act: the "Rail Splitters" includes four musicians dressed in suit and tie; two in cowboy attire; and one rube comic named "Shorty," billed as "the Dumbest Man in radio," in mis-matched suspenders, blacked-out teeth, and silly cap.[115] This station never lets its "family" audience forget that barn dance is premised on theatricality, not "nature" or history, and is first and foremost an act of labor.

IV. CONCLUSION: MAN-HUNGRY WOMEN AND SENTIMENTAL MOTHERS

Thus far, my discussion of authenticity in barn dance performance has incor-porated gender primarily as it manifests itself rather implicitly in the alter-nating feminizing and remasculinizing of male rube and blackface perform-ers (Minnie Pearl being the exception). Gender's relationship to country authenticity becomes more explicit, however, when critical focus shifts to the presence of women themselves in both rustic and sentimental roles. (Inter-estingly, I found no evidence of female barn dance performers taking up blackface, though, as M. Alison Kibler has shown, such a tradition existed in vaudeville.[116]) Recent cultural historians have challenged the commonplace notion that country music was a male-dominated industry until the 1960s by pointing to barn dance radio in particular as a site that readily incorporated women into its programming. While the new technology of radio proved to be one reason for this phenomenon—its sensitive microphones lent them-selves to the softer voices of female singers as opposed to the raw, loud voices of old-time "shouters"—the genre's developing ideology of rusticity had an arguably greater impact on women's emerging profile.[117]

In her work on popular *National Barn Dance* singer Linda Parker, for ex-ample, Kristine McCusker has argued that the barn dance construction of a traditional rural past paradoxically hinged on *middle-class* notions of femi-ninity. Two prominent and early visionaries of the WLS program, Bradley Kincaid and John Lair, recast the Appalachian South as a nostalgic emblem of timeless tradition whose centerpiece was the "sentimental mother" figure. In a series of 1929 radio addresses, Kincaid sought to downplay the region's uncivilized hillbilly image by foregrounding its pure and inherently moral mountain culture, which was typically preserved by women. Kincaid's proto-typical maternal figure cherished not only conventional gender roles but also artisan crafts and talents, such as weaving and the singing of traditional En-glish ballads. Lair soon capitalized on this gendered image in the early De-pression years by configuring barn dance programming itself as an "aural refuge from modern times"—like the bourgeois home, it was likened to having a "therapeutic" effect on both its urban and rural audience members who found contemporary life disorienting and unsatisfying.[118] In a time of rapid change and loss, during which women frequently became the family breadwinners, such a message also reclaimed domesticity as the preeminent "salve" for economic and cultural wounds. According to McCusker, Lair's resuscitation of the sentimental mother role as the epitome of this soothing tradition thus ushered in a new phase of rustic iconography accentuating distinctly middle-class, rather than working-class, cultural codes.[119]

The intertwined class and gender politics of such imagery becomes more complicated, however, when positioning the Linda Parker figure against female rube performers such as WLS's Lulu Belle or KMOX's Cousin Emmy. McCusker persuasively documents that Lair originally created the Parker persona by transforming the real singer Jeanne Muenich from an unsavory Midwestern "delinquent" into an idealized Southern middle-class Sunbonnet Girl.[120] He nevertheless felt the need to create another kind of female presence on the barn dance stage (first at the *National Barn Dance* in Chicago, later in Kentucky on his *Renfro Valley* program) that amplified the coarser rendition of rusticity already being developed in country's song and performance. As recounted by Michael Ann Williams, Lair encouraged another aspiring female singer, "Lulu Belle" Myrtle Cooper—who did, in fact, hail from rural North Carolina—"to develop a bold and sassy persona to contrast with Parker's sweet and demure one." Modeled specifically on earlier vaudeville performer Elviry Weaver in her calico dress, old-fashioned laced-up shoes, pantaloons, and trademark chewing gum, Cooper played the independent hillbilly gal buffoon to the hilt. As a "female clown," she challenged "the femininity, class status, and acculturation associated with the civilizing woman" of stage tradition.[121] Significantly, this counterimage quickly surpassed Parker's middle-class ideal in terms of audience popularity and won her the 1936 title "Radio Queen of America." Lair admitted, "Lulu Belle just took the show away from her."[122]

Moreover, despite their subversive flouting of middle-class gender norms, these comic performers had the capacity to serve one prized symbolic function of femininity: representing domesticity for their modern fans. Jeanne Muenich may have reinvented herself to simulate a refined woman "whose music, voice, and character tamed a world out of control from her radio microphone," yet McCusker uses precisely the same phrasing to describe the decidedly lowbrow effect of the rube performer called "Cousin Emmy"—her "music" equally "seemed to tame a modern world out of control." Indeed, despite her off-stage identity as a sharp, hard-driving business-woman, Cynthia May Carver accentuated her rustic "motherly role" on radio.[123] This role takes on heightened importance during the honky-tonk era as the nostalgic emblem of a rural feminine art decidedly lost in the *post*war "modern" world of material affluence and hedonistic individualism. But in the 1930s, rube barn dance comics and vocalists such as Lulu Belle and Emmy could paradoxically embody the part, especially Lulu Belle, who radiated Emmy's warmth and country charm but also, upon marriage to fellow WLS performer "Scotty" Wiseman, became prominently featured in the station's monthly magazine *Stand By!* as a dutiful wife and mother.

In the 31 October 1936 issue, for instance, Lulu Belle writes her own piece to thank fans for crowning her "Radio Queen" and presents herself as "an everyday gal from the hills of Carolina" who was "a-crawlin' around on the floor" with her ten-month-old daughter when she got the news of her award. She attests, "It's fun being settled in one place, and having a real home, and being able to do my own cooking. Scotty says I'm getting pretty good at it, too." A year later, she's gracing the cover in a telephone pose, checking up on her daughter, properly left at home, before a performance. Affectionately dubbed the "Mother Goose Hill-Billy" by the article's subheading, she adopts the most significant title of all when she walks in the living room door, for once home, she "sheds the title of Radio Queen . . . and becomes Mrs. Scott Wiseman, mother of Linda Lou."[124]

Rather than configuring rural femininity in strictly middle-class terms, then, barn dance imagery blended the more genteel "sentimental mother" with the "everyday gal" in its domestic vision of traditional folk culture. (Sunshine Sue, of Richmond's *Old Dominion Barn Dance,* served as another example of this hybrid figure in the later 1940s and early '50s and as such will be discussed later, in the context of honky-tonk.) Bradley Kincaid may have crafted a picturesque, "properly" feminized version of Appalachian culture to compete with a more sensationalized hillbilly tableaux, but as John Lair and George Hay recognized, both lowbrow and highbrow audiences sought—albeit for different reasons—a female representative of that culture who was, to paraphrase Hay, "closer to the earth." A variety of long-standing prejudices against women in theater often literally eclipsed their presence on stage by a phalanx of male entertainers sporting black, hick, or cowboy masks.[125] Yet performers like Myrtle "Lulu Belle" Wiseman periodically emerged as live incarnations of the mythologized rural past celebrated in song: a vibrant feminine force preserving family mores and traditional mountain arts. She undoubtedly threatened the more sanitized representations of female folk culture in her on-stage antics or in her published statements about old-time music: "You'll never find the words 'love' and 'dove' in a mountain song. . . . You *will* find the fundamentals . . . for any real-life episode . . . a practical joke, a wreck, a murder, a child bride."[126] But Lulu Belle's private identity as conventional wife and mother increasingly blurred with this public persona to produce a more temperate domestic image. The next chapter explores how this variant of gendered authenticity proved as haunting for male honky-tonk artists in the postwar period—if not more— than the racial and class masquerade employed by their minstrel and rube counterparts. Not surprisingly, it had equally decisive yet ultimately far more damaging consequences for female performers.

CHAPTER 3

"After Dark": Honky-Tonk Music,

Postwar Modernity, and the

Masculinization of Country Identity

Now I'm a man, don't like to complain
The troubles I've got'll drive a man insane
I love that woman and I don't get far
She's got a cold, cold heart
She loves a hot guitar

—Ted Brooks, "Cold, Cold Woman and a Hot Guitar" (1952)

No longer would honky-tonk music be the music solely of beer-
drinking and dancing on a good-time Friday night. Country music
would take honky-tonk to the dark obverse of that carousing spirit
as well: remorse and guilt and world weariness. Honky-tonk music
would come to be a howl of abandon followed by a lament of an-
guish.

—Nick Tosches, "'Honky-Tonkin': Ernest Tubb, Hank Williams,
and the Bartender's Muse"

In the *late* twentieth century, music that originated in small Texas taverns in
the 1930s and reached its zenith in the early 1950s acquired a distinctive
moniker—"honky-tonk"—and an even more palpable image that parted
ways with barn dance hokum to redefine country authenticity: the hard-
driving, often brutally raw sound of male heartache in a "dark," alienating
modern world.[1] But in its midcentury moment, it took part in a shifting "roll
call" of names for the music at large, including "hillbilly," "country," "country
and western," and "folk," and was far less autonomous than more recent ac-

counts suggest. The music certainly spoke of "honky-tonks"; its most cele-brated stars performed in them; and its evolving discourse began to produce an identifiable sensibility immersed in those "bright lights," "hot guitars," and "world weariness." Its signature style, however, was consistently entan-gled with—and to some degree dictated by—surrounding music of the era, from barn dance's mixture of Western swing, traditional folk, and pop, to the 1950s renegade upstart rock 'n' roll, as well as country's own later foray into pop instrumentation, the Nashville Sound.

I argue that what we now know as honky-tonk music did not so much abandon barn dance's ideology of rusticity as reconfigure it for U.S. postwar and subsequently Cold War culture. And once again, gender and race be-come crucial coordinates in its construction, as well as its consumption. As noted earlier, barn dance radio eventually reached a national audience di-verse in geographic region and cultural tastes. One group in particular, which had contributed to a wave of Northern migration in the 1930s and early '40s, proved essential to its success: displaced Southerners who now worked in and inhabited Northern cities but whose identities remained tied to their prior home culture. Similar (but not identical) to their *post*–World War II counterparts who returned from military service and/or relocated in search of jobs and promised prosperity, these early Southern migrants experienced prolonged homesickness and proved responsive to nostalgic visions of a shared rural "past." Additionally, both barn dance and honky-tonk staked at least a measure of their authenticity claims in live performance, despite the rise of the record industry, "chart placement" beginning in 1944, and later domination by Nashville's explicitly commercialized recording studios.

However, the postwar "crisis" in gender relations, precipitated by women's record-setting participation in the wartime workforce, trans-formed country music's representation of both the personal and the regional past. Predominately written and performed by male artists, honky-tonk mu-sic largely mourned the loss of women as the embodiment of a mytholo-gized "home" place rather than the loss of the past itself, which in the post-war era appeared antediluvian, an impossible space of return. "Home" thus became refashioned as a public and masculine domain—the honky-tonk—rather than a private, domestic space, when rural femininity could no longer represent a utopian ideal. The illicit urban tavern, while the seeming an-tithesis of the family-oriented, down-home barn dance, became its ironic twin in one important sense: both in fact functioned as a kind of patriarchal locus delimiting women's participation in their respective communities precisely through nostalgia for an imaginary domesticity that signified a traditional, yet vanishing regional or home culture. The liminal juke joint's free-flowing alcohol, fevered dancing, and preoccupation with sexuality may have permitted a novel kind of "carnivalesque" abandon for modern country audiences, but it hardly overturned all of rural culture's deeply entrenched conventions.[2]

At the same time, honky-tonk's new public version of "home" facilitated a performance style noteworthy for its strikingly different relationship to racial identity. Barn dance performers sought refuge in minstrelsy (at least in part) as a "cover" for both class and gender anxieties. The feminized white male rube figure functioned as one limited and risky strategy for embracing hillbilly identity, its excessiveness ensuring the very presence of poor white Southernness within popular culture yet simultaneously threatening both performer and audience identification with that foolish rustic character. Donning blackface offered another, albeit ironic, route to such presence, while converting an imperiled white masculinity into an equally excessive representation of black male sexuality. But as minstrelsy began its decline as a performative mode during the mid-1940s and the honky-tonk style gained ground, gender supplanted race as a central masking device in the music: in other words, white rural masculinity became reconfigured as modern and "strong."

Bill Malone and Michael Bertrand have persuasively argued that transplanted white Southern working-class men in Northern cities were subject to more acute forms of emasculation in urban settings, yet they discovered a new geographic and psychic space in which to "reassert their manhood."[3] Blackface no longer served as one primary vehicle for such gendered performance, though honky-tonk music itself was strongly informed by the blues and, as several critics have pointed out, racial mimicry resurfaced most notably in rockabilly.[4] Preeminent honky-tonk artists Ernest Tubb and Hank Williams may have literally crossed paths with Jamup and Honey on the Opry stage and in road shows during the postwar period, but their emphasis on "sincerity" signaled a new relationship between performer and audience.[5]

This chapter approaches honky-tonk performance in two distinct phases: (1) the postwar phase, or what I am calling "first wave," covering the years 1945–52 (the latter date essentially marking Hank Williams's death[6]), when the honky-tonk male's desire for middle-class domesticity was writ large in song texts, followed swiftly by disillusionment; and (2) the "second wave," or the 1950s Cold War era, when women artists such as Kitty Wells and Jean

Shepard emerged against a backdrop of the nascent civil rights movement as well as the rockabilly scene to "answer" this music's initial construction of gender relations. The "third wave," encompassing Buck Owens's West Coast Bakersfield Sound, will be briefly examined in the chapter's concluding segment as a reinscription of honky-tonk's masculinist paradigm, even as it arguably introduces a more abstract version of "home." This schema aims not to replicate standard accounts of the genre that typically bypass or marginalize women's presence but to create a nuanced and accurate study of honky-tonk as a performance genre dominated overall by white men of Southern working-class or poor origins and as an increasingly corporatized business dominated by white professional-class men.[7]

I. FIRST WAVE: THE POSTWAR MILIEU

Thanks to pioneering feminist historians, the U.S. postwar era, traditionally touted as a time of "peace and prosperity," is understood as a time of upheaval rather than resolution when the critical lens shifts to women's experiences in both the private and the public spheres. Significant scholarly debates concerning women's racial, ethnic, and class diversity have dispelled any claims to a monolithic female experience in this period, emphasizing that certain populations of women had not only always worked, as seen in the Depression era, but continued to do so after the war ended.[8] In 1940, 11.5 million of them contributed to the labor force despite lingering hostilities against married women in the workplace, and after the United States entered the war, this group comprised 50 percent of defense workers. By 1944, one-third of women in the defense industry were former housewives, new to full-time employment. Some, particularly on the West Coast, working in the aircraft industry, were able to retain their jobs throughout the 1950s.[9] Others successfully found employment in "pink-collar" positions after the war ended, "downgraded" to lower pay and status but not "permanently expelled from the labor force."[10]

Yet most agree that dramatic shifts in women's work opportunities and conditions, as well as concomitant changes in gender ideologies, created another kind of "war" on the home front.[11] Millions of women who had become accustomed to full-time employment during a wartime economy, filling the positions of men in the armed services, were summarily dismissed when those men returned. Mary Bufwack and Robert Oermann describe the situation in their capsule portrait of the era:

75 percent of women at work said they wanted to keep their jobs, but in some cases women were dismissed from their positions within one week of V-J Day. The aircraft industry laid off 800,000, mostly women, two months after victory in Japan. Women fell from 25 percent of the automobile workforce in 1944 to 7.5 percent by early 1946. In 1945, one in four women was dropped from her factory job and nine out of every ten women got pay cuts. Female autoworkers in Detroit took to the streets with signs reading, "Stop discrimination because of sex."[12]

And every facet of popular culture—magazines, radio programming, films, advertising, music, and television—endorsed this phenomenon in a variety of ways by casting women's postwar national "duty" as homemaker rather than plant employee. Even during the war, advertisers for modern household devices had framed women's employment as a temporary "fight" in order to gain, as the Eureka vacuum cleaner company insisted, "a little house of your own, and a husband to meet every night at the door." After the troops came home, women of all classes, if not all races, were put on notice that "the personal side of reconstruction is women's work."[13] As this thumbnail sketch goes, Rosie the Riveter, perhaps the most iconic image of wartime women workers, transmuted into June Cleaver, beckoning women back into domesticity (though even Rosie, as her theme song pointedly reminded listeners, had a Marine boyfriend named Charlie).[14]

Yet this campaign initially faced an uphill battle. Divorce was at an all-time high in 1946 due to war-torn marriages and women's newfound independence as wage-earning heads of their households. Servicemen returned home shell-shocked yet often much more worldly, their small-town horizons and values no longer relevant or appealing. And rural Southerners who migrated north for wartime work felt intense displacement and loneliness as their own sense of local culture and speech clashed with urban practices. Men, too, thus needed to be lured into the postwar reconsolidation of domestic life, though they had a different role to play as middle-class bread-winners.[15] Finally, *working-class* identity during the 1940s experienced a momentous sense of transformation as well. The wartime economy attracted sizable new populations of workers (African American, rural, and female), "disrupting traditional networks of paternalistic authority and control, and encouraging the growth of new cultural forms in factories and in working-class neighborhoods."[16] An unprecedented series of strikes helped solidify such class consciousness yet paradoxically also led to the securing of a stable middle-class wage, which made the 1950s suburban nuclear family ideal appear accessible and desirable to many working-class men and women.

Honky-tonk music may have emerged during the 1930s at the edge of south Texas oil-boom towns, taking its definitive shape as a barroom cultural form, but it flourished in this postwar climate of mingled optimism, bitterness, and longing. Barn dance programming would continue to hold sway throughout the 1940s and '50s, particularly the Opry and later variants such as Shreveport's *Louisiana Hayride,* yet it strained to keep intact amid changing social forces. Honky-tonk—with its amped-up sound, shuffle beat, and candid lyrics—had a freshness and adult edge. Though it gained national currency on the radio and jukebox, it retained its affiliation with a distinctly working-class audience at once exhilarated and alienated by modern culture.

George Lipsitz thus fittingly chose a 1946 song popularized by Ernest Tubb, "Rainbow at Midnight," to encapsulate the U.S. postwar "national ambivalence between fear and hope" (and to serve as the title of his study).[17] While the song itself isn't steeped in the kind of blue-collar imagery now emblematic of the honky-tonk genre, it usefully reminds us of that genre's early optimism, though it became increasingly overshadowed by despair. Even more significantly, "Rainbow at Midnight" explicitly links that optimism to what Lipsitz calls "a distinctly male fantasy": a future rooted in domestic family life. In the song, a soldier returning home from the war sees an improbable rainbow in the night sky that comes to symbolize his sweetheart and their love. The home he promises to build "in the country" then serves as a "heaven" on earth for the couple and their children, whom they'll name "after the rainbow."[18] The lyrics alone paint a rather generic picture of a soldier's dream, and Lipsitz's analysis centers on its promise of "restored patriarchal authority as the penultimate reward for wartime sacrifice"—a promise pervading popular culture overall in the postwar period. Indeed, the song seems a tailor-made response to the 1942 government-sponsored radio program *To the Young,* which told young American men and women that the war was "about love and gettin' hitched, and havin' a home, and some kids, and breathin' fresh air out in the suburbs."[19]

But "Rainbow at Midnight" became a top *country* hit when sung by Ernest Tubb. It clearly resonated with his audience, who bought half a million copies of the record released on Decca's new 46000 "hillbilly" series.[20] My point is that honky-tonk music was as susceptible to this gendered vision as any popular Tin Pan Alley–style song crooned by Eddy Arnold on the Opry. It is equally important to recognize that the song equates such "heaven" with a rustic country cottage, not a suburban tract home. Honky-tonk's particular approach to nostalgia becomes a crucial component in this first-wave representation of working-class gender relations.

After all, the tumultuous war years had exposed the underside of this romanticized ideology, as infidelity, abandonment, and divorce tore lovers and families apart. More than any other contemporary musical genre, honky-tonk confronted—in many cases, obsessed over—this situation in its now-classic roster of "cheating" and heartache songs. In fact, the flip side of "Rainbow at Midnight" offered the song "I Don't Blame You" (cowritten by Tubb), recounting a wayward husband's adultery and subsequent regret. More telling, Tubb recorded "Answer to Rainbow at Midnight" in 1947, undoubtedly capitalizing on his prior hit yet also articulating, just one year later, its naivete; in this rendition, Tubb's returning soldier discovers his lover has left him for someone new and laments, "my rainbow has lied."[21] To be sure, more than a bit of happenstance is involved in the pairing of songs on 78″ records, and one can find a whole host of seemingly contradictory themes in honky-tonk songs assembled for jukebox play. But these tensions have significance beyond sheer marketplace trial and error. They resonate with class, gender, and racial politics of the era and thus need critical unpacking to deepen our understanding of country authenticity in this first, most iconic phase of the music.

II. THE HONKY-TONK HABITUS

Before launching a detailed look at this period's two most revered male performers, Ernest Tubb and Hank Williams, the discussion must begin with what I am calling the honky-tonk "habitus": that complex of daily practices, tastes, knowledges, and beliefs shared by the music's working-class audience and ultimately situating the tavern or bar as the locus of authentic experience and feeling, the listeners' alternative "home." I draw on Pierre Bourdieu's concept and term here to emphasize that the music and its affiliated discourses constitute an informal system of dispositions, perceptions, and actions rather than "simply" a preference, say, for the steel guitar sound. That system is not at all inborn or "natural"—it is a product of particular economic, cultural, and social conditions—yet it tends to be unconscious. Individuals learn and internalize specific behaviors, attitudes, and tastes, producing a sense of identity based in community or belonging with others and often linked to a particular location.[22]

Country music scholars Bill Malone and Joli Jensen have established the basic lineaments of this state of mind and its "home" place (both real and symbolic), despite differences in interpretation. Malone declares that honky-tonk music in the postwar era was not only "the most valid expression in song of the world view of the Southern working class" but a strictly masculine one: like the songs played on its jukebox or by its featured musicians, "the honky tonk was a man's world" of both camaraderie and violence. While lonely patrons could always find companionship with their own stiff drink or barstool compatriot, they might also stumble into a fight or two, as "drunken oil field roughnecks or industrial workers playing cowboy worked out their fantasies or tested their macho impulses in the competitive arena of the barroom." Malone reads such potentially dangerous "encounters" as "a ritualized expression of manhood." Sisters, wives, mothers, or sweethearts, on the other hand, were barred from such community, and those who dared to cross the threshold "were not respected." The prototypical "honky-tonk angel"—a single woman haunting the bar scene for drink, sex, attention—"was both a lure and a threat," as she signified such "potential in all women." Finally, Malone gestures toward establishing the racial identity of this space: though he believes the music's name "probably has urban black origins . . . by the 1930s it had come to be identified with roadhouses generally frequented by Southern whites." By the mid-1940s, the term had become synonymous with any small club or venue offering alcohol, music, and dancing.[23]

Jensen usefully approaches the honky-tonk site as an actual live setting for musical performance and class community but also as a "self-conscious construction" of authenticity produced by songwriters of the era, as well as recent scholars and journalists commenting on this music (such as Malone). Drawing on her own ethnographic study, she proposes that honky-tonk as music and locale "embodies the long-standing tension between downhome and uptown that characterizes country music"—communal but also urban. To retain an imprimatur of country authenticity, it is represented, then, "as a downhome haven in a heartless uptown world," a "pocket" of familiarity in a disorienting modern culture. But while corroborating that the honky-tonk is literally and figuratively "a man's world," Jensen proceeds to outline a "dialectic" of larger "tensions" within its song texts that makes possible a more nuanced gender schema for this habitus than previously allowed. In "Country vs. City," for example, "the rural-urban tension . . . is played out as a tension between purity and corruption" in which women are deemed "especially susceptible to the lure of urban life." The rural "home" may now slip from the grasp of the displaced Southern man because he himself has been "tainted" by the city, yet the woman's transgression is much greater, it seems to me, since she can no longer function as a stable signifier of that mythic "pure" home space ("green, welcoming, often with mother or girlfriend wait-ing"). This is confirmed in another dialectic offered by Jensen, "High Class vs. Working Class," in which elite culture often appears accessible to trans-planted rural women who can momentarily "pass"; men, however, "stay in their own world of faded jeans, callused hands, and rough but honest ways."[24] In the city, women have more fluidity and, what's more, the *desire* to "trespass" into forbidden class territories.

The honky-tonk tavern in this model thus becomes reconfigured as a masculinized "home" for its patrons. Jensen notes that the bar may be "the antithesis of the mythological hills of home" but is nevertheless "structured by their absence"—a significant observation with much greater gender im-plications. She argues that "what defines the honky-tonk world is the *loss* of Eden, the absence of the hills and hollers" (even though they may have left those hills due to joblessness, restlessness, and the like). But that rural utopia was typically feminized, affiliated not only with a traditional but with a do-mestic—specifically maternal—place. Honky-tonk discourse wistfully in-vokes this "lost" world yet highlights its impossibility in an urban and modern setting—not only are its values incongruent and out of step, but more criti-cally, the rural woman can no longer embody them. The juke joint may, as Jensen proposes, be depicted as a "hollow" substitute for "true companion-ship and real beauty," but in this mythology, "that raunchy, neon-lit bar with its cheap beer and even cheaper solace is [now] called *home*" for its abject working-class male clientele.[25]

Nostalgia clearly underpins the honky-tonk habitus, further entangling its gender, racial, and class codings. However, unlike the pastoral landscape or the rugged frontier peopled with the quaint "folk" whom middle-class, ur-bane listeners sought in barn dance imagery, this genre's yearning for a rural past in a postwar world may very well have a different function for those ac-tually intimate with that "lost" home. Kathleen Stewart's ethnographic re-modeling of nostalgia, though based in the discursive practices of 1980s West Virginia coal camps, resonates with this midcentury version of a dislocated local culture, whose denizens may similarly express nostalgia, "not as tourists taking in framed scenes from a maintained and exercised distance" but as "exiles" who are "inescapably haunted by the images they dwell in." Cultural memory combats "those things that 'try' to erase someone"—like those poor/working-class rubes and minstrels of barn dance performance striving to remain visible despite the fact that their "history" may have already left "'marks'" on them, "even as bodily scars."[26]

When considered in the context of Stewart's model, honky-tonk music al-

lows these migrants "to reconstitute their lives in narrative form, a story designed to reassemble a broken history into a new whole." This is not, as Stewart notes, a "simple nostalgia for a 'dying culture'"; in song and performance,
it constructs a "*present* based not on 'fact' or 'solid ground' but on a faith in
human fictions that drives them to continuously dis-member and re-member
the model of what it is to be 'human' in order that it can include them and
their lives as they now know them."[27] I quote Stewart extensively here to emphasize that honky-tonk nostalgia often mourns the loss of a collective per-
sonal/regional/class cultural past yet does not pretend, as barn dance often
appeared, to revive that past wholesale. Its songs offer up strikingly *new* imagery and sound to conjure a present "structured by the absence" of what has
been lost: unfaithful spouses, empty beer glasses, blinding city lights. Nevertheless, the nostalgia reconstituting this "broken history" still stakes its vision
of the past in a distinctly gendered ideology equating the feminine with an
ideal but now obsolete "home" and thus banishes women (both real and
imaginary) from the new one relocated in the public sphere.

As one instantiation of a "man's world," the honky-tonk habitus openly
hinges on a model of working-class masculinity equally informed by such
nostalgic reframings of past and present. The feminization haunting rural
Southern men of the poor and working classes during the 1930s and early
'40s resurfaces here in postwar alienation and plays itself out in primitive
"rituals of manhood," within or alongside the honky-tonk bar, that help shore
up masculine identity. At the same time, these gendered rites reflect the kind
of raw emotion now emblematic of honky-tonk music and, within a dominant
cultural schema, can in fact be identified much more strongly with the feminine—that is, the nonrational, the nonintellectual. Countering the trite imagery and predictable, if stirring, instrumentation characterizing much of the
era's romantic pop music recorded by both women and men, honky-tonk
boasted excessive feeling in lyrics, vocal styling, and song arrangement.
Singers "went for unabashed theatricality. They wailed; they moaned; they
whimpered; they shouted; they pleaded; they cried. With slurred phrases,
bent-note effects, vocal breaks and slippery yodel techniques, they practically wept in tune."[28] The genre's popularization of electric guitars and
drums—initially implemented to be heard over the "din" of raucous barroom
patrons—helped drive that emotion home. Malone points to the introduction of the pedal steel guitar in 1954 (during the second wave of the genre)
as a key development in this music in no small part because it mimicked the
honky-tonk singer's "whine" and argues that such instrumentation "both attracts and repels" because it prompts "elemental, and often cathartic, im-

pulses and emotions . . . a vision of emotional pain and isolation and weakness that we have all shared."[29] What Malone finds potentially discomforting, I propose, is not simply the honesty of such gut-wrenching emotion but its conventional gendering. "Whimpering" and "whining" are ostensibly the province of women and children, not men.

Yet honky-tonk songwriters and performers typically recast and subsequently embraced such passion as white "working man's blues." While white Southern working-class masculinity traditionally prized brawn over sentiment and thus emerged in physicality rather than "feelings," it nonetheless conveyed strong—I would emphasize raw or crude—emotion.[30] In barn dance performance, this primitiveness at once epitomized and stigmatized the white rube character, resulting in a feminized comic persona that appealed, for different reasons, to both working-class and middle-class audiences. Honky-tonk representation, however, had the potential to rewrite this formulation, insisting that strong feeling is the only viable response to alienation and marginalization in the modern city. Richard Leppert and George Lipsitz go so far as to argue that Hank Williams rejected the "dominant 'heroic' image of masculinity" in this period, writing "songs about heartbreak and failed personal relations" that posed "the body and the psyche as crucial terrains of political struggle in the postwar era."[31] Still, rather than identifying *with* the feminine, as Leppert and Lipsitz maintain about Williams, much honky-tonk discourse positions itself against both women and middle-class men. Its stereotypic wail functions as a collective lament that protests both a classed *and* a gendered universe, pitting "Us" against "Them."[32]

While Malone and similar champions of this music designate such emotion as (too) authentically "real" for most consumers who prefer "intellectual" distance,[33] other scholars emphasize its self-conscious performativity. Whether envisioned as a "poetics of intensification" or an abject "*burlesque* of the American dream*,"[34] honky-tonk songs in this alternate critical model function not as sincere reflections of a singer's heartache but, as seen earlier in Jensen's work, as a stylized stance that knowingly references honky-tonk iconography. Identities are reflexively performed as excessive personae that resist as well as reinscribe normative conventions. While clearly rooted in such a paradigm, this book's approach to the conceptualization of country authenticity allows for even more ambivalence in this genre's evolving constructions. Like barn dance performers who adopted rube and minstrel masks within an amalgam of shame and defiance, honky-tonk singers participated in and perpetuated the music's scripted conventions with an equally conflicted or hybrid consciousness.

This chapter thus proposes a different kind of "mask" at work in the post-war country music scene that in some ways codes as no mask at all: sincere, hard-hitting emotion of transplanted white Southern working-class masculinity. While Ching rightly calls attention to the comic aspects of this deliberate and spectacular "lowly pose,"[35] particularly male artists' own avowed failure to meet *middle-class* gender norms, I believe such self-conscious performance is even more overdetermined, operating as much out of fear and anxiety as knowing bravado. As argued earlier, male honky-tonk fans and stars alike sought meaningful presence in a dominant culture that marginalized their own. Rather than relying on earlier representational strategies that alternately parlayed and deflected their abjection in a notably distorting fashion, they struck upon another stance that proposed to showcase their "true" subjectivity, even as the performers' propensity for popular cowboy attire hints at lingering insecurities about their legitimacy. Forgoing both "black" and rube posturing, they adopted a seemingly more transparent persona accentuating the vulnerability as well as strength of white working-class manhood forced to search for a new home. Of course, as honky-tonk develops into a recognizable and hence marketable genre, it serves as just such a literal and mythic site yet also reifies that "non"-persona into another veritable mask.

Aaron Fox's analysis of recent Texan honky-tonk subculture gets close to acknowledging such a mask when he discusses the "comedic fool" trope found in certain strains of the music (such as those explored by Ching). Arguably reminiscent of the barn dance rube, this figure displays "a certain kind of expressive foolishness" in his "babbling, overflowing, excessive character." Typically entertaining, the fool is "interpreted as both an unfair stereotype and a funny exaggeration, as a trope of explanation for actual, known people and for highly performative assumptions of the 'hillbilly' identity." But Fox contends that this comic tenor can swiftly transmute into the disturbing "antisocial silence" of the "tore up" fool consumed by sadness—perhaps an even more salient figure within honky-tonk discourse. Both variations clearly code as "stylized, poetic foolishness" marked by "distance between the performer and the fool s/he performs."[36] Fox would view this less as a "masking" device, however, than as a poetic one that expressly utilized such distancing to stage and reframe identity.

Yet the archetypal honky-tonk "fool"—either playing for laughs or crying in his beer—can at once function as a familiar circulating trope, prone to exaggeration, *and* as a "realistic" representation of an identifiable bar culture embraced by this music's audience. Eddie Noack's 1956 recording "When the Bright Lights Grow Dim" ingeniously illustrates this dynamic, invoking both the comedic and the "dark" conventions of the music. The song's narrator distinguishes between his honky-tonk persona of gaiety—"I'm the laugh of the party"—and the "lonely" self that emerges "when the bright lights grow dim." Addressing his absent lover, he confesses that "until you return, dear / I'll keep wearing a mask / That will hide how I'm feeling within."[37] On the most literal level, that "mask" is associated exclusively with the self-conscious pose of the "carefree and Gay" partier; the "real" man of feeling, unable to put the past "behind" him, remains submerged, accessible only to his sweetheart. That image alone can work for an audience equally experienced at splitting their identities. Here, the honky-tonk appears less a true "home" than a facade hospitable to only one mode of community. This narrator wants to *dispose* of his mask. Yet his abject self also resonates as another self-evident trope of the genre—one that paradoxically permits individuality or freedom from masquerade. Since "When the Bright Lights Grow Dim" is itself a honky-tonk song, it also confirms that tavern culture can indeed be "home" to lonely men seeking to express their despair. The song's strict binary collapses when viewed as part of a larger discourse.

This illusion of transparency is facilitated by honky-tonk's shift from a "black" to a "white" performative schema. While barn dance programming continued to feature blackface comedy in its postwar lineup, this irrepressibly modern genre jettisoned explicit racial mimicry, which served as an earlier vehicle for fostering class solidarity, as well as racist ideologies. Perhaps most importantly, blackface provided its white performers access to an imaginary strong masculinity represented largely as animalistic sexuality. As Michael Bertrand argues, a similar strategy of racial appropriation next erupted in mid-1950s rockabilly, a hybrid term that "implied integration by alluding to the consolidation of 'white' hillbilly music and 'black' rhythm and blues." He astutely notes that the rockabilly generation was constituted by the *children* of honky-tonk's central fan base of older resettled Southern workers, and thus their "first brush with modernity signaled promise, not failure; the future, not the past." Unlike their parents' generation (but echoing their grandparents' devices), rockabilly fans seized upon black masculinity as a "tool" to help register their unique identities; they "*consciously* and *conspicuously* emulated African American male urban style."[38] Honky-tonk's departure from this tradition in the interim is thus equally "conspicuous": as a genre, it was clearly allied with black musical forms—especially in the frequent covering of Jimmie Rodgers songs, themselves explicitly steeped in African American blues—yet it neither engaged in crudely "blacking up" nor unabashedly claimed black male cultural trappings.

Honky-tonk song and discourse turned to white working-class masculinity as a new performative strategy to manage insecurities fueled by dislocation and loss. Not quite "urban" but no longer "rural," this modern identity dared to claim itself, at least within the honky-tonk habitus, as the "norm." Explicit modes of racial impersonation could be retired. Both whiteness and masculinity, signifiers of dominance, appeared accessible to this population even if its class Otherness threatened that access outside the tavern world. Stripped of more obvious masks, honky-tonk music could parade itself as the "real" thing—at least on one level. James Smethurst offers another plausible reading that complements mine in his study of the relationship among the blues, country music, and rockabilly. He suggests that honky-tonk music in the late 1940s and '50s actually "gained a national currency (as opposed to a specifically southern currency) as a 'white' cultural marker in no small part because of its official identification with southern white workers and farmers and its relative lack of publicly visible African-American artists and audiences." Countering the conventional wisdom that rockabilly destroyed honky-tonk with its even newer sound and youthful swagger, Smethurst posits that "publicly 'miscegenated' rock and roll" in fact allowed honky-tonk (at least initially) to thrive because the former served as a dangerous example "to which country could be opposed."[39] In other words, racist objections to rockabilly's direct links to black culture could find refuge in honky-tonk's "white" coding, driving its popularity and record sales. While this theory primarily targets the music's iconography and consumer reception, it also encourages further probing of songwriters' and artists' investments in the reclamation of whiteness. Smethurst reminds us that there is yet another "Them" to be reckoned with in honky-tonk representation.

III. ERNEST TUBB AND HANK WILLIAMS: DON'T LOOK NOW (BUT YOUR BROKEN HEART IS SHOWING)

Two postwar honky-tonk male stars dominated the genre, engineering and subsequently symbolizing its sound and affect. Certainly others who preceded them helped set the stage for its formulation as a recognizable new trend in "hillbilly" music. Al Dexter's 1936 recording of "Honky Tonk Blues" introduced the term into the country lexicon, and his later, self-penned "Pistol Packin' Mama" (1943–44) became one of the decade's biggest country hits. Louisianan Ted Daffan's "Born to Lose" (written in 1941, released in 1943) embodied "the essence of the honky-tonk credo" in its lines "I've lived my life in vain / Every dream I dreamed has only brought me pain."[40] And Floyd Tillman's recordings of "Drivin' Nails in My Coffin" (1946) and "Slippin' Around" (1949) helped immortalize drinking and cheating as honky-tonk's twin vices. But Ernest Tubb and Hank Williams defined this music for their contemporary audiences, especially in the mid-to-late 1940s and early 1950s, and even more so in the later twentieth century for fans and music critics engaged in their own mourning ritual for a lost country authenticity. Nick Tosches speaks for many when he writes: "The passing from glory of Ernest Tubb and the death of Hank Williams were the end of something. To be sure, there have been great country singers since, but country music itself seems to have lost much of its greatness. . . . We have entered an age of Lite Beer and Lite Country Music, an age of all things Lite."[41] Although Williams has come to eclipse Tubb in this countermythology as a legendary spectacle of artistic brilliance and personal self-destruction—indeed, it is nearly impossible to "see" Hank apart from the aura of tragedy and spirit of hagiography sparked by his death at the age of twenty-nine—both performers made distinctive and essential contributions to the honky-tonk habitus outlined here.

Ernest Tubb

Apart from his role as stylistic innovator and galvanizing performer, Tubb's status as a honky-tonk icon rests on two (perhaps conflicting) aims: to champion the music's "sincerity" *and* to embody "respectability." His life history, vocal style, and songwriting all reflect his suitability for, and faith in, an authentic connection between entertainer and audience. As Tubb biographer Ronnie Pugh sums up: "His concerns were their concerns, voiced without frill, without metaphor, without simile, in a sparse, rough-hewn, down-to-earth style. . . . Listeners knew what he was singing about and identified with his viewpoint."[42] From a young age, he had lived a life in sync with theirs. He was born on a cotton farm in tiny Crisp, Texas, in 1914, and his family migrated by covered wagon across the state in search of work after the postwar cotton bust, yet he suffered greater hardship when his parents divorced. Tubb's spotty formal schooling came to an abrupt end as he was initially forced to take on full-time farm work for his mother and then, during the start of the Depression years, itinerant work as a ditch digger, truck driver, and eventually Works Progress Administration construction-crew employee, before his fascination with Jimmie Rodgers' music led to a star-crossed chance at a far different career.[43]

That experience resonated in his voice—a baritone profoundly ordinary yet instantly recognizable. Though he initially mimicked Rodgers's yodeling style while playing live on a San Antonio radio station, a tonsillectomy in 1939 transformed his vocal range and forced him to sing in his everyday register. He won fans' allegiance precisely because he sounded so familiar, so like themselves. Interviewed late in life, he confessed, "I'm not saying I'm a good singer, but I sing like I feel, I think you can tell the feeling is there," adding, "I want my music to be simple enough, so that the boy out there on the farm can learn it and practice it and try to play it." Tubb's voice was the litmus test of cultural as well as musical sincerity, highlighting his affiliation with Southern working-class men (and boys) who may have moved north yet still prized their rural roots and values.[44]

But while his signature vocal style retained its small-town Texan flavor, his music's sound and lyrics became increasingly contemporary and "urban." As the owner of a modest San Angelo tavern in 1940 (dubbed the "E&E"), Tubb became acquainted with new honky-tonk jukebox fare such as "Honky-Tonk Blues" and incorporated its elements into his own compositions and recordings. At the same time, he grew impatient with its more light-hearted, "insubstantial" themes centered on carousing and drink. During the war years, then, Tubb brought together the somber tendencies of old-time ballads with amplified instrumentation.[45] His first true hit recorded for Decca in 1941, "Walking the Floor Over You," introduced the trend, setting a tale of contemporary romantic woe to a lively beat—in Tubb's estimation, "a little bouncy thing"—punctuated by electric guitar.[46] The song's success spurred Tubb to feature this new instrument in future recordings and live performances, and in 1943, he brought his electric sound to the Opry, in effect ushering the country's now-premiere barn dance program into the modern age. While Tubb's voice epitomized George Hay's Opry anthem, "keep it down to earth, boys," his band's instrumentation caused some initial consternation for the program's founder, yet the audience's enthusiastic reception, leading to several unusual encores, must have mattered most to Hay as he welcomed Tubb and his successors back to the Opry stage.[47]

Tubb and his "Texas Troubadours" rode a wave of popularity in the postwar years as his songs continued to excite listeners with their newfound realism—typically addressing disappointment and heartache in romantic or marital relationships—and pulsing rhythm. While hardly sporting matinee-idol looks, Tubb was a magnetic performer in this period, likened to both Elvis and Sinatra for his sexual appeal.[48] Indeed, in his music, on stage, and even in film, Tubb cultivated a new mode of masculinity. His costuming certainly capitalized on de rigueur cowboy imagery to signify strength and dignity—an everyman hero in rustic guise—yet his lyrics emphasized personal vulnerability and dramatic emotion.[49] He could serve as a more generic national figure voicing servicemen's domestic concerns ("Rainbow at Midnight") yet simultaneously register as a country artist exploring white blue-collar men's modern hopes and fears.

Tubb's songwriting throughout the 1940s popularized this abject honky-tonk persona. While bemoaning the wages of alcoholism in his covers of standard fare such as "Warm Red Wine" (1949) and "Driving Nails in My Coffin" (1946), he clearly relished the part of the lovesick victim or fool. "It's Been So Long Darling" (1945), recorded one year before "Rainbow," mines similar thematic territory of wartime separation and impending romantic reunion, but even in this national moment of optimism, Tubb skillfully captures his narrator's underlying anxiety, as well as sensitivity, as he anticipates his homecoming: the length of separation weighs on his mind, leading him to assure his sweetheart that he's "kept every vow" yet to admit that "just the thought of seeing you / it scares me through and through." He hopes she'll still be waiting for him as before, and though the day he'd left she'd been the one to cry, "that whole day long," he now pleads, "please don't blame me if I cry."[50] This song appears to have its own "answer" in "Those Tears in Your Eyes (Were Not for Me)" (1946), in which a similar male protagonist concludes that his lover's tears as he left for war were in fact shed for another man. Here, there is no anger, just devastation: "I don't know who to blame / but you have brought me shame / Cause those tears in your eyes were not for me."[51]

A year later, however, "Don't Look Now (But Your Broken Heart Is Showing)" takes grim satisfaction in the cheating woman's own abandonment, crowing, "now I guess you know my dear / what it means to be blue." At the same time, the song's chorus (and title) feature that split self so emblematic of this genre: "Don't look now / but your broken heart is showing / That smile upon your face cannot fool me."[52] Within the song's narrative, the unmasking at work solely targets an unfaithful female lover; yet it also, I would argue, addresses all spurned men who are subsequently left "in deep sorrow." As in Eddie Noack's later "laugh of the party," their masculine identity is more palpably threatened by such "misery."[53] Yet the song predicts that they will inevitably be exposed; their concealed emotions will eventually crack through. Honky-tonk music thus materializes this surreptitious feeling—enacts the unmasking—while demonstrating that "misery," in fact, loves company. The juke joint is full of other men nursing "broken hearts." Even Tubb's signature patter with his band members, as in this song's "Awwww, come in Jimmie," which beckons lead guitarist Jimmie Short, illustrates such community. It momentarily breaks the narrative frame, reminding listeners that they're actually hearing a musical performance, yet it also participates in and hence reinscribes that narrative by calling on the vocalist's own honky-tonk "pals" to complete the story.

Two other songs from Tubb's postwar output, however, complicate this composite portrait of gender relations. "Mississippi Gal" and "Filipino Baby" (neither written by Tubb) return to that initial search for domestic harmony, though this time the quest is refracted through overt racial coding. Both invoke "Rainbow"'s cottage-and-family imagery as haven for a "roamin'" man or soldier, whose respective "gal" and "baby" sit contentedly waiting. The former song's eponymous "Mississippi gal" embodies the South with her "big smile" and distinctive drawl, and its lyrics assure us that it is "down south" where "dreams come true." Yet this "gal" transforms into a mammy when Tubb, conjuring Al Jolsen, sings, "I'd walk a million miles for a great big southern smile." Here he exploits, rather than eschews, blackface imagery signifying a more conventionally nostalgic white vision of the Southern past. The romantic and the regional blur to produce an even more disturbing concept of home, where white and African American femininity converge in a reified portrait of servitude.[54]

"Filipino Baby," though written in the 1930s about a soldier serving in the Spanish-American War, was originally recorded in 1946 by Cowboy Copas, another country performer. But Tubb's version that same year became a bigger hit, and with the recent war in the Pacific as a backdrop, it makes a striking contribution to his own body of World War II songs, as well as to this era's popular cultural representations of Asian women. The soldier's island love, a black-haired Filipina whom he calls his "treasure and pet," in one sense reads as another version of mammy, the counter to all of those white American girls abandoning the home place for the workplace: in her "little rustic cottage in the far-off Philippines," *her* "heart beats true for him and him alone."[55] Sketching out this GI's fascination with an exotic locale, the song essentially rewrites the state of gender and race relations in the United States. As the soldier returns to "claim" his brown-skinned girl, the story's culmination in a wedding arguably fulfills, rather than unsettles, his country's greater imperialist mission both abroad and at home.[56] With these two recordings,

Tubb discloses another level of anxiety that persists in honky-tonk's refashioning of working-class masculine identity. Although he refrains from literally adopting a minstrel pose, his song choices demonstrate that blackface tradition remained a compelling vehicle for inhabiting a "virile" position of power and surfaced at surprising moments in his work.

Tubb's staging of "sincere" white male vulnerability in his best-known songs of this period thus bears a complicated relationship to his ensuing campaign for the music's respectability. His now-legendary warning, "Smile when you call me a hillbilly," is frequently cited as a kind of cultural call to arms by a man who single-handedly forced his record label to change its catalog appellations for Southern music in 1948.[57] As Pugh documents, Tubb was profoundly offended by the term *hillbilly* used to describe his music and upbringing, and as he achieved a greater degree of commercial success, he felt emboldened to launch several initiatives to win respectability for himself and other country entertainers. To transform record catalog categories, he proposed the alternative term *country,* telling Decca producer Dave Kapp, "Most of us are from the country originally—call it country music." When Kapp countered with the term *cowboy,* pointing to the previous popularity of Western music, Tubb suggested a compromise: "Country and Western."

By 1948, Decca's catalog had replaced its "Hill Billy Records" designation first with "Country," then with "Country & Western," and by the early 1950s, other record companies and trade papers, such as *Billboard,* had followed suit.[58] Tubb approached the Opry with a similar mission, persuading emcee George Hay to "quit saying hillbilly" in his broadcasts to "elevate" the music for the Opry audience.[59] Scholars point to other groundbreaking ventures as well, such as the 1947 Nashville opening of the Ernest Tubb Record Shop, where Tubb made country music records readily available with a mail-order service and went on to air his WSM *Midnight Jamboree* program. His organization of the Opry's first wildly successful debut at Carnegie Hall that same year serves as another oft-cited example. This latter historic event prompted another now-famous quote from the singer, who strode on stage and drawled, "Boy, this place sure could hold a lot of hay," as a way to both play up and deflate his fish-out-of-water setting (along with his Manhattan audience's stereotypical expectations).[60]

More needs to be said, however, about Tubb's *intertwined* campaigns for musical sincerity and industry respectability. On the one hand, he was combating a particularly cartoonish rural image: as he told Hay, "a lot of people . . . think of somebody sitting out somewhere making moonshine liquor, . . . barefooted, with a long beard."[61] His honky-tonk realism worked to counter such imagery, providing the live audience with a performer whom many welcomed as a mirror image of themselves and the listening audience with a new and bracing look at postwar working-class life. But that vision also offered up an ambiguous picture of white masculinity, no longer coding as hayseed primitiveness yet equally raw in a class context *and* potentially feminized when transmuted into the honky-tonk loner's excessive sadness. As hinted at a moment ago, Tubb's search for legitimacy may very well have been prompted by the same kind of shame voiced by his songs' endless jilted lovers, as well as by a righteous anger.

It's also curious that he recorded and later released songs with the pejorative *hillbilly* in their very titles, such as "Hillbilly Fever #2" (1950), "Hillbilly Waltz" (1972), and "My Hillbilly Baby" (1957). This last song was initially recorded in 1945 but released much later on Tubb's first LP, appropriately titled *The Daddy of 'Em All* (1957), which fittingly included "I've Got the Blues for Mammy" and "Mississippi Gal" and featured a cover photo of the seated artist holding a scepter—a regal image establishing Tubb as "the" patriarch of authentic country with "down-home" trappings.[62] That album was re-released and repackaged some time in the mid-to-late 1960s as an "affectionate album tribute" titled *My Hillbilly Baby and Other Big Hits!,* this time with a much more provocative cover: a sexy woman in a daringly low-cut "Daisy Mae" patchwork blouse, with a hint of bare midriff, sporting a "come-hither" gaze.[63] While I agree with Rachel Rubin that such brazen cornpone images can be read overall as a critique of those who indulge in "the exploitation of 'hillbilly' for titillation," in this case, I'm not so sure.[64] To begin with, Tubb had very little say about his albums' cover design,[65] and this one especially seems an outlier, produced for the quick sale of older hits—precisely the kind of marketing maneuver that would take advantage of such "titillating" fare. But conceptually, this female hillbilly image, popularized by Al Capp's comic strip *Li'l Abner,* also seems irrelevant to Tubb's larger protest of Southern caricature, as both his rhetoric and his songs focus predominantly on men.[66] And the song itself, covered but not written by Tubb, more likely trades in rather than challenges such stereotypes. According to its "country boy" narrator, its "sweetest gal," still far too young to marry, serves as just another rustic substitute for "songs about mountain shacks and moons."[67]

Even if a tongue-in-cheek representation—which again, to my mind, seems unlikely in this instance—both the song and the album cover risk misreading, a strategy perhaps embraced by other country artists, but not by one so sensitive to disrespect. Instead, Tubb's "hillbilly baby" functions as another variant of his "Mississippi Gal." While her cover image fails to share the latter's "great big southern smile," both represent a composite imaginary of Southern womanhood that this performer, along with his male fans, still longed for (and one that his "*filipino* baby" could reasonably pretend to fill). Her striking sexuality seemingly invokes the stock honky-tonk angel figure, but she represents a strictly rural fantasy of male pleasure. Indeed, a song Tubb recorded one year later (1958) more explicitly conveys this era's gender conservatism. "Educated Mama" chastises a book-loving woman for being "cold as an iceberg and romantic as a fish," *un*schooled in making her man happy. While an ostensibly comic tune premised on class divisions, its couplet "I'm goin' to the graveyard and dig a place I found / For anyone as dead as you belongs deep in the ground" offers a far more sobering take on modern women's "betrayal" of earlier social rules.[68] As much as Ernest Tubb can be credited with spearheading a new industry discourse about country music, as well as a new model of masculinity via the honky-tonk genre, his work was ultimately as susceptible as anyone's to conventional gender ideologies.[69]

Hank Williams

Tubb's musical innovations and sincerity pact with his audience helped give rise to what many consider the brightest honky-tonk luminary, but Hank Williams ultimately foiled his predecessor's respectability campaign by living his life as the most excessive "hillbilly" of all. And his fans loved him for it. While Tubb struggled with his own alcoholic tendencies and early marital strife, such private troubles rarely informed his public persona as a successful country artist.[70] His authenticity was grounded largely in a hardscrabble past rather than an unstable present. Williams, on the other hand, established a newly heightened mode of identification between performer and audience—in some cases, despite his best intentions. His volatile marriage to Audrey Shepard, public displays of drunkenness (the latter culminating in his notorious firing from the Opry in August 1952) and premature death demonstrated that he was a bona fide natural as a honky-tonk star, no "better" than his barroom cohorts. Like many of them, he never quite assimilated to urban modernity; the rural primitive in him won out. Williams may have been the first country artist to achieve lasting crossover appeal on the popular music charts—"the first writer on a regular basis to make country music, national music"—but he was beloved by his fans as an icon of low Southern culture.[71] He appeared not so much an "individual genius" but a medium for his audience, "letting its current flow through him."[72] For all of the arguable performativity of this persona, it created a new autobiographical standard in country music that has since attained mythic proportions.

Williams' authenticity in the postwar music scene, then, largely rests on the conflation of his private history and public identity. But even if his prolific body of songs fails to take an exclusive autobiographical tack, the work encapsulates his sincerity. Like Tubb's, Williams' voice attracted attention for its very commonness, yet his distinctive yodeling and plaintive whine surpassed the Troubadour's to capture the honky-tonk sound *and* outlook: the meeting ground of the rural and urban, past and present, tradition and modernity. Although he reportedly patterned some of his vocal phrasing on Tubb's, he idolized Roy Acuff's plain singing for its "heart-on-the-sleeve sincerity" and, at the height of his own fame, declared Acuff "the biggest singer this music ever knew. . . . For drawing power in the South, it was Roy Acuff, then God. He'd stand up there singing, tears running down his cheeks."[73] Williams not only prized such emotion, he claimed it as the province of what he pointedly deemed "hillbilly" culture: "When a hillbilly sings a crazy song, he feels crazy. . . . He sings more sincere than most entertainers because the hillbilly was raised rougher than most entertainers. . . . He is singing about . . . the hopes and prayers and dreams and experiences of what some call the 'common people.' I call them the 'best people.'"[74] While apparently preferring the term "Folk Music" to describe his own artistry,[75] Williams here, late in his short life, felt compelled to resurrect and reclaim the more derogatory label in a much-cited 1952 interview with the magazine *Nation's Business,* whose reporter and readership clearly represented the antithesis of his own fan base. In this context, *hillbilly* becomes a clever sobriquet of class pride as Williams concludes: "There ain't nothing strange about our popularity these days. It's just that there are more people who are like us than there are the educated, cultured kind."[76]

This brand of authenticity has a particularly interesting relationship to the larger habitus informing honky-tonk music. As many have observed, Williams' haunting voice put a rustic stamp on whatever he sang, despite his own songs' eventual entry into the popular music market in the hands of Tony Bennett and other similarly sophisticated vocalists.[77] And perhaps even more so than Tubb, Williams articulated through his vocal performance and lyrics a new mode of white working-class masculinity rooted in deep emotion. Insisting that his songwriting put a premium on "feelings about things,"[78] he focused on the "common" man's sense of loss, fear, anger, and dread as he negotiates the modern urban landscape. Leppert and Lipsitz convincingly focus on Williams' own abject body as the root of such transgressive emotion, arguing that his "deformity (spina bifida), addiction, . . . [and] unnatural thinness" flouted "the model of the self-reliant, self-contained in-shape and battle-tested postwar male." Acutely aware of his own marginalization within a dominant representational system, they contend, Williams challenged traditional gender norms and their concomitant narrative conventions, particularly "romantic optimism."[79]

Yet as Tubb's songs demonstrate, a break from *middle-class* masculinity cannot necessarily be equated with an embracing of the feminine nor guarantee that the performer remains wholly impervious to social messages about masculine entitlement. Williams certainly recasts the social "center" in his music and traffics in its despair—for every upbeat song like "Hey, Good Lookin'," there are ten more in effect wailing "I'm So Lonesome I Could Cry." But this avid reader of mass-marketed romantic tales and comic books laments the absence of romance and/or the domestic as much as he resists its simple-minded fantasy. Furthermore, his fabled stage magnetism demonstrates that he could repackage that feeble body as an equally self-confident and sexualized emblem of working-class Southern manhood.[80]

Williams' two most illustrious songs *about* honky-tonk culture, "Honky Tonk Blues" and "Honky-Tonkin'," serve as a telling entrée into his complicated vision of the Southern migrant's postwar dislocation and sense of "unease."[81] While not released as a single until 1952, "Honky Tonk Blues" was initially recorded in 1947 and expertly delineates the rural/urban tension on the minds of honky-tonk audiences in the mid-to-late 1940s. This song's speaker abandons his "home down on the rural route" for the pleasures of the city, signified by its addictive juke joints, yet he soon gets caught up in a virtual vortex of dancing and drinking to the "jumpin'" music as a panacea for his urban "blues." The song's chorus, however, ambiguously attributes those blues to the honky-tonk experience itself: as Barbara Ching notes of Williams as a whole, "rather than celebrating urban amusement, his songs say that honky-tonkin' masquerades as consolation for leaving the country."[82] The young man vows to "scat right back" to the rustic homestead to escape his "worries" and in the song's written but unrecorded last verse finds solace in his "Ma and Pa"'s sensible rural values and discipline. Here, the country functions as a seemingly safe haven, a locale of moral authority and plain good sense.

At the same time, the song's infectious melody and playful, as well as soulful, yodeling demonstrate for the listener just why the honky-tonk more frequently than not wins out. This is not to suggest that the song's nostalgic portrait of home should thus be read as "purely theatrical,"[83] for as noted in prior examples, it's in keeping with the split honky-tonk subject to pit the "real" self against his "partying" mask. (Indeed, Escott employs similar imagery when describing the artist himself, asserting that "from an early age the core of Hank Williams became a thing known only to himself, masked by the molassified haw-haw that led people to think that they were his closest friends."[84]) My point is that even honky-tonk songs dedicated to a kind of self-critique—an examination of the culture's dangerous seductiveness—often musically enact that seductiveness so successfully that they create a competing "home place" for the audience, unsettling the rural/urban binary originally animating their narratives. The fervor that causes this dancing narrator to literally wear out his shoes cannot help but serve as a compelling contrast to his staid farm life.

This latter dynamic certainly rings true in the second song, "Honky-Tonkin'," written in the same year and released as an MGM single in 1948. This time, though, its steel guitar, fiddle, and rhythm guitar highlight the lyrics' celebration of the honky-tonk as a place to forget one's blues, which suggestively begin *outside* the city limits. This male speaker urges a disconsolate "sweet mama" to bring her own money and join him on an excursion to the bright lights, where they'll drink and dance their cares away. Williams joyfully sings the refrain, convincing us that "honky-tonkin'" can also offer its own considerable rewards.

Both songs seemingly challenge, rather than replicate, gendered conventions of the genre, as "Honky Tonk Blues" equates the country homestead as much with "pa" as with "ma," and "Honky-Tonkin'" allows a rural woman of indeterminate background—that is, not necessarily a corrupted "angel"—to crash the "man's world" of the urban juke joint. Both may, to a certain extent, betray Williams' lifelong obsession with what Ching calls "masculine failure," as, in her reading, the two songs emphasize the male narrators' inability to succeed in an urban setting.[85] But it is precisely that abjection that gets rewritten in postwar honky-tonk music as working-class male reality, and in these two particular cases, Williams' buoyant arrangement and delivery infuse such reality with a lighthearted spirit. It might be more accurate to conclude that both song narratives' dramatizations of honky-tonk culture invoke or draw on popular gendered ideologies of the rural/urban dichotomy yet incorporate several permutations that leave an opening for different interpretations.

His countless songs of *romantic* failure, however, establish another, less generous context for such work, particularly when their gender politics are under scrutiny. Though their emphasis on private "feelings" recalls Tubb's accounts of male emotional vulnerability, Williams takes this facet of love songs to unprecedented heights. To a degree, I concur with Leppert and Lipsitz that such songs offer a sober alternative to typically mindless romantic ditties and thus have the *potential* to expose traditional gender ideology *as* fiction.[86] But more often, the songs register a deep sense of betrayal aimed not at romance narrative itself but at women who have failed to comply with the script.

On one level, the heart imagery pervading this body of songs works in accord with Tubb's paradigmatic "Don't Look Now," underscoring the daily existence of both a performative self and a true one. In the most iconic Williams tune of all, "Your Cheatin' Heart," the male speaker chastises his unfaithful lover by issuing an unusual warning: her "real" self, the heart, will ultimately reveal itself in guilt and pain; citing Tubb's first honky-tonk hit, Williams predicts, "you'll walk the floor / The way I do / Your cheatin' heart / Will tell on you."[87] Written shortly after his second divorce from Audrey, the song undoubtedly has an autobiographical element driving its emotion. As Escott notes, its language may now be "part of the stock-in-trade of the country tunesmith, but Hank's subtextual chisel and thirst for vengeance still make the overfamiliar phrases spring to life."[88] Despite its highly personal "scalding bitterness," however, its imagery also functions more generically as part of honky-tonk thematics focused on the unmasked wounded male.[89] A Williams song recorded the preceding year, "My Heart Would Know," establishes as much when its spurned speaker admits, "my lips could tell a lie, but my heart would know." Here, he distinguishes between the "I" of his speech and the heart's knowledge, a division replicated throughout the song in lines such as "I could tell my heart that I don't miss you." Ultimately, this "cryin'" rather than "cheatin'" heart will "tell on" him as well. In "Take These Chains from My Heart," even the pretense of such masquerade is gone as the heart explicitly represents the self: "take these chains from my heart and set me free."[90]

Read against an evolving cultural backdrop of gender upheaval and reconstitution in the postwar and Cold War periods, such songs contribute to honky-tonk's bold aim to carve out a new position for the male country music performer. They indeed "locate the societal in the most personal and private terrain of sexual love"[91] and in doing so, as seen earlier with Tubb, stake out a different model of authentic masculinity even as they risk refeminizing the image of poor/working-class Southern white men. Yet that "private terrain" remains subject to the most compelling kinds of social expectations and pressures, provoking a dangerous slippage from opposition to allegiance and back again.

Williams may have "presented a masculine voice that longed for reconnection to the feminine," as Leppert and Lipsitz claim,[92] but I would reframe that longing as a privileging of feeling and a frustrated desire for traditional romantic/domestic happiness that can't help but erupt in his work. The hopeful love song "If You'll Be a Baby to Me," for instance, envisions a generically rural home life—he plows and churns the milk, she cooks and "keeps the home fires burning"—that can't be explained away solely as an egalitarian vision of "shared labours," characteristic of a vanishing "agrarian cyclical" culture.[93] Undoubtedly, this song can be read as a more nuanced mode of nostalgia, outlined earlier by Kathleen Stewart: preventing the erasure of an entire region or class community's history. Nevertheless, it entirely romanticizes that domesticity (and by extension, that history)—perhaps because it is not a scenario that Williams himself ever experienced as a child or as an adult.[94]

Barbara Ching is much more on the mark in this regard when she asserts that in his *abject* love songs, Williams typically "portrays himself as the victim of a loose and abusive woman."[95] The "subtextual" vitriol of "Your Cheatin' Heart" can be detected in other similar songs lamenting the "coldness" of modern women's hearts. His hurt and anger lead him to take a more blustering posture in "You're Gonna Change (or I'm Gonna Leave)," which advises that "the way to keep a woman happy" is to "love her ev'ry mornin', bawl her out at night."[96] In "I'm a Long Gone Daddy," the narrator follows through on the prior song's threat by taking the initiative to abandon his lover, a nagging "ball and chain" who "used to be nice and sweet."[97] In some ways, the latter single's B-side recording, "Window Shopping" (1952), neatly sums up the gendered model of failed romance typically celebrated in Williams's song catalog: modern women can't be trusted to commit to a lasting relationship as they're too distracted by other possibilities. They "don't feel love," "don't want real love," they're just "window shoppin' that's all."[98] The shopping metaphor also handily reflects these songs' critiques of such superficial women as the embodiment of material excess in an era of unparalleled consumerism.[99]

Williams's notoriously volatile relationship with his wife certainly informs this perspective. Legendary for her off-key singing, foul temper, and driving ambition, Audrey often assumes a near-villainess role in Williams's mythobiography, but like most assertive women in the 1950s, she seems too easily cast as a domineering shrew—distasteful *because* strong-willed. Like Lucy Ricardo seeking her share of Ricky's limelight at the Tropicana nightclub, she desperately wanted a career in entertainment and harangued her husband to record with her. And like Lucy, she chafed against the era's traditional notions of femininity. Escott writes that her "duets with Hank were like an extension of their married life—she fought him for dominance on every note."[100] Her frequently violent spats with Williams reveal that he in fact desired—at the very least in fantasy—a more conventionally domestic wife. While Audrey was pregnant with Hank Jr., Williams momentarily curtailed his drinking in order to function as the traditional paterfamilias, but their fights soon resumed.[101] His "cross-complaint" to the divorce that Audrey filed in 1952 vividly catalogs what Williams perceived to be her "infidelity" to the gendered functions of wife and mother:

> The first years of . . . married life were troublesome, because of the inattention of [Audrey] to her home and husband. . . . [She] refused to appreciate the obligations of married life, denying her attentions and affections to her home and husband, insisting that she too was an entertainer and singer of ability. . . . [She had] no interest or disposition to [stay] at home . . . but has always insisted upon traveling about, acting independent and free of all marital restraint.[102]

While Audrey was undoubtedly a difficult woman to live with, Williams discloses here his own romantic attachment to dominant gender constructions. As with "Rainbow at Midnight" or his own "If You'll Be a Baby to Me," he wants the cottage ideal, and Audrey clearly wasn't "interested" in keeping their "home fires" burning.[103]

The urgent "politics of emotion" embodied in his songs thus operates at another, decidedly less progressive level, always in tension with the work's more recognizably oppositional qualities.[104] Williams refashions hillbilly masculinity as rustic sensitivity yet demands that women in the same class culture remain restricted by dominant models of feminine identity. Indeed, at times those love songs suggest that modern women's refusal of conventional gender norms *produces* such abject emotion. Like other honky-tonk male artists of this period, he mourns the absence of the domestic home place and actively seeks it out in his music, in effect expecting women to "continue to compensate for . . . the individualism" in his changing world.[105] His signature "drifting," accentuated in the name of his band, the Drifting Cowboys, and his alias "Luke the Drifter" (to record his gospel tunes), marks the failure of that search.[106]

Hank Williams converted a positionality of weakness into strength by conflating hillbilly music with the blues, his voice "a capsulised history of a

... regionally-ghettoised people,"[107] who experienced bewildering transition and erasure in the postwar period. As is well-known, African American men such as the street musician Rufus "Tee Tot" Payne gave him invaluable music "lessons" in his youth, and he embraced their style while dispensing with formalized racial masks.[108] But his brand of honky-tonk music asked women to adopt an equally repellent mode of masquerade in which they also had conflicting investments, inciting a musical dialogue with few genuine "answers."

IV. SECOND WAVE: KITTY WELLS AND JEAN SHEPARD

Honky-Tonk after Hank

After Williams quietly slipped into a drug-induced death in the backseat of a Cadillac on New Year's Day, 1953, twenty thousand mourners packed the funeral held in his hometown of Montgomery, Alabama, from everyday fans to country music luminaries such as Roy Acuff, Ernest Tubb, and Webb Pierce. As many have commented, the same music industry that had turned on the singer in the final months of his life, exasperated by his increasingly unprofessional behavior, now posthumously consecrated him as the "Immortal."[109] Although Pierce and Lefty Frizzell had appeared in the late 1940s and early '50s as significant honky-tonk singers and songwriters, and Tubb continued to have a thriving career throughout the next decade, Williams "personified" the genre. And as demonstrated by Tosches's tribute, quoted earlier, more recent critics tend to agree; his passing constitutes an equivalent death knoll for the original flourishing of what is now deemed "hard country."[110]

The gender politics of this last term aren't terribly subtle and are replicated in Richard Peterson's "hard-core"/"soft-shell" schema of country music, as well as Jeffrey Lange's division between "primal honky-tonk" and "soft honky-tonk," though both models allow for a few women artists in the "hard" category.[111] Historicized overviews of country music in the Cold War era tend to fuel this gendered paradigm, as Joli Jensen and Diane Pecknold have documented. Journalists and academics alike often position honky-tonk as the commercial "victim" in this era of not only the exciting novelty of rock 'n' roll—which offered a patently youthful version of masculine bravado—but rock's antithesis, the up-and-coming Nashville Sound, which with "its angelic backing vocals and orchestral strings" was deemed "the soggy reverie of the postwar suburban wife" by the early 1960s.[112] To be sure, the consolidation of the country industry during this period dramatically transformed the production, consumption, and marketing of its music. The swift rise of what is now known as Nashville's "Music Row" provided unforeseen opportunities to country performers but also enforced an overwhelmingly commercialist ethos that measured artistic success by chart placement of individual recordings.[113] Country music indeed experienced a crisis in the 1950s as it scrambled to establish itself as a viable financial venture. The point here is that analysts looking back on the era frequently, and seemingly unselfconsciously, employ its same gendered prescriptions as they reconstruct the history for later audiences. Despite both Tubb's and Williams's forays into the same feminized sphere of private emotion soon to be equated with the Nashville Sound, honky-tonk music's broader agenda of remasculinization left women artists precious little access to the genre, and its subsequent lionizing by later generations of male commentators has reproduced such marginalization.[114]

Nonetheless, female performers managed to gain a foothold during the music's next incarnation in the 1950s, and one went so far as to emerge the reigning "Queen of Country Music." Kitty Wells's breakthrough commercial success as a honky-tonk singer literally paved the way for lesser-known artists like Jean Shepard and Charline Arthur. A 1953 *Billboard* article entitled "Gals from the Hills: Kitty and Goldie Start Country-Girl Search" baldly announces the material stakes in this venture while also exposing the double standard exercised by the music industry:

> Ever since Kitty Wells hit with a big-selling disk on "It Wasn't God Who Made Honky Tonk Angels" and Goldie Hill followed with "Let the Stars Get in My Eyes," diskery a.& r. men [record labels' artists and repertoire representatives] have been scouring the hinterlands for additional girl country singers in hopes of coming up with one to rival the sales racked up by the two Decca artists. . . . While it is true . . . that girl vocalists in any musical field are never as consistent in sales as are the male singers, the country field has always been a tough one for fem thrushes.[115]

After honky-tonk transformed authenticity standards for country music as a whole, female performers' options for signifying rusticity and/or the "real" appeared to narrow even further: essentially, to continue perpetuating the prewar barn dance roles of either rube comedian, as epitomized by Minnie Pearl, or country sweetheart, as did Sunshine Sue, host of Virginia's *Old Dominion Barn Dance,* in a profoundly changed postwar scene.

But as the *Billboard* piece hints, honky-tonk inadvertently created a third possibility: the "answer song" phenomenon that allowed women like Wells and Hill to record musical "responses" to top-selling songs by male artists such as Hank Thompson's "The Wild Side of Life" and Ray Price's "Don't Let the Stars Get in Your Eyes." As demonstrated in prior years and particularly during the 1940s, when popular performers such as Ernest Tubb "answered" their own hit songs, the practice had always proved an easy way to maximize profitability.[116] In the 1950s, however, women not only inserted themselves into the previously predictable formula in order to sell records—they reconfigured it. Rather than simply replicating a prior hit's mood, melody, and basic lyrics, their new version of the answer song frequently had the potential to contest its very premise, functioning as a galvanizing countertext. Honky-tonk music's frank examination of private relationships, often culminating in a critique of modern women's wayward behavior, certainly made it risky for female performers to identify with the genre and, by association, its honky-tonk angel prototype. But its unprecedented subject matter also seemed tailor-made for the rise of a new and explicitly gendered "dialogue" addressing postwar changes in both the domestic and the public spheres.[117] Before turning to Wells and Shepard as two representative, if quite different figures of this second honky-tonk phase, I'd like to analyze the answer song model more fully as a discursive tool at once enabling and limiting female artists' agency.

Rethinking the Answer Song

As outlined earlier, honky-tonk songs sought to counter the cultural invisibility of poor/working-class Southern white men transplanted to urban spaces of work and pleasure. Yet their hard-won presence as alternately carousing and despairing protagonists of modern narratives is predicated on the absence of women who haunt these musical texts as either cherished signifiers of a lost past or more vexing contemporary emblems of lost purity. Increasingly, the latter dominated the genre: hardened women daring to make their own presence "out where the bright lights are glowing . . . drawn like a moth to a flame."[118] Joe Maphis and Rose Lee Maphis's 1952 hit "Dim Lights, Thick Smoke (And Loud, Loud Music)" encapsulates this structural dynamic, addressing such interlopers by juxtaposing two polarized versions of home: "A house and little children mean nothing to you . . . the only home you know is the club down the street."[119] As with all binary structures, such imagery cleverly incites yet also forbids response. At the very least, it dictates the formal as well as conceptual parameters of answer songs and restricts the material setting in which women artists might actually perform them.

The answer song thus cannot genuinely represent any monolithic "woman's perspective," as several critics have proposed.[120] It matters less that men wrote most of these songs, in any case, than that they consistently respond to a prior text already embedded in a gendered ideology that the "answer" song cannot help but reproduce as well. As Katie Stewart argues of male honky-tonk "sad" songs, "the image of the absent, or unrelentingly hard-hearted woman" *itself* "confirms and intensifies the sad song poetic and its male space of desire"; but more to the point here, that image "is actually given voice in female response songs . . . which bespeak a 'realist' counterattack," yet even this "belittling back talk . . . adds to the poetics of intensification and provides . . . more proof of its meaningfulness."[121] As with blackface or rube comedy, the very repetitiveness of this citational practice inevitably reconstitutes its gendered performances.[122]

At the same time, Stewart's approach to the female answer song as performative "backtalk" usefully engages with influential feminist theories of women's discourse to envision the response dynamic as a tool of resistance. Stewart contends that in those West Virginia coal camps of her study, women's speech in effect stages the larger discourse—throws it into relief *as* a construct—so that it "fragments and externalizes any assumed feminine character."[123] A welcome addition to the critical framework surrounding this song form, Stewart's reclamation of women's "backtalk" still appears too invested, however, in reading such discourse as resistant critique. Putting a more cautionary twist on that model, I prefer to view honky-tonk answer songs as "inlays on . . . existing inscriptions" with the *potential* to "reopen cultural forms to history."[124] Akin to barn dance minstrelsy skits, they can certainly call attention to the ideological assumptions underlying the caricatures that they dramatize (here accentuated as categories of class and gender, rather than race).

Depending on the song, this "inlay" will be produced more through mimicry than through explicit opposition—within Wells' body of answer songs, for example, "I'll Always Be Your Fraulein" as opposed to "It Wasn't God Who Made Honky-Tonk Angels."[125] At other times, as David Sanjek notes of African American women blues singers who used the music's inherent patterning to "'go public' with attitudes and points of view that the dominant society . . . wished to expurgate," answer songs openly appropriated the honky-tonk character of the modern "good-time" gal to expose the genre's gendered formulations.[126] But as with these analogous modes of performance (blackface and blues), women's answer songs are peculiarly overdetermined forms that rarely lend themselves to a rigid interpretative frame. In Wells's and Shepard's renditions—as well as in their own original songs—gender practices may be "externalized as discourse" *yet also* prove susceptible to, rather than simply defy, "internalization as identity."[127]

Kitty Wells

Like Tubb's and Williams', Kitty Wells' authenticity as a honky-tonk performer first registered in her singing voice—stark, rustic, encompassing the immediacy and pathos of earlier Appalachian music, as well as the heartache of modern private dramas. But as with her male counterparts, Wells's personal history and professional persona also made her ideally suited to represent the conflicts of the transitional postwar era. A Nashville native, she could hardly claim to have lived the culture of deep Southern rurality, but her working-class childhood was steeped in those values. Her own experience as a laundress and housekeeper during the early Depression years helped reinforce her bonds with and empathy for working people.[128] Church and family were the mainstays of her youth as well, introducing Wells at a young age to musical performance as she sang gospel songs with her sisters and mother. After marrying aspiring musician Johnnie Wright at the age of eighteen, she assumed she'd simply settle into life as a homemaker and mother and initially did so, performing only sporadically with her husband's act.[129] Robert Oermann thus rightly notes that "her deep roots in older traditions made her the perfect embodiment of the difficulties of adjusting to America's new morality" in the later 1940s. Wells's unlikely subsequent stardom was grounded in such tradition. At a time when country music was dominated by male artists, she found a niche in part because she paradoxically signified "Victorian-influenced old-country culture" and thereby posed no seeming threat to either the industry or conventional gender codes.[130]

Thus, even as Wells became best-known for songs that voiced the desires, laments, and indignation of the honky-tonk angel, as a female entertainer she could never risk blurring the line between her "real" and her performative selves. She ushered in a different mode of sincerity for women trespassing into honky-tonk musical territory. While "E. T." and Hank could embody its cultural habitus (albeit different ends of the spectrum), she had to accentuate her own outsider status. More precisely, she had to assure her fans and colleagues that she privately remained an emblem of (or at least professed allegiance to) their mythologized rural past even as she frequently performed as its antithesis in her music—and as a hard-working singer herself further threatened to expose the obsolescence of such gendered imagery. (Even her stage name was borrowed from an old folk song, "Sweet Kitty Wells," reaffirming her ties to tradition.[131])

Honky-tonk's trope of the split self takes on another function, then, when women step into the spotlight, as their personal authenticity is located in the perpetual *division* between biographical and performative identities. In answer songs, the dynamic becomes yet more complicated as the female singer in some ways necessarily engages with the trope in its endemic form when she responds to the original male text. Her "angel" persona both adopts a traditionally "hard" masculine identity ("tough," independent) and contests its very conception, while the typically anguished male lover of the former song signifies another mode of masculinity affiliated with "soft" emotion. It remains essential, though, that she also be capable of having her "cold" exterior "melted" to reveal her properly feminine core.

Wells's first and most infamous answer song, for instance, immediately announces itself as a transgressive text in that it collapses distinctions between two polarized women in honky-tonk discourse, the victimized wife and the cheating angel. "It Wasn't God Who Made Honky-Tonk Angels" opens with the female narrator ensconced in a bar, listening to the jukebox play Hank Thompson's recording of "The Wild Side of Life."[132] In that song, the jilted husband, like so many others in honky-tonk music, condemns his ex-wife for her sexual appetite, infidelities, and attraction to the night life, and because she has heartlessly refused to listen to his entreaties by letter or phone, he resorts to songwriting. Its key statement, which inspires the anthemic title to Wells's song, offers an essentialist interpretation of her behavior: since "God made honky-tonk angels," they will "naturally" return to a life of "sin." They are inherently corrupt. But in Wells's narrative, that song's refrain prompts "mem'ries" that tell quite a different story of cause and effect. Her protagonist used to be a "trustin' wife" betrayed by her own straying husband; in turn, she defiantly charges men with "the blame" for transforming "good girls" into "angels." "Honky-Tonk Angels" effectively rewrites "The Wild Side of Life" on multiple levels, revealing the actual power relations often determining women's fates and as such declaring the angel prototype an ideological construct of the honky-tonk genre. Within this song's logic, there is no inherent separation between the private and public selves that Wells herself was expected to model, as its narrator claims to be *both* a traditional and a modern woman.

Significantly, however, outside of the song's narrative frame, Wells the performer needed to reinstate such divisions. The male author of "The Wild

Side of Life" could openly promote his song as an autobiographical text and in fact performed it at a local bar frequented by his ex-wife.[133] Wells's success depended precisely on a convincing counterpersona. Her now-legendary 1954 honor from Tennessee governor Frank Clement serves as just one (extreme) mode of public discourse seeking control over her professional image, assuring her fans that "Kitty Wells, in addition to her artistry, has demonstrated that she is an outstanding wife and mother in keeping with the finest tradition of southern womanhood." Her very first appearance in *Country Song Roundup,* accompanied by the banner "A Star Is Born," established this message while ostensibly forecasting her imminent fame: "Today, as Mrs. Johnnie Wright, . . . Kitty is the proud mother of two lovely girls and one boy. . . . Though Kitty Wells spends a great deal of her time doing personal appearances and radio shows, she is a mother first, singer second," and thus "a lovely picture of fine American womanhood."[134] Such images abound in popular fan magazines of the period, whose photos frequently position Wells as the literal center of her musical family.

They also dominate the promotional copy and artwork for her recordings.[135] Her 1959 album suggestively titled *After Dark* serves as one especially striking example. Its back jacket touts her "sincerity, great warmth and feeling" yet hastens to cast her vocals as "folk artistry" of the highest order to discourage any hint of correspondence between her private experience and her "artist" persona. Those listening to her "songs of sinful sadness and broken romance" will be relieved to learn that "in her magnificent performances there is no real sadness."[136] The album's jacket front visually reinforces this schism: in her requisite barn dance gingham, Wells appears in the foreground caught midsong as if on the Opry stage; behind her, an out-of-focus backdrop reveals an illicit couple clad in contemporary urban dress.

For her part, Wells was more than content to embody domesticity in her private life as fervently as she portrayed the fictitious "queen" of "Heartbreak U.S.A." When Roy Acuff early on insisted to her husband that "you can't headline a show with a woman," it was Johnnie, not Kitty, who protested such sentiment, and she confesses that she recorded her now-signature song simply because she was "looking for a hit just like everybody else"—at the very least, she hoped to pocket the union-scale fee for completing the recording.[137] And as several others have commented, despite its quasi-feminist cachet, "Honky-Tonk Angels" can from another vantage point also appear more Victorian than modern, conveying the sense that the fallen woman is "more to be pitied than censured."[138] As it happens, one year earlier Audrey Williams had written and recorded the single "Leave Us Women Alone,"

The Queen of Country Music prefers a living room sofa to a "throne." Kitty is widely respected as a mother and homemaker by all who know her.

Kitty Wells in *Country Music Life*, June 1966: "The Queen of Country Music prefers a living room sofa to a 'throne.'" (Courtesy of Country Music Hall of Fame and Museum.)

which anticipates the basic sentiment of "Honky-Tonk Angels" but issues its critique with more sass and directness, perhaps due to her own public positioning as just such a failure of femininity: "If it wasn't for women what would you / do / Who would you tell your lies and your / troubles to."[139] It's fitting that Minnie Pearl, who found success in a nonthreatening female comic role, recognized the intertwined class and sexual politics dictating both women's subsequent fates in the industry (Audrey's poor singing notwithstanding!) when she declared, "Kitty is a lady . . . some tramp could never have done it [made a career singing such songs]."[140]

Nevertheless, Wells seemed to have a knack for courting controversy in her music. In her 1936 radio debut as a duo with her cousin Bessie, she sang a Carter Family tune, "Jealous Hearted Me," that the station management found so explicit that it cut them off in midperformance, a foreshadowing of the Opry's initial ban on her first number-one hit.[141] She may have insisted that she'd never been a feminist, but as she recently confessed, she clearly enjoyed "the womenfolk getting back at the menfolk" in her songs.[142] Furthermore, much like barn dance predecessors such as Lulu Belle, Wells' ability to combine her private and professional lives as she built her headlining career on the road demonstrates her own tenacity in merging two different versions of "home." It also dramatizes women artists' unusually fraught path to authenticity in the honky-tonk period.[143]

Wells's commercial launching of the female answer song in "Honky-Tonk Angels" thus functions simultaneously as "backtalk" to and reinscription of dominant gender codes pervading not just the honky-tonk genre but 1950s popular culture at large. Her subsequent variants on the model essentially remained faithful to its strictures. Three recordings in the year following her breakthrough success, 1953, encompassed such tensions. Her next single answered Webb Pierce's "Back Street Affair" by reminding the audience that it is the "other woman" who ultimately "pays" for such indiscretion. The first half of the song restates Pierce's basic narrative, affirming the woman's ignorance of her lover's marriage ("Yes, I thought that you were true when I fell in love with you"), yet the second half establishes a critical difference in how the two are judged. While Pierce's version claims that they both bear the burden, Wells's insists that "you didn't count the cost, you gambled and I lost / Now I must pay for that backstreet affair."[144] Once more, she takes on the persona of the fallen woman whose passion gets the better of her ("my will was not my own"), but only in the context of her initial innocence.

A more light-hearted early "answer" hit, "Hey Joe," may actually be more oppositional, as it invents a bold female subject completely absent in the original song recorded by Carl Smith. Set in a honky-tonk, Smith's version offers a male narrator who playfully warns his friend Joe that he'll steal his irresistible dance partner; however, no women speak in his rendition. Wells's narrator similarly addresses Joe, but as an assertive female onlooker eager to take advantage of his newly single status—not the "girlie" traded between the men. Though replicating the melody and silly wordplay featured in the original ("lovey dovey," "jolly dolly"), "Hey Joe" conjures a woman who commands, "Go put on your dancin' shoes and I'll help you forget your blues / I've simply got to have you for my own."[145]

That song's promise dimmed, however, in "My Cold Cold Heart Is Melted Now"—a fascinating rejoinder to both "Cold Cold Heart" and "Your Cheatin' Heart" that Hank Williams also wrote (with Johnnie Masters) but never recorded commercially. Set to the tune of the latter song, "My Cold Cold Heart Is Melted Now" employs a distinctly humbled female speaker repenting her "dark" past. Unlike most of the other modern women wreaking emotional havoc in Williams's narrative, this one admits her guilt and relishes her pain because, just as the male speaker in "Your Cheatin' Heart" predicted, it signals the revival of her heart—that key emblem of feeling venerated within the genre. With this twist, Williams acknowledged women's capacity for a deeper subjectivity—a recognition of "core" or unmasked identity—yet limited its parameters to his own fantasies of true femininity. In this short span of time, Wells thus came full circle in her roster of answer songs by enacting honky-tonk's most elusive figure: an "angel" who takes full responsibility for and laments her "sin."

When formally liberated from this "response" structure, Wells discovered that her independent songs in this era would still inevitably constitute a reaction to honky-tonk imagery, hampered by its conventions. In other words, all songs, to some degree, would function as answer songs. As suggested by its jacket copy, the aforementioned album *After Dark* offered a powerful distillation of the genre's themes if also, by this date, its now-waning sound, situating a few of her singles ("The Lonely Side of Town" [1955], "Your Wild Life's Gonna Get You Down" [1959]) within a stirring collection of songs articulating women's multiple perspectives. Wells certainly traverses more predictable terrain here, exploring the effects of infidelity by occupying the twin roles of devastated wife and lover, but she is also allowed to voice more complicated emotions. Representative phrases drawn from honky-tonk nomenclature–"slippin' around," "your wild life," "bright lights," even "shoppin' around"—circulate in this song cycle, verifying Wells's "credentials" to participate in this genre.

In some cases, they cluster in such a concentrated form that they threaten to reify the experience. "Lonely Side of Town's" string of references sketch out a convivial honky-tonk world in opposition to the female speaker's material and psychic site of abandonment, simply designated "the lonely side of town." As in many comparable songs recorded by men, such naming initially appears to position loneliness *outside* of the honky-tonk purview, replicating a familiar split between the carefree carouser and the anguished, alienated self. Here, that split is explicitly gendered as well as externalized, divided between the cheating male and his "lonely" wife. Rather than accept her fate or chastise her husband, however, this narrator longs to join him across town. Tired of "walking with these blues since sun down," she glances at the distant bright lights and wishes she weren't exiled from their promises.[146] Like other self-reflexive songs in the genre, this one finally relocates loneliness within the honky-tonk paradigm. Yet its closing declaration also suggests women's desire to steal across that threshold and, be they fans or performers of the music, claim its "home" space as their own.

"Honky Tonk Waltz" finds the wife of "Lonely Street" now acting on her desire but unexpectedly occupying the position of abject barroom loner rather than bon vivant. She's wandered uptown but remains alone with her "lost" heart, the surrounding "laughing crowd" oblivious to her sorrow.[147] A particular song encompasses and repeatedly broadcasts her loss, blurring the jukebox record with Wells's own "honky tonk waltz." Rather than retreating to her "lonely room," however, she chooses to stay at the bar after the crowd leaves, letting loose her tears. Unlike men who utilize the honky-tonk as a place to hide behind a mask, she eventually indulges her emotions there, momentarily healing the split between performative and "real" selves.

"I Heard the Jukebox Playing" offers another permutation of the suffering-wife role. Reminiscent of "Honky-Tonk Angels," it relies solely on jukebox imagery to signify the honky-tonk lifestyle, here heard over the phone by a suspicious wife weighing her husband's deceptive words against competing background noise of music and laughter.[148] As in so many answer songs, this narrator contrasts a man's speech with his actions and her own situation, opening with the lines, "You *said* that you'd be happy with a baby on your knees / But *here I sit* with him in my arms and *you're slippin' around* on me."[149] As the steel guitar and fiddle overtake Wells's song, they also stand in for the overheard music within the narrative, which prompts the speaker to realize, "that couldn't have been no radio 'cause it had a honky-tonk sound." The song's repetition confirms her worst fears. There's no internal resolution this time—just heartbreaking realization. But once again, the self-reflexive nature of the music establishes Wells's version of honky-tonk as a legitimate, even iconic representative of the genre.

Not surprisingly, *After Dark* has its share of fallen angels as well, but they subscribe to a revised formula made possible by Wells herself. The title song revisits the sentiments of her earlier chart-topping single "Paying for That Backstreet Affair," condemning a woman's illicit lover for remaining "scandal free" while she suffers the gossips' tongues. "You're Not Easy to Forget" gives voice to a woman who haunts honky-tonks in the aftermath of an affair. She freely admits that she seeks solace in both drink and physical affection as pleasant diversions yet still searches for genuine love. Finally, the album's closing song, "They Can't Take Your Love," offers a further twist on this position by casting the female speaker's devotion as itself a kind of social rebellion, blurring the line between feminine excess and virtue. Employing Cold War imagery to capture her battle against unspecified authority figures who oppose her relationship with a "reckless" lover, she advises, "So while they plan their next attack, let's really play it smart / and build a wall of defense around our hearts."

Written by a woman, May Hawks, the song does convey an unusual understanding of women's compromised agency in conducting private relationships. Honky-tonk men may receive unsolicited advice about their romantic partners from their barroom pals, but few contend with forces that actually attempt "to plan [their] life" as this narrator does. Released one year after Wanda Jackson's blistering cover of "Fujiyama Mama," which likens women's sexuality to the atom bomb, the song ingeniously deepens its social critique through its Cold War references: the era's "symbolic connections among the fears of atomic power, sex, and women out of control" here become invoked and overturned as the forbidden lovers are cast as victims, rather than perpetrators, of the "attack."[150] Clearly, Wells the performer was no feminist firebrand, but *After Dark* demonstrates that women could succeed at appropriating, while also replicating, honky-tonk music. This particular "inlay" on previously "encoded" texts indeed finds opportunities to reimagine its form, destabilizing—if not entirely reinventing—honky-tonk's gendered blueprint for country authenticity.

Jean Shepard

Wells was undoubtedly a trailblazer in the country music field, claiming many milestones: the first song by a woman artist to reach number one on the *country* charts (and remain there for six weeks); the first woman artist to record a country LP (*Kitty Wells' Country Hit Parade*); the first female vocalist to become a member of the Opry in the 1950s.[151] She accomplished other industry feats as well that remain impressive by today's standards, such as winning the "top female vocalist" category in country fan and trade magazines for fourteen years and placing thirty-eight singles in the Country Top 10.[152] But as even *Billboard* recognized about country music's "fem singers" in the 1950s, which certainly included Wells, they typically caught a break through their affiliations with men already ensconced in the business.[153] Even in the wake of Wells's stardom, such gate-keeping continued to hamper women's efforts to join the honky-tonk firmament.

While maverick performer Charline Arthur has emerged in recent historiography as the most notable casualty of country's masculinist practices during this period, Jean Shepard may serve as the more instructive example: a bold honky-tonk singer and musician whose uneven career reflected her ability to both epitomize and defy the music's gendered mythologies.[154] Born into a large sharecropping family that moved from Oklahoma at the close of World War II to California's San Joaquin Valley, Shepard could certainly claim the kind of authentic rural identity so familiar to honky-tonk's established audience in the early 1950s. She also shared the same veneration of Jimmie Rodgers's music as Tubb and Williams, learning to yodel by wearing out her father's cherished secondhand collection of Rodgers's records. At the same time, she departed from the traditional model for "girl" singers. While attending high school in the postwar period, she formed an all-girl band, The Melody Ranch Girls, that whetted her appetite for country music performance—so much so that she fled an early marriage when her new husband wanted to squash her career plans in hopes of keeping her, in Shepard's parlance, "barefoot and pregnant."[155]

A chance encounter with Hank Thompson in 1952, when the "Wild Side of Life"/"Honky-Tonk Angels" dyad was at the peak of success, proved a fitting turning point, verifying Shepard's promise but also the industry's gendered constraints. Impressed with her talent, Thompson all but assured Shepard of a recording contract with his West Coast label, Capitol Records, but she waited half a year or so due to the reservations harbored by Capitol's country A&R chief, Ken Nelson. Following in the footsteps of Opry host Roy Acuff, as well as fellow industry executives, Nelson was loathe to devote Capitol's resources to a solo female performer, declaring, "There's just no place in country music for women," while adding the telling caveat, "But every band needs a girl singer." Upon subsequently witnessing the seventeen-year-old Shepard perform with an all-male ensemble, singing Wells's current hit and playing bass, Nelson was apparently placated, reassured that she was just a "little mite of a girl with this big bass . . . whacking away."[156]

Despite Shepard's breakthrough rise as a solo artist now lauded in critical commentary, her career was shaped by this entrenched commitment to women's decidedly marginal "place" in country music, especially its honky-tonk niche.[157] Capitol's publicity machine borrowed Nelson's dismissive language to accentuate its new vocalist's diminutive size and status, as well as her physical assets, introducing this female "country and hillbilly singer" as a "vivacious blonde," a "tiny vocalist (she's barely over five feet)," and the "little girl who sings in a full voice as clear as a bell."[158] Unlike Wells, always prominently linked to her husband and children, Shepard posed an initial image problem and was thus marketed throughout the 1950s as the unthreatening "girl-next-door." *Country Song Roundup,* for instance, touts her as the "Girl with the 'Big Heart'" who "behind the big voice" is simply "a cute blonde girl who . . . weighs a small 100 pounds" and whose "big friendly smile and . . . warm personality . . . [make] you feel as though you have known her all her life."[159] Due to her songs' frequently frank lyrics or adult themes and her "balls-to-the-walls" voice—standard issue for male honky-tonk–industry and fan magazine discourse strategically underscored little "Jeannie"'s feminine, rather than "cold," heart.[160]

Shepard's early recording experiences reflected such anxiety. Her 1953 debut record, "Crying Steel Guitar Waltz," took up the classic abject honkytonk position with an inventive spin, blaming its female narrator's romantic woes on the genre's signature instrument, the steel guitar. It proved a commercial failure, despite Capitol's decision to add the name of famed steel guitarist Speedy West to the record's label to offset worries about a woman's "selling power."[161] (Interestingly, Kitty Wells recorded the song later that same year as the B-side to "Paying for That Backstreet Affair.") She achieved her first number-one hit not as a solo artist but as the "duet" partner of male newcomer Ferlin Husky, with a record evocative of Tubb's postwar paeans to domesticity, "Rainbow at Midnight" and its "Answer"—but this time recrafted for the Korean War era as "A Dear John Letter."[162] Initially dismissed by Nelson as an antiquated piece with outworn sentiments and "corny" language, the single was paired with Shepard's cover of a recent pop hit, "I'd Rather Die Young," which Nelson predicted would be the big seller. Yet significantly, it was "the record where that ole boy's doing the talking"—referring to Husky's featured recitation—that shot to the top.[163]

"Dear John" narrates a woman's confessed betrayal of her sweetheart, a soldier overseas, in the form of a letter. While it begins with Shepard's poignant vocals, the song's emotional center undeniably rests in Husky's voice-over, as he opens and then recites the rest of her message. Although the song may indeed have appeared a throwback in both theme and arrangement, it also seems well suited to early 1950s gender conservatism, casting Shepard as the equivalent of honky-tonk's modern femme fatale who cheats on her darling (with his brother, no less) while he serves his country. The song's structure reflects the era's gender politics as well: we actually hear very little of Shepard on this recording, as the male part in this "duet" takes over her first-person narrative. (Ironically, the first pressings of this record omitted Husky's name, listing Shepard as a solo artist.) Husky's tremulous recitation of the letter simultaneously conveys her heartlessness, as well as his character's devastated hopes for socially sanctioned family life, reviving men's postwar naivete that "the fighting was all over and the battles have all been won."

The one-million-selling record clearly resonated with both country and pop music audiences, launching Shepard's career. Predictably, it also spawned its own answer song, "Forgive Me John," which this time intriguingly sought to "repair" the woman's reputation by voicing her regret over marrying her lover's brother. But despite lamenting "the awful wrong I've done," she remains a static and marginal figure, eclipsed by her soldier's response.[164] Husky resumes his role as central narrator, soberly informing her that while other men are returning home to reunite with their parents and wives, he cannot accept her as a sister-in-law, nor will he allow her to betray his brother. Reaffirming the equation among traditional femininity, domesticity, and an abstracted notion of the nation, he melodramatically concludes, "There's nothing for me to come home to now / so I'll re-enlist and live my lonely soldier's life." Perhaps to elicit a bit more sympathy for both songs' tainted female personas and, by extension, Shepard herself, "Forgive Me John" was paired with "My Wedding Ring," which, similar to the still-popular "Honky-Tonk Angels," provides the "back story" for that archetype by telling the tale of "a mother that was once a happy wife" yet, like "Dear John"'s soldier, was "left without a future" when her husband abandoned her for another. Encouraging women listeners' identification with her plight, Shepard convincingly sings, "I'm just a girl like so many others / neither good nor bad / maybe a girl like you."[165]

Literally overshadowed by men in her early recordings as well as on tour, where Husky functioned as both her road manager and her legal guardian until she turned twenty-one, Shepard admitted much later in her career that she had been "very meek and mild" in those initial years.[166] Nevertheless, her status as a single "girl" throughout the 1950s allowed her to emerge as another female voice in honky-tonk who attempted to "talk back" to its gendered inscriptions. Dressed early on in alternately cowgirl or modest contemporary attire, she signified modern country femininity as a compromise between Wells's old-fashioned barn dance look and rockabilly women's more outrageous or sophisticated costuming. (Wells and Shepard are even figured as such in *Rustic Rhythm*'s "Fashions on Parade" segment in the July 1957 issue, with Wells representing Opry styling and the latter, though pictured in Western wear, touted for her "assorted variety of wearables." Wanda Jackson is featured in a prior issue that year sporting fringed sheaths "fashioned for glamour.")

Even when appearing in what initially seems a conservative context, she clearly functions as another kind of transitional gendered symbol within honky-tonk discourse who appeals to younger female fans with forward-looking aspirations. *Country Style USA*, a military recruitment show taped throughout the 1950s and early 1960s that interspersed musical performances of country stars with formal bits promoting army recruitment, provides one instructive example. Shepard leads off her segment with a feisty 1955 tune of domestic discord, "Sad Singin' and Slow Ridin'," which anticipates Loretta Lynn's later "Don't Come Home A'Drinkin' with Lovin' on Your Mind." (She follows with a more standard honky-tonk ballad, "If You Can Walk Away" [1956].) What's more, her appearance strategically precedes a recruiting segment targeting young professional women who have finished college and envision themselves as army officers sitting on the "right side of the desk." In staged banter with recruiter Charlie Applewhite (a recurring figure on the program dubbed "Your Opportunity Man"), Shepard approves the segment's message, enthusing, "That's a real opportunity for all the girls out there!"[167] The army's ideologically muddled depictions of military service as both patriotic "duty" and labor advancement, helping women escape the domestic enclave as well as concomitant subordination in the workplace (the "right side of the desk"), suits Shepard's equally hybrid image—one part traditional, one part modern.

And while recording her share of formal answer songs to such hits as Webb Pierce's "There Stands the Glass" (her 1954 version bemoans "The Glass That Stands Beside You"), "little Jeannie Shepard" also managed to release a song that same year that arguably ranks as the "most feminist recording" by any honky-tonk female vocalist.[168] Like "Honky-Tonk Angels," "Two Whoops and a Holler" (written by Shepard's former duet partner, Ferlin Husky, using one of his myriad pseudonyms) exposes the double standard at work in contemporary gender codes but encompasses a far greater range of images and practices than sexual agency. Set to a rollicking Western swing beat, the song critiques men's sanctioned ability to "let loose" in the public sphere by drinking, smoking, drinking, and cheating, while women who do "one foolish little thing" are stigmatized as the "lowest thing in town."[169] More daringly, it poses women's unpaid domestic work as the much greater "responsibility" than men's work and in its final verse invites women to organize as a collective force to "rule the world." While Wells's comparable songs typically adopt a tragic and martyred air, this one has an ostensibly comic feel yet simultaneously radiates ominous energy and urgency. It's no wonder that "Two Whoops" failed commercially as a single, though it did resurface on her 1959 album *This Is Jean Shepard*.[170]

Shepard's remaining body of work throughout the 1950s largely operated within honky-tonk's restricted circumference by alternately replicating and refashioning its gendered morality tales. Even more dramatically than Wells, Shepard adopted the "angel" persona in a number of guises, depicting unrepentant sexual desire as much as regret, in songs such as "Don't Fall in Love with a Married Man" (1954), "Other Woman" (1956), "Thief in the Night" (1958), "You'd Better Go" (1958), and "I Hate Myself" (1958). Yet her first LP, *Songs from a Love Affair* (1956), is now considered a landmark work as the first country music *concept* album recorded by a woman—three years before Wells's *After Dark*—and within the honky-tonk oeuvre demonstrated that deep and complicated feeling was not an exclusively masculine province. The album's anatomy of a young woman's romantic history allowed Shepard, as Dave Sanjek observes, "to display a broad affective register that more adequately represented the range of female emotion than the restricted emotional palette of earlier Country performers."[171]

Yet by constructing a narrative from the album's song sequencing, the back jacket copy actually works to flatten out this text's complexity and adult affect in order to present a palatable image of its performer. It accomplishes the kind of distancing between female vocalist and material seen all along in Wells's career and thus, similar to *After Dark*, underscores the artifice of both. "No performer in the field of country music is better suited to interpret the many moods of a girl in love than pretty Jean Shepard," it cries. Sanctioned as a "Hank Thompson discovery" and "permanent member of the Grand Ole Opry," the "charming Miss Shepard is known best for the sweet quality of her voice and her meaningful phrasing of every word." Yet neither her voice nor multiple stances in this album's "story of . . . a girl too eager to give her heart" can be dismissed as such. While the promotional text bills the narrative as that of a "longing heart"'s initial betrayal and final recovery, culminating in new love and marriage, the album's trajectory of songs in fact offers no such closure, and Shepard's vocals are nuanced, full of pain. Its centerpiece, "Hello Old Broken Heart," most immediately recalls Billie Holiday's "Good Morning, Heartache" but also clearly mimes the split-self trope favored by male honky-tonk artists.[172] Here, the heart is reified as a separate entity—a recurring nuisance to be shooed away—yet it eventually becomes a signifier for this narrator's identity ("I promised myself that I'll see you no more, / but you have me crying as you did before"). Rather than suggesting a kind of immaturity or fickleness associated with female youth, the album's exploration of the protagonist's "many moods" in the aftermath of a love affair establishes her solidity—her very humanness. Although the collection includes the optimistic "I Married You for Love," that tune occupies the penultimate slot on the album. "It's Hard to Tell the Married from the Free" closes out this narrative, warning both single and married women about modern men's deceptive nature.

Shepard's public image transformed at the close of the decade when she married fellow country artist Hawkshaw Hawkins in 1960 and shortly thereafter became the mother of two young boys. The two performers had met while working on the *Ozark Jubilee* and, openly following in the footsteps of Hank Williams and Billie Jean Eshliman's spectacle of a wedding in 1952, married in front of four thousand fans during a roadshow that was also broadcast on the radio.[173] Though still occasionally resurrecting earlier Western trappings in her costuming and performances—for a brief time, she and Hawkins toured as a Wild West show featuring cowboys, Indians, and horses—she was now eagerly inserted into domestic iconography by fan magazines profiting from this celebrity marriage. But her transmutation from sunny teen to wife and mother took an entirely different cast after Hawkins died in the same 1963 plane crash that killed Patsy Cline. Shepard was suddenly thrown into the media spotlight in the role of young widow, and her later presence as a new kind of solo artist was shrouded in an aura of both tragedy and anxiety. A publicity piece in *Music City News* two years after the crash reassured Shepard's (and Hawkins's) fans, as well as industry insiders, that she may "enjoy a solid career in country music," as the headline trumpets, but not at the expense of her children. A sobering version of Wells, Shepard was now figured primarily as a modern single mother who worked to support her family. The article's five photos documented her continuing normal daily domestic activities, whether "romping" with her sons in the yard, "watching TV after supper," or reading a bedtime story "when moma [*sic*] gets home from a trip." The sole photo alluding to her status as a recording artist actually deprofessionalizes her as well, acknowledging that she "turns to the electric organ for relaxation."[174]

During this mourning period, she released several singles that revived the thematic touchstones of her honky-tonk recordings from the prior decade, such as "When Your House Is Not a Home" (1963). But such attempts could not elude the recontexualization of her career in terms of her private identity. Instead of potentially redefining the gendered notion of "home" in honky-tonk discourse, for instance, this song about a husband's absence was perceived as an elegy to her own personal loss.[175] The sassy "Second Fiddle (To an Old Guitar)" (1964) went on to become a solid hit, and while its title was subsequently borrowed for a film showcasing many of country music's reigning stars in a convoluted yet oh-so-familiar plot pitting lowbrow country against highbrow opera, it can also be understood as gendered "backtalk" within the genre itself: another kind of answer song protesting women's marginal status as honky-tonk artists.[176] Interestingly, however, its B-side was the sentimental and explicitly biographical song "Two Little Boys," which family friend Marty Robbins wrote for Shepard about her two sons in the wake of Hawkins's death. Even Shepard's "comeback" song, "Second Fiddle," was thus shadowed by her representation as traumatized mother, tempering its transgressive possibilities.

V. CONCLUSION: "'RUSTIC'-ALLY YOURS"

Jean Shepard's "rebranding" in the early 1960s offers another, less celebratory perspective on that decade's resurgence of honky-tonk on the West Coast—a rock 'n' roll–influenced style now synonymous with the Bakersfield Sound popularized by Buck Owens and Merle Haggard—and revived in Nashville itself via consummate honky-tonk stylists like George Jones. These later incarnations of honky-tonk's "hard" sensibility typically accentuated its masculinized discourse of authenticity to counter the musically overproduced and culturally sanitized Nashville Sound dominating country by the mid-1960s. Women performers like Shepard continued to be excluded from that discourse despite "down-home" class credentials and equally "sincere" emotive vocals (not to mention the nascent "rights" discourse percolating in the era's public sphere). Like Wells, Shepard remained a stalwart of the Opry (where she still performs), but her recording career took numerous fitful turns as Music Row steered her music away from old-school honky-tonk to take on a more contemporary sound. Ironically, Shepard emerged as an outspoken critic of "pop" country music in the 1970s, defending the same "traditional" style that she considered her own in the 1950s yet by the next decade struggled to retain amid its revival in California and much-maligned demise in Nashville.[177]

Cold War culture's infatuation with domesticity continued to influence the gendering of country authenticity throughout the 1950s and the transitional era of the early-to-mid-1960s in country fan magazines' at times surprising (re)configurations of "home." Popular publications such as the well-known *Country Song Roundup* and now faded *Rustic Rhythm* explicitly negotiated a fraught relationship with country's barn dance legacy, reembodying its intersecting ideologies of gender, race, and rusticity even while documenting and promoting postwar shifts in musical style, costuming, and societal mores. Such tensions were most evident in the magazines' coverage of country performers, which often highlighted the stars' modern middle-class domestic lifestyles yet insistently framed their music as American "folk" culture.

Country Song Roundup, published bimonthly by American Folk Publications, operating out of Derby, Connecticut, billed itself as a "Hillbilly/Folk/Western Picture Magazine" and printed lyrics to songs by past favorite artists such as Jimmie Rodgers, as well as more recent stars like Hank Williams. At the same time, as Peter La Chapelle has demonstrated, features such as "Meet the Mrs." or "Kiddie Korner" accomplished a "restructuring of the family iconography of country music" by converting barn dance radio's fictitious "family" of stage characters into a suburban "male breadwinner and a subordinate female homemaker with offspring in tow." Photo spreads of performers' spacious modern homes indeed serve "as both monuments to class mobility and testaments to the usefulness of a docile, domestic femininity."[178] Women such as Wells might be the occasional focal point of one popular feature, "At Home with the Stars," but they are carefully positioned in that locale as mothers and wives, not as talented professionals.[179]

Rustic Rhythm, launched later in the decade out of a Manhattan office also publishing *Teen Life* and *Mystery Digest,* offered similar coverage of country celebrities' material affluence and domestic spaces (as noted earlier about Shepard's image, it also boasted a monthly "Fashions on Parade" feature focusing on individual female stars). Yet as its name suggests, the magazine declared a mission of preserving country authenticity by focusing on "true folklore . . . representative of an altruistic America's way of life."[180] The magazine's female editor, Frieda Barter Gillis, signed each of her columns "'Rustic'-ally yours," stating in her inaugural issue, "In the vernacular of folk music's theme, may we close on the note that to profit by the best in each of us, we must always be good to one another."[181] Here, rusticity seemingly signifies the antithesis of postwar commercial excess, proposing a return to feminized social relations "profiting" from genuine "altruism" or care, rather than greed. Tennessee governor Frank Clement, however, hints at another interpretation of Gillis's language in his letter of congratulations (reproduced on official state stationery) proclaiming country music "the heartbeat of America": invoking Cold War nationalist fervor, he insists that "country music is a way of life—our way of life . . . and as long as we can give free expression in words and music to this way of life, democracy as we know it, under God, will continue to flourish."[182] This capitalist rendition of authenticity competed with Gillis's throughout the magazine's shelf life, though the latter's emphasis upon women's moral duties within the rural household could also obviously be fashioned to work in concert with the McCarthy era's vision of vigilant mothers preserving American values.[183]

On balance, the text's representation of "folk" music is in fact quite eclectic, encompassing rockabilly and pop currents in country, as well as honky-tonk and more traditional fare. Yet its formal rhetoric avers that it is filling a niche for those fans dedicated to "old-time" or "Western" music and, by extension, "folk" values. Thus, a letter from "Bakersfield Record Co." envisions *Rustic Rhythm* as a "truly beautiful monument to that fine phase of music in America, western and folk music," and thereby relegates its subject to a "phase" of the past, while a letter from "the Hicks Family" of New Hampshire explicitly links "old-time music" to the enduring mountain heritage of their "Great Grandmothers." Industry insiders and fans alike employ notions of authenticity clearly informed by earlier barn dance discourse, but the latter have faith that "the sound of a folk tune" can nostalgically suggest that "things were just as wonderful as today's country music makes you feel they must have been *and still are.*"[184]

This fan missive epitomizes Gillis' perspective, framing traditional rural culture as a feminine enterprise: a most conventional home for folk arts and family customs that can resist modernity's crass individualism and commodity fetishism. Such reclamations of rusticity might initially appear to be at odds with the magazine's routine nod to stars' luxurious lifestyles. But in fact, they accentuate the conventional gender coding of these features, which insist that the true domain of popular female performers like "Sunshine Sue" is the home.[185] This at times strained juxtaposition of the old and the new— musically, culturally, ideologically—clearly resonates within honky-tonk itself. Both the music and the fan magazines share an understanding of the nexus point between the two: an imaginary rural femininity bestowed with the responsibility of transmitting the values and traditions of local "folk" cultures to future generations who have left the familial and regional home place. But while both sets of representations perpetuate the "truth" of this mythology, honky-tonk holds modern women accountable for its failure in practice. The fan texts, particularly *Rustic Rhythm,* persist in peddling counterimagery ingeniously supplied by the stars themselves, their private lives a striking contrast to the looming abject personas of their songs. (Hank Williams, conveniently dead by the time these publications appeared, served as fodder for another mode of mystification.) In their pages, women can in fact still embody the domestic home and the home of country music's folk culture while ensconced in suburban modernity.

Buck Owens' revitalization of honky-tonk in the 1960s, then, becomes significant not simply because his sound marked a new modern phase in the music but because his Bakersfield movement arguably added a different piece to that music's gendered model of authenticity in its reconceptualization of "home." As Rachel Rubin has suggested, early 1960s country music in California offered a voice to those rural Americans comprising an "urban diaspora" as they migrated during the 1930s and '40s from Oklahoma to migrant work in California's San Joaquin Valley (Jean Shepard's family among them). At once "describing a new multiracial and modernized setting" and reflecting a palpable "homesickness," Owens's souped-up version of honky-tonk constituted a "self-conscious" mode of nostalgia equating the notion of "home," Rubin argues, with a regional "birthplace"—a more abstract, "iconic South" articulating "a sense of roots and pride that speaks in dialogue with migrants' position as Okies in California." Yet this shift in iconography takes on further importance when considered within the history of honky-tonk music and culture and from a feminist vantage point, for it conceived of home not as a strictly private, domestic arena nor necessarily as the stand-in for a feminized folk culture but as the *idea* of communal Southern identity (distinctly not "a particular remembered place").[186] It created a public version of home that had the potential to transcend the strict parameters of the honky-tonk bar.

At the same time, as in honky-tonk of the prior generation, this new music retained a similar fascination with performers' own biographies as a kind of authenticity litmus test. As Rubin notes, "Tracing for audiences the trajectories of their own relocations, giving voice to their struggles and successes, the singers' life stories become public property." My exploration of this "public" transmission process in postwar and 1950s honky-tonk, especially in the tortured route it often takes for women performers, demonstrates that such determinations of "sincerity" are as much dictated by gender as by class or race. That Merle Haggard claims "the most emblematic biography in Bakersfield country music"—in effect occupying Hank Williams's esteemed position within postwar honky-tonk—reveals an ongoing masculinist paradigm structuring this music and its accompanying fictions of identity.[187] Bakersfield's construction of home as a distinctly public imaginary thus cannot help but draw on its earlier counterpart's traditionally conceived notions of gender as it locates authenticity in a prototypically masculine life story.

Loretta Lynn's songwriting in this decade reverts to a much more concrete and personal representation of home as a domestic space, yet she takes up where Jean Shepard left off by rewriting honky-tonk's gendered script from a distinctly feminist perspective. While "I'm A Honky-Tonk Girl" (1960) and "This Haunted House" (1964) safely remain in the mold made famous by Wells, songs such as "You Ain't Woman Enough to Take My Man" (1965) and "Don't Come Home A'Drinkin' with Lovin' on Your Mind" (1966) add a new confidence, even aggressiveness, to the women's repertoire.[188] I believe Lynn's most significant contribution, however, lies in her ability to conflate her private life, song persona, and professional image. Unlike prior women in either barn dance or honky-tonk, who had to establish a *discon*nect between these three representational components, Lynn elevated her life story to the same iconic status as men's. Despite the fact that her music itself often subscribed to the new "countrypolitan" sound under producer Owen Bradley's direction, Lynn the performer definitively embodied rusticity. Her Appalachian childhood became the stuff of mythobiography in her signature song "Coal Miner's Daughter," but she refused to serve as an emblem of that folk culture's ostensibly feminine reticence. Instead, Lynn exposed another dimension of white rural existence, where home could be a battleground as well as a nurturing space. Equally important, she carried such toughness into the present and dared to sing about it, inserting women performers into the country authenticity narrative established and dominated by men. In chapter 4, I turn to Lynn's *written* autobiography, *Coal Miner's Daughter*, as a highly influential yet critically neglected intervention into such gendered ideologies—a model for other female country performers complicit in yet compelled to "answer" the industry's representations.

Coal Miner's Daughters: Women (Re)Write Authenticity in the Country Music Autobiography

> Somebody said I should write all these memories down. But it ain't like writing a song. . . . I'm not pretending I know how to write a book—not even a book about me. . . . The first thing I insisted was that it [*Coal Miner's Daughter*] sound like me. When all those city folks try to fix up my talking, all they do is mess me up. . . . This is MY book. Instead of using Webster's Dictionary, we're using Webb's Dictionary—Webb was my maiden name.
>
> —Loretta Lynn, preface to *Coal Miner's Daughter*

> As I passed among the tables in my costume, speaking to people, smiling and saying Howdy, an incredible thing happened to me. I felt myself moving out of Sarah Ophelia Colley into Minnie Pearl. I felt more uninhibited than I ever had felt doing her before, but it was more than that. I BECAME the character.
>
> —*Minnie Pearl, An Autobiography*

In her mid-1970s memoir *Coal Miner's Daughter,* Loretta Lynn divulges with typical candor one supreme and long-standing irony of country stardom. Though she continually reminds the reader that she "ain't never forgot" where she came from, she confesses: "It's a strange deal. I'm supposed to be a country singer, writing songs about marriage and family and the way normal folks live. But mostly I'm living in motel rooms and traveling on my special bus with my private bedroom in the back. I don't even open the shades in my bus anymore."[1] This remark, framing her life story in its opening pages, not only recognizes the structural contradiction that imperils any popular country music performer's claims of biographical authenticity. It registers women artists' particular constraints as they navigate the strained ties among this music's history of gendered iconography, their own class and regional histories, their private or familial commitments as adult women, and their public personas as recording artists and touring performers. Lynn is haunted by the realization that success profoundly unsettles identity: both literally and figuratively, it compels the self to "travel." But as she has always been aware—and as the careers of Lulu Belle, Kitty Wells, and Jean Shepard have demonstrated—the stakes are much higher for women within country's evolving discourses. Alternately embodying home as a composite site of private domesticity and public folk or Southern rural culture from country music's earliest years through the early 1940s, then its antithesis as the "cold" quintessence of postwar and 1950s modernity, and finally its suburban equivalent in the sugary arrangements of the Nashville Sound in the 1960s, female performers indeed experience a "strange deal" as working entertainers whose material survival in the industry depends upon both meeting and flouting its impossible standards.

By the time Lynn had written the song "Coal Miner's Daughter" in 1969 and followed it with her co-authored autobiography of the same name in 1976, honky-tonk's bracing sound and maverick attitude had been usurped by the Texan "Outlaws" movement headed by the hippie triumvirate of Waylon Jennings, Willie Nelson, and Tompall Glaser (another predominantly male club). Moreover, Music Row's controversial shift to popular musical arrangements in the prior decade had produced a veritable identity crisis epitomized by the likes of crossover artists such as Olivia Newton-John and Lynn's own sister Crystal Gayle. "New Traditionalism," which sought to revive the appeal of honky-tonk vocals and themes in a distinctly "softer," more modest equivalent, had yet to emerge but in the early to mid-1980s would launch a style initially dominated by male performers yet swiftly broadened to include female acts such as the Judds and Reba McEntire.

However, as much as the *songs* of the 1970s and 1980s constituted embattled texts in the ongoing war over the meaning of modern country identity, I want to argue that the country music memoir is an equally significant, yet typically overlooked participant in the skirmish. As the prior chapter observed, the very notion of autobiography proves to be one of country's most cherished components in part because it is linked in country music historiography with the authentic sincerity of "hard" country.[2] Forever exemplified by Hank Williams, such performers abandoned earlier performative guises, such as the rube and minstrel "masks," to honor their class and racial roots in (some variant of) the mythic rural past; they unabashedly reveal themselves to their audiences to emphasize that they remain "just like" the men (and occasional woman) in the crowd. As Richard Peterson notes, they appear someone "who could easily have been a farmer, truck driver, housewife, or hairdresser instead."[3] When this concept takes material shape as a cultural form, literary genre, or narrative formula—that is, the published celebrity autobiography—it in fact becomes particularly useful to the hard country construct since it explicitly addresses the relationship between the past and the present, precisely through the intertwining of private and public histories.

Male performers have certainly utilized the formal memoir as an opportunity to validate their authenticity credentials (as well as to maximize profits generated by their music), yet female artists, out of necessity, have put it to more strategic use.[4] Lynn predictably pioneered country music's version of the genre as a whole (preceded only by Johnny Cash's *Man in Black* in 1975), and *Coal Miner's Daughter* both drew upon and reconfigured the masculine mode of autobiographical narrative circulating more informally in country song and discourse. Akin to the honky-tonk answer song, autobiography provided women performers in these troubled decades of country another possible vehicle for establishing their own cachet as authentic country artists, exploiting *and* rewriting the music's gendered cultural scripts. Memoir offered the potential to challenge persistent representations of the Southern past as a domestic, bucolic temporality and the present as a largely feminine preoccupation with modern sensual and material pleasures. At the same time, the woman's autobiographical text can function as an uncanny re-creation of earlier fan magazines like *Rustic Rhythm,* performing a similar sleight-of-hand that permits its constructed image simultaneously to emblemize tradition and modernity.

This chapter explores *Coal Miner's Daughter* alongside the published memoirs of five other legendary women performers who represent three different eras in country music and who, with the exception of Colley Cannon, have become synonymous with their "personal" histories: Tammy Wynette's *Stand By Your Man* (1979), Sarah Colley Cannon's *Minnie Pearl: An Autobiography* (1980), Naomi Judd's *Love Can Build a Bridge* (1993), Dolly Parton's *Dolly: My Life and Other Unfinished Business* (1994), and Reba McEntire's *Reba: My Story* (1994). It is crucial to add, however, that these texts contend with one more set of expectations intrinsic to autobiography as a genre. Though four of the six autobiographers in question are noted songwriters, as well as singers (Lynn, Parton, Wynette, and Judd), they cannot, in the realm of published life story, automatically adopt the persona of "author." As Lynn so boldly relays in the epigraph fronting this chapter, one identity does not necessarily translate into the other—particularly within an industry that until quite recently showcased its own lowbrow tastes. The published memoir, in other words, cannot be conflated with autobiographical song: situated within the arena of *literary* discourse, it establishes unique conditions of authorship and reception.[5] These texts betray considerable anxiety about the act of writing itself, and the collaborative or ghostwriter plays a significant role in both quelling and compounding the star-author's apprehension. When rusticity and modernity are simultaneously in demand, the professional writer can alternately accentuate and deflate the authenticity of his/her subject's "country" life narrative. I thus begin by surveying formal properties of the memoir genre in order to emphasize the inherent performativity of identity in country's autobiographical tradition and to illuminate the unique dilemma of the female country performer as she enters this discursive arena.

I. CONSTRUCTING THE COUNTRY MUSIC MEMOIR

Tracking the "I" of Country

Until recently, autobiography criticism focused almost exclusively on life narratives written by educated white men and clung to notions of a singular, authoritative, and whole "self." But contemporary autobiography theory, spearheaded by feminist scholars, favors postmodern models of subjectivity and has thus entirely transformed our understanding of the "I" dominating autobiographical writing. Supplanting the humanist model of selfhood with a dynamic, fragmented subject positioned by and in multiple discourses, this criticism has often argued that it is women writers in particular who begin with the assumption that "selfhood is mediated."[6] In turn, their life narratives challenge both the content and the form of traditional autobiography, offering fragmented, private "confessions" in place of the typically seamless and linear recounting of major lessons and triumphs experienced as an autonomous individual in life's intellectual and public arenas.[7] The result has been a virtual explosion of critical material on (as well as examples of) women's autobiography that underscores the inherently fictive nature of the autobiographical enterprise.

But all too little analytic work has been produced about the contemporary life stories of, as Philippe Lejeune calls them, "those who do not write":

"common people" who cannot imagine adopting the mantle of "writer"—who often lack the very skills to do so—and need another's assistance to tell their narrative. Lejeune's study of the collaborator/editor/translator/ghostwriter's role in such texts most clearly resembles feminist examinations of the transnational power dynamics underwriting transnational women's life stories published in the West.[8] In both instances, the written autobiographical form can appear alien or forbidding and requires another's participation or intervention. But from Lejeune's perspective, the ghostwritten text proves the key to understanding autobiography as a whole because it so dramatically exposes the artifice of all autobiographical writing. The very practice of ghostwriting suggests that no autobiography can parade itself very long as a transparent reflection of the author's life:

> It is not the inauthenticity of these books that people condemn, but the fact that they let the cat out of the bag. They cast suspicion, no doubt legitimately so, on the rest of the literature. On a certain number of points, autobiography by people who do not write throws light on autobiography written by those who do: the imitation reveals the secrets of fabrication and functioning of the "natural" product.[9]

An admitted "pastiche" produced by multiple authors, ghostwritten autobiography operates as a kind of "floating writing" that "negotiates between the model's [subject's] supply and the public's demand," as well as "narrative forms currently on the market." As Lejeune goes on to note, in many ways "the real author is the public itself" (through its "desire and obliging credulity").[10]

However, the "public" harbors different expectations for different types of lives. Celebrities almost by definition seem the antithesis of the "common man," though some, as Richard Dyer has demonstrated, have achieved a (twisted) version of the latter.[11] Lejeune himself similarly distinguishes between French "hero" and "antihero" autobiography, emphasizing the fictive nature of that distinction:

> A LIFE (that is, a written and published story of a life) is always the product of a transaction between different postures, and the determination of the "author," in the case of an acknowledged collaboration, depends above all on the type of effect that the book has to produce. It is not a metaphysical question to be solved in the absolute; it is an ideological problem, linked to reading contracts, to the possible identification with "persons," and to relations of class.[12]

My contention is that country music autobiography in many ways illustrates the blurred boundaries between two such "hero" and "antihero" modes. On the one hand, the six texts I am examining here clearly fall into the former category, recounting the unusual and model lives of those who have "made it." They are celebrities who have become, as Lejeune puts it, "owners of their life . . . and make of it the place for passing on social values." Accordingly, in such cases the very presence of a ghostwriter must be erased or effaced. "Heroes" must appear as if they possess the sophistication, the cultural capital, to write their own story.[13] Yet country authenticity presumes humble origins, anti-intellectualism, and literary naivete. Indeed, Lynn, Parton, and Wynette, who hail respectively from Kentucky coal-mining, Tennessee sharecropping, and Mississippi farming families, highlight their grindingly poor, modestly educated backgrounds in their autobiographies—and the former two have virtually fashioned their musical careers out of such pasts. (The other three have college educations and approach the problem of authorship somewhat differently, though only Cannon claims membership in the cultured middle class—more on this later.) These women's narratives, then, also function as "common" or "antihero" autobiography whose value derives chiefly from the subject's very membership in a "culture defined by the exclusion of writing" and hence virtually *demands* a collaborator or ghostwriter to ensure the celebrity author's rustic authenticity.[14] Their autobiographies maintain a notable tension between, and complicate further, these two subject positions: that is, the "common" voice of the Southern girl who still remembers picking cotton and the worldly perspective of the glamorous woman whose very name has become a material end unto itself.

Aaron Fox's approach to the de- and renaturalization of country music similarly focuses on the division between song*writing* and song*speaking* (i.e., singing/performing). As initially outlined in chapter 3, Fox argues that the country songwriter must take "ordinary" or "plain" language ("drawn largely from working-class social contexts") and rework it into discourse recognized as "poetic" yet still serving as a signifier or marker of "everyday" culture.[15] This "denaturalized" effect is primarily produced by all manner of verbal play, including country music's love of puns and clichés. The country singer, however, recovers the "natural" quality of the text through his/her "ordinary" vocal performance. (In the context of honky-tonk, for instance, Ernest Tubb would serve as an exemplar of this dynamic.) According to Fox, the voice itself embodies the entire de- and renaturalization process: "The nasal, rough, timbrally distinct and/or accented voices of most great country singers are at once unique and ordinary, an effect which spins a story about both the uniqueness (denaturalisation) and the ordinariness (renaturalisation) of the figure of the singer."[16]

Clearly, the voice of the published literary text must accomplish a similar "fit" between exclusivity and commonness—between high and low. And just as the songwriter in country music has traditionally been effaced by the celebrity singer performing his or her work, the professional collaborative or ghostwriter is often hidden behind the star-author ostensibly telling her own story. But in written discourse, that writer continues to control the performed product; it is he or she who de- and renaturalizes the country autobiographical narrative by both fabricating an educated, "authorial" star voice and miming her "ordinary," "country" one. (In the fascinating case of Sarah Cannon, however, the terms are reversed—and in exaggerated fashion—by Colley herself when she disrupts her own story to "speak" as Minnie Pearl.) These jarring voices in the text attempt to meet the demands of two contrary or seemingly incompatible cultural forms.

Live performance in itself would seem to encompass a similar dynamic, for as Fox notes,

> After denaturalising themselves through a marked form of fancy dress, highly stylised stage movements, and other familiar trappings of the distanced, aesthetic experience of staged musical performance [here, literary discourse], country musicians partially renaturalise the marked distinction between the stage and the dance floor by breaking the performative "frame" which separates them from their fans. Songs are frequently introduced with stories which relate them to the singer's biography, which is presented as an exaggerated version of a biography common to the singer and their audience. Songs are thus explicitly claimed to be about "the real lives of real people."[17]

Here, it is audience identification with the singer's own life story that finally appears to shatter that "performative 'frame,'" overcoming or negating its distancing effects. But this self-conscious, stylized notion of performance, helpful as it is in suggestively revealing the performativity inherent in all daily experience, is ironically denied permission to represent itself as such within autobiography by the laws governing the genre. As we will see, "breaking the frame" in published country music autobiography is a much more furtive process, involving both an insistence upon and a denial of that frame's very existence.

II. MAPPING THE FEMALE COUNTRY
AUTOBIOGRAPHICAL TEXT

My analysis begins with a brief schematic look at how the six texts in question attempt to negotiate between the form of discourse to which the star-authors are "naturally" linked—that is, song or comic skit—and the literary form of memoir. Interestingly, half of the collaborative writers treat the text *as* a kind of compendium of songs, with titles of the performer's past and present hits serving as the book title and/or chapter headings. Wynette's entire narrative is encompassed by the title of her most famous and controversial song, "Stand By Your Man." Lynn's is similarly fronted by her signature song, "Coal Miner's Daughter," yet also includes snatches of lyrics as epigraphs to individual chapters. Judd most explicitly conflates memoir and song, as the title (*Love Can Build a Bridge*) and chapter headings ("Mama, He's Crazy," "Guardian Angels") comprise a Judds' greatest hits list. Additionally, these three autobiographies dramatically intertwine the stars' professional and personal histories at yet another level by inserting songs overtly autobiographical ("Coal Miner's Daughter," "Guardian Angels") and non ("Stand By Your Man") into key moments of the authors' "real"-life narratives. Most often, this practice further authenticates their stories, though on occasion it calls attention to the ironic disparity between the "facts" of their lives and the fiction of their songs and on the whole reminds the reader of their celebrity status.[18]

The other two singers' autobiographies settle for main titles that simply declare their first names—Reba, Dolly—and subtitles that suggest a confession of truth: "My Story," "My Life and Other Unfinished Business." (Interestingly, Cannon's text, which doesn't belong in this category for obvious reasons, is the only one to use the term *autobiography*.) Their deviation from the pattern might be explained by their status at the time as "crossover" artists. Though both began their careers as "New Traditionalists," joining Randy Travis and Alan Jackson in rescuing country from its more synthetic pop sound, they each attained their greatest commercial success with increasing excursions into mainstream territory. That status does not exempt their autobiographies from the pressures of country metanarratives; if anything, it intensifies certain expectations. But it does suggest that at the time of writing they were perhaps marketing their life stories to a larger, more diverse audience. McEntire's text, in fact, put a new spin on said tradition: her book appeared on store shelves simultaneously with her latest and least "country" recording. Boldly tied in a calculated commercial maneuver, promotional materials for both beckoned the reader/listener to "read" Reba's "mind."[19]

But while preserving numerous connections to songwriting and singing, these written texts also clearly code as another mode of discourse: first, they all contain photos of the star, which authenticate identity in ways that both complement and depart from those appearing on CD covers and in liner notes; and second, they all employ a professional writer. These two distinctive formal aspects have a complex relationship to one another.

The Photo Album

All six autobiographies incorporate a chronological series of photographs of the performer and her various family members, from past and present, to accomplish two (seemingly conflicting) goals: to record her transformation from "ordinary" girl into star (the "hero" mode) and to insist upon her enduring country authenticity (the "antihero" mode). In asking the reader to treat these images as what Paul Jay has termed "visual memory" in the autobiographical text,[20] the photo insert attempts to close the gap between the "real" and the "performing" selves—to achieve a kind of damage control as new identities (or fragments thereof) seem to proliferate in the narrative. These star-authors most immediately seek what Roland Barthes, in his study of photography, claims that we all seek in self-portraiture: neat correspondence between (changing) visual image and "core" self. Barthes confesses:

> What I want . . . is that my (mobile) image, buffeted among a thousand shifting photographs, altering with situation and age, should always coincide with my (profound) "self"; but it is the contrary that must be said: "myself" never coincides with my image; for it is the image which is heavy, motionless, stubborn . . . and "myself" which is light, divided, dispersed.[21]

Such distinctions between the "outer" and "inner" can no more suffice or succeed, of course, than simplistic correlations between the past and present. The scrapbooks offered in these autobiographies, meant to illustrate both, are as much themselves a construction as the individual photos are.

But as seen earlier in the industry's representation of country performers on album covers and in fan magazines from the postwar period through the 1950s, even this typical maneuver had different implications for female honky-tonk performers like Wells and Shepard, caught in country's double bind. Rather than collapsing the distinction between private self and performative persona to ensure authenticity, their publicized images needed to accentuate a definitive break between their biographical and public identities—more precisely, they needed to demonstrate that *off*-stage, they still coded as traditional domestic women (preferably mothers), rather than modern honky-tonk denizens. Within this historical context, opting instead to close that gap between one's "common" past and "exceptional" present accrues certain risks for these star-authors, even those of later generations. Some clearly approach this route to authenticity as an act of reclamation—taking the same privilege as male performers—while others attempt to hedge their bets with strategies reminiscent of that earlier era.

The texts' use of photo captions helps to expose the naturalizing intent of such visuals. In almost every instance, captions are written in the first person to amplify the sense that the star is in full control of her image, as well as to verify that such images are trustworthy or "real," taken from the star's very own collection. Lynn's book specializes in this approach. Explicitly titled "My Photo Album," the insert offers intimate, down-home commentary on the pictures, such as the following caption, accompanying one early shot of young marrieds Loretta and Doolittle: "That cute little guy I'm cuddling up with is my husband, folks. I sure look different myself, don't I? Well, I was around twenty-one years old and was taking care of four kids and didn't have much time or money for myself. Heck, I had just about figured out what was causing all them kids." The other texts offer similarly comic observations. Captions may make note of visual discrepancies between the past and present, often joking about outdated costumes, hairstyles, and the like. But again, they almost always function to give the illusion of authorial control and static identity—through the years, essentially the same "girl" lies underneath the teen dungarees, cowgirl fringe, and sequined gown. The captions thereby attempt to construct a seamless line connecting private histories and contemporary public lives.

At the same time, certain recurring key images destabilize that identity by *de*naturalizing it, documenting the star-author's progress in sharply clashing visions of rural poverty and glamorous wealth. Almost every memoir, for example, specifically includes comparison/contrast photos of houses, juxtaposing the original dilapidated family homestead with the contemporary mansion. Here, the reader detects the strain in the caption "voice" more clearly. While still attempting to make light of her shift in fortune—typically offset by another photo of the star herself cooking "country" food in that huge state-of-the-art kitchen—there is a lingering sense of pride *in* her metamorphosis. She wants us to recognize this "other" identity as much as she alternatively downplays its existence.

Captions written in the third person, however, truly expose the artifice at work. Judd's photo inserts curiously highlight her determined transformation from Diana Ellen Judd Ciminella into beloved celebrity "Naomi." Informal snapshots of the star as young hippie mountain mother and nurse accompany grainy photos of early Judds performances, as well as professional publicity shots, to round out the panorama of images. Yet the third-person point of view provided by the captions works against any sense of neutral "documentation." The reader cannot help but interpret each successive image as a calculated pose or performance. (Indeed, one childhood photo caption calls attention to such a practice by noting that Naomi is "posing—as usual."[22]) And as is true time and again, Cannon's autobiography finally serves as the best example of such performativity, throwing into relief both of these photo-caption strategies. Its own shifts between first and third person underscore its utterly self-conscious distinction between Sarah Colley Cannon, the "real" woman, and Minnie Pearl, her stage persona. Photos of the former, off-stage, are claimed as "I," while those of the latter are entirely distanced: "The publicity photo of Minnie Pearl, her first, was taken in November 1941"; "Minnie as a troop entertainer in World War II." Yet as I will demonstrate later in this chapter, Cannon has difficulty maintaining this distinction in the text itself. Reared within an entirely different class strata, she, too, seeks an authentication that these photo captions strangely belie.[23]

Authorial Voice

Photo captions, then, often provide one means of controlling or modulating the star-authors' identities by tying together disparate images with an ostensibly consistent and "natural" voice. Their narrative voices as a whole, however, must accomplish something else entirely. These autobiographies persist in subordinating the collaborative or ghostwriter's presence, striving to maintain the spontaneity and vernacular speech that their fan-readers expect. Yet they also reveal awareness of a conflicting set of expectations that requires the collaborative writer to perform major work on the text to meet the demands of elite discourse. One such prominent writer of choice for country stars, Tom Carter, has confirmed that many ask him to "make me sound more intelligent than I am," admitting, "I had one artist who scarcely even wanted to read the manuscript. He told me, 'Just make me sound smart.'"[24]

Coal Miner's Daughter illustrates the complexities of this dynamic. Intensely aware of her ungrammatical dialect and fourth-grade education, Lynn is, as hinted earlier, unusually candid in the preface about her need to hire writer George Vecsey to help her "talk" through her memories for the task of publishing an autobiography. In "About Me and This Book," she even explains her criteria for his selection:

> The way I did it was this: the writers have always been really nice to me, and I've always enjoyed sitting and talking to 'em. But we finally got together with this one writer who used to live in Kentucky, name of George. He knows my part of the country real well; he's visited the coal mines and he's been up to the hollers, so he speaks my language. Now for the past year he's been traveling with me and Doolittle.[25]

She then assures the reader of the text's truth, in both content and style: "You can bet your last scrip penny I checked out every word before they sent it to the book company. And if I didn't think it was true, out it went. The first thing I insisted was that it sound like me." Concluding with her tongue-in-cheek reference to "Webb's Dictionary," Lynn invites her fans to apply the following test of authenticity: "So when you're reading this book, just try to *picture me up on stage,* singing my songs and clowning around, and *try to hear me saying* 'Butcher Holler.' Then *you'll know it's me.*" She conflates image, voice, and identity here, while simultaneously admitting that the voice is a fabrication carefully crafted by Vecsey. Even more interestingly, he is likened to a kind of analyst who elicits and faithfully records material from Lynn's unconscious. The preface's opening vignette recounts her tendency to talk (and fight!) in her sleep, then addresses the reader: "What does it mean when you carry on in your sleep like that? Somebody said it means you've got something on your mind. I said, 'I KNOW that.' I ain't got much education, but I got some sense. To me, this talking is almost like I've got things inside me that never came out before." Such "things," equated with the memories that comprise her life story, enter her official autobiographical text through Vecsey, who proceeds to capture their "hillbilly" flavor throughout the narrative yet clearly filters them through a slightly more standard mode of speech and narrative structure.[26]

Vecsey's quite visible role in the memoir's production thus both challenges and underscores its veracity, ironically preserving Lynn's authentic identity. And the "ruse" works: *Journal of Country Music* critic Bob Allen, writing on the phenomenon of country music memoirs, looks back rather nostalgically on *Coal Miner's Daughter,* praising its "almost guileless forth-

rightness or utter lack of premeditation" and ranking it with classic "folk literature," even as he recognizes that the book is "written with—well, let's be
frank here—written by *New York Times* veteran George Vecsey."[27] Their
joint venture seems to have set the standard by which the succeeding texts
have been measured but also, it would seem, a standard against which those
same texts react, for the very laws of authenticity governing Lynn's voice apparently proved a bit too excessive or stringent. For the other collaborative
writers generally have far less acknowledged roles, even as they have equally
shaped narrative structure and produced narrative voice. Their concealment
or erasure suggests a heightened awareness of the "hero" strain in autobiography, matched by modern country music's increasing distaste for the rube
stereotype.

It may be linked as well to the artists' education levels. Those star-authors
with high school diplomas, Wynette and Parton, make only vague references
to their "assistants." *Stand By Your Man* simply lists the author on the title
page as "Tammy Wynette, with Joan Dew." *Dolly* thanks Buddy Sheffield for
"the use of your computers, the one on your lap and the one on your shoul-
ders."[28] Those with college educations take still a different approach, curiously relegating their writers to the status of "researcher" and/or transcriber.
McEntire's acknowledgments page goes so far as to designate Tom Carter as
"co-author" yet lists his tasks as "interviewing people, gathering all the facts,
listening to all the endless stories, and typing it all up."[29] Judd begins her acknowledgments with a Lynn-like pronouncement of ignorance but quickly
inverts the roles of writer and celebrity-author:

> I've never even read a book on how to write a book. One night when I was
> praying about whether I could do this or not I got a message: The Judds' lives
> had a voice of their own—just sit perfectly still, be silent, and listen to it.
> That's what I've done for the last two years secluded at my farm, Peaceful
> Valley. I got so far into it I walked through a hole in time and really got out in
> the cosmic lost and found. Larry, Wynonna, and Ashley claimed me and
> pulled me back in. . . . Gee thanks, Bud Schaetzle, for assistance with some
> of the preliminary research, "grunt work" as you put it, to help me get orga-
> nized so I could concentrate on writing this book.[30]

Only Cannon—laying claim to the most elite educational background of the
six (Nashville's exclusive Ward-Belmont College)—gives her collaborative
writer explicit credit, thanking "her friend" Joan Dew as "the most patient of
all writers" and for the "fun!" they shared.[31] She has perhaps the least to lose
in such disclosure, since her own highbrow status is secure; yet in her Min-

nie Pearl persona, she is also, like Lynn, appealing to an earlier version of country authenticity that only becomes further enhanced by Dew's presence.

These various methods of handling the ghostwriter dilemma can thus ultimately be explained not simply by education or class but by the particular definition of authenticity that each performer seeks to achieve in her published life story. Lynn's book perhaps creates an image too uncomfortably hayseed for the succeeding generations of women in country music. It offers an increasingly obsolete, though still nostalgic mode of rusticity in official country music discourse. The subsequent autobiographies adopt a modified version of "Webb's Dictionary," liberally sprinkling each chapter with rural Southern phrases or witticisms (Judd is especially fond of this device) to capture as "natural" a voice as possible. But they also attempt to preserve the illusion that they themselves "wrote" these narratives, taking equal credit for the literary as well as countrified panache. Judd and Parton, for instance, make special note of their lifelong love of books and intellectual aspirations, even as they play up their lasting ties to their most colorful hillbilly relatives. At times, then, these texts seem to want it both ways, shifting among several identities. Their star-authors attempt to occupy both discursive positions, caught in another double bind. In the context of country, they need their collaborative writers, but in the context of (literate) dominant culture, they must possess the skills to tell their success "stories."

(Masculine) Loss and (Feminine) Desire

The professional writer's presence may finally prove to be a source of anxiety (and mystification) precisely because it exposes that paradox—reveals, in fact, the complexity, if not impossibility, of being at once "ordinary" and "unique." And as suggested in this chapter's opening lines, the dilemma has an expressly gendered dimension. Loretta Lynn's seeming cliché about the contradictions of country stardom has its roots in what is finally a highly intricate dialectic attempting to reconcile, within the confines of a single genre, low and high culture, country music's past and present, authenticity and commercialism. As such, it also invokes the music's honky-tonk legacy of associating folk tradition with a once-prized domesticity now lost to the profane attractions of modern urban culture. As depicted earlier in the songs of Ernest Tubb and Hank Williams, Southern women lured by the "bright lights" of postwar optimism and prosperity betrayed their cultural contract to embody and preserve their communal rustic heritage, leaving men to rail against its absence. Echoing Aaron Fox's twin country "metanarratives" of

"Loss and Desire," men ostensibly value "the old and the worn out" and are "unable to forget the past" ("Loss"), while women seek individualistic "fulfilment through the consumption of objects" ("Desire").[32]

In theme and form, these autobiographies can be said to enact such Loss, performing a "reconstruction of the past through an 'archaeology' of highly objectified memories."[33] Through their very structure—including song motifs, photo inserts, and coauthorship, as well as organization of the story itself—they attempt to recover, to revalue, the performers' pasts, displaying not only their valuable country roots but also their feminine allegiance to tradition. Yet that structure also necessarily precludes any fully successful recovery mission. The texts' celebrity-authors must equally come to terms with the elusiveness or irretrievability of their earlier "ordinary" selves—and as such their seeming loss of feminized authenticity—as they succumb to the material luxuries and pressures of celebrity existence. In telling their full life story, they are forced to reckon with and subsequently lament the competing narrative of "Desire" that marks their stardom. Though few, if any, romanticize their early poverty, they suggest that they've traded in one set of values for another. Modernity's "'false' language of the market," representing commercial success and a kind of jaded immorality, pales beside tradition's "'authentic' language of emotion,"[34] which comes to signify the past, private relations, and the "dream" of artistry uncontaminated or compromised by the music industry.

Fox's "Loss/Desire" model is intended to encompass a more Marxist ethic in the music, challenging capitalist cultural norms. As Fox explains, Loss, the inverse of Desire, resists reification: "Whereas the metanarrative of Desire makes feelings and people into 'things,' the metanarrative of Loss turns 'things' into speaking, feeling presences."[35] A feminist reading of this dialectic, however, demonstrates that women in country discourse can also be reified *as* the past and dismissed as its vilified opposite when they resist such mystification—especially the case when this model's examples derive almost exclusively from honky-tonk culture (Hank Williams, Webb Pierce, George Jones).[36] The autobiographies under investigation here suggest that ideologies of tradition and modernity are not always so self-consciously deployed. They depend upon and reinscribe, as much as they negate, myriad dominant narratives of authenticity.

Certainly in the decades in which Cannon, Lynn, Parton, and Wynette were building their careers, country discourse equated women's *gender* authenticity with nurturing domesticity, especially motherhood—the single mode of conventional femininity most available to poor Southern white women. Earlier chapters demonstrate that women country artists, unlike male performers, who could pose as active sexual and romantic agents in their public as well as private lives, were strongly discouraged from adopting any remotely suggestive stage persona; until the 1950s, they could not perform solo on the road or anywhere on stage with a man, except in the guise of an advertised family act, for fear of seeming impropriety.[37] During the 1960s, a few women dramatically broke the mold. Miniskirted Jeannie C. Riley, for example, profited from the changing times with her best-selling single about an unconventional mother, "Harper Valley PTA," but her own career proved short-lived. And as I will later discuss more extensively, Parton successfully challenged the rules for female performers, but hers is an exceptional case with its own contradictions. Less exaggerated variants of sexualized artists have now become the norm, of course, transmuted into a tamer, professional kind of glamour: Wynette certainly visually coded as a star in that tradition; McEntire, who has traversed both categories in her career, moving from "New Traditionalist" rancher to reigning Vegas-style diva to recent Broadway star, can shift between the two in her performances through costuming alone. But the memoirs attest that this group of artists is still quite mindful of the industry's lingering attachment to the sentimental mother role.[38]

A breakthrough artist like Loretta Lynn would seem to introduce another model—woman as nonsexualized *working* body—but that potential doesn't quite materialize in her songs or performance style. She speaks for women connected to male working bodies in the public sphere—husbands, fathers, sons—and who certainly labor in the home themselves as wives and mothers. Yet her most famous songs emphasize the often fractious relations between men and women in that space, rather than the gendered chores themselves. Additionally, while Lynn's version of feminism has transformed country music lyrics for women, it has had surprisingly minimal effect on their stage presence: with her puffed-sleeve, floor-length dresses, she herself visually reprises past "mother" or "sweetheart" stage roles. It would seem, then, that for women in country music seeking authenticity, the only truly acceptable avenue—to represent tradition within a domestic context and as such to encourage female fan identification—was, and in some ways remains, motherhood.

Yet it is precisely in this sense that these autobiographies' success stories rank as distinctly gendered "failures" of country authenticity. As working female celebrities, these figures forfeit not only their traditional pasts but also their present maternal identities. By "choosing" the tour bus over (or as the single means of maintaining) the glamorous mansion, they lose their claim to "home" altogether. As suggested earlier, these texts struggle to adopt a narrative form and voice that at once verify and preclude an ordinary identity for their star-authors. And as women, much of that identity finally entails a private domestic life preempted and compromised, if not erased entirely, by their unique status as successful performers. The later discussion will sift through the "archeology of memories" embodied by these texts in order to chart how they navigate the overlapping minefields of tradition and modernity. To accommodate these competing demands, my six texts seem to have adopted two different strategies. Lynn, Judd, Wynette, and McEntire foreground their maternal identities throughout their autobiographies, frequently reducing themselves *to* mothering bodies. Parton and Cannon "compensate" for their lack of maternity by capitalizing on other modes of class visibility available to women in country music. In these ways, they attempt to preserve the qualities of both their country and their literary personas.

III. MATERNITY AND MODERNITY

Lost and Found Motherhood

As my capsule discussions of the six autobiographies suggest, five can call upon some version of an authentic country past. Lynn's and Parton's Appalachian childhoods are perhaps the most famous, but the others also possess personal histories of considerable, if not equal, cachet: Wynette picked cotton and trained as a beautician before heading to Nashville; Judd looks back to her Kentucky ancestors for musical inspiration, weaving their rustic personalities (and rather grim photographs) into her own tale; and McEntire can lay claim to her father's ranching business, as well as her own experience as a young ranch hand and rodeo rider.

It's telling, then, that the four star-authors who can also lay claim to motherhood choose to launch their memoirs by highlighting the centrality of their children's births, rather than their own. *Love Can Build a Bridge* explicitly begins with the birth of daughter Wynonna (initially named Christina), and while the scene quickly invokes a "duet" metaphor that forever blurs Judd's roles as mother and professional singing partner, it primarily emphasizes the unique harmony of their parent-child bond:

When the nurse brought my baby in, I looked into her face and saw myself—her eyes, her skin, her expressions, her spirit. . . . A broad and mischievous grin lit up her face, a sign that told me in no uncertain terms that this was a child to be reckoned with, a child who would be worthy of great things. . . . I was terrified, elated, proud, and complete. . . . Wynonna and I were instantly one, a partnership, a team—just the two of us against a frightening and unknown world. On that spring day in 1964, we began our wonderful duet, a blend of heart, mind, and soul that continues to this day.[39]

Stand By Your Man opens with another version of the birth scene: the emergency room of a Birmingham, Alabama, children's hospital, where Wynette's premature infant daughter is fighting a harrowing bout of spinal meningitis. Both opening episodes seem calculated to capture the stars' fierce determination to be good mothers. Judd's experience is obviously much more celebratory, but both scenes register the tremendous fear, as well as strength, of two young women (one eighteen, the other twenty-three) facing the responsibilities of single parenthood. Wynette's story is especially powerful, detailing the gruesome condition of her daughter's body, along with her own physical and emotional exhaustion as she remained quarantined in the hospital room.

Significantly, both vignettes take place before either woman has achieved stardom. It is as if we must "meet" them not as children themselves nor as celebrities, but in their definitive moment as everyday women (Judd uses the word "humble") named Diana and Wynette.[40] These unorthodox initial episodes serve as preeminently authenticating material for their life stories yet encompass from the beginning both Loss and Desire. They document Wynette's and Judd's "ordinary" pasts via their positions as materially poor but emotionally rich caregivers, while also foreshadowing the changes that success will bring. Wynette confides:

I had never felt so alone in my life. My husband had left me. . . . I was making only $45 per week at the beauty shop, trying to support myself and my children on that, and living in a $23-a-month government housing project apartment with bare concrete floors and a few scarred pieces of old furniture. . . . I was twenty-three years old and I had reached the lowest point of my life. If someone had told me at that moment that the next ten years would bring fame and wealth, I would have said they were completely crazy. All I kept thinking was . . . if Tina dies I know I can't take it, but I don't know how I'll take care of her if she lives.[41]

Here, she yokes her past, present, and future together so that her success ostensibly saves both her child and herself. But the passage finally functions as a lasting character reference for Wynette, who proves she has the "right stuff" both to sustain her family and to become a country legend. Much later in the autobiography, however, she finds herself musing on the price of superstardom, which has given her children unimaginable material rewards but deprived them of mothering. She recounts the process of writing one of her most dramatic concert songs, "Dear Daughters," whose lyrics include the stanza, "You've had to grow up much too quick, and you've done it on your / own / You did it without Mama / 'Cause Mama wasn't home."[42]

Judd initially prefers to cast this tension between the past and present as "a modern fairy tale,"[43] importing yet another narrative form into her text, but the rags-to-riches cliché wears thin as the Judds' growing fame continually separates Naomi from her other daughter, Ashley. Though this second child makes sporadic appearances in the narrative and joins mother and sister on the book jacket, the text makes clear from the very beginning that Judd's life story reads strictly as a Naomi/Wynonna duo. The reader becomes increasingly disturbed by Ashley's neglect even as Judd strives to justify the situation as the fulfillment of "their" dream. As commoner Diana Ciminella transforms into self-crowned "Queen of Everything" Naomi Judd, her authenticity grows more dependent upon her maternal identity, yet that identity becomes at once accentuated and compromised by her public persona.

Reba: My Story and *Coal Miner's Daughter* function as interesting frame texts for these two examples, laying bare their strategies. Of the four, McEntire's text begins the most traditionally by sketching out her family history. But the book is first effusively dedicated to her young son, Shelby: "For every second I have watched, laughed, cried, and marveled at every little 'sing' you do. You have given me the greatest five years of my life. Hopefully, these words will keep you familiar with your family, past and present, and also give you an idea of what it is your Mama does and has been doing for the past thirty-nine years." The preface continues this line of thought by explaining, "Part of the reason I'm writing this book is that I want Shelby to understand what the traditional McEntire cowboy life was like."[44] These references lay the groundwork for the memoir's later celebratory chapter on childbirth and countless photos of mother and son, including one while pregnant, in order to capitalize on McEntire's predominant image during the late 1980s and early '90s in celebrity and women's magazines, and often in her stage show, as a doting mom.

All work together to offset the counterportrait that evolved in her meta-morphosis from rather plain and wholesome cowgirl to sexy, sequined glam queen, perhaps best represented by what McEntire refers to as that "infa-mous low cut red dress" that caused such a stir at the 1993 Country Music Association award show. The memoir is in fact quite mindful of this latter im-age and immediately attempts to neutralize any damaging effects in its open-ing lines by mentioning, and then dispelling, a recent threatening tabloid headline: "REBA STOLE OUR HUSBANDS." McEntire's mission to "set the record straight about my marriages and other matters" is accomplished in part by the text's calculated trade-off of her performative vamp role for her "natural" maternal one.[45] Aware that her stage persona has violated a seem-ingly outmoded but still powerful gender code governing country music's representation of the female body, she seeks to minimize the threat of her sexuality by meeting (and hence reproducing) that code's standards in her own life story.

Reba's polarization of the maternal and the sexual is only more open in its intent than Wynette's and Judd's texts. The latter two also clearly flirt with the fine line McEntire negotiates in her stage presence. Their respective life histories—Tammy's five marriages and celebrity affairs, Naomi's infamous wild streak—provide more than enough material to provoke suspicion about their claims to "feminine" country tradition. (Indeed, one male commentator on country autobiography seems positively obsessed with Wynette's sexual status, remarking, "Most [!] of Tammy's story relates events of her sex life, with an astonishing number of men for a good ole Mississippi girl."[46]) To en-sure a properly gendered version of class authenticity, they thus equally need to promote their own maternal sensibilities—to find a permissible means of becoming Judd's "bridge" joining together the past and present/Loss and Desire/tradition and modernity.

Lynn's autobiography, however, succeeds in presenting a uniquely de-mystified construction of motherhood. Her hillbilly identity is as much tied to her experience as a fourteen-year-old mother as to her rustic relatives. Her text has the most to gain, one could say, from equating her womanhood with motherhood. The preface is perhaps the most obvious in this regard, serving as a powerful location for establishing the star-author's authentic abjection:

People know the basic facts about me, how I was married when I wasn't quite fourteen and had four babies by the time I was eighteen. . . . I was just a kid— didn't know nothing—picking strawberries in the fields with my babies on a blanket, under an umbrella. I'd change a few diapers, my fingers all rough and dirty, give 'em a few bottles, and go back to picking. So when I sing those country songs about women struggling to keep things going, you could say I've been there. It's like that hit record I had in 1975, "The Pill," about this woman who's taking birth-control pills so she won't have no more babies. Well, they didn't have none of them pills when I was younger, or I'd have been swallowing 'em like popcorn. See, the men who run some of the radio stations, they banned the record because they didn't like what I was saying. But the women knew. Like I say, I know what it's like to be pregnant and nervous and poor.[47]

But as this passage begins to suggest, unlike the song's somewhat romanticized treatment of such conditions, *Coal Miner's Daughter* offers an unflinching and essentially unapologetic look at reluctant—as well as absent—mothering. Compared to the other memoirs, there's remarkably little sentiment surrounding her children in the narrative as a whole, few dramatic scenes or rustic tableaux. (Though like Wynette, Lynn occasionally regrets missing out on her later children's everyday lives.) Her representation as an "ordinary" Appalachian woman daringly emphasizes her *lack* of traditional maternal "desire." Moreover, the sole woman in the text who comes closest to exemplifying the role, Lynn's mother, actually threatens to overturn the entire myth by couching her "healing" ways not in feminine white folk culture but in her Cherokee heritage (and at the time of writing, "Mommy" was still dubbed "The Squaw" for her "special powers").[48]

Lynn's struggle to survive as a mother while still a child herself prompts tremendous sympathy from the reader—so much so that her professional life codes as much as escape and release as family betrayal or personal sacrifice. Recounting her early relationship with her husband, Lynn resents that she "went directly from Daddy to Doolittle" with no time on her own and recognizes, "I still don't have complete control over myself."[49] In the preface, she similarly admits that "being on stage is . . . the only time when I really feel grown-up and in control of things." Interestingly, then, Lynn is most conventionally "maternal" in those scenes representing her relations with her male back-up band, "The Coal Miners": they call her "Mom," she calls them "my boys"; they offer her "protection," she offers them "fussin'" and food. She thus finds yet another means of intertwining the private and public, past and present, modes of her identity. Her views on sexuality equally depart from the standard script. Announcing "I'm not the backward little country girl I was then," Lynn writes openly about her disappointment in marital sex, charging, "There's plenty of songs about how women should stand by their men and give them plenty of loving when they walk through the door, and that's fine. But what about the man's responsibility? A man is supposed to give his wife a good time, too. Let him be tender with her once in a while, too."[50] Her story comes the closest to presenting the adult female body in all of its Southern "reality," encouraging a very new ground of identification with her female audience.

Lost and Found Presence

Perhaps no two female country performers present a more startling visual contrast than the remaining star-authors, Cannon and Parton: the wallflower and the sex bomb, the gawky country mouse and the outrageous queen of glitz. Although they represent opposite poles of the spectrum, each enacts an explicit performance of country femininity. The absence and excess of embodiment, they appropriate two alternate models circulating within country music discourse, the plain and ostensibly "innocent" country girl and the seductive "angel." But since both appear such obvious caricatures, Cannon and Parton face, in different ways, an especially vexed pursuit of authenticity in the fashioning of their memoirs. Their life stories cannot help but denaturalize or complicate notions of the "real" as they epitomize less legitimate variants of tradition and modernity.

Minnie

A famed comedian, rather than singer and songwriter, Cannon is most notably distinguished from the others on a number of additional counts. As one of the oldest members of the Opry, she signifies a prized, if also by 1980 outdated, form of rusticity; yet she married "late" in life, never had children, and as a young single woman in the 1930s and '40s braved her own way as a road performer. Additionally, her entire stage persona hinged upon physical *undesirability*. Most important, her stage act was never able to make autobiographical claims: "Minnie Pearl" is the fictitious character developed over time by a woman born to cultured Southern gentility.

Cannon's memoir is thus beset by an entirely different set of anxieties concerning both gender and class authenticity. Though her lack of conventional femininity arguably (and ironically) proved to make her image that much more rustic in the sense that it encouraged her to take on the rube stereotype, it clearly haunts her consciousness throughout the text. As with her elite background, her betrayal of gender normativity threatens to brand her as an outsider, a transgressor. As she and collaborative writer Joan Dew recount her life history, they struggle with the star-author's "right" to "be" Minnie Pearl. Indeed, though the comic works with a much more self-consciously constructed stage persona than most of the others, she at times seeks—and at other times claims—a conflation of her self and her performative identity.

Minnie Pearl: An Autobiography registers this desire early on by beginning with two variants of the birth scene. The "Introduction" actually opens the narrative with Cannon's own career achievement, crystallized by the 1975 Country Music Association Hall of Fame Award. But in quoting the plaque's dedication, she documents the birth and merger of her two "selves":

> Humor is the least recorded but certainly one of the most important aspects of live country music. No one exemplifies the endearing values of pure country comedy more than Minnie Pearl. Born Sarah Ophelia Colley in Centerville, Tennessee; educated at fashionable Ward-Belmont College; joined the Grand Ole Opry in 1940. Her trademark—the dime-store hat with the dangling price tag and shrill "Howdee! I'm just so proud to be here!" made her the first country music humorist to be known and loved worldwide.[51]

She experiences "joyous hysteria" upon winning the award not only because it confirms her acceptance by the country music industry but because she herself can finally feel, and accept, the Minnie "within" her. (Later she refers to the character as her "alter ego.") Yet much of the narrative's drama concerns the performer's own resistance to or suspicion of this ostensible transformation. As she puts it, "The truth is, if Sarah Ophelia Colley had had her way, there never would have been a Minnie Pearl."[52]

The next chapter, containing her birth scene "proper," begins with the line, "I was a mistake from the start." While embedded within a narrative that intertwines stories of her parents' pasts and her own early years in order to point up her "idyllic childhood," that opening sentence belies her recurrent misgivings about her destiny to occupy two entirely different worlds. It was a "mistake," she discovers from her well-born parents, to aspire to lowness ("I'm certain my mother and father had never come into close contact with anyone who made their living standing on a stage 'cuttin' the fool,' much less spending a lifetime as a clown").[53] Her lighthearted story in this chapter of being "sold" to a family of gypsies by her father, to teach her a lesson when misbehaving, can be read as a coded description of her later career. She wants to "be" Minnie but fears being tainted by her "dark," common sphere.

As she charts the gradual evolution of the Minnie Pearl character, how-

ever, Cannon is at pains to emphasize her love of the "simple" mountain culture Pearl ostensibly represents. She modeled Minnie on an old woman she
met while working as a traveling stage director for the Wayne P. Sewell Company, which produced entertainment shows for small rural Southern towns.
Generously allowed to board with the impoverished woman and her family,
Cannon grew "fascinated" by their mountain dialect and manners. She relays: "They were funny people, witty people, who didn't know they were being funny, and didn't try to be. . . . The way these people expressed themselves had an innocence and a wit about it that charmed me." She soon
mimes their ways by adopting the character of a bashful young country girl
dressed in what the comic believed was an appropriate costume (a "tacky
straw hat," a dress made of "sleazy organdy"). Interestingly, she distinguishes
this persona from the rubes of country comedy: "There has been a miscon-
ception over the years that Minnie Pearl originally wore painted-on freckles
and had one front tooth blacked out. This is not so. I never intended her to
be a caricature. I dressed her as I thought a young country girl would dress
to go to meetin' on Sunday or to come to town on Saturday afternoon to do a
little trading and a little flirting." In fact, at various moments in the text, Cannon portrays Minnie as the medium for a seemingly universal rather than
strictly Southern past, concluding, "I think one of the reasons Minnie Pearl
has found so many fans is because she retains some of . . . [the] . . . guileless,
childlike innocence that characterized my formative years."[54]

Yet other comments, making rather classist distinctions between the performer and her character, suggest that the persona indeed operates as a rural
caricature. Cannon based part of the act on another young woman's comedy
routine, singing horribly off-key as a "funny old country woman." She notes,
"This wasn't real country music at all, but a parody that was so silly you absolutely laughed yourself sick." Many of the Pearl sketches she's performed
over the years and reproduced in the text, in mountain dialect, certainly fall in
this category, poking gentle fun at Minnie's ignorance. The tale that opens
chapter 17 ironically underscores this point. Meeting ad-agency executives
during her first years working the Opry, Cannon plays herself, noting: "I had
on a smart suit . . . and I carried on a brief conversation. . . . I didn't talk like
Minnie Pearl; I talked like Sarah Ophelia Colley. After all, my parents had
spent a good deal of time and money teaching me to speak properly. (I read
without moving my lips, and I can carry on a relatively intelligent conversation
when I want to.)" Later, she is astonished when the show's ad men fire her
from the Opry's network segment for being "not authentic." While she relishes their poor judgment of the Minnie character ("Poor old thing, she's only

lasted 40 years!"), she clearly fails to see how her discourse in the autobiography itself reveals her need, on one level, to retain her own class heritage.[55]

Minnie's distinctly unfeminine traits further weakened Cannon's grasp on that elite background. But interestingly, she experiences conflicts with gender expectations long before she "becomes" Minnie Pearl; it is in fact Sarah Ophelia's own early version of "gender trouble" that ultimately leads to her character's creation. She notes that her "natural inclinations" to be both a "tomboy" and a "showoff" as a young girl thwart her mother's attempts to "raise a little lady." Yet soon, she dreams of becoming a "romantic princess," as well as a respected dramatic actress. Both plans are derailed by one critical moment recounted in chapter 4, when she overhears one of her mother's friends call her "a plain little thing." She brings the gender and class components of this moment into sharp relief, writing: "What that woman said made a deep impression on me, and it was actually a help many years later when I finally had to face the fact that my future lay in comedy, not drama. Remembering her words made it all come together, because I knew I could never be the beautiful lady leaning over the balcony tossing her scarf to the handsome knight." The text immediately juxtaposes this memory with another: her failure as a last-minute beauty contestant in a PTA pageant run by her mother. The audience's cruel laughter as she strolls out to the tune "A Pretty Girl Is like a Melody" transmutes into comic appreciation when Colley decides to pantomime the contestant role ("I decided, 'Well, I'll give them a show'").[56] Together, the two scenes demonstrate the complex roots and implications of Cannon's comedy. While she appears to equate gender transgression with a particular kind of low cultural performance—because she is "plain" and masculinized, she is limited to "cuttin' the fool"—her stint on that high school stage also reveals that gender itself is a performance. To "be" a woman is to enact an explicit act or set of behaviors that she proceeds to ape.

More often than not, however, Cannon's commentary within the autobiography continues to insist upon the naturalness of gender. In other words, by choosing to "become" Minnie Pearl, she chooses to strip herself of an ostensibly inherent femininity. Time and again, she notes her reluctance to make such a choice: "I wasn't ready to give up sex appeal and a feminine image to be a clown." Her apprehension over her own gender identity is exacerbated by two additional factors: participation in road life as a young single woman and failure to be a mother. The former receives much more explicit and often fascinating attention in the text. As mentioned earlier, few solo women performers were permitted this experience during the Opry's heyday, and it marked Cannon in numerous ways. On the one hand, her endurance of its physical and emotional trials makes her "one of the boys": "I didn't complain or whine or ask for any favors or special treatment because I was a woman. I took the rigors and changes just like the men." She enjoys the camaraderie and general excitement of touring. Yet her enthusiasm mustn't get too out of hand, for at the same time, she becomes branded as a particular type of woman, what Cannon calls a "'show girl' . . . different from their wives, mothers, sisters or girlfriends." Her attempts to negotiate these two positions give rise to several postures that include both "having a sense of humor" and "remain[ing] ladylike and deserving of their respect."[57]

Eventually, she opts for two other, more traditional, roles—wife to a dashing pilot named Henry Cannon and "mother" to her road "family." Cannon's marriage lends legitimacy as well as safety to her unusual lifestyle. She confesses, "If I had lived the road life alone for 27 years, I doubt seriously that I would be here to write this book!" It affords her the opportunity to display *Sarah Ophelia's* "true" feminine character, assuring the reader, "He was the first man who had ever *told* me what to do, and I liked it." Motherhood, the final test of gender authenticity within both Sarah's and Minnie's worlds, eludes her. But while biological maternity was "not forthcoming," her desire to be pregnant ("a longing I could literally *feel*") is for a time displaced and satisfied by the "maternal instincts" she directs, much like Lynn, toward her male touring partners but also her younger female cohorts.[58] The Minnie persona indeed finally serves as Cannon's "alter ego" or double, allowing her early and seemingly "unnatural" tendencies to continue their expression even as the performer herself settles for a more conventional gender (if not class) script.

Dolly

If Cannon's mimicry of "natural" rusticity assumes a desexualization of the female body, Parton's country femininity is a paean to the erotics of artifice. Every facet of her body has been exaggerated to match the outlandish dimensions of those infamous breasts: hair, cheekbones, lips, hips, height. And ever since she gained national exposure in the late 1960s through the early '70s on Porter Wagoner's television show, their grand sum has attracted as much attention as her accomplished musical talents (and exceptional business savvy). More than any other legendary female performer in country, Parton *is* body, though one that appears to both epitomize and defy the laws of nature.

Recent feminist cultural critics have made laudable efforts to understand the gender politics of Parton's image, envisioning her self-representation as a deliberate parody of dominant cultural norms for women.[59] Like Cannon's comic persona, then, is "Dolly Parton" an explicit invention with subversive undercurrents? Her autobiography provides another means of reading her performative gestures specifically in the context of country music history and discourse. Loss and Desire would seem to have particular salience here, as Parton's impoverished yet iconic Smoky Mountain childhood so markedly pales beside her current indulgence of material and "vain" pleasures. Her traditional past, elevated to the level of folk culture in the signature song "Coat of Many Colors," would seem to clash with her delight in the contemporary world of Hollywood as well as Music Row and in the creation of her own business empire. According to the dictates of country authenticity, she must make good in both her stage performance and in the example of her "true" life story one of the autobiography's central tenets: "Although I look like a drag queen's Christmas tree on the outside, I am at heart a simple country woman."[60]

Parton's conception of Southern "trash" culture holds the key, I think, to the apparent contradictions of her identity. She is one of the few women artists considered here to even use the pejorative term, but in her role as queen of country excess, she relishes its dangers as much as its directness. When she jokes, "It costs a lot to make a person look this cheap," she at once pays tribute to her own poor taste—the continuing legacy of her low-class roots—and *celebrates* her escape from the material deprivation that frequently accompanies it. In one sense, her current garishness is the "natural" extension, rather than betrayal, of her particular cultural history. Yet it also serves as a clear departure, specifically in its gendered form. For throughout the text, Parton equates "trashiness" with a femininity antithetical to the hillbilly "womanhood" surrounding her in the Parton household:

Womanhood was a difficult thing to get a grip on in those hills, unless you were a man. My sisters and I used to cling desperately to anything halfway feminine. . . . We could see the pictures of the models in the newspapers that lined the walls of our house and the occasional glimpse we would get at a magazine. We wanted to look like them. They didn't look at all like they had to work in the fields. They didn't look like they had to take a spit bath in a dishpan. They didn't look as if men and boys could just put their hands on them any time they felt like it, and with any degree of roughness they chose. The way they looked, if a man wanted to touch them, he'd better be damned nice to them.[61]

In this remarkable passage, she challenges a number of definitions and assumptions surrounding the relationship between gender and class in her culture: "cheapness" refers to the exhausted, plain farm women who must endure male gropings, rather than to the brightly painted magazine models; *they* were the ones who appeared *un*natural, unfeminine. The alternative provides Parton with a "model" of gender identity far more concrete and desirable than that inscribed within local Appalachian "sister" or "mother" images. It leads Parton to develop a trashy look quite the opposite of her own rural existence as the oldest daughter of twelve children: "I couldn't get my hair big enough or 'yaller' enough. Couldn't get my skirt tight enough, my blouses low enough. . . . I'd go into the four-for-a-quarter picture booth at Woolworth's, unbutton my blouse, push my headlights up with my arms, and take pictures." (126). She realizes that her early awkward experiments with makeup and dress occasionally made her resemble a "clown" (an image mocked much later in a color photo insert), but more often than not, they helped her feel "beautiful."[62] Much like Lynn, Parton critiques idealized renditions of women's experiences in rural culture—not by exposing the actual demands of motherhood, as in *Coal Miner's Daughter,* but by overturning the binary dividing "natural" and "unnatural" women. Adopting the look of a "loose" woman offered another mode of Otherness that seemed to bring her autonomy and agency, rather than powerlessness.

Parton's life story thus finally verifies her own authenticity by recuperating class abjection. In the recounting of her personal and public histories, the "sub"-humanity of poor white Southerners takes a more Desirable form that turns out to be an explicit construction of her intangible image and very real body. She is in fact quite candid about her efforts to deliberately reshape and augment the latter through cosmetic surgery, stating: "I have done it and will do it again when something in my mirror doesn't look to me like it belongs on Dolly Parton. . . . I feel it is my duty to myself and my public. My spirit is too beautiful and alive to live in some dilapidated old body if it doesn't have to."[63] Here, "Dolly Parton" becomes a separate, almost reified persona that her body literally creates. Yet in the end, I would argue, it doesn't quite function as a means of critical parody. Parton understands that gender is performance: achieving the "right" hair color, conforming to a seemingly impossible bodily ideal. But it is a performance she can pull off with astounding success. She doesn't so much confront (and subsequently expose) reification itself, as in Fox's proposed theory of the Loss/Desire dialectic. She exchanges the *class*-based objectification of her past for a *gender*-based one in the present. The Dolly character represents the embodiment of her personal "dream."

Her chapter on Dollywood essentially attempts to make the same point. Chiding those critics who dismiss the theme park as a vanity project, Parton insists that the business honors "her people," employing "mostly real hillbillies" to showcase mountain culture. At the same time, she planned the park to resemble old-time, small-town carnivals—the ostensible Other of that hardscrabble world. In the memoir, she recalls discovering her childhood cousin "Myrtle" as the "alligator girl" in a local sideshow and casts her as the symbol of her own quest: "I could understand her completely. After all, I wanted to leave the mountains too, and I wanted attention. She probably thought I was making fun or blowing her cover, but I just wanted to say, 'Hello, I understand. Be the alligator girl. Be whatever your dreams and your luck will let you be. . . . Give them a quarter's worth of wonder.'"[64] Rather than viewing her cousin's situation as a pathetic or shameful tragedy—as the exemplification of her white trash upbringing—Parton envisions it as an opportunity for escape, transformation. Myrtle's role in the freak show, of course, is in fact no more autonomous or divorced from class positioning and cultural expectations than Parton's wigs and spectacular silhouette. But Parton's autobiography as a whole suggests that *making oneself* into a spectacle, even an abject one, is better than being erased, ignored, or silenced altogether.

Dolly's most controversial moments, however, probably lie in two interrelated claims that brand her as the embodiment of modernity: explicit disinterest in motherhood and an eroticized approach to religion. Parton shamelessly conflates her life's three grand "passions"—music, God, and sexuality (art/spirit/body)—arguing that they "overlap and intertwine within me." Their coalescence, free of maternal pressures, constitutes the core of her identity. Like the carnival, a local abandoned chapel emerges as another key symbol in her life narrative, the site of emotional and spiritual solace during Parton's adolescence. It attracts her attention precisely because it functions as a shrine to teen "sin and vice," a repository of used condoms, empty beer bottles, and crude sexual graffiti. Singing hymns while studying the church walls' "dirty pictures," she suddenly has an epiphany: God "meant" her to be both an artist and "a sexual being." She concludes: "I was validated. I was sanctified. I was truly reborn. . . . The joy of the truth I found there is with me to this day. I had found God. I had found Dolly Parton. And I loved them both." This alternate claim of authenticity is at once transgressive and traditional, provoking and repelling critique. Her seemingly profane impulses—enjoyment of sexual pleasure, being body, and being "unique"—have spiritual sanction. Later in the text, she can thus make the following blithe statement about motherhood: "I have never been pregnant. I don't know what that feeling is like. I think God has different purposes for different people. Some women are meant to be mothers and grandmothers. I was meant to be Aunt Granny."[65] Of the six women performers under consideration, she may have discovered the least confining and yet most legitimate means of utilizing autobiography to "answer" country's gendered dictates.

IV. CONCLUSION: STILL WOMAN ENOUGH

In *Bodies That Matter,* Judith Butler proposes that a performative act is in itself a "congealment of the past which is precisely foreclosed in its act-like status," concluding, "In this sense an 'act' is always a provisional failure of memory."[66] As much as it explicitly tries to mine (and mime) a past that signifies the "real," the country music memoir, like its musical equivalent, cannot escape its own particular mode of performativity. Reproducing a set of norms that constitute country authenticity while paradoxically striving to meet literary cultural standards, it rewrites the history of disenfranchisement (personal/regional/class/gender) so that it simultaneously accomplishes a merciful "failure" *and* a fulfillment of "memory." Lynn is fond of claiming "what you see is what you get," but the reader gets so much more in all of these texts. From barn dance masquerade to honky-tonk "sincerity," country artists have devised various strategies for establishing meaningful visibility in dominant class culture, and at this juncture women performers have had to contend with an additional history of marginalization within their field. Whether a coal miner's daughter or an alligator girl, these star-authors perform their past and present lives with a vengeance, insisting that they, too, are "bodies that matter" to country music.

Intriguingly, Lynn felt compelled to pen a "sequel" to her groundbreaking memoir in 2002. Titled *Still Woman Enough,* it narrates the twenty-seven years that followed not simply the first book's publication but, more notably, its 1980 film version—as she puts it, "after the final credits for *Coal Miner's Daughter* rolled across the screen."[67] As Lynn astutely observes in this comment, Hollywood's cinematic rendition of her autobiography, starring actress Sissy Spacek, had essentially come to define her life story for the American public.[68] It transported the singer's image and personal history into millions of suburban cineplexes, small-town theaters, and uptown movie houses and thereby won her an ironic form of crossover fame. "Lorett-y" was no longer simply a country music icon but the rube darling of popular culture, frozen in time, as well as the more abstract embodiment of the "American Dream" broadcast daily in the Smithsonian Museum of American History. According to Lynn, the film also tampered with her own version of the truth—"building a sort of myth around Doo and me and our marriage"—which prompted her (at least in part) to tell "the rest of the story" anew.[69]

In the early twenty-first century, however, Lynn's updated autobiography arguably serves a different cultural function within the country music industry. Long neglected by country radio and record producers, she until recently appeared more relic than idol, despite her ardent older fan base that keeps her on the road to perform her beloved string of hits. The new memoir title clearly marks Lynn's passage from "daughter" (and wife) to independent "woman" over the past decades, but it can also be read as an arch rejoinder to the music's lingering gendered mythologies *and* to Music Row's betrayal of its traditional roots. (The song title from which it derives, "You Ain't Woman Enough," similarly put country music on notice in 1965.) This second coauthored text works to revive her very presence within the country "scene" and to some degree also speaks collectively for the other women of her generation, such as Tammy Wynette and Dolly Parton, whose stars similarly faded in the commercial music market.[70]

Interestingly, then, although mainstream country largely continued to ignore Loretta Lynn, with the exception of dutifully honoring her image as a static emblem of the music's traditional past, an upstart movement branded as "alternative" heard her plea for current recognition. In the late 1990s and beyond, artists from the emerging alt.country genre (especially women) turned to singers like Lynn and Parton as both inspirational vocalists and trailblazing figures in the industry, and "independent" record labels began wooing them back into the studio.[71] Lynn launched her comeback with the unlikeliest of partners, Jack White of the alternative band the White Stripes, who produced and arranged her new collection of songs as the album *Van Lear Rose* in 2004. Although White isn't designated an alt.country artist per se, he clearly flirts with that genre and offered to work with Lynn in a Nashville recording studio.[72] (In the liner notes, she even enthuses, "I can see a little of [Lynn's legendary country music producer] Owen Bradley in that young man!") *Van Lear Rose* wasn't played on Top 40 country radio, but it topped many alt.country playlists that year, revitalizing Lynn's career for a distinctly different fan community.

My final chapter will explore this alt.country phenomenon as the most recent and influential purveyor of authenticity discourse. Although mainstream country continues to fret about its crossover identity and thus necessarily engages, from time to time, with a pastiche of authenticity narratives, it has been supplanted, I would argue, by alt.country rhetoric—a new mode of "backtalk" (and accompanying musical production) that has gained purchase with not only a new generation of listener but one affiliated with elite, rather than low, cultural capital. Despite this shift in demographic, it is making in-roads into the transformation of modern country itself. Alt.country's *post*modern approach to authenticity, however, offers an ostensibly respectful but deeply problematic reclamation of traditional country music. While paying "homage" to the forgotten masters of the music, it frequently operates with a detached sense of irony that nevertheless has the potential to revive the music's masculinist history and iconography along with its earlier rustic sound.

CHAPTER 5

Revivals, Survivals, and the Future of Authenticity: Alternative Country's Reclamation of Rusticity

> Not too long ago, to "be country" meant that you had been cast by a geo-socio-economic accident of birth into an almost automatically adversarial relationship with the dominant urban/suburban culture; in effect, you belonged to a cultural ghetto. Now, it's a simple matter of free consumer choice. Anybody can make the choice, no questions asked, no attitudes implied.
>
> —Patrick Carr, "Will the Circle Be Unbroken? Country's Changing Image"

When writing the "story" of country music near the end of the twentieth century, Tony Scherman, like many of his fellow music journalists, denounced the "self-eviscerating" tendencies of contemporary commercial country and glimpsed signs of genuine renewal not in Music Row's marketing slogan of "New Traditionalism" throughout the 1980s—epitomized by "vapid newcomers like Alan Jackson"—but in the "fresh style" of emerging artists such as Dwight Yoakam and Marty Brown, who within a year or two of Scherman's published musings would become key figures in the new movement known as "alternative country."[1] A diverse melding of honky-tonk, Appalachian, and alternative rock/punk traditions, "alt.country" music proceeded to take hold in the mid-1990s, gaining favor with similar anti-industry critics and like-minded fans by purporting to respect country's "true" class, regional, and stylistic roots. More than a decade later, it has emerged as a high-minded competitor to Top 40 country. Its performers embrace authenticity models of the past that have come to be either stigmatized or neglected in modern mainstream country, paying allegiance to earlier icons such as Hank Williams, Johnny Cash, and Merle Haggard. At the same time, the music retains certain late-twentieth-century accents that establish its contemporary currency, such as the Internet community and terminology that originally provided alt.country's fan base and official moniker. Other attempts at naming this genre throughout the decade and beyond hint at its hybridized style and ostensible ideological bent—"insurgent country," "Americana," "roots music," "twang," "honky-skronk," "thrashgrass," "grange rock"—while its most recent incarnation may be the most provocative of all: simply "American music."[2]

Yet despite encompassing a wide variety of artists—from Emmylou Harris and Steve Earle to lesser-known acts sporting tongue-in-cheek names like Trailer Trash, Southern Culture on the Skids, and the Drive-By Truckers—the term *alt.country* has evolved into a reductive insignia that promises little more than a hip reconstitution of country rusticity. As it has solidified as a genre, its tastemakers have fashioned a left-leaning cultural agenda embedded in a critique of red-state national politics that targets a younger, more high-brow audience both knowledgeable and appreciative of "authentic" music. Paradoxically, it has also come to wield an ever-increasing influence on the look, themes, and, to some degree, sound of mainstream country performers: from Faith Hill's fling as a down-home "Mississippi Girl" (see chapter 1), to Miranda Lambert's recent guise as a pistol-packing "Crazy Ex-Girlfriend." This chapter, then, brings my study toward closure by examining alt.country as a *post*modern movement that has appropriated the discourse on country authenticity, exploiting while also altering prior formulas.[3] While dubbed "modern twang" by one of its earliest and most enthusiastic proponents, David Goodman, alt.country music actually demonstrates a much more self-conscious approach—deeply engaged with the modern as it has become etched into country's representations of itself but also curiously detached. As Barbara Ching and I argue, alt.country typically strikes a sardonic or parodic pose in relation to country music history and cultural coding, suffusing its reverence of the "past" with irony.[4] Often lacking the biographical credentials that verified the class and/or regional authenticity of earlier country artists from the 1940s through the mid-1960s, alt.country performers may revert to vintage costuming to play the role or alternatively adopt a sophisticated distancing from their rustic forebears. The movement's rhetoric certainly expresses commitment to the revival and reauthorization of prior authenticity models charted in this book—particularly honky-tonk and "old-time" folk from the earliest era—but it can do so indiscriminately.

Drawing on Raymond Williams' theorization of "residual" culture and others' ethnomusicological approaches to music revivalism, this final chapter untangles alternative country's knotty class, gender, and racial politics in order to determine whether its valorization of country tradition can offer a genuinely oppositional, as well as more recognizably hegemonic, mode of country music culture. As Williams reminds us, any notion of literary or aesthetic tradition is intimately tied to the *contemporary* moment, its visibility defined and fueled by the interests of a dominant class. Within the context of country music, such "tradition" is defiantly common rather than exclusive, yet it remains "an intentionally selective version of a shaping past and a pre-shaped present, which is then powerfully operative in the process of social and cultural definition and identification." Alt.country's more utopian impulses, privileging artistic simplicity and organicism over crass commodification, have the potential to frame the music as an "alternative" or "oppositional" cultural form that permits previously repressed practices and values to be "lived and practiced on the basis of the residue . . . of some previous social and cultural institution or formation."[5] Nevertheless, as I will soon explore, most modes of "residual" culture become recuperated by dominant culture, and alt.country's revivalist sensibility indeed functions, like others, as a distinctly "middle-class phenomen[on]"[6]—unwittingly taking up the legacy of earlier barn dance constructions of "old-time" music and culture engineered by the likes of George Hay and John Lair for *their* middle-class spectators of the 1930s and '40s. In fact, alternative music artist Michelle Shocked, in a tart send-up of alt.country music, likens its posers to those "taking the subway home from a costume party."[7] Her own work throughout the last two decades has much to teach us about both classed and racialized constructions of American "roots" music, exposing yet also reframing the fraught ties to minstrelsy that underlie alt.country's performance of authenticity.

My analysis concentrates on alt.country's consistent fascination with classic abject tropes of country music history, particularly those connecting the past's "dark" lifestyle of violence, despair, and excess with current facets of rural, white trash, or working-class existence. Later in the chapter, I argue that male artists promoted by certain alt.country record labels, such as Chicago's Bloodshot Records, equate country authenticity with a specifically masculinized version of class authenticity, reveling in the "dirty white boy" tradition handed down by their dissolute heroes of the honky-tonk era. That period's mythic conflation of the modern and the primitive—electronic sound and brazen revelation of the "true" self—lays the groundwork for one gendered teleological vision leading from honky-tonk to rock to punk music.

To be sure, alt.country instrumentation and lyrics incorporate contemporary sounds and signifiers to connect the "past" to the present moment, yet this impulse plays out in unintentionally ironic ways. For despite these performers' attempts to adapt country tradition to the peculiarities of blue-collar life in the 1990s and beyond, they finally invest it with palpable nostalgia for an imaginary past. Birmingham's Drive-By Truckers, garnering praise from such cultural mainstays as *Rolling Stone* and the *Village Voice,* will close out the discussion as a male alt.country act that both typifies and considerably complicates this trend.[8] The chapter's final section turns to a group of female artists who appear equally attracted to narratives or markers of abjection— Gillian Welch, the band Freakwater, and Iris DeMent—yet take refuge in even earlier feminized models of country culture popularized by the Carter Family. As with prior women performers' appropriation of honky-tonk and autobiography, their work complicates our understanding of authenticity's continued presence in country music discourse. At times, their renditions of a Southern neogothic aesthetic simply reproduce alt.country's nostalgic revivalism, yet in other instances, akin to the Truckers, they interrogate the model with a more clear-eyed "survivalism."

I. THEORIZING OPPOSITIONAL CULTURE

While brashly iconoclastic and dedicated to cultural and stylistic *im*purity— that is, borrowing from a series of "radical" musical traditions including bluegrass, punk, blues, and honky-tonk—alt.country can nevertheless, at least in its beginnings as a verifiable movement, be positioned within a revivalist paradigm. As Neil Rosenberg has shown in the 1960s folk music scene, and as Tamara Livingston theorizes about the Brazilian urban popular music known as "choro," music revivalists share a common "cultural and political agenda" articulated "in *opposition* to aspects of the contemporary cultural mainstream" and "offer a cultural alternative in which legitimacy is grounded in reference to authenticity and historical fidelity."[9] Though alt.country often adopts a more playful posture in relation to its historical referents, be they Appalachian ballads, Outlaw country-rock, or "cry-in-your-beer" honky-tonk standards, it still demands that such marginalized forms of country music be *re*seen and restored as valuable bits of the country archive, as well as exemplars of a superior aesthetic abandoned by Nashville's corporate hit-makers. Similar to earlier folk preservation movements that sought to "collect and rehabilitate seemingly disappearing, seemingly premodern communities such

as the people of Appalachia, who symbolized the fragile persistence of authentic practice"—yet subsequently transformed these artifacts into marketable commodities—the alt.country industry reveres traditional country
music's "'emotional depth,' 'sincerity,' and . . . 'indigenous genuineness of dialect and twang.'"[10]

In her cross-cultural comparison, Livingston suggests that all music revival movements share both an oppositional and a pedagogical stance: to
teach, and thereby "improve," dominant culture by (re)introducing long-
buried values and cultural forms.[11] Composed of collectors, performers, and
writers, a revivalist community generates its own ideology, discourse, and eth-
ical code; creates its own organizations, festivals, and publications to dissemi-
nate its products; and founds its own counterinstitutions to produce contemporary variants of the revived tradition or style—all of which can be glimpsed
in alt.country's *No Depression* magazine (both in print and online); its Americana Music Association (AMA); and its numerous industry showcases, such as
the South X Southwest Music Festival. The mission is moralistic, rescuing not
simply a musical style or trend from cultural oblivion but a level of *taste* affiliated with cosmopolitan and urban, rather than mass and/or suburban,
lifestyles. Livingston rightly situates revivalism within a particular class habitus that divides culture into "modern" and "traditional" components and professes "certain aesthetic preferences" such as "precision in playing and of tone
production, tight arrangements, privileging of contrast over continuity." Frequently, the very choice of tradition reflects revivalism's class context—"associated *by the dominant society* with the minority's culture."[12]

Raymond Williams and Evan Watkins: Residuals and "Throwaways"

Raymond Williams' cultural materialist theory, currently enjoying a quasi-
"retro" revival of its own in an arguably *post*-postmodern academic climate,
helps amplify the politics at stake in revivalism but also allows for the possibility of a genuinely "alternative" culture.[13] *The Country and the City*, first
published in 1973, masterfully exposes the charged relationship among pas-
toralism, realism, rusticity, and urban aestheticism, establishing that "the relations between country and city . . . are not only of ideas and experiences,
but of rent and interest; of situation and power; a wider system." Williams
ends this now-classic study with the following commentary:

> It is significant . . . that the common image of the country is now an image of
> the past, and the common image of the city an image of the future. That

leaves, if we isolate them, an undefined present. The pull of the idea of the country is towards old ways, human ways, natural ways. The pull of the idea of the city is towards progress, modernization, development. In what is then a . . . present experienced as tension, we use the contrast of country and city to ratify an unresolved division and conflict of impulses, which it might be better to face on its own terms.[14]

Alt.country presents itself as a movement and musical genre at home with this tension while reframing the terms. Its "idea of the country" at the end of the twentieth century resembles just such an anticorporate, "natural" way of life, yet its "idea of the city" is less "modernization" than hipster sophistication. It accuses mainstream country radio of betraying traditional values and practices in favor of a mass-produced commodity that offers only a suburbanized simulacrum of the "country" to achieve popular appeal.

Yet as Williams demonstrates more fully in his subsequent exploration of the interplay between hegemonic and oppositional cultures, self-proclaimed alternative movements have a difficult time eluding a similar kind of co-optation. Insisting that dominant culture inherently works to incorporate any political or artistic movement that threatens its authority, he cautions that it "at once produces and limits its own form of counter-culture." His approach thus helps to decode the conflicted status of alt.country, which initially emerged as an ostensibly rustic alternative to the hegemonic urban culture represented by Nashville, Los Angeles, Atlanta, and New York but has since become incorporated into and celebrated by those bastions of cultural capital. Even those elements of a stubbornly residual mode of culture, which Williams distinguishes from the "archaic," are typically absorbed into the mainstream. Drawing on his prior work in *The Country and the City*, Williams illustrates this argument by pointing to "the idea of rural community," which he believes has the *potential* to function in opposition to urban industrial capitalism but is more typically recuperated as "fantasy or as an exotic . . . leisure function of the dominant order itself."[15] Evan Watkins' study of "obsolescence" in the contemporary era is similarly concerned with investigating how dominant ideology defines "pastness" and mystifies its own temporal scene. Arguing that "narratives of change . . . are about the determination of social position," Watkins maintains that current notions of cultural "extinction" are always predicated upon "conditions of both cultural and economic production *in the present*."[16]

Williams allows that "much of the most accessible and influential work of the counter-hegemony is historical: the recovery of discarded areas, or the redress of selective and reductive interpretations," which is certainly true of alt.country's mission vis-à-vis mainstream country music. Yet he warns that such efforts will be futile unless they can demonstrate how such excavated cultural "ruins" can be "clearly and actively traced" to the present moment. In other words, how might this (re)construction of the past also "ratify" hegemonic ideals?[17] All too often, alt.country's representations and proclamations lack such accountability, persuasively charting the selectivity of much conventional country music history yet failing to recognize how the movement's own "alternative" chronicle of the past equally validates prevailing social relations. Alt.country can at times successfully reference or mimic the past to signal protest against present conditions, while in other instances it produces its own androcentric historical "time-line" that reinscribes prior masculinized models of authenticity.[18]

Williams' concern to delineate the murky borders between hegemonic forces and self-professed alternatives thus usefully puts in check the more utopian (or merely self-aggrandizing) claims of this evolving movement. However, he is just as careful to approach hegemony as a "process" rather than a reified "system," occasionally subject to "authentic breaks" by what he calls "independent" modes or forms: "other kinds of initiative and contribution which are irreducible to the terms of the original or the adaptive hegemony."[19] Later sections of this chapter will demonstrate that certain alt.country artists have helped moved the genre in this direction by self-consciously approaching their music as a residual "trace" capable of powerful commentary on present class relations. As Watkins has suggested about the resistance strategies of all economically and racially marginalized populations who have been deemed "throwaways" in late capitalism, they salvage the past not to fetishize but to "repair" it as a means of "survival" in the present world.[20] I conclude the present section by turning to a performer who has served as both trenchant critic and (rarely recognized) pioneer of the alt.country movement and whose own meditations on the country/folk musical tradition have reinjected race as well as class into the contemporary discussion of country authenticity. In its own fashion, her work exemplifies both revivalism and survivalism.

Michelle Shocked: Reconfiguring the Minstrel Mask

In the March–April 2002 issue of *No Depression*, gender- and genre-bending performer Michelle Shocked provocatively announced her return to the music industry after a lengthy hiatus by both situating herself within and distancing herself from alt.country culture. Her ad for the just-released double album *Deep Natural/Dub Natural* questions the authenticity mania of much alt.country material by satirizing those performers who "dress up like moonshiners or Gram Parsons or buckaroos or Buckaroos, or inbred mountain maidens, guided by stylists who moved to Nashville from LA, sneering all the while at those horrible sellout Nashville hat acts while clinging desperately to one of the saddest marketing niches imaginable, trying all the while to look authentic and weather-beaten."[21] Well-versed in "shocking" the mainstream with her dramatic shifts in musical and visual stylings, moving from folk-punk to swing to bluegrass and gospel, Shocked here confronts the alt.country orthodoxy in the very "Ur"-text of the movement by exposing some of the troubling assumptions underlying much of the music's self-conscious mode of hillbilly masquerade. Yet her album recorded a decade earlier, *Arkansas Traveler*, engaged in a similarly pointed act of revelation and critique by drawing explicit attention to folk music's taboo connection to *racial* mimicry—blackface performance. Here, I bring *Arkansas Traveler* and *Deep/Dub Natural* together for a brief reading in order to position Shocked as an incisive theorist, as well as performer, of alt.country music. Her representation of the "natural" in both class and racial contexts helps illuminate what is deeply problematic but also potentially visionary in this "alternative" approach to country music.

Arkansas Traveler (Mercury, 1992), the final installment of her self-proclaimed trilogy, which also includes *Short Sharp Shocked* (Polygram, 1990) and *Captain Swing* (Polygram, 1989), pairs up traditional fiddle tunes popular during the antebellum and Civil War periods with Shocked's own original lyrics. (At least one commentator also identifies this album as the true progenitor of the 2002 *O Brother Where Art Thou* soundtrack phenomenon.[22]) Incorporating several standard minstrel show tunes, Shocked, as noted in the opening pages of chapter 1, argues in the liner notes that "a blackface tradition is alive and well hidden behind a modern mask."[23] But insisting that "'blacking up' should be done correctly," she eschews a photo of herself in such a pose for fear of stirring up "hatemongers" or "offending the delicate sensibilities of the politically correct." Interview commentary, in conjunction with the songs themselves, helps sketch out her vision of "appropriate" contemporary racial masquerade that is practiced "in a context of true respect for the cultures we ape."[24] Shocked primarily chooses to operate with the mask metaphor central to much modern academic theorizing on racial performance, and this is where I will focus my analysis.

Overall, Shocked makes a number of conflicting (and at times highly naive) statements about whites' relationship to blackface. In a 1992 Dutch radio program, she begins to elaborate on the motivations behind this practice. Emphasizing that minstrelsy has European as well as American roots, she frames the minstrel performer as "a person with a European perspective . . . for the first time meeting up with Afro-centric culture . . . and they say, 'Oh, I like this. I can do this. I have rhythm. I'm funky. I've got soul.'"[25] The reader might be tempted to detect some irony in this interpretation, but Shocked proceeds to lend it validity. When asked why whites "painted" their faces black, she replies:

> I think it was the very time honoured ritual of wearing a mask. When you put on a mask you can be something other than what you are. I don't believe that anyone really believed when they saw this person with black paint that they were black. . . . I think it was respecting the tradition of wearing a mask and once you're in that mask you become a different character. You become a soul singer!

For Shocked, then, the "mask" functions distinctly outside the parameters of realism and authenticity. When pressed about its racist dimensions, she attempts to clarify but finally gets mired in further confusion:

> Our understanding of it is racist but the history is a fact. It existed and the fact that we've tried to sweep it under the carpet, deny that it ever existed, rip it out of the history books, that's racist. . . . If you can't understand your own racism of the past you can't go forward. You can't take out the part that is unpleasant. You must accept it . . . but it's not racist. If anything, it's appreciation of a culture that has something very valuable to give.

For Shocked, that "value" lies primarily in "Afro-centric culture's" "impurity," its refusal to "segregate," to define—"putting all kinds of dance and music and rhythm and poly-rhythms together," unlike its "very box-like . . . very structured" Eurocentric counterpart. This sounds much like critics' delineations of Shocked's own musical trajectory, of course, which has consistently challenged boundaries of genre or form and functioned as a kind of aesthetic bricolage now claimed by alt.country. Yet her sense of the precise relationship between the minstrel mask and "African" culture itself—and her music's enactment of this complex dynamic—remains hazy. An implicit sense of identification seems to be at work in Shocked's model of blackface performance, allowing the white actor to "become" momentarily "black," though she emphasizes that spectators would never recognize the transformation as such. And this would certainly seem to be true of other examples from Shocked's own life history: in the same year *Arkansas Traveler* appeared, she joined a South Central Los Angeles African American Pentecostal church and initiated a protracted legal battle with Mercury Records over ownership of her material by citing the Thirteenth Amendment, outlawing slavery.[26] In both her personal experience and her cultural production, then, she has laid claim to an affinity with black identity, though the grounds for such imitation remain, at least on surface, quite simplistic.

At the same time, a promotional postcard for *Arkansas Traveler* takes pains to emphasize Shocked's own "low," transgressive *class* origins by painting her father as a romantically "dangerous" young carnival worker and establishing her status as an "illegitimate" child born out of wedlock to her fanatically conservative Mormon mother. Similarly, in an interview conducted in conjunction with the release of *Deep Natural,* she conveys a suspicion of current alt.country performers by noting that Gillian Welch (as just one example) is "probably too cool for the likes of me, I'm a little backward and hillbilly in my ways."[27] While not quite self-consciously linked to her own minstrelsy project, such tell-tale notions of class identity begin to hint at potential links between blackface and hillbilly representations, as well as between African American and poor white cultures, at times echoing the more erudite theories of scholars such as Eric Lott, W. T. Lhamon, and especially Robert Cantwell. Shocked's "soul singer" fantasies to a degree recall Lott's metaphor of "ventriloquism," wherein white performers donned the minstrel mask in order to express certain transgressive values and desires associated with "blackness"; yet the express sense of identification that Cantwell charts between Southern poor whites and blacks in the nineteenth century lends a wealth of documentation to back up what Shocked presents as mere "instinct" or supposition. In fact, she comes closest to Cantwell's formulation when puzzling through the phenomenon of African American blackface performers. Acknowledging that minstrelsy often promoted very "broad" and "stereotypical" roles, she claims many black performers "became seen as maybe collaborators with the enemy" but concludes that such offensive roles were actually "safe" for black performers—known and comforting to whites—and thus allowed a very literal kind of "survival" both on and off the mid-nineteenth-century stage.[28] *Arkansas Traveler* and *Deep/Dub Natural* take two different approaches to enacting such theories of racial performance and identification as Shocked works to ensure the continuing entwined presence of poor white and black cultures.

Only partly revivalist in mission, *Arkansas Traveler* functions more generally as a kind of travelogue celebrating both "life on the road" and cultural sampling. The songs themselves were recorded on a river boat, at a Georgia antique store, in Dublin, and at a friend's Chapel Hill home, with a host of guest musical collaborators. The album's alt.country anthem can best be summed up in the song "Strawberry Jam": culture needs to be a homegrown and collaborative practice to battle corporate and social hegemony. But when linked to minstrelsy, such "traveling" takes on another complicated set of meanings. The title song, a classic instrumental piece incorporating comic dialogue about a worldly traveler's encounters with a hayseed farmer, serves as the album's conceptual foundation, and in it, Shocked adopts the persona of cultured urbanite rather than rustic. Though ostensibly more sophisticated and clever, *she* is the one who is "lost" and ultimately bested by the hick (a cautionary tale for later alt. artists who position themselves in just this way, even while posing as the latter). The album's jacket cover offers one interpretation of this stance, inserting a contemporary hip image of Shocked into a stereotypic stage set frequently depicted in barn dance programs of the 1930s and '40s: a crudely painted backdrop of a ramshackle homestead with a receding rural landscape and Shocked, red kerchief slung on a stick, soaking her aching feet in a washtub with her grunge-era Doc Martens nearby. However, the album insert's back cover offers a counterimage, presenting Shocked as a respectable farm girl fronting an old-fashioned microphone. The artist keeps us guessing: Is this another mode of masquerade? If so, to re- or demystify notions of authentic rustic identity?

Arkansas Traveler opens with three original songs that neither introduce nor contextualize the later nineteenth-century tunes in any recognizable way. Indeed, the first two, "33 R.P.M. Soul" and "Come a Long Way," have a distinctly modern flavor (both musically and thematically), the latter a kind of surreal motorcycle odyssey through contemporary Los Angeles (Shocked's home at that time). Rather than establish a jarring contrast for the rural adventure about to follow, however, both help to create a fitting conceptual framework by contemplating the pleasures and dangers of border crossings. In the first song (joined by eminent black gospel and R&B artist "Pops" Staples), a young widow discovers alternate forms of "consecration" and "soul" as she exchanges the "hellfire brimstone blues" of the fundamentalist church for a young black lover on the "country side of town"; in "Come a Long Way," a Spanish phrase alluding to "illegal" crossings over the U.S./Mexico border serves as a mantra for its itinerant subject traversing from one side of the vast

Front cover of *Arkansas Traveler*. (Courtesy of Michelle Shocked, Mighty Sound, and Michelle Shocked/Campfire Girl Publishing.)

city to the other. Identity surely "travels" in these introductory song texts, preparing us for the momentary transformations sought after in the racial impersonation invoked by the later minstrel songs.[29]

Shocked takes these familiar melodies—some part and parcel of American culture, others now seemingly antiquated or forgotten—and indeed attempts to make them her own by adding or rewriting lyrics. In her hands, songs such as "Soldier's Joy" (featuring seminal 1990s group Uncle Tupelo), "Frankie and Johnny," and "Cotton-Eyed Joe" (accompanied by bluegrass/alt.artist Alison Krauss) become no simple period pieces but vibrant commentaries on war and gender politics, with transformed titles to match—respectively, "Shaking Hands" (about Civil War soldiers' morphine addiction),

Back cover of album insert, *Arkansas Traveler.* (Courtesy of Michelle Shocked, Mighty Sound, and Michelle Shocked/Campfire Girl Publishing.)

"Hold Me Back" (a new take on spurned womanhood), and "Prodigal Daughter" (a new take on "wayward" womanhood). However, the album's most notorious minstrel song, "Jump Jim Crow," is cleverly paired with "Zip-A-Dee-Doo-Dah," the sunny anthem originally written for Disney's 1946 film *Song of the South,* to recast the familiar theatrical roles of country rube/city slicker in an explicitly racial guise. Accompanied by blues artist Taj Mahal, she downplays the comic dimension of these stock minstrel types in order to embrace their enviable energy as "outlaw" figures: admiring Zip Coon's zesty "walking trick," she sings, "if I knew your secret I would make it mine." She then introduces a third black caricature, Tarbaby, to address both the racist history and effects of blackface performance but also to unsettle identity. Referencing both the white man "talking that jive" and the black man "trying to stay alive," Shocked suggests that it's impossible—and ultimately futile—to seek the authentic "jigaboo" among the white and black minstrels. Racist ideology, however, retreats from such a conclusion and typically resorts to mythology to mystify racial identity—hence Shocked's incorporation of the ironic Disneyfied coda to signify America's truly cartoonish understanding of race (nothing more than a "smiling" Tarbaby "wit de bone in de nose").[30]

Shocked's later work, *Deep/Dub Natural,* functions as a decoding device for this particular text, as well as more general commentary on the twenty-first-century alt.country scene. To begin, *Arkansas Traveler*'s closing visual image of Shocked-as-farmer eerily reappears on the cover insert to *Deep Natural,* this time as a colorful billboard erected over a color*less* small Texan oil town. Cheerfully touting "Effective Outdoor Advertising," the billboard emphasizes that Shocked is deliberately performing the role of "natural" yokel, sporting a similar straw hat and goofy grin yet hoisting a food product, rather than microphone, toward her viewers. Overall, the twin albums' recurring billboard imagery challenges conventional correspondences between sign and referent, representation and original, cultural construct and "nature." Read within the context of the album packaging's larger advertising motif, the billboard gracing the cover insert casts the earlier Shocked as a distinct commodity of Mercury/Polygram Records—or its "slave," as she argued in the 1990s—as opposed to any persuasive incarnation of Arkansan rube. As a whole, *Deep/Dub Natural*'s visuals offer a much more sardonic take on notions of imitation, belying the somewhat reductive, if admiring, interpretations of Shocked's infatuation with black musical influences (gospel, soul, reggae dub) promulgated by many reviewers. Initially claiming yet finally defying any easy dichotomy between voice and instrumentation, nature and technology, "deep" and dub versions, these paired recordings suggest that dub might well serve as Shocked's contemporary version of minstrelsy: a *self-conscious* performance of "Afro-centric" cultural identity that refuses simplistic constructs of authenticity.

Shocked introduces the billboard trope on the *Deep/Dub Natural* album cover, which pairs day- and nighttime renditions of "the natural"—fluorescent trees and sky—via large, seemingly transparent signs/mirrors promoting the titles to both albums. Both "deep" and "dub" versions of this same scene, respectively cast as light and dark, appear to be made of clear glass and finally blur the reflection or representation and the thing itself: foliage appearing within the frame, for example, also exceeds it, violating the border dividing copy or reflection and original. The insert, rather than listing song credits, lyrics, and the like, offers variations on this motif and as such seems to ex-

plore a number of possible options for the relation between sign and referent. As the "Effective Outdoor Advertising" strategy on the insert cover suggests, the first and most typical relation between the two is ideological, a willful *distortion* to promote a particular product or message. Page 3 of the
insert offers another example, superimposing a highly stylized image of a golf
course over a majestic photo of the Grand Canyon. The second option posits
a direct representation of the original: a billboard not functioning as a mirror
per se, as on the album cover, but seemingly offering an exact replica of the
stretch of road/landscape beside it. (Such mimesis is also enacted on the first
interior spread of the insert, which presents multiple "copies" of Shocked
herself in performance pose, an advertising poster for the album suspended
behind her: the proliferating images are exact, if literally faded, replicas of
the center figure.) Last, we have two examples of what might be deemed a
relationship of utopian transformation: a dry canyon becomes, on the billboard beside it, a verdant landscape with waterfall, and on the last interior
page spread we see a stretch of road at sunset, the accompanying billboard
remaining almost entirely empty of imagery except for the phrase "THIS
SPACE AVAILABLE" and some indecipherable graffiti. The insert's back
cover functions as a reprise of the front, yet the billboard is now advertising
Shocked's own cultural product among the oil wells, including the sequencing of song titles on both albums; her new record company's Web site address
(ironically incorrect); and ASCAP copyright info., which she pointedly titles
"2002 Minstrel Cycle Music."

This "cycle," as she envisions it, might then work in the following way.
Blackface (or hillbilly) performance certainly functions as another mediated
relation between an "original" and its imitation—between one referent already signifying "the natural" and what could only be a distorted and stylized
representation of it. In *Arkansas Traveler,* Shocked seemed at once to recognize and discount that inevitable mediation: she argued that "no one" would
mistake the copy for the original—and in the song "Jim Crow" questioned all
notions of racial authenticity—yet other times insisted that such masquerade
was a respectful tribute to that "natural" culture. In the later work, both conceptually and musically, dub operates as the race-inflected vehicle of imitation, yet with the aid of technological apparatuses, it quite deliberately transforms and *de*forms the original songs with which its "black" versions are
paired.

Deep/Dub Natural thereby registers a much more profound recognition
of the transforming effects of commodification itself, an unavoidable fate
even for those few artists like Shocked who manage to win legal and financial

control of their own artistic labor. To a degree, this thoughtful engagement with the very process of commercialization distinguishes her from the *No Depression* crowd whom she sought to reach with her advertising campaign: her critique of alt.country "dress up" more broadly argues that the genre is in fact an *unwitting* commodity advertising its own trumped-up version of "country" identity. But *Deep/Dub Natural* also presents a more utopian understanding of commodification reminiscent of Susan Willis' conception of blackface detailed earlier in this study: the notion that dominant meanings are subject to critique when they are exposed in highly contrived, reified forms. Both the billboard advertising Shocked *as* hillbilly and its vacant counterpart promising "This Space Available" demonstrate the power of the commodity to take on this transformative capacity. As I will now illustrate, this position anticipates but finally departs from alt.country's twin maneuvers: ironic detachment from its representational subject and faith in its own status as noncommodified art.

II. WHEN COUNTRY *WAS* COOL: ALT.COUNTRY, TASTE, AND MASCULINITY

As the alt.country "revolution" caught fire in the late 1990s, its purveyors became quite savvy about the politics of naming. Mindful of the demise of other recent musical trends (such as grunge) when achieving mass recognition, fans and performers continue to warn against labeling and hence codifying the music's "underground" style. In the pages of *No Depression* and on Internet listservs, they often eschew a single descriptive name, insisting, "It's just good music." Undoubtedly, stylistic differences in the early days distinguished the sounds of a purely "retro" group like BR5-49 (in its pre-2001 formation) from that of country-punk acts such as Angry Johnny and the Killbillies or, more recently, Hank III (Hank Williams's grandson, self-titled the "Honkytonk Hellbilly"). Music critic Bob Allen noted early on that the "only apparent shared trait" of such performers "is that they don't get played much on country radio."[31] Yet promotional and fan materials, performer interviews, and the music itself suggest common agendas, while the genre's increasingly institutionalization, marked by the formation of the Americana Music Association and its formal industry chart, belies its rhizomatic origins, even as some strains of the movement protest such consolidation.[32]

As Allen's comment suggests, this is music that strives above all to present a challenging "alternative" to commercial country. In most alt.country discourse, Nashville emerges as the principal Evil Empire, its Music Row conglomerates dismissed as stultifying "labs" or "factories" producing formulaic "ear candy" for the masses. Anti-Nashville songs practically constitute a subgenre of their own: Jason and the Scorchers' "Greetings from Nashville" (1983), Dale Watson's "Nashville Rash" (1995), Robbie Fulks's "Fuck This Town" (1997), and Heather Myles's "Nashville's Gone Hollywood" (2002), among others, validate artistic authenticity by choosing aesthetic quality and purity over popular taste and commercial success. Bemoaning "I'm too country now for country, just like Johnny Cash," Watson warns that the industry's "rash" of crossover pandering will "be the death of us," while Fulks more directly scorns its "moron market."[33] Such denouncements of Music Row hardly constitute a novel critique, as this study and many others have shown. Country's increasing derustification has proven to be the driving concern within the music itself over the past half century. Ever since smoother vocalists began occupying the Opry stage alongside "old-time" singers and the Nashville Sound replaced fiddles with violins, pop music's infiltration of traditional country has caused endless consternation among (a segment of) critics, performers, and listeners. And predictably, this latest installment of the "crisis" continues to operate with a gendered model of "hard" vs. "soft" country, arguing that mainstream or "Hot New Country" brought the 1990s radio scene to the same nadir as that of the late '70s: Garth Brooks and Shania Twain have become just as vilified as the earlier Crystal Gayle or Olivia Newton-John for catering to a fan base of "suburban moms."[34]

However, alt.country's punk origins and influences have also transformed the *tenor* of the critique, lending it a much more vociferous, acrimonious, and in some cases anarchistic air. Much of this edginess can be traced to the work of Bloodshot Records, founded in 1993 to produce and promote "Insurgent Country." Its product catalogs boast a Bolshevik-like bravado: "If you're new to the cause, pull up a chair and listen as we rail against the industry big boys and their ploys to cram worthless musical swill down the throats of a trusting, ill-informed populace"; "With your help, we can continue to churn out our CD and vinyl manifestos and slowly end the scourges of line-dancing, smoke machines, and 7th generation Nirvana rip-offs singing earnest professions of emptiness. . . . Help us keep our steel-toed workboots firmly on the throats of the rhinestone-encrusted enemies."[35] Early Bloodshot owner Eric Babcock emphasized the necessity of remaining on the cultural fringe. Calling his label "a reaction to the bastardization of country music by Nashville," he noted, "There's been a lot of talk—is this [alt.country] the next big thing? . . . It could be . . . but my gut feeling is that if it ever breaks out anything like the level of a Green Day [a contemporary punk band] . . . it will . . . [have] gone further away from us towards mass acceptance."[36] Other independent labels may offer less rancorous rhetoric, but they echo Babcock's sentiment about the dangers of being co-opted by hegemonic forces. Little Dog Records, for instance, entices fans by arguing that it has "been able to sign and develop the most creative artists, unfettered by the pressures faced by the majors," and adds, "we live by the adage that music is forever, so there's no room for mediocrity; it better be great!"[37] Jay Farrar, frequently deemed the cofounder of alt.country due to his work with the now-defunct but influential band Uncle Tupelo, resorted to creating his own record company, ActResistRecords, to ensure his artistic integrity and sustain an uncompromised solo career. (The insert material for his 2003 album *Terroir Blues* features a photo of the makeshift recording "studio" inside his home.)

The more politically progressive elements of this anticorporate posturing assert solidarity with an "authentic" working-class subjectivity. In commenting on the term *alt.country,* for example, *No Depression* editors Grant Alden and Peter Blackstock state outrightly, "To the mainstream music industry . . . it became code for 'doesn't sell'; to fans, it came to describe a network of hardworking bands that fused punk rock's DIY spirit to country music's working-class honesty."[38] Yet the music's claims to aesthetic integrity also rely on a discourse of cultural capital—what Barbara Ching and I call "alt.cosmopolitanism"—linking its "true art" to an urban audience with sophisticated tastes.[39] Its cultivation of "distinction," or what Richard Peterson and Roger Kern more broadly deem "discriminating omnivorousness," emphasizes a highbrow sensibility in spite of its ostensibly lowbrow cultural referent: that exclusive sense of aesthetic appreciation underlying other revivalist and alternative music movements.[40] As Mark Fenster pertinently notes of Buck Owens's attempt in the mid-1960s to distinguish himself as a "real" country music artist in opposition to the emerging Nashville Sound, "within the discourse that constructs a figure like that . . . as creating a flow of unmediated, creative and distinct communication between himself and his audience, . . . the status of his music as a commodity, dependent upon economic and communicative systems, is elided, left behind in claims of art and/or popularity."[41] And many alt.country artists enjoy underscoring the literary quality of their music in terms of both influence and aestheticism, leading *Vanity Fair* in 2006 to define alt.country as "cerebral, devoid of anything hick."[42]

To be sure, other performers included on the alt.country roster aren't quite so loathe to abandon the margins for a broader audience. One thinks of the band Wilco, fronted by Farrar's former Uncle Tupelo partner, Jeff Tweedy, which achieved star status on college radio and whose music has now been absorbed by the mainstream—part of the sound mix circulating in "Big Box" stores such as Target—despite having its highly acclaimed album *Yankee Hotel Foxtrot* eventually rejected by its big-budget label Reprise (AOL Time Warner). Or Ryan Adams, whose early stint with foundational alt.country band Whiskeytown catapulted him to stardom but who parlayed his solo venture into that most lucrative and telling mark of mainstream appeal, the Gap ad.[43] Even Robbie Fulks briefly moved on to Geffen Records before settling back in at Bloodshot (and now recording with another fringe label, Yep Roc Records). Still, nearly all performers in this genre cite the same three or four male names as musical heroes in the country pantheon: Hank Williams, Johnny Cash, Buck Owens, and Merle Haggard (with Gram Parsons, one clear predecessor in the not-too-distant past, often thrown in for good measure). While Nashville's Country Music Hall of Fame indulges in its own form of veneration, constructing a historical narrative in its core exhibition to preserve the reputation of now-faded stars, alt.country highlights such artists' marginal status on current country radio and pays tribute to both their "raw" sound *and* the "tortured," "twisted" nature of their personal lives.[44]

Not surprisingly, then, Hank Williams serves as a particular touchstone for this movement. Jon Langford, founder of British agit-punk band the Mekons and one-time frontman for the Waco Brothers, complains about the Williams "blackout" on mainstream radio by sneering, "Is he not pretty enough?" He continues, "There seems to be a well-conditioned aversion in this country to listening to someone who lays out unsentimental, naked feeling the way he did."[45] Killbillies' Angry Johnny similarly believes that "country punk" musicians are "the rightful heirs to Hank's throne. . . . This is what Hank would be doing now if he had a little bit more electricity at his disposal."[46] Volume 2 of the Bloodshot compilation *Hell-Bent: Insurgent Country* features Langford's original cover art of an angry Williams, slain with arrows, in classic martyr pose, and the album's liner notes amplify this image by serving as a manifesto for the radical arm of this music:

> We come to exhume Hank, not to canonize him. Unbury him not from the ground in which he achieves his final elusive rest, but from beneath the mounds of gutless swill which pass for his legacy. . . . Exposed to the air, ol' Hank could properly decompose and begin to act as fertilizer to his spiritual spawn, his dust scattering and regerminating in new mutations.[47]

Hank Shot Through with Arrows. Painting by Jon Langford, published as CD cover art for *Hell-Bent: Insurgent Country Vol. II.* (Courtesy of Jon Langford and Bloodshot Records.)

Protests to the contrary, however, alt.country most certainly does "canonize" Hank, along with later maverick male artists who established an "insurgent" legacy within country music. As a result, it produces its own selective counter-tradition. Shooter Jennings' anthem "Put the O Back in Country," which serves as one recent and highly disturbing example of this stance, receives the imprimatur of George Jones, whose initial voice-over proclaims that he's offering Shooter his assistance to "put the O back."[48] Thus, the *musical* legacy of such icons can be heard clearly enough in songs that faithfully reproduce the sounds of earlier eras, as in Robbie Fulks' clever yet heartfelt paean to Buck Owens, "The Buck Starts Here," or BR5-49's cover of Webb Pierce's "I Ain't Never."[49] It also reverberates in the more contemporary effect of Jason and the Scorchers' "Drugstore Truck Drivin' Man," Jay Farrar's *Sebastopol,* or Hank III's punk-infused "Blue Devil."[50] But to my mind, the most significant dimension of this "twang revolution" is its construction of authenticity as a classed and gendered *lifestyle* marked by danger, violence, and volatile emotion that is subsequently marketed to upscale consumers.[51] If many of these performers are engaged in the act of "exhumation," what exactly is being unearthed and reincarnated?

"Risin' Outlaws"

The movement's punk roots, as hinted earlier, have certainly shaped its predilections, imagery, and outlook, forcing it to reconcile with country's "lost" heroes along highly particular lines. Dallas Clemmons has suggested (in a rather reductive formulation) that though punk essentially sought to "shatter traditions" and country is a music "steeped in tradition," the two share "common themes" of "alienation and self-destruction."[52] Angry Johnny of the Killbillies emerged as one early and confrontational example of those intersecting impulses. Announcing that he was returning country to its "'dangerous' roots," his band's *Hankenstein* (1996), intoxicated as it was with violence, claimed to reach back to staples of country music's "darker" heritage: "'We've got drinkin', bar rooms, cheatin', killin'.'" Clemmons concurred, noting that the album's "ragged cover of 'Frankie and Johnny' . . . serves notice that murder and mayhem . . . are nothing new to country music."[53] The Killbillies' Web site furnishes further evidence for this claim, presenting "Killville, MA" (the band's fictitious "home") as a "twisted universe . . . where it's an eye for an eye, . . . a shotgun blast for a shotgun blast . . . a place where true love's 'bout as common as an honest politician, and thank God almighty, . . . whiskey's served in a bottle not a glass."[54] Langford similarly underscores the comparison, observing that while punk was often seen as the "antithesis" of country, many young punkers listened to Williams and Cash because they recognized a similar "self-destructive streak" in the latter's songs and personas.[55] Hank III certainly serves as testimony to such an unlikely hybrid lineage, a "Risin' Outlaw" for the twenty-first century, as influenced by AC/DC and Black Flag as by his own (in)famous family members.[56]

Alt.country discourse as a whole, however, is rife with similar (and astonishingly repetitive) images, themes, and terminology. Joel Bernstein, for instance, praised Robbie Fulks's early album *Country Love Songs* for music that was "mostly of the dark and twisted classic country sort, where love is a gateway to Hell."[57] Not coincidentally, the folk ballad "Knoxville Girl," recounting a young woman's bloody murder, has undergone a pointed revival in alt.country circles. Gary Louris of the Jayhawks effuses, "It represented the twisted dark country side that belied the whole goofy stupid country stuff you'd often hear. . . . It showed how complex a country song could be."[58] This is, then, a "revolution" seeking at least in part to recover or reinstate a specific tradition within country music culture—one that purports to reveal that culture in all of its genuinely sordid splendor. It departs from prior modern efforts within the industry to reclaim country's roots, such as the aforementioned New Traditionalism, since these tended to focus less on abject themes and more on musical style. This wing of the alternative movement clearly invests country authenticity with particular gendered and racialized class codes that might best be summarized by the title of Johnny Russell's 1973 working-class anthem, "Rednecks, White Socks, and Blue Ribbon Beer." Penned in a decade far removed from the honky-tonk era, the song nevertheless taps into and in some senses reinstates a mythic 1950s subculture of proud white blue-collar masculinity, in which "There Stands the Glass" still plays on a highway tavern's jukebox and the patrons "don't fit in with that white collar crowd / [they're] a little too rowdy and a little too loud."[59] Alt.country discourse often performs a similar conflation, piling up signifiers of an equally obscured "past" to be memorialized and celebrated.

Such representations function as far more than simple portraits of class "realism," as David Cantwell has argued.[60] Popular country performers of both past and present have certainly been cognizant of the music's affiliations with poor rural and working-class people and have long traded on such class-based tropes, but they typically accentuate the respectable rather than the retrograde. It is a fairly short reach back, however, from the 1990s brand of alt. "insurgency" to a strain of music criticism that embraces the dissolute side of country identity. Nick Tosches remains, I would argue, the indisputable leader of this journalistic "rat pack."[61] Originally published in 1977 but reissued in 1996 by Da Capo Press, his book *Country: The Twisted Roots of Rock'N'Roll* is an at times exhilarating yet ultimately patronizing romp through the "darker areas of country music's history." Sporting chapter titles like "Stained Panties and Coarse Metaphors" and "You're Going to Watch Me Kill Her," the book revels in the vulgarity and violence of country's past, committed by both its lesser lights and its bona fide stars and often directed at women. While replete with examples, the book's particular fixation on Jerry Lee Lewis serves as fitting illustration: "Talk about rock-and-roll depravados: Jerry Lee makes them all look like Wayne Newton. Talk about honky-tonk heroes: Next to Jerry Lee, they're a bunch of frat-party pukers. . . . Jerry Lee can out-drink, out-dope, out-fight, out-cuss, out-shoot, and out-fuck any man alive. He is the last American wild man, *homo agrestis americanus ultimus.*" Tosches delights in linking Lewis's signature song "Great Balls of Fire" (1957) to mass murderer Charlie Starkweather, who on the day of the record's release "thrashed and skidded through Nebraska and Wyoming murdering and murdering and murdering. How many times did Starkweather gnash and grin with sexy delight as 'Great Balls of Fire' crackled through his radio."[62] Reading Tosches's prose, one can easily identify the model for Bloodshot Records' own bluster. (In fact, one Bloodshot act, the Starkweathers, is named after his bloodthirsty hero, and in its at once poignant and condescending ode to "Little White Trash Boy," the band betrays a similar lingering fascination with this culture's low-rent tragedies.[63])

Tamer examples of this tendency can be found in more recent country music commentary. Nicholas Dawidoff seeks to recapture the "Spirit of Jimmie Rodgers" in the country scene and, after reviewing the personal demons of "real" stars such as Johnny Cash, Bill Monroe, and George Jones, finds its promise in alt.country. Dawidoff dismisses 1990s Top 40 country for its artifice and commercialism (embodied once again by Garth Brooks), and like Tosches, though perhaps less cynically, he measures authenticity in terms of hell-raising behavior both on and off stage: "When Ira Louvin destroyed his mandolin or Johnny Cash kicked out the footlights at The Grand Ole Opry, it was no contrived bad-boy rock act, but spasms of misery from men whose music also suggested their tortured souls. Brooks is a pop star masquerading as a country singer, a yuppie with a lariat."[64]

Such fixations on the raw and profane in rural culture of the past—transmuted into certain celebrity lifestyles and decaying industrial locales of the present—suggest an all-too-familiar slumming when they are perpetuated by nonmembers of that culture. Borrowing Dawidoff's own language, I contend that a "bad-boy" posture indeed characterizes the alt.country movement. *No Depression*'s early coverage of the Bottle Rockets certainly highlights such a pose, as writer Jeff Copetas exults in the fact that the band members seem like veritable "dirty white boys"—the kind to drink cheap beer, drive a truck, and run a gas station.[65] He thrillingly describes their album *The Brooklyn Side* as "a country-rockabilly trip through white-trash America—trailer parks, beat-up cars, cops, couch potatoes."[66] The occasional blatant misogyny found in Tosches's work has been tempered, and many more women performers are getting their due, but as Shooter Jennings and others illustrate, this can still resemble a club where Gen-X males, adopting names like "The Inbreds," play at being "good ole boys."

Some acts take a more obvious tongue-in-cheek approach to white trash chic. Early "newgrass" group One Riot One Ranger described one band member as "rising from humble beginnings, forced to eat little but rocks and dirt," another as the "love child of Hank Williams Jr. and Tammy Faye Bakker."[67] In a similar vein, Bloodshot Records promoted The Handsome Family's *Milk and Scissors* by crowing, "Blacker than Johnny Cash's wardrobe, scarier than George Jones on a pill freakout, and as cheerful as Flannery O'Conner [*sic*] and William Faulkner playing gin rummy. Hide the knives and listen."[68] North Carolina's Southern Culture on the Skids, more reminiscent of the campy B-52s, celebrates the excess of a specific class locale with songs like "Daddy Was a Preacher but Mama Was a Go-Go Girl" and "Biscuit Eater."[69] The self-conscious performativity of these latter examples was taken to the extreme by "Unknown Hinson," the redneck caricature created in the mid-1990s by session musician Danny Baker. With blacked-out teeth and "backwoods drawl," Hinson aped a "jailbird wife-beater with a six-gun and a quick temper," singing lines like "Wear somethin' sexy if yer gonna talk." Baker said of his persona, "It hits home, but how can you take this moron seriously? . . . He's a cartoon, but he's the last one to know it. The joke is always on him."[70]

The Drive-By Truckers: Remapping the "Southern Thing"

Like Michelle Shocked, the Drive-By Truckers are all too aware of the "joke" on Southern culture epitomized by such masquerade. They have devoted their last eight albums to its examination and, through their reincarnation of "three-guitar" Southern rock, finally put it to raucous rest. Alternately defying and embodying male alt.country acts, they demonstrate the genre's oppositional potential when it is produced by those who consider themselves "survivals" of a working-class community and culture facing extinction in a post-NAFTA climate. Granted, they express nostalgia for "big, dumb" Southern rock, not country per se—and, accordingly, for the 1970s of their own adolescence, not the 1950s of their parents' youth.[71] But their music for the most part constitutes an admirably clear-eyed reminiscence of the past, aiming to demystify what *Southern Rock Opera* calls the "duality of the southern thing": uncomfortable truths about the entanglements of class, gender, and race in post—civil rights Southern identity. Founding band member and prolific song/storywriter Patterson Hood admits to an earlier shame over his perceived "redneck" roots, reflected in his exodus from northern Alabama and preference for intellectual punk rock rather than country (or for the iconic music of his locale and generation, Lynyrd Skynyrd). Critiquing white liberal elitism, he scoffs in "The Southern Thing," "You think I'm dumb, maybe not too bright / You wonder how I sleep at night," yet he clearly felt the sting of such representations in his youth.[72] His discovery of traditional country music came later, after a move to Athens, Georgia, in his early thirties, when he discovered a community "really hard-core into Loretta Lynn and old country stuff. . . . It was almost like I had an epiphany from it. I'd had a great-uncle who was always watching 'Hee-Haw.' I didn't want to watch 'Hee-Haw.'"[73] Hood also returned to the hard rock/metal bands of his youth—Molly Hatchet, 38 Special, AC/DC—to which he pays tribute in "Let There Be Rock."

The resultant mix at times reinscribes the gender, if not class, politics of other alt.country male performers who regret *never* watching *Hee-Haw* and are making up for it now. Exhorting listeners to "TURN IT UP LOUD!" the Truckers play amped-up music equally "hard" and bigger than life as that of the original honky-tonkers (as well as any generic garage band), similarly utilizing electric guitar *and* voice to unleash pent-up emotion. Patterson Hood rivals Hank III in evoking Hank Sr.'s plaintive whine—both Alabamian storytellers who connect with their audiences through their distinctive vocals—but the Truckers' lead singer amplifies such lines of connection by marrying the 1950s lineage to 1970s stadium rock 'n' roll. Additionally, however, the band's very name and early album title, *Gangstabilly,* suggest a third point of reference, not only drawing on rap and hip-hop music's sonically and thematically *gendered* markings but recalling country music's earlier class-based claims of identification with African American culture. The "Drive-By" modifier accentuates the band's male "outlaw" positionality, particularly underscored in its 2004 album *The Dirty South*, while simultaneously reconstructing the legacy established by the Waylon Jennings brand of country desperados in the 1970s. Though this gesture can be seen to suffer from the same romanticist tendencies plaguing similar acts of racial appropriation—be they contemporary white suburban teenage boys miming rap artists' dress, speech, and mannerisms or, perhaps more to the point here, barn dance minstrel performers' excessive mode of masquerade—its potentially racist *and* masculinist effects are at least somewhat tempered by the music's self-conscious deployment of such tropes for politicized commentary.

As with both honky-tonk and more recent hip-hop cultures, women in the Drive-By Truckers' universe initially appear a nagging avatar of reality to be escaped via the road and bottle or replaced by a temporary "angel"/groupie. Album cover illustrations by Wes Freed call further attention to such clichéd framing, creating a kind of gothic trucker art featuring cars, guitars, and busty women. Yet when examined more closely, the songs and their packaging demonstrate that these musician-writers are alternately indulging *and* critiquing their texts' adolescent male leanings. Reminiscent of honky-tonk's dichotomous split between the "night life" partier and the emotionally devastated loner, their narrators ultimately reveal individual weaknesses and longings—the underside to "gangstabilly" affectation. Attempting to blunt criticism of the albums' cover art, Hood could be offering broader commentary on their music as a whole when he admits: "I know a lot of people had real problems with the artwork, . . . but, to me, that was the kid in those songs. That was Cooley [band member/guitarist/songwriter Mike Cooley] at 12, and that was the kinda kid who wanted to be Steve McQueen. He's leaning up against a shitty old car that he really wishes was a muscle car, and the girl ain't too hot, but she's warm, and it's someone else. All that rang true to me."[74]

While *Southern Rock Opera* explores young blue-collar Southern masculinity in the 1970s, *Decoration Day* (2003) offers a brilliant study of its present formation, outlining the costs of such posturing. "Marry Me" cautions, "Rock'n'roll means well, / but it can't help telling young boys lies"—especially those with little else to fuel their dreams.[75] This is Springsteen territory, as several critics have recognized, but the Truckers, with their Southern spin, take a particularly brutal look at this population's vulnerability.[76] The venerable excitement of rock performance eulogized in the prior album becomes, on *Decoration Day,* a numbing grind. "Hell No, I Ain't Happy" and "Marry Me" document the emotional hazards of life on the road and serve as pleas for a meaningful alternative. "Heathens" still clings to boyish rebellion, exulting in being an outsider and living life to the "fullest" without answering to anyone—"She ain't revved till the rods are thrown." At the same time, this song's narrator admits to some culpability in "the dangers I pose to myself."[77] "Sounds Better in the Song," written and performed by Mike Cooley, mourns one such danger, the loss of a lover tired of waiting for her aspiring rock star to come home. The stubbornness of "Heathens" resurfaces here in a famous line from Skynyrd's classic anthem "Freebird," only to be exposed as self-defeating bluster: "And 'Lord knows, I can't change,' / Sounds better in the song / than it does with hell to pay." Many of *Decoration Day*'s songs demonstrate that the band can genuinely extend its gaze and empathy directly to women, especially its final tune. "Loaded Gun in the Closet" is a devastating portrait of working-class marriage wherein the balance of power is maintained by a well-placed, and as yet unused, weapon. The wife's daily deprivations are certainly recognized and cataloged, yet the song's chilling closing lines perform perhaps the greatest critical work on the album as a whole: "But she's got a loaded gun in the closet / And it's there anytime she wants it / And her one and only man knows it and / that's why he put it there in the first place."[78]

This nuanced depiction of the everyday tragedies befalling men, women, and children in economically depressed communities suffuses the band's follow-up effort, *The Dirty South,* which juxtaposes two Southern "outlaw" sensibilities: the folkloric romance of the so-called Redneck Mafia recounted in films such as *Walking Tall* (1973) and the quiet desperation of laid-off workers turned small-time drug dealers and thieves.[79] "Puttin' People on the Moon" sketches out the tale of those suffering not only from escalating cancer rates but from what Patterson Hood calls "rocket envy"—"a non-diagnosable psychosis" affecting those who live in proximity to the NASA Space and Rocket Center in Huntsville, Alabama.[80] Its narrator, previously employed at the Ford auto plant, resorts to "runnin' numbers" and peddling "a little blow" during the Reagan years to support his family, yet it is his wife's death from cancer that seals his bitterness. Working at the Wal-Mart, he muses, "I wish I'z still an outlaw, was a better way of life."[81] The cycle of songs detailing the myth of Sheriff Buford Pusser confirms this supposition by instilling a bit more glamour into the outlaw archetype. The bootleggers battling Pusser get their due here, one boasting, "I put more lawmen in the ground than Alabama put cottonseed" ("Cottonseed"), another snarling, "don't piss off the Boys from Alabama / Better take it like a man" ("Boys from Alabama"). Yet their more recent counterparts contemplate suicide ("Lookout Mountain") and find themselves back at the bar "waking up" from their dreams and hoping to "kill the goddamn lonely, goddamn lonely love" ("Goddamn Lonely Love").[82]

Though their music is often unabashedly autobiographical, the Drive-By Truckers don't stake claims in most forms of authenticity, except perhaps two: that borne of tremendously hard work and that rooted in "a very strong sense of place."[83] Their songs clearly seek to understand the relationship between class marginality and abjection at a specific time and in a specific location. Mindful of the Southern poor and working class's seeming obsolescence in a late capitalist economy, they represent their music's "lost" boys as survivals of a residual culture; like their honky-tonk predecessors, they attempt to ensure the very visibility of their vanishing communities. But unlike many of their alt.country cohorts, they don't go so far as to naturalize class identity—they know the dangers of careless class marking all too well. Their work challenges the logic that reads white trash culture (the accent, the musical preferences, the racism) along such lines. In other hands, a song like "Deeper In," about consensual brother/sister incest, or "Decoration Day," narrating a long-standing hillbilly "feud" between rival families, might serve as comic or exotic fodder. Situated among the band's other narratives, however, both songs merely extend the possibilities of class representation. Even their early manifesto "The Southern Thing" attempts to establish contemporary affinities between Southern African Americans and whites while also acknowledging the viewpoint of those infatuated with "guts and glory and Rebel stands," declaring that "to the fucking rich man, all poor people look the same."[84]

I thus agree with critic Adrien Begrand that the band excels at "telling a simple, straightforward, from-the-gut story . . . with no hint of irony, satire, or oblique hipster blathering that masquerades as profound poetry," but argue that such an approach shouldn't translate into another version of David Cantwell's "realism."[85] With few exceptions, the Truckers resist the reification of authentic class identity. In doing so, they offer another model of negotiating earlier country music performative traditions prized by contemporary alt.country enthusiasts. Many male artists prefer adopting the honky-tonk pose to fashion their own stage personas but actually *write about* the contemporary equivalents of the hillbilly. That is to say, they themselves borrow the trappings of those earlier hard-living messengers of primitive emotion yet produce musical texts rife with comic rube imagery.

But aside from those acts that deliberately aim to function as little more than "white-trash slideshows" reducing "working people to big-haired caricatures with funny names,"[86] these performers might exploit their white trash representations in order to distance themselves from, rather than embrace, the abjection they appear to seek in their "bad boy" guises. Alt.country's rhetoric of distinction and irony depends on this disconnect, converting its middle-class listeners' tenuous identification into aestheticized consumption. The Drive-By Truckers take another route in their exposé of the diminished dreams available to Birmingham's working-class males. They exchange one kind of marginality for another infused with ostensible glamour rather than shame—the masculine version, oddly enough, of Dolly Parton's brand of performativity—all the while understanding the futility of this maneuver.

III. ALT.COUNTRY WOMEN'S PERFORMANCE OF THE PAST

Despite alt.country's androcentric tendencies, one can look rather fruitlessly for feminist critical interventions. Cheryl Cline, self-proclaimed "editrix" of the webzine *Twangin'!*, launched her own not-so-quiet war on this music's masculinist parameters and practices a decade ago when she introduced her spinoff 'zine *Country Grrl*, yet few appear to have joined her at the barricades. Cline turned the tables on the alt.country movement by casting its various impresarios as the new industry "big boys'" (a favored Bloodshot epithet) suppressing women artists even more effectively than their Music Row counterparts. Scrutinizing pertinent Internet mailing lists, as well as radio and magazine music charts, Cline noted that "women in country music outside the mainstream are shot by both sides. They're ignored by the alternative country scene because they're women. They're ignored by the grrl and women's music movements because they're country." She envisioned *Country Grrl* as not simply a showcase for previously "invisible" female musicians but "a place to air out stuffy old assumptions about women, men, and country music, to ask pointed questions and get some real answers or else; to shine a light on discrimination and sexism, and to generally rile up things that are past due for a good riling."[87] Since then, a handful of others have heeded her call. Mary Bufwack and Robert Oermann supplemented their pioneering work *Finding Her Voice: The Saga of Women in Country Music* with a substantial chapter titled "Meeting the Millenium: Female Country Triumphs," which concludes with an enthusiastic if brief overview of numerous female alt.country artists. Barbara Ching explicitly critiqued *No Depression's* "macho nostalgia" in her 2004 essay "Going Back to the Old Mainstream: *No Depression*, Robbie Fulks, and Alt.Country's Muddied Waters,"[88] and, as noted earlier, she and I most recently initiated a broader feminist analysis of the movement in the introductory essay to our coedited volume *Old Roots, New Routes*.

Yet as the Bufwack/Oermann book and much journalistic coverage demonstrate, the critical discourse tends to remain rather celebratory when the focus shifts to alt.country's female proponents, neglecting to consider how women artists often continue to share the movement's problematic assumptions about class authenticity. Women performers' imagined relationship to (various versions of) country music history and tradition greatly dictates their response to the fetishized codes of authenticity established by male artists. Although they certainly represent the entire stylistic spectrum on the alt.country roster, a fair number have gravitated toward a different version of rawness than their male equivalents: "old-time" Appalachian music of country's earliest beginnings. While this stance arguably works as a quasi-feminist intervention into alt.country gender politics in its reclamation of traditional country music historically associated with women, it also at times subscribes to revivalist tendencies grounded in class elitism. As with the men, however, other voices have also emerged to document the "traces" of poor and working-class peoples who have doggedly survived despite their growing obsolescence in the Reagan, Clinton, and Bush years.

This section concentrates on the work of three representative acts: Gillian Welch; Freakwater, fronted by singer-songwriters Catherine Irwin and Janet Bean; and Iris DeMent. All have attracted considerable attention from the alt.country press, as well as earned increasingly mainstream acclaim, though Welch has emerged the most consistent favorite in both arenas. But while each has become associated with the signature sound and spirit of the Carter Family, differences in class identity and stage presence also pose some challenging contrasts. Early in her career, Welch often adopted the most extreme visual masquerade of the four—looking, notes *Washington Post* reviewer Richard Harrington, "as though she'd stepped out of one of Dorothea Lange's Depression-era portraits"—yet is an ex–University of California, Santa Cruz, student hailing from upper-middle-class Hollywood.[89] As one of fourteen children in an Arkansan farming/factory-working family, DeMent sings songs of loss and want that are often genuinely autobiographical and has continued to battle crippling stage fright throughout her career. Of the three, Louisville-based Freakwater retains the most marginal presence in the industry, its members operating on genuine shoestring budgets with tiny independent label Thrilljockey and, as such, bolstering their musicianship with waitressing and house painting. Irwin and Bean typically opt for flannel shirts and jeans while engaging in esoteric banter for their audiences—in keeping with their punk pasts, they might seem most at home with the college radio crowd. All three acts seek to rescue an older, seemingly outmoded *class* sensibility or way of life, embodied in an equally outmoded and *feminized* musical form, from obscurity. As such, each can also be said to be reviving women's longstanding role as folk culture preservationists through their very work as songwriters and performers devoted to the old-time genre and perhaps specifically appropriating the bluegrass genre for women: boldly mingling, in the Carter Family tradition, prewar feminine parlor and mountain stylings with postwar masculine bluegrass reproductions of such stylings. Yet their similarities are not nearly as significant as their differences, as Welch's preoccupation with "Revival" (the title of her first album), DeMent's enactment of "survival," and Freakwater's interrogation of authenticity in any guise expose key fault lines in the "country grrl" contingent.

The Carter Family and Female Folk Song Preservationists

The Carter Family remains one of the most revered acts in country music and also happens to function as one iconic image of alt.country itself: their 1936 song "No Depression in Heaven," covered by Uncle Tupelo with manic intensity in 1990, inspired the title of the first alt.country online discussion group and eventually the journal, which appeared in 1995. The Carters are particularly viewed, however, as the touchstone for a certain musical and cultural era captured in the work of Gillian Welch, Freakwater, and Iris DeMent. Most journalists and popular commentators conjure up a handful of tropes associated with the Carter repertoire, such as "dead baby" songs, rape and murder ballads, or bittersweet laments, to signify the tradition of mountain music preserved by these women artists. However, they fail to sketch out the larger implications of this stylistic influence. Scholars of the music almost always situate the Carter Family within what is now called the "parlor" style of singing characteristic of American rural life from the turn of the century through the 1930s.

That style, as its name suggests, is almost exclusively domestic: the preferred performance space for women with singing talents and yearnings, typically distinguished from the "assembly" tradition featuring male musicians in public settings such as dances.[90] Additionally, both styles took on corresponding class connotations, the former "genteel" and "sentimental," accentuating the individual voice (which led to duets), the latter rough and "scallywaggy," with a more collective or social air. Richard Peterson divides the two, in fact, into the "soft-shell" and "hard-core" stylistic categories he traces throughout the history of country music, noting that the parlor vocal tradition (in its many guises) was marked by more "polished and dignified interpretations of songs rather than . . . the hard-edged outpouring of raw emotion." Music critics such as Tosches who privilege "hard" country hardly mince words when summing up the Carters' contribution to country music history: "Mother Maybelle Carter's influence as a country-music instrumentalist is equal to that of, say, Rudy Vallee."[91]

It might seem odd, then, for the duet harmonizing of cousins Sara and Maybelle Carter, working out of this feminized musical context, to achieve legendary stature within both the mainstream and the alt.country industries. Robert Coltman's groundbreaking early scholarship has helped to illuminate their role in complicating this music's gendered appeal. Citing Maybelle's unique guitar-playing technique along with Sara's distinctive voice, he argues that "the parlor idiom was . . . to be entirely remade by the Carters, who gave it brawn, substance, distinction and a cutting edge." They were "avant garde," inventing a "marriage" of assembly-style "hard instrumental rhythms" and parlor-style singing.[92] The group's literal patriarch and manager, however, also contributed greatly to their success—both then and now, commercial and iconic—by "collecting" and later copyrighting songs from a variety of sources that captured a traditional rural sound. A. P. Carter, in other words, was a master of borrowing heavily from gospel, popular, and cowboy trends to invent "songs that [merely] *seemed* old-fashioned."[93] The Carters thus transformed the parlor genre, reinfusing it with a seemingly more masculine rustic aura, and in doing so also helped produce certain notions of country authenticity perfectly suited to alt.country's later revivalist agenda.

The Carter Family may have made women newly visible as *public* performers and even highlighted those ballads of heartache, desire, and loss that claimed to speak from women's perspectives, but they equally, at the behest of RCA Victor front man Ralph Peer, helped create a culture of nostalgia during America's Depression years. Despite the eventual breakdown of their own family structure after A.P. and Sara's divorce, as well as recordings such as "Single Girl, Married Girl," which chronicle married women's plight, the group continued to represent traditional values: songs such as "Mid the Green Fields of Virginia," "Picture on the Wall," and "You Are My Flower" appeared to sentimentalize, in the words of Bufwack and Oermann, "a time that was fast slipping away as the world rocked through the Jazz Age, plunged into economic chaos, and slid inexorably toward World War II."[94] The Carters' refashioning of old-time musical form was thus offset by the content of their material, whose images of romanticism helped stimulate barn dance and honky-tonk preoccupations with "home" as a feminine space of both family nurturance and folk culture preservation.

The anxiety surrounding such societal transformations also emerged in the efforts of middle-class female ballad collectors in this era (approximately 1910 to 1940), whose work was intimately wedded to the Carters' mission. Such "song catchers" as Dorothy Scarborough, Louise Rand Bascomb, Ethel Park Richardson, and Maude Minnish Sutton sought to champion a distinctly female Appalachian cultural heritage—"all that is native and fine"—in which mothers handed down folk songs to their daughters much as one would a quilt or heirloom.[95] Yet in the process of study and documentation, the preservationists often indulged their own mingled idealism and condescension.

Folklorist and journalist Sutton, for instance, portrays one North Carolinian backwoods mother as "an Italian Madonna with . . . blue-black hair combed smoothly back from her olive brow," whose voice was "like a ring dove." In a newspaper article, however, she retreats from such highbrow aestheticized imagery to create a more naturalized portrait that critiques all that is disturbing about modern American culture: "How I hate to see the stupidly obvious moving picture take the place of this real literature, and jingling syncopated ragtime replace the living wail of these 'lonesome tunes.' Their crudities are as much a part of the folk to whom they belong as the rhododendrons are a part of the mountains."[96] While hardly as transparent and simplistic, alt.country can echo such sentiments in its critique of modern country music generally, as well as in its explicit connection to such ballad collectors in the 2001 film *Songcatcher,* which featured several alt.country women artists—including Gillian Welch and Iris DeMent—in the film and on the soundtrack.[97]

Few of these early twentieth-century folk preservationists could speak from the sobering experience of Emma Bell Miles, the most celebrated female folklorist of her generation. Her 1905 *Spirit of the Mountains* helped launch the genre and anticipated by nearly two decades Cecil Sharp's landmark *English Folk Songs from the Southern Appalachians.* At the age of nineteen, Bell, the daughter of missionaries and a one-time student of the St. Louis School of Art, met and married Tennessee mountain man Frank Miles, and her subsequent battles with searing poverty, endless childbearing, and lingering, untreated illnesses—leading to her death from tuberculosis at the age of thirty-nine—certainly informed her unvarnished study of mountain culture. Miles's language soared when paying tribute to the endurance and wisdom of female elders—"prophetesses . . . [who] . . . are repositories of tribal lore"—yet became unusually grounded when exploring the hardships of daily life, especially as they wracked the female body.[98] Her book's final warning about the "oncoming tide of civilization" bearing down on Appalachia had less to do with Maude Sutton's disdain of "cheap gramophones" than with Miles' prescient understanding of the exploitative modern wage labor taking over the mountains. Most of the other "culture workers" remained tourists in the field, their essential distance from its lifestyle allowing more mythic pronouncements and gestures.[99]

Bluegrass: "Folk Music with Overdrive"

Despite these and other checkered efforts to promote "folk" music as the native solution to modernity's ills, by the 1940s the Carter-style sound and look appeared anachronistic, frozen in time. As this study has charted, "old-time" images of authenticity had been tempered by others such as "Sunbonnet Girl" Linda Parker of the *National Barn Dance,* as well as black and white rube figures. They would not be revived again until the advent of bluegrass— that other predominant musical and vocal style admired by this group of alt.country women artists. Yet bluegrass was and remains, by all accounts, a masculinized folk genre. It reinvents the assembly tradition, joining a "high lonesome" male voice with furiously fast, "aerodynamic" instrumentals.[100] Its keening sound is certainly emotional; however, as Robert Cantwell argues—referencing not only Bill Monroe but, I would wager, Hank Williams—the "singer is as virile and straight as a Douglas fir." In both the past and the present, female vocalists and musicians have largely been dismissed as too frail (or inept) to withstand bluegrass's sheer energy.[101]

However, the music has been deemed distinctly "modern," as well as primitive, for at the same time it can claim a self-conscious referentiality: "Bluegrass seems to be as much *about* music as it *is* a music." Cantwell conceives of bluegrass as "a body of musical resources which Monroe's music had retrieved from obsolescence" and as such argues that it "redesigned" old-time music for "the modern world." Bluegrass thus represents yet another variant of nostalgia production, fashioning "an imagined community ambiguously situated in the 'years ago' and in the emblematic 'hills of old Kentucky'"—an "avenue into the past . . . neither personal nor historical but fabulous." Cantwell envisions this mythology as either curiously benign—a "pure form" of the "American historical imagination"—or a morally superior act of recovery that restores dignity to an entire rural class.[102] Yet as in prior incarnations such as barn dance, as well as later variants such as alt.country, it is clearly energized by, and itself represents, other currents of social power. Furthermore, if in fact "bluegrass *is* the original alt.country," as Steve Earle insists, its own notions of authenticity—like honky-tonk, alt.country's other predominant influence—might find an especially vexed translation in postmodern culture, particularly since performers would seem to have an entirely different arsenal of production techniques at their disposal.[103] Like their male contemporaries, alt.country women artists negotiate quite a complicated relationship to their representations and actual studio productions of an ostensibly more "primitive" historical moment—one that has, in certain socioeconomic contexts, contemporary equivalents.

Time as "Revelator": Dislocation and Memory

Revivalist attempts to replicate an earlier recorded sound are fraught with an array of problems and assumptions. As I will explore momentarily, vintage technology at once allows and precludes authentic representation of the past, whose medium is most principally voice. It seemingly captures the "real" in all of its nuances, preserving the imperfect as well as harmonious. Yet as Cantwell suggests, we inevitably measure the genuineness of that voice according to our own fabricated designs:

> The very devices through which . . . hillbilly musicians chiefly addressed their audiences, the radio and phonograph, inevitably threw a kind of dust over the brightest and most lucid music. . . . By their incapacity to recover the subtler lights of the audial spectrum, the old recording and transmitting devices . . . seemed to shut the speaking or singing voice up into a suitcase. . . . Anyone who will compare the old recordings, or reissues of them, to contemporary musicians playing in the same style . . . will feel the difference at once: the new recordings, though often quaint, are flat and irresolute, shallow and ultimately tedious . . . But the old recordings, like the voice of a sweetheart, wife, or mother to whom the long-distance connection does not quite connect you, seem somehow just out of reach, melancholy, dreamlike, set in the acoustic half-light of another time and place whose veiled image rises to consciousness under the promptings of an old song.[104]

Despite these female performers' varying efforts to "fix" particular moments of history, identifying with a specific locale and subjectivity via a past musical genre, the referent finally eludes—they and their audiences are left with a distinct sense of *dis*connection. At times, as in much of Freakwater's music, such disconnection is precisely the point. Yet in other texts, such disconnection runs the risk of becoming idealized and ultimately reviving that earlier sensibility. Cantwell, for example, struggles to stay in control of his own critical posture in this passage as he revels in the ostensible "dreaminess" of "old recordings," likened to women's voices over the long-distance wire. Similarly, in seeking to reinstate older feminized musical forms, artists like Welch can appear to fetishize precisely their obsolete, irretrievable qualities. Revivalists may want to ensure the renewed presence of an outmoded music or culture, but unlike survivalists, they to some degree relish its impossibility. Obsessed with the notion of dislocation, all of these performers in their self-conscious ruminations on time feature memory as a strategic, if fragile, bridge between the past and the present.

Gillian Welch: Vintage Technology, Vintage Identity

Since her debut in 1996, Welch has achieved enormous critical success, likened by one journalist to a "kind of down-home-storytelling, banjo-wield-ing Jedi."[105] That success has undoubtedly been bolstered by her associations with the Coen brothers' hit film *O Brother, Where Art Thou?*, contributing to its multiplatinum soundtrack, as well as showcasing her acting talents in the film.[106] But Welch works a distinctive power all her own with the acoustic artistic project she has called "American Primitive."[107] Her early Web site bi-ography proclaimed her a "neo-traditionalist" who "draws from early sources of American roots music." Exemplified by the appropriately titled *Revival* (1996) but true enough of her later albums as well, her work evokes "a rustic, rich, and bittersweet past with an austere story-telling honesty" for contem-porary times. In that single sentence, Welch's promotional material proposes a meaningful nexus between the past and the present. But the music as a whole fails to articulate the precise grounds of the connection. Like the quote itself, her songs suggest a continuity of form rather than content: a spare, genuine narrative line. More often, others commenting on her music stress the tim*elessness* of her songs' themes. Richard Harrington, reviewing a 1997 performance, admires the "plaintive minimalism" of her style, recap-turing "the unvarnished imagery and melodic simplicity of country music's roots, when nothing ever seemed wasted—notes, words or emotions." He goes on to note, however, that "her best songs are like thick pieces of moun-tain wood whittled into beautiful decoys, only it's not wood but common-place experience that Welch transforms into something lasting in songs that address such essential concerns as family and community, love and loss, sin and salvation."[108]

Before exploring Welch's musical texts in detail in order to test these claims, I want to examine self-reflexive explanations of her actual sound—how she conceptualizes the production of such "decoys" through voice, in-strumentation, and studio equipment. In published statements, Welch her-self refers less to the Carter Family as her musical forebears than to slightly

Front cover of Gillian Welch's *Revival*. (Courtesy of Gillian Welch and Acony Records.)

later bluegrass brother duos such as the Stanleys and Delmores, particularly the Blue Sky Boys. "I'm a fool for those two part harmonies," she confesses. "I think there are some very interesting and unique sensibilities that are embraced by the Appalachian bluegrass and brother teams. The gritty and abrasive qualities and very intense vocals are what I love."[109] This "grittiness" serves as Welch's ultimate marker of authenticity. As she says of her more recent album, *Soul Journey,* "We wanted this record to be anti-manufactured—it's almost anti-professional, really."[110] Welch is especially fixated on the vocals' "impurity" in these earlier recordings, made possible by the studio's recording equipment: "The Stanley Brothers made two live records on the Rebel label back in the Fifties that corrupted me forever. These records are just the shit! They're singing into these old tube mics, and every time the vocals get loud there's this great distortion which is all part of the sound. If it was too clean it wouldn't be the same."[111] To achieve this effect herself, she and musical partner, guitarist, and background vocalist David Rawlings deliberately recorded some of *Revival*'s songs in lo-fi. In fact, their producer for that first album, T-Bone Burnett, sought out the equipment used by none other than alt.country idol Hank Williams. Welch explains: "We wanted the record to sound real and tough . . . real and small, with everything mashed together and one thing fighting through another. It gives the songs character. Everything was live, nothing was buried, everything was bleeding into everything else and it sounded great."[112] Her "minimalist" aesthetic, in other words, consists of a kind of tonal dissonance that has, it seems, a cultural counterpart in the period itself.

But which period? As a whole, Welch's music approximates this "mashing" and "bleeding" together of styles, genres, and tropes culled from "early" country and folk: 1920s mountain ballads, mid-1950s bluegrass, 1930s gospel; moonshine stillhouses and small-town "barroom girls." As hinted earlier, she celebrates this approach as a form of bricolage, yet in a sense its "American Primitive" label has a different, reifying effect. The distinctive edges dividing decades, years, and historical moments become blurred. In a fairly recognizable gesture—much like previously noted song catchers such as Scarborough and the Library of Congress's more well-known Lomax brothers, Opry founder Hay, and bluegrass "father" Monroe—Welch appropriates what she finds useful for representing the past, which is seemingly more "authentic" because it is "unvarnished," "live," and thus ostensibly "real," yet produced through vintage recording techniques. Interestingly, she insists that her music is "not a throwback" or "a mood thing" at all, arguing, "I didn't set out to recapture . . . [an earlier era]. . . . It's most natural to me. That's what my voice and writing are most suited for." Not a self-conscious performance, imitation, or recovery effort, then, but an unusual, "natural" vehicle for reflecting the *present* world: "To me they're contemporary songs. . . . I just choose to write in a traditional vein."[113] But as her songs demonstrate, Welch has indeed constructed a vintage notion of authentic identity to accompany her older sound. At most, her work functions as an ironic illustration of Raymond Williams' argument that notions of tradition always point to ideological conditions in the present. *Time (the Revelator)* (2000), perhaps her most acclaimed album to date, attempts most dramatically to break out of such constraints, but it too ultimately succumbs to earlier conceptual formulas.

Perhaps more than any other female alt.country artist, Welch gravitates toward "dark" anthems, narratives, and details. Class abjection becomes the principal feature of early twentieth-century rural life recovered in her musical creations. Almost all of *Revival*'s songs tell tales of wrenching poverty, deprivation, and disenfranchisement that result in disconnection or displacement. A few, like "Barroom Girls" and "One More Dollar," glimpse the poignant fates of those who are destined to leave their mountain homes in pursuit of work but are reduced simply to "last night's spangles" or gambling debts. Both options, rigidly gendered, sever their protagonists from their families and, seemingly, their pasts. More frequently, narrators such as "Orphan Girl" and the sharecropper of "Annabelle" have suffered similar fates through no action or fault of their own. Both have lost "ties of kinship" ("Orphan Girl") through the cruel vagaries of a hardscrabble existence: for all of her backbreaking work as a sharecropper, for instance, Annabelle gets a twofold "handful of dust"—a pittance of money and her daughter's death. But both call upon their faith to endure their pain: the former knows that when she's called to "God's table," she'll meet her heavenly and earthly family, "no more an orphan girl." Annabelle matter-of-factly states, "We cannot have all things to please us," relying on her union with Jesus to explain "why."[114] Yet the gospel strains that would seem to conjure a vision of religious community—an old-fashioned evangelist "revival"—in fact underscore a more overwhelming sense of fatalism and alienation.

"Tear My Stillhouse Down" serves as one quintessential example of this dynamic, arguably serving as the set piece for *Revival* as a whole. A rousing number featuring militaristic percussion, the song conveys an old moonshiner's shame over her sinful life. Convinced that her "whiskey machine" serves as Satan's home, she pleads, "when I die tear my stillhouse down."[115] Interestingly, for this narrator, viable codes of class respectability lie not in permanent visible markers, such as a tombstone's gold-plated sign, but in the complete *erasure* of others that had remained only partially hidden: "leave no trace of the hiding place where I made that evil stuff." Producing neither material nor spiritual "profit," her whiskey still is the preeminent sign of low-class Otherness. In the present, however, it is also a striking sign of obsolescence—the nostalgic figuring of an outdated, and now somewhat mystified, rural culture. In attempting to revive this figure into the present, Welch finally values it precisely *for* its archaism: the moonshiner's desire to eradicate the emblem of her shame becomes a vehicle for Welch's seemingly contrary desire to preserve it. The song thus fetishizes not only the narrator's past—represented by the stillhouse—but also the seeming emptiness of her spiritual request to "tear it down." Religion accentuates, rather than combats or relieves, her character's abjection.

Of her five albums, *Time (the Revelator)* is by far the most ambitious (and the first, significantly, produced by Welch and Rawlings on their Acony label). As its title suggests, Welch here becomes much more self-conscious about time's symbolic value and uses, rendering this work a knowing meditation on *musical* history grounded in Smith's and Lomax's folk music anthologies. The "past" that gets refashioned here has its familiar, if disquieting moments of jarring dissonance—references to Elvis, John Henry, and Abraham Lincoln jostle up against Steve Miller lyrics and a "present" of cell phones and MP3s. If anything, this later album is also positively saturated with earlier spiritual or biblical themes reflecting her own alt.utopia: exodus, emancipation, resurrection, and salvation. Yet with *Time,* Welch focuses as never before to plead for a specific form of cultural "revival" located surprisingly not in Mother Maybelle's Appalachian holler but in Graceland, Elvis's own strange version of bricolage. Within this album's own interior narrative, it is 1950s rock 'n' roll that ultimately trumps Lincoln to emerge as the *modern* Great Emancipator.

The album opens with the title track and sets the stage for this text's ensuing exploration of time's "revelatory" power. Though specifically invoking the blues with references to Mississippi John Hurt and Blind Willie Johnson (the term *revelator* itself), as well as snatches of lyrics from Jimmie Rodgers' "California Blues," the song's own arrangement and instrumentation channel a quieter folk tradition.[116] That blending issues one challenge to Welch's audience: Does the amalgam work, or has something been lost over the decades? What is the ground bed of authenticity? Form appears to mirror content, as this tune's narrator warns his lover that he's "not what I'm supposed to be." His dissembling act is vulnerable solely to the scrutiny of time, which will eventually reveal whether he's "a traitor."[117] The rest of the album proposes to answer his query, illustrating just how time both unmasks and understands "the imitator."

"April the 14th—Part I" and its companion text, "Ruination Day—Part 2," serve as *Time's* principal anchors, putting all surrounding songs in conversation with one another. Both, drawing on the early blues and folk catalog of "disaster" songs, compress centuries and decades by orchestrating several cataclysmic events happening on the same date in history—Lincoln's assassination, the *Titanic's* sinking—around the demise of a traveling, two-bit, late twentieth-century band.[118] The song's narrator haunts the "red-eye zone" of urban nightlife, observing the sad travails of a no-name musical act yet still stirred by the mythology of the "rock 'n' roll" life.[119] On "Ruination Day," she resumes her everyday life even as "the iceberg broke / and the Okies fled /

And the Great Emancipator / Took a bullet in the head." The effect is a collapsing of history and a leveling of perspectives: the great and small, high and low, come together to give this narrator's wistfulness a singular poignancy and urgency devoid of irony. *All* of these events become infused with a kind of grandeur and tragedy. The slow melodic cadence of "April the 14th—Part I" is replaced by a harsher, repetitive chant in Part II, lending its multiple instances of "ruination" an even greater sense of fury and power.

Significantly, two other songs are positioned between these companion pieces, serving as a conceptual bridge or key decoding their murkier meanings. The first, "I Want to Sing That Rock and Roll," recorded live at the Ryman Auditorium, eerily re-creates the sound of 1950s and early 1960s folk groups and thus reinscribes Welch's earlier vintage taste. Here, however, the referent point has shifted somewhat to celebrate the introduction of distinctly modern electronic instruments, pointing to a new kind of "salvation" for those longing to be heard above the din: "I want to sing that rock and roll / I want to 'lectrify my soul."[120] This song revives the prior narrator's desire by returning her to popular music's earlier roots. Rock's demise in the prior text here experiences a spiritual rebirth as prior allusions to slavery and emancipation are recast in musical terms, positing a more accessible "glory land" where one can imagine clasping the "savior's hand."

"Elvis Presley Blues," the next track, conjures up just such a deity: another monumental figure who suffered an untimely and unseemly death. This clever elegy manages to both humanize and lionize the first "king" of rock: a naive "country boy that combed his hair / Put on a shirt his mother made / And went on the air"; a gyrating wonder likened to a dancing girl and "Harlem queen"; a force of nature creating a new religion, shaking it like a "holy roller . . . with his soul at stake."[121] Welch ultimately equates Elvis with folk hero John Henry, the mythic slave and railroad worker who used sheer strength of will and body to compete against a steam drill, though his victory culminated in his own premature death. (Henry makes another cameo appearance in the album's epic closing track, this time linked to Johnny Cash.) Together, the two songs put another spin on the "April 14th" mosaic, as ruination now comes to signify the death of a singular artist who set popular music on a whole new course, only to be derailed by others' greed and corruption.

This second pairing of songs also helps amplify the final two selections, "Everything Is Free" and "I Dream a Highway." For Welch, perhaps the most pernicious emblem of postmodern technology is the MP3, which has sounded a unique death knell for the music community. "Freedom" here resonates with a capitalist ethos run amok—the freedom to exploit songwriters' and performers' creativity. She laments that her body of work will be "given away" yet recognizes that she'll continue to make music "even if it doesn't pay." She ends, though, with a warning: "If there's something that you want to hear / You can sing it yourself."[122] *Time* thus resurrects the battle between humans and technology in numerous guises, rooting for those earlier, now-mythic figures (John Henry, Elvis) who reenvisioned, and paid the highest price for, freedom. By the time we reach the fourteen-minute "Highway," it is clear that Welch's music has become the most direct route back to the past she treasures. (She recorded the album in Nashville's famed RCA Studio B, which served as the locus, ironically enough, of the Nashville Sound.[123]) Cash, the King, Gram Parsons, and Emmylou Harris are all paid (oblique) tribute in this poetic paean to country music history, whose concluding stanza points to a period of bleakness, stasis, deprivation: "What will sustain us through the winter? / Where did last year's lessons go? / Walk me out into the rain and snow / I dream a highway back to you."[124] The highway metaphor finally suggests a rather linear notion of time, where music allows us to move both backward and forward, positioning the past so that it mechanistically, if necessarily, informs the present. Welch thus may rely less on literal masquerade as her career has burgeoned, but her music still performs a kind of aesthetic "conjuring" that professes implicit faith in an authentic original. *Time (the Revelator)* functions as its own "anthology" of "vanishing" "sacred texts"; like those by Smith and Lomax that it explicitly references, it aims to "capture a disappearing American tradition and to evangelize on its behalf."[125]

Unlike some male alt.country artists, Welch considers her work absolutely sincere—no irony for this "orphan girl," despite the fact that she downplays the self-consciously scripted elements of her work to offset her ill-fitting class background. Instead, Welch underlines her instinctive pull towards early country material, asserting, "I must have a natural inclination toward the stuff. . . . I guess I had the groundwork—the sponge—to absorb it." Most music critics have agreed, echoing Bill Friskics-Warren's sense that "despite the fact that Welch wasn't raised dirt poor in some East Tennessee hollow, her grasp of the emotional and spiritual reach of old-time country music is undeniable."[126] One former bandmate from her Santa Cruz years put it more bluntly in a recent interview: "'She got a lot of shit when she first started playing, because she wasn't a hillbilly. . . . Like you have to have black lung to write about mining. If she did all the things she writes about, she'd be dead by now."[127]

However, it is not Welch's "grasp" of old-time music that I question but her use of it and, finally, its implications. She is undoubtedly a highly compelling artist and performer, but it is precisely her ease at stepping into this reconstructed world that I find troubling. As will be clear momentarily, when Freakwater takes the stage, the band members almost take pleasure in the disjunction between their late-twentieth-century visual presence and the sound they produce with voice and instrument. They harbor few, if any, illusions about their "natural" relationship to earlier rural culture. And as suggested earlier, the contemporary trappings of their songs usually work to highlight, rather than erase, the nuanced distinctions between a representational past and present. Welch seems unwilling to take this responsibility for the performative elements of her persona, embodied by, but certainly not limited to, her deliberate vintage costuming. Her work at times enacts a disquieting version of what Eric Schocket calls "class transvestism," establishing unwitting links to her male counterparts.[128]

Freakwater: Deforming the Genre

Though their albums have always garnered enthusiastic critical reviews, Freakwater can scarcely claim to be a household name. Like Welch, they have appeared on numerous alt.country compilations and contributed to the soundtrack of a small independent film (*The Slaughter Rule* [2002]), yet they have failed to parlay that exposure into a broader market share for their own artistic efforts.[129] This marginality may be due in part to their exceptionally spare rendering of old-time music (both covers and original tunes), which can seem halting, off-kilter, excessively raw. Some attribute such style to their very earnestness. As music journalist Allison Stewart comments: "Their desire to protect early twentieth-century country and bluegrass tradition . . . is almost palpable. Whatever else Freakwater are, they aren't kidding."[130] It is clear that Catherine Irwin and Janet Bean have methodically researched this most rustic of country music genres, situating their work within its rich, if often underappreciated, history. Yet others protest that the work isn't traditional *enough*. Jon Weisberger's *No Depression* review of *End Time* (1999) rehearses his past objections to Freakwater's approach—"flouting, or at least ignoring, important aspects of the traditions created by Sara and Maybelle Carter and Ira & Charlie Louvin," indicated by "wobbling pitches" and "sloppy . . . timing"—and continues to lament their "distinctive habit . . . of mismatching lyric and melodic phrases."[131] Indeed, they are guilty as charged. Although they might initially be mistaken for a "country music appreciation society,"[132] their prior work with punk bands and evolving maverick vision ensures that Irwin and Bean quite deliberately *deform* the genre of old-time music.

Compared with Welch's oeuvre, their songs seem remarkably fresh and contemporary. Although it is their fellow dedicated revivalist who accentuates her ties to the present in her publicity materials and the Freakwater women who appear to delight in being "stubbornly anachronistic,"[133] it is the latter who most successfully articulate the (tenuous) continuities between the 1920s, 1930s, and the contemporary moment. They accomplish this in part through pairing older musical styles and arrangements with modern references and stories—a tendency that surfaces sporadically in earlier work but takes a stunningly intricate form in both *Springtime* (1997) and the later *End Time*. As the group's chief songwriter, Irwin also amplifies this effect by associating *both* the past and the present with fragmentation, loss, displacement. Equally important, as Weisberger's critique fails to recognize, the songs' very form in fact mirrors the lyrical content: their unique and often "disorienting" time shifts accentuate the sense of dislocation and disjunction.

At first glance, the works on *Springtime* seem to conform to a familiar pattern, a predictable roster of grim mountain tunes awash with sin, whiskey, and, most notably, death. Brought dramatically to life by the ragged vocals of Irwin and Bean and untempered strains of banjo and fiddle, such "Gothic bluegrass numbers" have become Freakwater's "stock in trade,"[134] so much so that more than a few commentators have pointed to the "irony" of the album's optimistic title. Without careful study, their individual songs can seem virtually interchangeable, a simulacrum of early country music. Yet rather than simply imitate various stylistic staples of an old-time repertoire, *Springtime* weaves fragmented narrative lines or themes throughout its various songs. "Heaven" and "Flat Hand" jointly eke out the tale of a woman haunted by her child's death or disappearance, while "Lorraine" and "Louisville Lip" allude to specific incidents of racist violence and oppression. Together, these latter two suggest pronounced links between what would initially appear a distinctive past and a more modern present, connecting a Klan lynching to the "mythic" story involving Louisville local hero Muhammad Ali, who allegedly threw his Olympic gold medal into the Ohio River in protest over a town restaurant that refused to seat him. Other songs incorporate urban or contemporary images, such as the car wreck in "Binding Twine" and the Tilt-a-Whirl in "Slowride," while still others settle for modern terms or words (the Pentagon in "One Big Union" and varieties of 1970s Dodge car names—the "Swinger" and "Dart"—in "Scamp"). Few, if any, of these signs have an obvious function, meaning, or even presence; they surprise and challenge the listener, who must usually piece together errant details to grasp the reference at all. (Perhaps the most "old-fashioned" song on the album is contributed by temporary band member Max Konrad Johnston, who writes and performs the romance ballad "Harlan.")

Encased within distinctly traditional forms, these tropes do more than merely update the convention of old-time music, as Welch's songs often do, comprising a "catalog of universal woes" where one temporal mode of disaster substitutes for another (cf. "April the 14th" Parts I and II).[135] The songs don't entirely erase the differences between earlier and contemporary decades: "Even one big union," Freakwater laments, "can't help us now." Citing old IWW/labor songs and slogans, they cleverly sing, "which side are you on has [now] got more angles than the Pentagon."[136] At the same time, rather than compromising or diluting the kind of rustic authenticity associated with this earlier genre, markers of modernity often only serve to enhance it. *Springtime,* like Freakwater's prior albums, clearly reveres the strength and resourcefulness that often underlie a bleak existence—especially as lived by poor or working-class women. Irwin's and Bean's voices themselves perfectly illustrate this quality (both live and recorded, with or without amplifying equipment) in their stark, roughhewn power. They extend this energy into the present without arguing for an unbroken line or continuum.

Both fragmented and linked together, this song series' structure illustrates its greatest preoccupation: the desires, dangers, and failures of being "bound" to a person, place, or condition through memory. "Twisted Wire," for example, begins with images of fetterment and entanglement as its female narrator contemplates her former lover, whose hands are "bound." The recurring refrain makes such images chillingly concrete as its "silver hoops of silver wire" emerge as "shackles," which in turn become linked with lies. Reinforcing the analogy between handcuffs and false narratives, it concludes, "It's in your hands, but not in mine / Twisting wire / Twisting lies."[137] "Binding Twine" returns to such imagery by initially introducing tropes of *discon*nection: a "tug of war" over the reality of a past relationship.[138] The female speaker, however, remains seduced by the "simple messages" of remembrance and asks her ex-lover to "bind my memories in twine." In both songs, memory becomes just as much a "shackle" as a comfort or release—relentless, it needs to be contained and verified, so that it doesn't evolve into another criminal act of deception.

While *End Time* represents a new kind of artistic venture for this group— tripling the number of participating musicians (including ex–Waco Brothers drummer Steve Goulding), adding both electric and percussive instruments to create a much fuller sound, and showcasing Bean's talents as songwriter as well as vocalist so that she takes credit for fully half of the original compositions on the album—it continues to mine familiar thematic ground. As with Welch's own career progression, Freakwater demonstrates in its most ambitious production to date a near obsession with the workings of time.[139] Richer instrumentation allows for greater experimentation, so that later styles of country music, such as honky-tonk, receive more substantial treatment. Yet this album privileges personal rather than musical history. Here, time typically *fails* to serve as a solemn "revelator" in any sphere, in any capacity. Just as the romanticized highway trope ultimately crystallizes Welch's understanding of the relationship between past and present, *End Time* finally offers its own much more cynical counterpart: the "cheap watch."

Indulging Irwin's penchant for dark puns, the album kicks off with "Good for Nothing," whose narrator announces, "I've been good, and I've been good for nothing."[140] The song as a whole returns to one standard Freakwater emblem: the spring "showers" of its opening line quickly lead to waters that purport to offer baptismal salvation but instead drown those with true self-knowledge (cf. *Springtime*'s "Washed in the Blood"). An endless round of drinks submerges this speaker, whose fate curiously invokes Welch's *Titanic* trope: "many times I've watched my own self drown / Clinging fast to my lucidity / Like a life raft that's slowly sinking down." Like other personas conjured over the course of the album, this one clings fast to her bitter memories of the past, snarling that she'll never "forgive" or "forget." "Cloak of Frogs," a most ironic waltz, revisits such imagery, yet from a different perspective. This narrator turns on her radio to hear a preacher singing "to me, to the fallen": "Take me to the river / Wash me in the water."[141] She is seemingly contrite, rather than rebellious, accepting its address. Unlike Welch's moonshiner, who seeks to erase all outward "trace" of her sin, this speaker understands that such evidence remains at the core of her personhood, a "mess" that she embodies. At most, it can be "mislabeled" in the semblance of being "born again."

Several other songs written and sung by Bean are much more reflective of her own recent personal experience, which included a divorce from long-time partner and collaborator in the band Eleventh Dream Day. "My History" and "Written in Gold" offer yet another perspective, then, on the album's central concern with time. Arranged like a mid-1960s country torch song, the first recounts a woman's decision to break with her "history" of a dying marriage. Rather than celebrate her tenth wedding anniversary, she issues her husband divorce papers, attempting to break with her past passivity. Previously protecting herself from the truth—"waiting for it all to drop like a big new year's ball"—she discovers that such knowledge resonates, rather than "drops" with a singular finality, and that in the end it can still fail to teach us much of anything: "I thought that surely the answers would be revealed / We'd know it'd all been for the better . . . But I'm haunted by these words instead."[142] Similarly, in "Written in Gold," the lasting mark of a now-absent wedding ring illustrates the complex process by which one's personal history stubbornly remains, tattooing the body itself with the memory of marital vows: "Paler skin under a band of gold / . . . Now nail[s] her to the words she swore."[143] The "words" that finally "haunt" both of these female speakers certainly threaten to collapse the past and the present, extinguishing any hope for a new space or identity from which to "begin": "Evermore means something that it never did before."

Yet Irwin's sassy "Cheap Watch" offers another kind of cautionary tale about time's slipperiness, where the danger lies in just such a compression of history. In this saga, distortions of time—a bar sporting yearlong Christmas lights; an unreliable timepiece that, when "wound up," makes the hours "fly"—become equated with distortions of human truths. This narrator refuses to take a passive approach to her failed relationship, her "little white teeth wound around what sounds like more cheap lies," and warns that she's going to reveal the truth. And nothing could be made plainer than her own much more accurate and active accounting of time: "One foot on the gas, two feet from Tennessee / The little hand on the twelve-gauge and the big hand swinging free."[144] Like Bean's rueful heroines, this one momentarily appears to linger over her painful memories as she drinks another beer in that tavern where time appears frozen, but she finally frees herself from its pain.

Freakwater's tenuous membership in the newly chic alt.country "club" thus derives not only from critics' imposition of rigid authenticity standards but from the group's own resistance to any collective ethos—its distaste for "binding twine." Irwin is mystified by bluegrass "purists" like Weisberger, protesting, "We don't claim to be playing bluegrass. . . . Anybody who knows anything about it knows that that's not what we're doing and that we couldn't play true bluegrass music if we tried."[145] Yet she's equally frustrated by other alt.country associates, tongue firmly in cheek, who find them too dour. The band's first stint at the increasingly popular South X Southwest festival to promote *End Time,* for instance, seemed futile: "There doesn't seem to be any point." Concert reviewer and interviewer James Murray comments, "Freakwater know all too well that, in this Society of the Spectacle, only the poseurs taste success and recognition. Those who are real get little or nothing."[146] While his distinction here between the performative and the "real" is far too simplistic, Murray's observation at least recognizes the "spectacular" function of much alt.country, echoed by Bill Friskics-Warren: "In contrast to the trailer-park kitsch of most alt-country bands, Irwin and Bean didn't just woodshed with a clutch of Buck Owens LPs and a Southern Lit reading list and come out making records."[147]

Perhaps most important, Freakwater is all too aware of the performativity inherent not only in such "kitsch" but in country music's entire tradition. In a recent interview with Neil DeMause, Irwin and band bassist David Wayne Gay take on the very notion of authenticity to indict none other than their own musical "ancestors,'" the Carter Family. Irwin begins, "The whole issue of authenticity is really just a music writer's invention to me. I mean, I don't even know what people mean. Do people think that when they hear 'Under My Thumb' or something?" When challenged by Gay, who goads, "You know what it means. Like, Little Richard vs. Pat Boone doing 'Tutti Frutti,'" she notes, "Well, Little Richard wrote that song. But when you hear just a normal person singing a . . . Rolling Stones song, you don't think, 'Did he *really* meet a gin-soaked barroom queen in Memphis?' Is that authentic?"[148] When discussing reception of their own music, she admits, "I feel like we're being accused of something I never even was trying to get away with in the first place. I never pretended that I was riding to Chicago on horseback or something." Gay adds, "Even the Carter Family was part of the folk revival, back when they were doing that, right? They were part of a revival," to which she retorts, "They were part of basically swiping stuff from people who knew less about copyright laws than they did. They were exploiters of the less literate."

As its musical trajectory also attests, Freakwater harbors few illusions about revivalism, rejecting the very idea of a natural or authentic rusticity. Band members' attachment to "dark" material may occasionally flirt with fetishization of abjection itself (a by-product, perhaps, of an earlier punk sensibility), but they don't make the mistake of *conflating* such a condition with a particular musical or cultural heritage. It seems significant that even the band's name, which turns out to be a term for moonshine whiskey, was in Bean and Irwin's initial estimation their own neologism—a "made-up word they considered meaningless."[149] Appropriately, their devotion to originality brings them closest to one of country's earliest versions of authenticity.

Freakwater may offer one of the most intellectual interpretations of the past currently circulating in alt.country performance, but its cerebral approach isn't steeped in the kind of ironized distance characteristic of alt.country as a whole.

Iris DeMent: The Way We Should

At the turn of this new century, Iris DeMent all but disappeared from the alt.country roster. Somewhat reminiscent of Freakwater, this may have been the result of her decline in marketable productivity, recording just one new original album, *Lifeline* (2004), since *The Way I Should* in 1996 (though she continued to serve as a prolific guest artist on other albums). Her controversial decision to end concert appearances to protest the U.S. war in Iraq no doubt also contributed to her seeming vanishing act. Her appeal as an alt.country performer is thus, in the context of this study, both predictable and unique. Her voice has attracted more interest—at times, sheer fascination—than that of almost any other female alt.country artist in this genre. "Part Kitty Wells, part Sarah Carter . . . and part Loretta too," it has been deemed "remarkable," "amazing," a "hillbilly voice . . . the likes of which haven't been heard since the Carter Family, but with the modern passion of an Emmylou Harris."[150] For many, it serves as DeMent's own reigning marker of authenticity, achieved not through the technology of 1950s microphones but through her own "honest" roots in hard-core country culture.[151] Though threatening to become a reified thing of its own in such critical commentary, DeMent's voice eventually gets traced back, through her own songs and research, to her personal life history. Her negotiation of this biographical narrative, marking her genuine ties to a fading cultural rusticity, produces another version of alt.country survivalism.

To begin, DeMent's affinity for earlier strains of country music can be detected in both the form and the content of her songs, but her old-time currency has never been limited to a set of generic rural props and lyrical conventions. She is not drawn to the macabre or gothic as much as to the stark truths of "ordinary" life. Similar to the other female artists under discussion, her music over the course of four albums has become increasingly shot through with modern images and markings. As John Hoppenthaler writes, "The influence of roots legends like the Carter family is obvious, but DeMent has infused into her musical inheritance an urgent sense of what it means to be alive and awake in the contemporary world."[152]

This contemporary gloss is most obvious in *The Way I Should,* which takes on current political problems with much more candor and indignation than any of her prior work. Songs like "There's a Wall in Washington" and "Quality Time" locate DeMent very much in the present as they denounce the fragmentation of contemporary family life: their respective cultural icons, the Vietnam Veterans Memorial and a drive-thru McDonald's, link together misdirected state power and individual solipsism. In the same vein, "Wasteland of the Free" functions as a veritable protest anthem and, as such, is perhaps the most alien to those fans seeking a more purist strain of alt.country, though it showcases her trademark clarity of vision and speech. Attacking corporate lies and excess, the Christian right's hypocrisy, and the Gulf War ("We kill for oil, then we throw a party when we win"), the song sums up her analysis in its blasting chorus: "Living in the wasteland of the free / Where the poor have now become the enemy / Let's blame the troubles on the weak ones / Sounds like some kind of Hitler remedy."[153] Though she has suffered some critique for this new bent, DeMent remains steadfast: "My songs are an outgrowth of . . . where I come from. . . . I heard many stories about hard times and these were part of my life. But now . . . the more I hear and learn about the world and all the injustice that goes on . . . it makes me realize that maybe I should begin writing more and more . . . so that more people understand what we are really facing."[154] Along the way, she has experimented musically as well, offsetting her acoustic arrangements with a more electric sound. In fact, at the end of a particularly raucous duet with Delbert McClinton that closes *The Way I Should,* DeMent declares defiantly, "Now ain't *that* old-timey!"

In some ways, this juxtaposition of past and present clearly recalls Freakwater's approach and performs a similar function. DeMent wants to highlight the struggles of common people and, through her songs' mingling of style and substance, outlines that struggle's history. But she also has a strikingly personal investment in recovering the past. It represents a certain array of "old-fashioned" values that she seeks to reclaim—but not as vintage mementos or kitsch, for which Freakwater's work, at least on surface, can be mistaken. Her songs serve as relics of her own family history, symbols of a class position and lifestyle that, like her family itself, have threatened to become obsolete in the late capitalist era. Earlier songs such as "Our Town" allude to the demise of small working-class communities, urging her neighbors to recognize "the sun settin' down on" their livelihood and common experience.[155] In an interview with *The Progressive Populist,* DeMent comments on the inspiration for her later song "The Way I Should," noting:

I was trying to express . . . that in this world we live in, or at least in America, there's a lot of pressure to work your butt off and get a bunch of stuff. And if you don't have a bunch of stuff, you're not very well thought of here. That's just a fact. I knew when I was a kid, it dawned on me that because we didn't have a bunch of stuff and because my dad was a janitor, I understood how this society was set up, that somehow we were left [behind].[156]

Much of her realist project thus involves sheer documentation of this class-marked condition as it persists into contemporary life, arguing for its validity and ensuring its survival. She expresses the desire to materialize her vanishing world in the sights of a class culture and structure hostile to her own.

And for DeMent, that impulse paradoxically demands that she record the light along with the dark. Her first album, *Infamous Angel* (1993), has been called "a sweet celebration of life—a joyous romp through love, home, and family, and with a sly wink that hinted that she wasn't as innocent as that pure voice might indicate."[157] Though songs like "When Love Was Young" anticipate the striking somberness of her later classic "Easy's Gettin' Harder Every Day," there remains in this signature work the same playful spirit that surfaces in much of her writing as a whole. Surprisingly, this lighthearted characteristic most often marks her gospel tunes. DeMent had an intensely religious upbringing, growing up in the very center of the evangelical church, and though she renounced that church in her adolescence, she has never denied her spiritual curiosity and interests. Her pantheistic outlook is celebrated in "Let the Mystery Be," "The Shores of Jordan," and "Keep Me God," while her most recent album is entirely devoted to traditional spirituals (some dating from the Civil War era) that served as solace, she confesses, in a spate of "hard times."[158] Evocative of Welch's own forays into old-time religious music, DeMent's approach nonetheless results in a more nuanced treatment of country gospel conventions, not quite ironic *or* exoticized—the equal, perhaps, of Shocked's reinvention of minstrel music. She openly wrestles with her questions about traditional Christianity yet is unafraid to claim her faith.

DeMent's purely autobiographical songs about family life, however, seem positively airbrushed at times, potentially compromised for some audiences by their excessive sentimentality. Throughout her oeuvre, "home" is an alternately sacrosanct space, condition, and theory, blurring the spiritual and the domestic, heaven and family. It is the ultimate "Destination" for all "infamous angels" who seek love, forgiveness, and restoration, recalling earlier gendered renditions of "home" in country music that bestow the care of kin, rural community, and folk culture onto women. DeMent's mother undoubtedly plays such a role in her song narratives, whether honored in "Mama's Opry" for introducing her family to music by the Carters and Jimmie Rodgers or appearing as a haunting lead vocalist herself on the song "Higher Ground."[159] When looking outward, DeMent's vision doesn't remain so narrow: she recognizes that for others, home can be a treacherous place of sexual violence ("Letter to Mom") or numbing boredom ("Easy's Gettin' Harder Every Day"), a disappointing space of lapsed love ("You've Done Nothing Wrong") or parental responsibility ("Quality Time").[160] But when DeMent writes about her own private history, she focuses squarely on the ideal—on the redemptive power of community. While her entire second album, pointedly titled *My Life,* serves as an autobiographical text inspired by her father's recent death—replete with home photos of parent and child—it is "Walkin' Home," from *The Way I Should,* that best encapsulates her approach to the familial past. Reprising the quieter, more acoustic sound of DeMent's best-known work, this text features the narrator traveling down familiar roads of her hometown and, via memory, reaching her childhood. Embodied in her mother's voice and her father's presence, it is a place of essential knowledges: "Old worn out couches and a bunch of kids / Four to a bedroom and all mom's plates were chipped / But I never knew about the things I missed."[161] "Home" fundamentally positions this singer-songwriter, anchoring her identity in authentic yet seemingly passé or equally "worn-out" principles— "good or bad, it's where the deal was done." To protect the ground bed of such identity, DeMent perhaps cannot afford to explore what she and her thirteen siblings may, in fact, have "missed"—both emotional and material deprivations.

Overall, however, the tension between place and displacement becomes a central preoccupation of DeMent's work, a complex code for the intertwined past and present. She articulates a dialectical relationship between the two in a 1997 interview with John Hoppenthaler. When he remarks upon the "ghosts" that appear to "haunt" her music—"your dad's, surely, but also the dead of Vietnam, the spirits of childhood memories that rush through the hills of the past"—DeMent responds by tracing a rather dizzying line of connection between father and daughter:

> I grew up in southern California, and my dad had come from this island in Arkansas—actually in the middle of a river that ran between Arkansas and Missouri. The whole time I was growing up, I had this sense of this place where we came from, and my dad really longing for this place and missing it a whole awful lot . . . . While I grew up, I tried to identify and be close to this

person who had this real sense or aura about him of missing something from the past, and so I consequently ended up feeling very connected to this place that I didn't grow up in because of the stories he'd tell. . . . I always had a sense that that place I never saw was my home—that's where I came from. So maybe that's why, in a lot of my songs, I have that sense of being connected to these things that are dead and gone, but they're not dead and gone on the inside of people.[162]

In this recitation, DeMent overcomes her own threatening dislocation from the ancestral homeplace precisely through identifying with her father's loss. His desire for home gets passed down and thus becomes a kind of stand-in for the thing itself. And once again, the past materializes through reminiscence, through persistent memory. As suggested earlier, however, her most self-consciously autobiographical songs resist the implications of this dynamic. "Childhood Memories" seems almost naive in its recollected pleasures of catching fireflies, buying penny candy, "playin' church around the old piano stand." Here, DeMent flatly rejects alt.country's penchant for a distinctly grim bit of Americana. The last stanza reassures that "no matter where I roam" on "life's highway," she can construct her own bridge back to home's pastoral currency through her memories.[163] DeMent's cover of the 1951 Lefty Frizzell tune "Mom and Dad's Waltz" similarly displays her naked sentimentality, confessing she'd "walk for miles" to tell "mama and daddy" of her steadfast love.[164]

These traveling byways undoubtedly recall that other "highway" to history imagined by Gillian Welch. But I would argue that the two operate in overlapping, yet finally quite different spheres. Despite the powerful rusticity of her singing voice, DeMent's notion of a private sincere identity to be recaptured or reclaimed might initially strain credulity for a certain kind of alt.country listener, evoking trite mainstream country more than trendy "twang." Yet her survivalist vision of family and class community has the potential to function as a nascent resistance strategy. Her music instructs us in an "alternative" use for alt.country nostalgia—not simply rewriting, inventing, or appropriating the past but, as is earlier suggested about seemingly "extinct" class populations and cultures, salvaging outmoded traits to remain visible in the present.[165] This practice entails not so much Welch's fascination with the past as an inherent understanding of its value—a familiarity with that "throwaway" culture's habitus and will to survive but also its capacity to be equally erased *and* "revived" through varieties of exploitation. DeMent, along with alt. artists such as the Drive-By Truckers, Michelle Shocked, or even relative newcomer James McMurtry in his anthem of working-class rage, "We Can't Make it Here," grasps that those deemed obsolete are in fact "indispensable to" contemporary power relations.[166] Welch's brand of revivalism finally becomes an inadvertent illustration of just such a dynamic, reproducing alt.country's troubling class politics even as her work as a whole attempts to flout the genre's conservative gendered conventions.

IV. CONCLUSION: THE COUNTRY AND THE CITY REDUX

Richard Peterson has suggested that even in the early decades of the twentieth century, working-class audiences "quickly tired" of old-time country music performers (such as Fiddlin' John Carson and WLS's Bradley Kincaid), but "middle-class anti-modernists," from corporate titan Henry Ford to amateur song collector Jean Thomas, "tried to perpetuate that old-timer image as part of their own ideological agendas."[167] Seventy years later, the alt.country movement has inadvertently revived this phenomenon. The professed antithesis of late capitalist ideology and practice, it nevertheless often similarly positions both traditional and mainstream country as the "rearguard to their avant-garde."[168] That early class divide in audience taste has also reemerged, ringing another change on Raymond Williams' country-city dialectic. Several performers have in fact explicitly commented on an urban/rural divide in country music preference and accessibility. Gillian Welch, for instance, notes that "in the Seventies, it was hard to find records by The Carter Family and The Blue Sky Boys in a little town in Virginia. In Los Angeles, it was no problem at all. You get a lot of people out of the bigger cities playing the music. Folks in North Carolina grew up with access only to Top 40 music."[169] Hank III still encounters such a split, admitting: "I'm sick of headlining these little redneck, honky tonk dives where they play disco music before you go on and you have to put up with people who don't even like country music. . . . The best place for us to play is in the cities. No one seems to want to hear country music out in the country, but in the city, people are starved for it."[170] Patterson Hood echoes Hank's lament when he tells an interviewer, "The South has been the toughest region for us to break."[171] As Williams cautioned, the "idea of rural community" is almost always more serviceable than the thing itself.

But despite Hood's comment, the Drive-By Truckers' music comes closest, I think, to grasping the utter complexity of Southern and/or rural audience's responses to their own representation in the American popular imagination. *Southern Rock Opera, Decoration Day,* and *The Dirty South* cannot help but critique the alt.country allegiance to authenticity when they reveal *everyone's* continuing investments in the privileges of modernity—and illustrate how such privileges remain marked by middle-class forms of whiteness and masculinity. Revealing what is at stake in the distinction between "revival" and "survival," Hood's band joins what is perhaps an unlikely alliance with alt.country artists like DeMent and Freakwater, yet it demonstrates the necessity of getting beyond what are by now well-worn conceptual paths singularly tracking gender, race, and class in order to achieve a truly useful understanding of the relationship among country music's past, present, and future.

Country Girls, "Unglamorous" Mothers, and Redneck Women: The Refeminization of Authenticity in Recent Mainstream Country

Staking out an alternative history of country music focused on racialized and gendered representations of country authenticity, this study in its opening pages traces a compressed arc of images: from the Grand Ole Opry's explicit and now execrable mode of blackface and hillbilly performance in 1950, to Faith Hill's more palatable, yet equally mannered version of rustic masquerade in 2005. The improbable entrée of Rissi Palmer to mainstream country radio in 2007—the first African American female artist to break *Billboard's* Hot Country chart since the late 1980s—poses a further dilemma for such inquiry. At first glance, the singer-songwriter's debut single "Country Girl" serves as a welcome rejoinder to earlier models of authenticity—the counter to calculated simulations of both "black" and "white" country identity. Yet upon closer inspection, Palmer's popular anthem proves a suitable successor to a line of comparable songs, from Ernest Tubb's "Mississippi Gal" to Hill's "Mississippi Girl." This closing look at the current terrain of country music authenticity considers Palmer alongside another unlikely newcomer to Top 40 country, alt.country/folk artist Lori McKenna, and concludes with a nod to mainstream "Outlaw" Gretchen Wilson to highlight new (as well as persistent) challenges facing country iconography.

"Country Girl" boldly asserts a definition of country grounded in attitude and mores rather than geography, socioeconomic status, race, or cultural lineage. Matched by soul-infused vocals and instrumentation, the lyrics insist that country is primarily "a state of mind no matter where you're from"; its infectious chorus chants, "you don't have to be a Georgia Peach from Savannah Beach to / show the world you're a country girl."[1] Jettisoning traditional authenticity markers such as regional accent and Southern "kin," Palmer claims country music for a young woman-of-color born in Pittsburgh and raised in the exurbs of St. Louis.[2] Nevertheless, the song's address to a distinctly gendered audience reverts to the most conventional ideologies of white country femininity to articulate its unorthodox message. This breakout performer may resist the need to showcase rural roots to bolster her authenticity credentials, but like so many women artists examined earlier, she succumbs to country's long-standing narrative of domesticity to establish her legitimacy.

Palmer engages in her own revivalist project by celebrating feminine virtue: the heralded foundation of rural folk culture perceived in the early *twenty-first* century to be another lost "art" in need of preservation. She advocates "pride" in the strong moral upbringing exemplified by family matriarchs; her country "state of mind" is equivalent to "living like your grandma done." Whether signified by Sunday gospel services or a "sweet as molasses down home style," this identity hearkens back to earlier portraits of the "sentimental mother" or country sweetheart first popularized in barn dance programming and whose obsolescence was subsequently mourned in so many postwar honky-tonk songs. Addressing her female listeners as "ladies," Palmer beckons those who subscribe to such roles, no matter their skin color or birth place, to recognize and "show" themselves as "country girls" (Cheryl Cline's "country *grrls*" need not apply).

For an African American woman, obviously, such referents are even more overdetermined than for a white woman of any class strata. On the one hand, Palmer's persona reassures her audience that she is neither a wayward "angel" of the honky-tonk variety nor a more contemporary "ho" from the Southern hip-hop universe. She must recast the particular intersectionality of race, gender, and class in country's representations of authenticity that allows certain poor white women to claim feminine status yet denies their African American counterparts, via the legacy of blackface performance, similar standing. Yet minstrelsy offers up its own racist variant of the virtuous Southern woman, and a particular line in Palmer's song eerily invokes it by echoing Tubb's mammy-like icon in "Mississippi Gal": "I'm the kind of girl says it with a smile." In the song's video, Palmer presents herself as nothing less than a proud and independent woman-of-color whose hair, clothing, and jewelry all boast an Afrocentric sensibility—a somewhat startling incarnation of "country" femininity. Yet she needs to convert outdated gender scripts into a hip, youthful stance in order to bring the musical and visual texts' dissonant elements into a semblance of coherency.

Ironically, "Country Girl" cannot help but recall another relatively recent song recorded by an African American woman. Erykah Badu's 1999 single "Southern Girl," featuring beatboxer and former Roots musician Rahzel, poses a more overtly politicized challenge to white rural representations of country authenticity.[3] While the neosoul tune traverses a range of musical genres, its lyrics remain fixated on the "dirty South," that mythic territory ruled by both the Drive-By Truckers and Southern rap artists. It constitutes the converse, in other words, of Palmer's anodyne vision. Here, the country "home" place occupies both public and private spheres, affiliated as much with the "burning church" of the civil rights era as black Southern cultural and familial traditions (hairstyles, fried food). Rather than depict country identity as an abstract code of moral conduct, this Dallas-born singer-song-writer locates its coordinates squarely in the African American neighbor-hoods of the Southern United States. Moreover, "Southern Girl" is an auto-biographical song promulgating an altogether different image of "countrified" girlhood. Badu exalts not only her Southern drawl but her "dirty mouth," gleefully putting her listeners on notice: "can't nobody fuck with me." Nevertheless, she too appropriates the term "L.A.D.Y.," with all of its white genteel connotations, for herself.

Palmer's earnest reinscription of country femininity—not so much con-testing the definition as broadening the category to include any young woman with proper "training"—should prove far more marketable. She has recently appeared in the pages of long-running country fan magazine *Country Weekly* (touting her "old-fashioned" corn bread recipe), as well as per-formed on the Grand Ole Opry's radio and television programs.[4] Though still often treated as a "novelty" in the industry who has yet to attract a major la-bel, she garnered another endorsement after her debut song's release that may prove a more meaningful measure of commercial success. The Star-bucks conglomerate packaged "Country Girl" as part of a four-song EP, which resulted in the kind of mass exposure needed to position Palmer in iTunes' Top 5 country artists, in the company of mainstream stars such as Brad Paisley, Taylor Swift, Tim McGraw, and Carrie Underwood.[5] The song's veneer of liberal multicultural politics echoes its musical blending of soul, country, and pop arrangements, a rather benign form of hybridity that can appeal to diverse (and notably younger) fans as well as to music insiders. That combination leads *Billboard*, for example, to enthuse that "Country Girl"'s "soul-country smokiness . . . proves genres aren't as segregated as they sometimes seem on paper."[6] Its more conservative *gender* outlook can be either obscured or highlighted, depending on the audience, but it certainly seems key to securing Palmer's foothold in commercial country.

Another seeming "outsider" to the industry by geography and musical style, Massachusetts singer-songwriter Lori McKenna is similarly poised to achieve unanticipated mainstream country stardom on the basis of her songs' familiar domestic imagery and themes. Yet for most of her fledgling career, McKenna appeared much more the doppelganger of alt.country performer Iris DeMent than her most recent champion, Faith Hill. More than any other current alternative female artist, McKenna dramatically conveys the class knowledges of country music so evocative in DeMent's work.[7] Her equally raw, haunting voice and tales of fading blue-collar life outside of Boston's city limits evoke a comparable "survivalist" bent despite their Northeastern, rather than Southern, grounding. Album titles like *The Kitchen Table Tapes* (2003), *Bittertown* (2004), and *Unglamorous* (2007) be-speak McKenna's outlook as a working-class mother of five who, like De-Ment, charts the desperations pervading her own small town yet also fears its eclipse. Her songs are peopled with restless and neglected stay-at-home moms, ex–high school jocks working dead-end jobs, and suicidal boys who married too young. The bedraggled housewife of "Stealing Kisses" urges neighborhood girls to "run" from a similar fate, while "How to Survive" doc-uments the crippling silences of a couple worn down by the numbing grind of their domestic and work lives.[8] Both songs explore the sheer *drudgery* of this class-bound world's efforts to remain visible and viable. Yet McKenna also captures the distinct pride in such community. The narrator of "One Man," for instance, objects to the gentrification of her neighborhood— houses so monstrously large that their occupants "never even see one an-other in the dark"—and remains confident that "one man, one town is all I need."[9] Like both DeMent and Palmer, McKenna is also well aware of the power of religion to serve as a salve for larger wounds, though her female narrators typically attempt to flee its oppressive grasp.[10] Her music serves as another mode of "witnessing" the living presence of working-class culture in all of its complexity.[11]

Despite the title of her most recent album, however, McKenna's music and persona have undergone an undeniably "glamorous" makeover, at odds with the gritty domesticity of her prior work. After Hill recorded three of McKenna's songs on her top-selling 2005 album *Fireflies* (including "Stealing Kisses"), she became the singer-songwriter's most celebrated as well as influential fan and engineered her breakthrough into Top 40 country radio. In

2007, Hill invited McKenna to join her on *Oprah* and on tour, granting the alt.artist enormous media exposure and a priceless endorsement. *Unglamorous,* produced by Hill's husband Tim McGraw, received sophisticated packaging, as well as state-of-the-art production values that helped soften McKenna's trademark vocals. She herself experienced a comparable transformation, disseminated widely on Country Music Television: insistently marketed as an everyday "wife and mother," but with the aid of glossy photo shoots and celebrity hairstyling, she appears more reminiscent of Hill than of her song heroines—a long way from the edgy image of her *Bittertown* period. Predictably, the album's title track (and recently released single) veers from her stark vision of home life toward a more romanticized tableaux heralding the "beauty" of frozen dinners, cable-free television, dirty laundry—the 2007 counterpart to Phil Vassar's late 1990s country pop hit, "Just Another Day in Paradise."[12] While she eschews the exploitative fascination with class abjection so rife in other alt.country music, here her work and persona reach too far in the other direction by resuscitating country's myth of ostensibly unvarnished yet noble domesticity. Earlier, McKenna brought respectful *visibility* to working-class motherhood; this song dilutes, if not erases, such experience by sanitizing it for the mass audience of crossover country.[13]

Other selections on the album certainly complicate this scenario, including "How to Survive," "Written Permission," and "Drinking Problem." Yet the lyrics and melody to "Unglamorous" specifically serve as the inspiration for McKenna's Country Music Television Web page and interviews filmed for the program *Unplugged at Studio 330*—as well as her own independent official Web site—which not only aggressively tie the artist to current commercial product but, more important, underscore her Everywoman maternal identity. The single's autobiographical music video, replicating the formula seen earlier in country music memoirs and songs like Hill's "Mississippi Girl," embodies the song's larger ideology of exalting the home place: tender shots of McKenna in the kitchen with her young son flash against older family photos and small-town locales to establish her own gendered version of class authenticity while also blending with glimpses of McKenna the performer (live concert footage, in the recording studio, at home with guitar). As with female stars past and present, this comforting composite portrait trumpets her overriding commitment to motherhood. In one interview, she ranks her professional career a distinct second, insisting, "God was rewarding me for having all of these children."[14]

While occupying notably different positions along the mainstream continuum, Rissi Palmer and Lori McKenna confront, resist, perpetuate, and above all illuminate the entrenched demands of country music's authenticity narrative in the first decade of the twenty-first century. Both have admirably tested the limits of the genre by injecting new racialized and class definitions of "country" identity into its discourse and music. In this sense, they join recent African American "hick-hop" performer Cowboy Troy, whose work admittedly remains on the margins of commercial country radio yet has drawn new listeners to the music as a whole, and his better-known Muzik Mafia compatriot Gretchen Wilson, whose blockbuster hit "Redneck Woman" revived the indecorous features of poor white country culture for mass consumption. Yet Wilson also serves as an instructive counterpoint to the two in her relationship to the music industry's gendered expectations for female country stars. Unlike most women vocalists of the honky-tonk and Nashville Sound eras or newcomers like Palmer and McKenna, she has managed to promote her own "white trash" feminine persona as a viable mode of authenticity—one that is enhanced, rather than tempered, by her private status as a single mother.

At the same time, she has taken this gendered persona in a new direction. In barn dance programming particularly, representations of poor white rural women typically blurred traditional categories of masculinity and femininity and subsequently played up one or the other: either the comic assertive "spinster/single gal" to defuse the transgressive potential of the image or the treacly "sentimental mother" to restore its respectability. Wilson's brand, however, has come to achieve another, "outlaw" cachet. She has emerged as "one of the boys" (the title of her most recent album) in the contemporary country field, equating "redneck" womanhood with the same masculine bravado admired in hard country male performance. She may extol the virtues of Wal-Mart lingerie in her signature song—and even model it in the video—but she remains one of the very few young women topping today's country charts who just as ardently claim masculine terrain as their own.[15] It is perhaps her bid for the most stigmatized mode of class visibility (and arguably the central point of "Redneck Woman"'s lingerie reference, which champions both the pragmatism and the "questionable" taste of low-class culture). Shunning both Palmer's "good home training" and McKenna's turn to airbrushed domesticity, Wilson challenges the gendered limits of mainstream "Country Girl" constructions. She does so, however, with a novel return to the origins of this music's fabled rusticity. Less masquerade than mission, her music and surrounding iconography position the white female *hillbilly*—gender hybrid, class "primitive"—as the next archetype of country authenticity.

NOTES

Chapter 1

1. The program can be heard on *Hank Williams: Live at the Grand Ole Opry,* CD 2 (AFRS Show #116, 18 Feb. 1950) (Mercury Records, 314-546 466-2, 1999).

2. Biographer Colin Escott establishes that Williams owned Emmett Miller's recordings of the song (1925 and 1928) and contends that the young star modeled his yodeling style on Miller's "note for note." See *Hank Williams,* 91.

3. The liner notes to this two-CD set specify that "Aunt Jemima's Plaster" was "written and first recorded by" Foley's former WLS *Barn Dance* costars Lulu Belle and Scotty, but the song bears striking resemblance to a nineteenth-century song titled "Aunt Jemima's Plaster, or, Sheep-skin Bees Wax No. 2." See the Library of Congress's online collection "American Songs and Ballads," particularly the segment "Nineteenth-Century Song Sheets": http://memory.loc.gov/cgi-bin/ampage?collId=amss&fileName=sb1/sb100 (accessed 17 July 2007).

4. Cultural historian Pamela Grundy combines impressive archival research with incisive analysis to examine the Crazy Water Crystals' Depression-era ad campaign in her essay "'We Always Tried to Be Good People.'" She envisions a somewhat similar ideological aim for this laxative product's promotional religious rhetoric, "offering temporary relief to residents' intestines and working permanent change on their cultural traditions" by equating "control over a bodily process" with control over personal character (1591, 1595).

5. Michelle Shocked, *Arkansas Traveler* (Mercury Records, 512 101-2, 1992).

6. Songwriters John Rich and Adam Schoenfeld, on *Fireflies* (Warner Bros., B0009X7768, 2005).

7. Similarly, one reporter wryly notes: "It seems transparently designed to be her *Jenny from the Block* [Jennifer Lopez's hit single]. . . . She's very successfully had this glamour-girl image, but she was a little too successful for her audience and for country radio. Now, like J. Lo, there's a need to come and say, 'I'm not this uppity snob; I'm the same girl I always was'" (Mansfield, "Country Stars Find Their Way Back to Roots").

8. Hartigan, "Name Calling," 41–56. On this issue, also see legendary country music historian Bill Malone's discussion of his own academic career in his inter-

view with Cecelia Tichi (Tichi, *Reading Country Music,* 292–96), as well as his article "Country Music and the Academy," and Barbara Ching's piece on academics' elitist perspective on country music ("Acting Naturally").

9. For one overview, see Richard Peterson's *Creating Country Music.*

10. For a representative view, see almost any issue of *Country Music* magazine, especially Patrick Carr's work, or Chet Flippo in *Rolling Stone.* For a more cynical rendition of this position, see Nick Tosches' incendiary critiques in *Rolling Stone* or in books like *Country: The Twisted Roots.*

11. See Bill Malone's *Country Music, U.S.A.,* for one now classic example.

12. Peterson, *Creating Country Music,* 33; Ching, *Wrong's What I Do Best,* 4. Also see A. Fox, *Real Country;* Jensen, *Nashville Sound;* Pecknold, *Selling Sound.*

13. As stated in the original subtitle to Mary Bufwack and Robert Oermann's 1993 edition of *Finding Her Voice.*

14. Bufwack and Oermann, *Finding Her Voice,* xiii. Also see Wolfe and Akenson, *Women of Country Music.* I want to emphasize that both of these volumes represent important breakthroughs in country music historiography and provide scholars with indispensable information about female performers. I take issue with their analytic approach to gender.

15. Jensen, *Nashville Sound,* 27; Ching, *Wrong's What I Do Best,* 30.

16. McCusker and Pecknold, "Introduction," xx. I make use of this volume's essays later in the study.

17. In their excellent introduction to *Knowing Your Place,* Barbara Ching and Gerald W. Creed include a section entitled "Emplacing Race, Class, and Gender" to flesh out their notion of "recognizing rusticity" (22–28). And as I will discuss in chap. 3, Kathleen Stewart similarly acknowledges the complexity of rural identity formation: she envisions her study of discourse in the coal camps of southwestern West Virginia as "itself a kind of back-talk to a gender analysis of an earlier feminist theory which explained gender asymmetry in universal gendered dichotomies (i.e. domestic/public, nature/culture, reproduction/production)" (44). See "Backtalking the Wilderness."

18. For articulations and critiques of "dual systems" theories, see Hartmann, *Unhappy Marriage of Marxism and Feminism.* For work on intersectionality, see Crenshaw, "Mapping the Margins"; Collins, *Black Feminist Thought.* For such theorization in a transnational context, see Kaplan and Grewal, *Scattered Hegemonies.*

19. Acker, *Class Questions,* 39.

20. For an excellent bibliography and essay collection that serves as an "archive" of this field, see Hennessy and Ingraham, *Materialist Feminism,* as well as the volume's introductory essay, "Reclaiming Anticapitalist Feminism" (1–14). Also see Janet Zandy's body of work, including the two edited collections, *Liberating Memory* and *What We Hold in Common,* and *Hands.*

21. Acker, *Class Questions,* 50; Skeggs, *Formations of Class and Gender.*

22. Cook, *From Tobacco Road to Route 66,* 50; Harkins, *Hillbilly,* 7. I explore these images more extensively in chap. 2.

23. Butler, *Bodies That Matter*, chap. 3, "Phantasmatic Identification and the Assumption of Sex," esp. 95–103, 111–19.

24. Butler, *Bodies That Matter*, 3.

25. Butler begins to recognize such a dynamic in her discussion of queer vs. gay and lesbian identity politics, yet she urges "collective disidentifications" (*Bodies That Matter*, 4) with regulatory norms rather than identification with abject positions, as the latter, she argues, always reproduces exclusionary logics: "the strategies of abjection wielded through and by hegemonic subject positions" will still "structure and contain the articulatory struggles of those in subordinate or erased positionalities" (*Bodies That Matter*, 112).

26. Butler, *Bodies That Matter*, 26.

27. Lott, *Love and Theft*, 68.

28. See, e.g., William J. Mahar's *Behind the Burnt Cork Mask* and Susan Gubar's *Racechanges*, as well as W. T. Lhamon's work, which I discuss later. For similarly nuanced scholarship that predates Lott, see Roediger, *Wages of Whiteness*; Rogin, "Blackface, White Noise"; Ostendorf, "Minstrelsy and Early Jazz."

29. Lhamon, *Raising Cain*, 139.

30. See my *Class Fictions*, especially the first two chapters.

31. In this formulation, hard country stars such as George Jones and David Allan Coe willfully do battle with both elitist values and mainstream country's naive image of "country" identity; they wholeheartedly embrace their own abjection: "Unlike gilded Trumps and yuppies in tasteful suits, hard country stars rise and shine due to the darkness of the background they create. Since their success lies in a formulaic articulation of failure, it can only be given plain and disdainful stage names like 'the Possum' and 'the Hag.' . . . Instead of striving for the good life, hard country singers unabashedly portray themselves and their listeners as the 'low other' of American culture" (Ching, *Wrong's What I Do Best*, 29, 33). I am not disputing the basic outlines of such posturing but suggesting that at times Ching stops short in her analysis of such performers' engagement with it.

32. A. Fox, *Real Country*, 42. See also Fox's "Jukebox of History" and "Beyond Austin's City Limits."

33. As I document in greater detail in chap. 2, a handful of critics have paved the way to a more nuanced discussion of country's adaptations of minstrel show practices, and I am certainly indebted to their research in this study: Charles K. Wolfe, Nick Tosches, and most notably Robert Cantwell.

34. See Shank, *Dissonant Identities*, 35–36.

35. See Pecknold, *Selling Sound*, on the commercialization of country music during this period and its effect on the new production techniques and styles dubbed within the industry as the "Selling Sound" (133–67).

36. Citing prohibitive costs, the editors of *No Depression* ceased publishing the magazine in print form with its seventy-fifth issue, May–June 2008, but retained its presence as an electronic publication.

37. While data on fan demographics is always subject to change, one substantial study, based on a self-survey conducted by the Internet alt.country listserv Postcard2 (or P2), demonstrates that the typical member of this group is a white

male, in his thirties and a white-collar professional. See Richard Peterson and Bruce Beal's "Alternative Country."

38. The cover story of *No Depression*'s Summer 1996 issue concerned Jamup and Honey comic "Honey" Wilds and featured a photo of Hank Williams flanked by the blackface duo. See Grant Alden's "Wilds, the Innocent."

Chapter 2

1. Ad in *Billboard*, 8 June 1940, p. 18; review in 4 May 1940 issue.

2. See Wolfe, *Good-Natured Riot;* Nick Tosches' provocatively titled chapter in *Country: The Twisted Roots*, as well as his impressive research on minstrel performer Emmett Miller, collected in *Where Dead Voices Gather;* and Robert Cantwell's *Bluegrass Breakdown*, esp. the chapter "Tambo and Bones: Blackface Minstrelsy, the Opry, and Bill Malone."

3. Lott, *Love and Theft*, 4 (my emphasis).

4. McCusker, "'Bury Me Beneath the Willow,'" 7. For other recent work emphasizing the importance of barn dance radio's nationwide market, see Harkins, *Hillbilly*, esp. 78–87; Lange, *Smile When You Call Me a Hillbilly*, 19–66.

5. Peterson, *Creating Country Music*, 99. See Diane Pecknold's *Selling Sound* for an in-depth account of barn dance radio's business foundations. Pecknold argues that hillbilly music in this early period "can reasonably be interpreted more as an adjunct of radio broadcast advertising than as a part of the music industry until well after World War II" (17) and "served as a portent of modernization even as it nostalgically invoked the rural past" (24).

6. Harkins, *Hillbilly*, 7, 6; McCusker, "'Bury Me Beneath the Willow,'" 8; Biggar, "WLS Barn Dance Story," 106.

7. For an overview, see Harkins, *Hillbilly*, 95–98; Peterson, *Creating Country Music*, 81–94; Malone, *Country Music, U.S.A.*, chap. 5; Lange, *Smile When You Call Me a Hillbilly*, 83–85.

8. McCusker, *Lonesome Cowgirls and Honky-Tonk Angels*, 33.

9. This is W. T. Lhamon Jr.'s term (*Raising Cain*, 21).

10. Rourke, *American Humor*, 74.

11. Willis, "I Shop, Therefore I Am," 194. Other scholars have made additional useful contributions to this discussion: see Saxton's "Blackface Minstrelsy and Jacksonian Ideology"; Rogin's influential "Blackface, White Noise"; Gubar, *Racechanges*.

12. Rourke, *American Humor*, 11, 100.

13. R. Ellison, "Change the Joke," 49 (two quotes) (my emphasis).

14. R. Ellison, "Change the Joke," 53, 48 (two quotes).

15. Mahar, "Ethiopian Skits and Sketches," 181; Lott, *Love and Theft*, 7.

16. Lott, *Love and Theft*, 25.

17. Lott, *Love and Theft*, 6, 39.

18. Lott, *Love and Theft*, 66, 92, 68 (two quotes), 71 (two quotes).

19. Mahar, *Behind the Burnt Cork Mask*, 1.

20. Mahar, *Behind the Burnt Cork Mask*, 330 (my emphasis).

21. Mahar, "Ethiopian Skits and Sketches," 184–85. In *Behind the Burnt Cork Mask,* Mahar elaborates: "The blackface mask in those circumstances did not reflect white perceptions of black culture but served as a vehicle to express the disappointments and doubts of those 'others' (including whites themselves) who dwelt on the margins of political power, economic comfort, and relative security in jobs, homes, and private life" (41).

22. Mahar, *Behind the Burnt Cork Mask,* 192.

23. Lhamon, *Raising Cain,* 4, 22. However, Lhamon does pay tribute to Rourke in his preface to *American Humor,* claiming that she produced "the first theory of American culture" (xiii) but that its "minstrel portion . . . arguably its subtlest and most original feature, ran up against a closed door" (xxx).

24. Lhamon, *Raising Cain,* 21, 6 (two quotes), 35, 52, 65, 44.

25. Lhamon, *Raising Cain,* 6, 110. This statement is prompted by Lhamon's reading of *The Jazz Singer,* which he believes has too often been interpreted as "eager replacement of ethnicity or Jewishness with whiteness" (*Raising Cain,* 107). He counters, "Jack Robin needs the blackface mask as the agency of his compounded identity" (110).

26. Lhamon, *Raising Cain,* 42 (my emphasis), 139.

27. Willis, "I Shop, Therefore I Am," 189.

28. Willis, "I Shop, Therefore I Am," 190, 188. Willis offers up Michael Jackson (of the late 1980s) as a modern example of this dynamic, arguing that his "physical transformations are his trademark—a means for bringing all the sexual tensions and social contradictions present in blackface into a contemporary form" ("I Shop, Therefore I Am," 190). Contrast her view with Lauren Berlant's more totalizing conception of the commodification of "blackness" taking place in the novel and film versions of *Imitation of Life:* "We have seen that in modern America, the artificial legitimacy of the citizen has merged with the commodity form: its autonomy, its phantasmatic freedom from its own history, seem to invest it with the power to transmit its aura, its 'body,' to consumers. . . . But the films and the novel give the lie to the American promise that participation in the national/capitalist public sphere has emancipatory potential for the historically overembodied" ("National Brands/National Body," 133).

29. After formulating this concept, I discovered the work of several other scholars analogous, yet not identical, to my own. Rachel Rubin proposes that "19th century blackface minstrelsy . . . is an obvious source and referent in . . . hayseed performances" within modern country music ("Sing Me Back Home," 106), noting that the comedy "rescues a viewer from likeness to that figure" (107). Anthony Harkins argues that in appropriating the term *hillbilly,* some performers and audience members participated in "a form of self-mockery . . . [that] removed some of the word's stigma and defined their own identity" (*Hillbilly,* 94). McCusker speculates that the rube antics of vaudeville performer Elviry Weaver served as solace to those in the audience "who worried their own rural naivete made them something to laugh at" (*Lonesome Cowgirls and Honky-Tonk Angels,* 11).

30. Smith-Rosenberg, "Davy Crockett as Trickster," 93.

31. Rourke, *American Humor,* 36–37.

32. Smith-Rosenberg, "Davy Crockett as Trickster," 96, 98, 105.

33. Rourke, *American Humor,* 62, 42. Charles Wolfe has researched Crockett's relationship to certain songs in the minstrel tradition, as well as documented his role as a fiddler. See "Davy Crockett Songs."

34. Roediger, *Wages of Whiteness,* 98. James Dorman argues that *coon* became a popular term for blacks in the early 1880s, though earlier black images were associated with the raccoon. See "Shaping the Popular Image of Post-Reconstruction American Blacks."

35. Smith-Rosenberg, "Davy Crockett as Trickster," 101, 107–8. Harkins makes a similar point in his discussion of the mountaineer image that initially managed to supercede the hillbilly, though he focuses on the former's refiguring of the latter's racial identity—"mountain whites" who represented "racial and religious purity" (*Hillbilly,* 43).

36. Lott, *Love and Theft,* 102.

37. Albanese, "Davy Crockett and the Wild Man," 83.

38. Rourke, *American Humor,* 99.

39. Lhamon, *Raising Cain,* 190, 256–57, 189 (two quotes) (my emphasis), 191.

40. Cook, *From Tobacco Road to Route 66,* ix, xiii.

41. Cook, *From Tobacco Road to Route 66,* 4.

42. Cook, *From Tobacco Road to Route 66,* 17; Flynt, *Dixie's Forgotten People,* 40.

43. Arnold Toynbee, quoted in Flynt, *Dixie's Forgotten People,* 15.

44. Tosches' reporting on Miller first appeared in his book *Country: The Twisted Roots,* 102–8 and 118–19, followed by a series of articles in the *Journal of Country Music* and finally published in book form in *Where Dead Voices Gather* (2002). While elsewhere in this book I take Tosches to task for his gender politics, here I express only profound respect for his unflagging investigative skills.

45. Tosches, "Strange and Hermetical Case," 39; Tosches, "Emmett Miller," 27.

46. Tosches, "Strange and Hermetical Case," 39.

47. Tosches, "Emmett Miller," 32; Tosches, "Strange and Hermetical Case," 41.

48. Tosches is quoting the 1927 *Macon Telegraph* ("Emmett Miller," 32–33).

49. Tosches establishes that Miller was an auto mechanic, his father a fireman ("Emmett Miller," 32–33).

50. J. M. Mancini casts Miller as one exemplar of early country music's market-driven "interracial modernity" in "'Messin' with the Furniture Man.'" Mancini makes a compelling claim for situating this music as a neglected example of modernist "hybridity" (211), particularly focusing on its "interracial circulation" among black and white musicians and early references to "consumer culture" (213).

51. Tosches, "Emmett Miller," 34.

52. R. Cantwell, *Bluegrass Breakdown,* 241.

53. R. Cantwell, *Bluegrass Breakdown,* 265 (my emphasis).

54. Ostendorf, "Minstrelsy and Early Jazz," 588.

55. The quote is from Vaillant, "Sounds of Whiteness," 26. A 1936 article in WLS's fan magazine *Stand By!* promotes the message of class unification as it recounts the diversity of fans who cluster outside Chicago's Eighth Street theater to view a *National Barn Dance* program: spying a couple in "evening dress" speaking to a newsboy in patched trousers, author Kathryn Swihart announces that "the Barn Dance is the one place in the world where all classes of people meet on common ground. . . . Those who are inclined to be a little reserved are soon talking to their neighbors as if they were old friends . . . swept into this whirlpool of merriment and friendliness that overflows from the old Hayloft." See Swihart, "From Near and Far," 3.

56. Ostendorf, "Minstrelsy and Early Jazz," 591.

57. Huggins, *Harlem Renaissance,* 258.

58. Lott, *Love and Theft,* 113.

59. See Tosches, "Strange and Hermetical Case," 44. He also documents here that another yodeling minstrel man and ex-Field employee, Al Tint, abandoned blackface entirely for the backwoods yokel character, touring with the Opry in 1935 and joining WLS's *National Barn Dance* in 1937 as a "real 'hillbilly.'"

60. I recognize, however, that WLS's *National Barn Dance* featured its own hillbilly characters ("Uncle Ezra," "Lulu Belle") and blackface comedians (principally "Spareribs"). The latter, played by Malcolm Claire, specialized in "fairy stories for children related in the soft dialect of the 'deep south' negro," as stated in a cover story about Claire in *Prairie Farmer's New WLS Weekly* (what would soon be titled *Stand By!*), 2 Mar. 1935, 15. I examine Lulu Belle specifically in the chapter's concluding section.

61. R. Cantwell, *Bluegrass Breakdown,* 13.

62. Twain quoted in Saxton, "Blackface Minstrelsy," 3; Rourke, *American Humor,* 174.

63. Wolfe, *Good-Natured Riot,* 21–22.

64. Wolfe, *Good-Natured Riot,* 13, 16.

65. Wolfe, *Good-Natured Riot,* 16 (two quotes), 17. For the photographs, see Wolfe, *Grand Ole Opry,* 16–21; Peterson, *Creating Country Music,* 69–80. Also see Harkins, *Hillbilly,* 80, 84–86.

66. Wolfe, *Grand Ole Opry,* 11.

67. Wolfe, *Good-Natured Riot,* 7, 22.

68. Hay, *Howdy Judge.*

69. Hay, *Howdy Judge,* 7.

70. Hay, *Howdy Judge,* 6, 7, 8, 13, 12 (two quotes).

71. Hay, *Howdy Judge,* 14, 15, 14, 15.

72. Hay, *Howdy Judge,* 16–17.

73. Hay, *Howdy Judge,* 25, 50.

74. Hay, *Howdy Judge,* 104–5, 105, 106.

75. Hay, *Story of the Grand Ole Opry,* 17.

76. Hay, *Story of the Grand Old Opry,* 10.

77. Wolfe, *Good-Natured Riot,* 126.

78. Hay, *Story of the Grand Ole Opry,* 17.

79. Wolfe, *Good-Natured Riot,* 225.

80. Hay, *Story of the Grand Ole Opry,* 19 (all quotes).

81. Lott, *Love and Theft,*123, 113.

82. Tsuchiya, "'Let Them Be Amused,'" 98. Tsuchiya uncovers examples of several corporate minstrel shows, such as Goodyear's Greater Minstrels in 1917, which included "comic skits in blackface . . . ragtime and dixieland music" (99), and Western Electric's Hawthorne Follies 1920 performance (103). After World War I ended, however, "surveys indicated that workers tended to avoid company recreation facilities" (100).

83. McCusker, *Lonesome Cowgirls and Honky-Tonk Angels,* 58–62.

84. See Green, *Country Roots,* 71–72; Cusic, "Comedy and Humor in Country Music."

85. Wolfe, *Good-Natured Riot,* 227.

86. Wolfe, *Good-Natured Riot,* 230.

87. Wolfe, *Good-Natured Riot,* 229.

88. Vaillant, writing on the emergence of local radio in Chicago during the 1920s and early 1930s, similarly notes that "music radio helped to domesticate and to gender excursions through the symbolic and sonic 'wilds' of African American music, blunting its forbidden or unseemly connotations" ("Sounds of Whiteness," 36).

89. White, *Book of Humor and Song,* 4, 5, 11.

90. These scripts can be found in the Country Music Foundation library's R. Lowell Blanchard collection.

91. The song was written by a woman, Hattie Nevada, in 1897 and went on to have a substantial presence within country music: first recorded by Vernon Dalhart in 1925, then by Bradley Kincaid in 1934, and later by Marty Robbins in 1983. It was also recorded by Jim Reeves and Hank Snow. For discussion of its vaudeville context, see McCusker, *Lonesome Cowgirls and Honky-Tonk Angels,* 11–12.

92. For Roy Acuff's minstrel history with a traveling medicine show in 1932, see Schlappi, *Roy Acuff,* 21. Jake Tindell, another entertainer in that show, joined Acuff's Crazy Tennesseans band as a jug-playing blackface comic and later worked with his Smoky Mountain Boys.

93. Lott, *Love and Theft,* 122.

94. The phrase describing Arnold is Bill Malone's in *Country Music, U.S.A.,* 236.

95. McCusker, *Lonesome Cowgirls and Honky-Tonk Angels,* 21.

96. The transgressive nature of this persona influenced off-stage identities as well. McCusker notes that Cannon "so successfully played an old maid that . . . George D. Hay called her 'one of the boys'" (*Lonesome Cowgirls and Honky-Tonk Angels,* 114).

97. See chap. 4's discussion of Cannon's autobiography for the origins of the Pearl character.

98. McCusker argues that Cannon used her alter ego Minnie Pearl to "police black behavior" in her support for political candidates opposed to the civil rights movement, the most notorious being George Wallace a decade later. See *Lonesome Cowgirls and Honky-Tonk Angels*, 121–22.

99. Jamup and Honey Opry scripts from the early 1950s offer more of the same: wives so promiscuous in their younger days that they are deemed "Satanic" (12 Aug. 1950) or "like a disease" ("so easy caught, and so hard to git $$$ [*sic*] rid of") (28 Mar. 1951), trapping Jamup into a shotgun union. Jokes about violence abound: "Jamup, you looks bad tonight, what's de Matter? Why do you go out and dround your troubles?" / "I cant, she wont eben go close to de water" (28 Mar. 1951). These scripts also display the uneven orthographic dimensions of the minstrel dialect they employed on stage:

> HON. And dats how cum your wife to quit you too. . . . Is you been goin wid any gals since your wife left you?
> JAM. You know I'm is, cause I'm a man about town and a fool about womens. . . . I'm goin wid a little ole gal now dat remind me of a new streamlined automobile. . . . She's got a perfect body, pleasing lines, built for speed, a great paint job, low back, beautiful lamps, snappy pick-up, terrific clutch, and Oh brother, what a tank capacity. (2 Feb. 1952)

100. Lott, *Love and Theft*, 147.

101. Lott, *Love and Theft*, 148.

102. For more information on Blanchard's career at WNOX, see Smyth, "Early Knoxville Radio."

103. Quoted in Alden, "Wilds, the Innocent," 50.

104. Quoted in Alden, "Wilds, the Innocent," 50–51.

105. Quoted in Hagan, *Grand Ole Opry*, 29. This sentiment also surfaces in an interview with traveling medicine show blackface performer Tommy Millard, who made several appearances on the Opry and on Knoxville's *Mid-Day Merry Go-Round* during the 1930s before a stint with Bill Monroe's fledgling Blue Grass Boys. Although he forswore blackface performance after receiving a complaint from a black preacher, his interviewer explains that "according to Tommy, back when he did blackface, it was really accepted by both blacks and whites and there were no hard feelings. . . . 'I've had colored people come around and talk to me, shake hands and they had no hard feelings, or anything like that'" (3). Millard subsequently adopted "the more acceptable" comic persona of a white country rube. See Erbsen, "Tommy Millard."

106. Quoted in Alden, "Wilds, the Innocent," 50.

107. Quoted in Alden, "Wilds, the Innocent," 51, 52.

108. Vaillant, "Sounds of Whiteness," 29.

109. During a more recent interview I conducted in Washington, D.C., in Sept. 2000, David Wilds very much wanted to *humanize* his father—sharing fam-

ily photos, home movies, and mementos—to offset the stigma now attached to "Honey"'s chosen profession. He also expressed some bitterness over his father's excision from contemporary country music history, stressing what seemed to be a seamless overlap between his father's public and private lives.

110. These letters were generously lent to me by David Wilds.

111. Also see Diane Pecknold's discussion of fan-based publications in the barn dance era. Focusing on "readers' interests in the mechanics of radio reception and the politics of radio broadcasting," such magazines "encouraged a sense of personal connection to stars through familial imagery but also fostered a more pragmatic form of identification through the promise that, as cultural producers, amateurs and professionals were not so far removed from each other" (*Selling Sound*, 40).

112. This might offer one way to understand the popularity of local barn dance "parties," as described by one fan of the WHO *Sunset Corners Frolic* program: "Every Saturday night a group of people reserve the Club for the evening and come dressed in overalls, straw hats, farm aprons, etc., and carrying anything from a milk stool to a pitchfork. They call it the 'Old Timers Club' and all their dancing is done to the music of the Sunset Corners Frolic." See "Over the Cracker Barrel."

113. Lott, *Love and Theft*, 59.

114. See McCusker, "Rose Lee Maphis," for an interesting discussion of barn dance as a site of women's work.

115. Both station albums can be found in the archives of the Country Music Foundation, which houses other representative barn dance scrapbooks, such as those from Wheeling, WV, and even Canada's CKNX *Barn Dance* on the Ontario Farm Station.

116. Kibler, *Rank Ladies*, 112–35. Kibler points to Sophie Tucker, the "World Renowned Coon Shouter," as "the most famous example of the link between size, beauty, and blackface for women in vaudeville" (129).

117. For a sampling of this kind of scholarship, see Kristine McCusker's work, cited earlier; M. Williams, "Home to Renfro Valley"; Lange, *Smile When You Call Me a Hillbilly*, 33–35.

118. McCusker, "'Bury Me Beneath the Willow,'" 5–11 (quote on 11).

119. McCusker, *Lonesome Cowgirls and Honky-Tonk Angels*, 37, 4–5.

120. McCusker outlines the situation: "The woman who performed as Parker . . . does not seem to have been as wholesome or as virtuous as Parker was. . . . She was born in Indiana, not Kentucky, may have been an illegitimate child, may have been a juvenile delinquent, and was probably singing in nightclubs when Lair discovered her" ("'Bury Me Beneath the Willow,'" 4).

121. M. Williams, "Home to Renfro Valley," 91; Alison Kibler, remarking on stock nineteenth-century theatrical roles for women, quoted in McCusker, *Lonesome Cowgirls and Honky-Tonk Angels*, 11.

122. Quoted in M. Williams, "Home to Renfro Valley," 91.

123. McCusker, "Bury Me Beneath the Willow," 5, 12, and *Lonesome Cowgirls and Honky-Tonk Angels*, 128, she quotes a *Time* magazine reporter (6 Dec.

1943, 62) who wrote of Emmy, "Every morning the notoriously noxious air of St. Louis is purified by the natural twang of real mountaineer goings on" (12).

124. "Girl on the Cover," *Stand By!* 18 Sept. 1937, 4.

125. See McCusker on ideologies governing women's presence on theatrical stages, especially in the South, where hints of "immorality" prompted solo female performers to be paired with fictitious brother or boyfriend figures as stage "chaperones" (including Lulu Belle in Chicago): *Lonesome Cowgirls and Honky-Tonk Angels,* 44; 139–40. Ironically, as McCusker notes, married male barn dance performers often gained reputations for their sexual improprieties.

126. As stated in a *Stand By!* forum on "what constitutes 'real American music'" (13 Nov. 1937), 3.

Chapter 3

"Cold, Cold Woman and a Hot Guitar," written by Ted Brooks and published by Acuff-Rose in 1952.

1. The first scholarly designation of the music as a subgenre called "honky-tonk" is attributed to Bill C. Malone in the 1960s: first in his 1964 University of Texas doctoral dissertation and then in his groundbreaking historical study *Country Music, U.S.A.* As chap. 5 will discuss more thoroughly, it has since come to signify a broader "movement"—"hard country"—often fetishized by male journalists and recent alt.country artists as "real" country music.

2. Barry Shank calls honky-tonks "magical places where promises were made and new possibilities of life could be imagined in the free recombination of repressed elements of the human," yet as a commercial medium the music offered an "increasingly rigidified, ritualized, and controlled . . . version of the carnival" (35). See his incisive reading of honky-tonk culture in relation to the Austin music scene in *Dissonant Identities.*

3. Bertrand, "I Don't Think Hank," 80; Malone, "Honky-Tonk," 120.

4. See Bertrand, "I Don't Think Hank," 59–85; Smethurst, "How I Got to Memphis," 47–64; Marcus, *Mystery Train.*

5. Tubb recorded in the Dallas studio of Bunny Biggs (future "Jamup" performer) in 1941 and later toured with Jamup and Honey in 1943 as part of an Opry tour package. See Pugh, *Ernest Tubb,* 88, 94. As noted in chaps. 1 and 2, Hank Williams's Opry performances coincided with Jamup and Honey appearances.

6. Williams died on 1 Jan. 1953.

7. Inevitably, however, I too have excised certain women artists from the discussion out of sheer necessity and regret their absence from this chapter: Mollie O'Day, Charline Arthur, Goldie Hill, and especially Rose Maddox, who provides another noteworthy example of a female country performer straddling pre- and postwar styles of music.

8. For three examples, see Gluck, *Rosie the Riveter Revisited;* Meyerowitz, *Not June Cleaver;* Coontz, *Way We Never Were.*

9. Gluck, *Rosie the Riveter Revisited,* 7–11, 13, 17.

10. Meyerowitz, *Not June Cleaver,* 4; Coontz, *Way We Never Were,* 31.

11. For an overview, see the following: May, *Homeward Bound,* which examines postwar constructions of the family as one version of "domestic containment"; Cott, *Public Vows,* 180–97; and Spigel, *Make Room for TV,* which primarily explores the relationship among television, postwar housing design, and emerging representations of "family unity."

12. Bufwack and Oermann, *Finding Her Voice,* 142.

13. Quoted in Cott, *Public Vows,* 188, 190.

14. Cott, *Public Vows,* 186.

15. On men's postwar trauma and the media's campaign to reinsert them into domestic life, see Spigel, *Make Room for TV,* 41–45; Cott, *Public Vows,* 189–90. On the middle-class breadwinner model of masculinity, see Pecknold, "'I Wanna Play House,'" which explores the effects of postwar ideals on the professionalization of the Nashville music industry in the early 1960s (88–95).

16. Lipsitz, *Rainbow at Midnight,* 20.

17. Lipsitz, *Rainbow at Midnight,* 45.

18. Lipsitz, *Rainbow at Midnight,* 45; "Rainbow at Midnight," written by Lost John Miller, recorded by Ernest Tubb in 1946 .

19. Lipsitz, *Rainbow at Midnight,* 45; *To the Young,* quoted in Cott, *Public Vows,* 187.

20. Recording stats documented in Pugh, *Ernest Tubb,* 111–12. Pugh notes that the song had previously been recorded by the Carlisles on the King label but hadn't sold nearly as well.

21. "Answer to Rainbow at Midnight," written by Lost John Miller and Ernest Tubb, recorded for Decca in 1947.

22. While Bourdieu's notion of habitus has been subjected to a thorough critique by scholars across the disciplines for its structuralist limitations and ostensibly bleak vision of individual agency, Bourdieu himself cautions against such readings, insisting that it is "not a fate, not a destiny . . . being a product of history, that is of social experience and education, it may be changed by history" ("Habitus," 45). For his original work on the concept, see *Outline of a Theory of Practice.* For later musings and qualifications, see *Invitation to Reflexive Sociology,* cowritten with Loïc Wacquant, and his essay "Habitus," in *Habitus. Habitus* usefully offers not only Bourdieu's reflections but twenty-first-century applications of the concept by a variety of scholars.

23. See Malone, "Honky Tonk," 120, 121, 122 (two quotes), 121 (two quotes), 128. Barbara Ching adds to this discussion, noting, "We all know what honkies are even though I don't think people remember that when they use the term 'honky-tonk'; according to [Cecelia] Tichi, 'the very term . . . is evidently black slang meaning 'white shack'" (*Wrong's What I Do Best,* 35).

24. Jensen, *Nashville Sound,* 19, 24, 27, 30, 29, 32.

25. Jensen, *Nashville Sound,* 24 (two quotes), 29, 25. The last quote is Jensen citing *Country Music* magazine editor Michael Banes, whose statement originally appeared in Peter Guralnick's *Lost Highway* (164).

26. K. Stewart, "Nostalgia," 235.

27. K. Stewart, "Nostalgia," 236, 237–38, 239 (my emphasis).

28. Bufwack and Oermann, *Finding Her Voice,* 144.

29. Malone, "Honky Tonk," 122, 127–28.

30. For this overview, I am drawing on both Malone's and Bertrand's essays. Bertrand argues that this group's "patriarchal ethos (independence, honor, dominance, and violence) typically manifested itself in the form of a physical presence that exuded self-assertiveness, aggressiveness, and competitiveness" ("I Don't Think Hank," 66).

31. Leppert and Lipsitz, "Age, the Body," 30, 22.

32. This binary construction is borrowed from Jensen's outline of themes in honky-tonk songs (*Nashville Sound,* 28).

33. Malone set the tone in 1982, when Top 40 country music was just on the verge of discovering "New Traditionalism," concluding that honky-tonk "is scorned by the country music industry because it is too country" and "dismissed by many of us . . . because it is too real": "too revealing emotionally to accept intellectually" ("Honky-Tonk," 127, 128).

34. For the former, see Katie [Kathleen] Stewart's "Engendering Narratives of Lament in Country Music," along with other work of hers cited in this chapter, as well as Aaron Fox's *Real Country,* which I will say more about later. For the latter, see Ching's study of hard country, *Wrong's What I Do Best,* especially chap. 2, "The Possum, the Hag, and the Rhinestone Cowboy," 30. As I will discuss later, Rachel Rubin's essay on the 1960s Bakersfield wave of country music also approaches nostalgia as a "self-conscious invocation . . . a lyrical strategy or poetic stance . . . that has allowed the music to speak for and depict rural Americans in the urban diaspora" ("Sing Me Back Home," 93).

35. Ching, *Wrong's What I Do Best,* 26.

36. A. Fox, *Real Country,* 98, 131, 97, 131.

37. Originally recorded on Starday Records, no. 225, in 1956.

38. Bertrand, "I Don't Think Hank," 61, 81, 62, 67 (my emphasis). Bertrand focuses on Elvis to sketch out his sense of the distinctions between rockabilly and blackface performance, arguing that "Presley's immersion in black music and style represented a novel and distinctive reading of southern tradition. . . . Rather than a modern-day blackface excursion into romanticized darkness . . . Elvis was adopting a masculine persona associated with actual working-class African-American males" ("I Don't Think Hank," 75). While I find Bertrand's reading of blackface performance oversimplified here and question his reliance in this theory on "actual" black men, I value the overall rubric he constructs.

39. Smethurst, "How I Got to Memphis," 61 (two quotes).

40. Written by Ted Daffan, released on Okeh Records. The quoted phrase is Nick Tosches' ("Honky Tonk," 47). Tosches's piece serves as the source for my general information here. Tosches also notes in passing that none other than Roy Acuff released a song titled "Honky Tonk Mamas" in 1938 (prior to his reign on the Opry).

41. Tosches, "Honky-Tonkin'," 174.

42. Quoted in Lange, *Smile When You Call Me a Hillbilly,* 166.

43. Pugh, *Ernest Tubb*, 5–7; 11–12; Tosches, "Honky-Tonkin'," 155.

44. Malone, *Country Music, U.S.A.*, 156; Guralnick, *Lost Highway*, 34. Barry Shank emphasizes that Tubb's sincere vocal delivery "was wholly a performance style," arguing that "thirty-five years after the first success of 'Walking the Floor,' he could still sing that song with the same emotive signs of genuine feeling" (*Dissonant Identities*, 34).

45. Tosches, "Honky-Tonkin'," 161; Lange, *Smile When You Call Me a Hillbilly*, 164.

46. Tubb quoted in Pugh, *Ernest Tubb*, 65. Pugh speculates that the song had an autobiographical bent, reflecting Tubb's own early marital troubles.

47. Lange and Pugh offer somewhat conflicting reports of Tubb's Opry debut: Lange emphasizes Hay's distress (*Smile When You Call Me a Hillbilly*, 85), while Pugh emphasizes the encores and Hay's overall praise of Tubb (*Ernest Tubb*, 85, 94), drawing on the Judge's 1945 *Story of the Grand Ole Opry.*

48. Fellow musician Charlie Walker recalls, "I've seen Elvis, and all the guys from every generation, the young girls trying to get to them after the show. Ernest, he had those thirty-year-old good-looking women trying to knock the door down to get to him . . . He was tall, and thin, and had those sharp-looking Western outfits." Fiddler Hal Smith concurs: "I remember women keeling over in Louisville when he sang there—they had to take them away on stretchers. He was as big as Sinatra, only with a different, country audience." Quoted in Pugh, *Ernest Tubb*, 110.

49. Tubb appeared in several Hollywood films: *Fighting Buckaroo, Riding West* (both filmed in 1942), and *Hollywood Barn Dance* (1947).

50. "It's Been So Long Darling," written by Ernest Tubb, recorded for Decca, published by American Music, Inc.

51. Written by Ernest Tubb, recorded for Decca in 1946.

52. Written by Ernest Tubb, published by Ernest Tubb Music, Inc.

53. That same year, Tubb recorded a song even more evocative of Noack's, "I'm with a Crowd but So Alone," but it didn't become a hit until released in 1951. See Pugh, *Ernest Tubb*, 127, for background details.

54. The song, written by Sam Nichols, Taylor McPeters, and Daniel Cypert and published by Hill & Range Songs, Inc., was originally recorded in Nashville in 1947 and re-recorded in 1956 along with an even more explicit "companion" song, "I've Got the Blues for Mammy."

55. Written by Billy Cox and Clarke Van Ness, published by Shapiro, Bernstein & Co., Inc.

56. I concede that the song's popularity may have also been stirred by the War Brides Act of 1945 and the Soldier Brides Act of 1947, which allowed, respectively, Chinese and American wives of American citizens to enter the United States.

57. Jeffrey Lange made Tubb's statement the title of his book. Rachel Rubin, as I'll explore later, analyzes Tubb's later album *My Hillbilly Baby and Other Big Hits!* as a self-conscious critique of the hillbilly stereotype, in keeping with this original directive. Interestingly, though, I have found no origin of or context for

his "smile" statement. Lange also includes other country artists such as Floyd Tillman and Red Foley in this name-changing initiative.

58. Pugh, *Ernest Tubb*, 132–34. *Billboard* had used the term "Folk Records" as the title of its chart for country records launched in 1944, but by 1949, "Folk" had been replaced by "Country & Western" and finally, beginning in 1962, by "Country" (Pugh, *Ernest Tubb*, 134). However, the publication still frequently employed the term *hillbilly* in the headlines of articles about country music into the early 1950s: "Hillbilly Nitery Makes Bow in Chicago July 1" (26 Apr. 1952); "A.&R. Men Search for Fem Hillbillies" (20 June 1953); "Hillbilly Center (54th St., NY) Not in Hills, But All Is Rosie" (31 Dec. 1949).

59. Pugh, *Ernest Tubb*, 133–34.

60. Lange, *Smile When You Call Me a Hillbilly*, 186; Pugh, *Ernest Tubb*, 134–37. Later in his career, Tubb related that this remark prompted a "very dignified" woman in the audience to "punch" her seatmate and exclaim, "My God! Talking about putting hay in Carnegie Hall!" (Pugh, *Ernest Tubb*, 136).

61. Tubb quoted in Pugh, *Ernest Tubb*, 133.

62. The epithet "daddy" is another interesting choice, certainly contributing to the album cover's associations with rural Southernness yet also injecting it with a dose of hipness borrowed from blues slang.

63. *My Hillbilly Baby and Other Big Hits!* does not have an identifiable release date, though it clearly appeared after 1965, as Ellis Nassour's back-jacket copy mentions that Tubb was elected to the Country Music Hall of Fame that year. Ronnie Pugh's exhaustive discography does not include the album.

64. Rubin, "Sing Me Back Home," 109.

65. Pugh, *Ernest Tubb*, 236–37.

66. See Anthony Harkins's *Hillbilly* for a cultural history of Capp's influential bit of popular culture (124–36).

67. Written by Rex Griffin, published by Peer International.

68. Written by Hal Willis and Ginger Willis, published by Tree Publishing Co.

69. Tubb's private life appears to reflect this influence. His first wife, Elaine, was reportedly restless as his stay-at-home wife during the earliest years of their marriage, when he was on the road. While she was instrumental in launching and working at the Record Shop, she was asked to quit by her husband. She sued for divorce on grounds of estrangement and loss of income (Pugh, *Ernest Tubb*, 141–43). His second wife, Olene, whom he married shortly thereafter, was profiled in *Country Song Roundup*'s "Meet the Mrs." column as "a wonderful homemaker" who "thrills to the responsibility of having to take care of their beautiful home" (no. 17, Apr. 1952, p. 13). This chapter's conclusion elaborates on this national fan magazine's constructions of gender relations.

70. On Tubb's drinking problems, see Pugh, *Ernest Tubb*, 140–41, 223–25, which recounts one "tragicomic" incident involving a gun that did make it into the local papers.

71. Wesley Rose, quoted in Goodson, "Hillbilly Humanist," 105.

72. Leppert and Lipsitz, "Age, the Body," 22.

73. Williams quoted in Escott, *Hank Williams,* 19. Escott notes that for his part, Acuff had little patience for Williams' personal failings, chiding, "You got a million-dollar voice . . . and a ten-cent brain" (20).

74. Williams quoted in Goodson, "Hillbilly Humanist," 110–11. The interview appeared in Rufus Jarman's "Country Music Goes to Town," 51.

75. Escott, *Hank Williams,* 46.

76. Williams quoted in Goodson, "Hillbilly Humanist," 111.

77. Bennett recorded "Cold, Cold Heart" in 1951 but was initially reluctant, telling Mitch Miller, "Don't make me do cowboy songs!" (Escott, *Hank Williams,* 143). Williams, Escott writes, "was happy to cash the checks that came when the palm orchestras played his songs," but he feared the practice was giving way to a "dilution" of his work (*Hank Williams,* 143–45).

78. Williams quoted in Goodson, "Hillbilly Humanist," 109.

79. Leppert and Lipsitz, "Age, the Body," 25, 22.

80. On his appetite for popular romance texts, see the film documentary *Hank Williams: The Honky-Tonk Blues.* Regarding Williams's sexual appeal, Garrison Keillor called him "the first really sexy hillbilly" ("'Lovesick Blues'"), and Minnie Pearl claimed that "he had a real animal magnetism" and "destroyed the women in the audience" (quoted in Roger M. Williams' biographical essay on Williams in *Stars of Country Music,* 245).

81. The term is Barbara Ching's (*Wrong's What I Do Best,* 75).

82. Ching, *Wrong's What I Do Best,* 54.

83. Ching, *Wrong's What I Do Best,* 55.

84. Escott, *Hank Williams,* 14.

85. Ching, *Wrong's What I Do Best,* 54. Ching argues that in "Honky-Tonkin'," the speaker is positioned as an unflattering "gigolo" who depends on a woman's money; in "Honky Tonk Blues," bar-hopping "becomes a compulsive repetition of failure," since the youthful narrator isn't tough enough to withstand the city and is kept "metaphorically down on the farm" (*Wrong's What I Do Best,* 54–55).

86. Leppert and Lipsitz, "Age, the Body," 28–29.

87. "Your Cheatin' Heart," recorded for MGM in 1952, released posthumously in 1953.

88. Escott, *Hank Williams,* 218.

89. In this sense, Audrey may have ironically put her finger on the truth when she suggested that her ex-husband had in fact "written the song about himself" (Escott, *Hank Williams,* 218).

90. Written by Hy Heath and Fred Rose, recorded by Williams in Sept. 1952 and reissued by MGM in 1953.

91. Leppert and Lipsitz, "Age, the Body," 31. I discovered after the fact that these two critics refer precisely to "Your Cheatin' Heart" and "Take These Chains from My Heart" to draw this conclusion.

92. Leppert and Lipsitz, "Age, the Body," 30.

93. Leppert and Lipsitz, "Age, the Body," 25.

94. Like Tubb's, Williams' childhood was marked by an absent father (a World War I veteran who never physically or psychically recovered from his war experience and remained in a series of Veterans' Administration hospitals for many years), which compelled him to seek work at an early age to help his mother, a church organist, make ends meet. For more details, see Lange, *Smile When You Call Me a Hillbilly*, 168–69; Escott, *Hank Williams*, 3–14. Patrick Carr, while otherwise fetishizing Hank as an icon of male rebellion, seems to agree with my claim here: "The bottom line is that the poor sonofabitch is beating his brains against the wall and tearing his heart out because when it comes right down to it, all he really wants out of life is a good, happy, loving Christian home and family. And he just isn't going to get it" ("Will the Circle Be Unbroken?" 344).

95. Ching, *Wrong's What I Do Best*, 60.

96. Written by Williams and recorded in 1949.

97. Recorded for MGM in 1947, released as a single in 1948.

98. The song's urban context can be traced to its writer, Marcel Joseph, a New York journalist. Escott surmises that Fred Rose assisted Williams on his diction in the song's recording, because the word *window* is "pronounced faultlessly—not as 'winn-der,'" and dismissively concludes that it "wasn't much of a song" (*Hank Williams*, 196).

99. Nick Tosches replicates such caricature when he casts "Fame and Fortune" as "those twin bitches from across the tracks" who "raised their skirts higher" and seduced Williams to his peril ("Honky-Tonkin," 168, 169).

100. Escott, *Hank Williams*, 67. Escott also snidely comments, "She wanted to be more than a happy homemaker, which would be easier to applaud if she could have sung even passably well" (*Hank Williams*, 66). Horace Logan, the program director for the *Louisiana Hayride* during Hank's tenure there, simply calls her "a pure, unmitigated, hard-boiled, blue-eyed bitch" (85).

101. Escott, *Hank Williams*, 85, 96.

102. Escott, *Hank Williams*, 187–88.

103. The song "Wedding Bells" furnishes another example: "I planned a little cottage in the valley / I even bought a band of gold / I thought I'd place it on your finger / But now the future looks so dark and cold."

104. The phrase is in Leppert and Lipsitz, "Age, the Body," 32.

105. Coontz, *Way We Never Were*, 41.

106. Ching notes that Williams's songs of heartache "often leave the singer psychically homeless, socially isolated, and almost inhuman—'like a piece of driftwood,' . . . rambling down the 'Lost Highway,' or mechanically walking the floor" (*Wrong's What I Do Best*, 61). Leppert and Lipsitz reference the "drifting" terminology to position Williams "as a fugitive from nearly any stable identity" ("Age, the Body," 31).

107. Leppert and Lipsitz, "Age, the Body," 27.

108. On "Tee Tot," see Escott, *Hank Williams*, 10–12, which claims that at the height of his career, Williams gave his childhood "mentor" "full credit" for his musical influence. See also Leppert and Lipsitz, "Age, the Body," 31. The latter text goes on to compare Williams's vocal styles, in his songs of unrequited love, to

Billie Holiday's and Nina Simone's; his similar "emotional intensity," Leppert and Lipsitz suggest, blurs the line "not only between genders, but between races as well" (32).

109. That title is derived from the "Special Hank Williams Memorial Issue" of *Country Song Roundup*, no. 24 (June 1953): 5. For descriptions of 1954's "Hank Williams Memorial Day," which included the dedication of an enormous marble monument, see Lange, *Smile When You Call Me a Hillbilly*, 171. For descriptions of the funeral, see Tosches, who cites the *Montgomery Advertiser*'s account: "They came from everywhere . . . dressed in their Sunday best, babies on their arms, hobbling on crutches and canes, Negroes, Jews, Catholics, Protestants, small children, and wrinkled faced old men and women" ("Honky-Tonkin'," 174).

110. Richard Peterson uses the term *personification* in his chapter title "Hank Williams as the Personification of Country Music" (*Creating Country Music*, 173). Also see the work of Patrick Carr and other previously cited scholars such as Malone and Lipsitz.

111. Lange, *Smile When You Call Me a Hillbilly*, 191. I will discuss Peterson's model more fully in chapter 4, represented by his article "The Dialectic of Hard-Core and Soft-Shell Country Music," and his discussion in *Creating Country Music*, principally 137–55. Lange's approach to phases in honky-tonk music departs from the norm by including Kitty Wells in the "primal" category and Carl Smith and Faron Young in the "soft" category, yet the gendered associations ascribed to these musical camps remain quite traditional.

112. Quoted in Pecknold, "'I Wanna Play House,'" 86. Jensen demonstrates that the *initial* industry discourse, however, cast the Nashville Sound as the commercial savior of country music, though she focuses less on the gendering of this campaign than Pecknold does. See *Nashville Sound*, 64–86.

113. See Pecknold's brilliant study of commercialism's impact on country music (*Selling Sound*, particularly chap. 2, "Country Music Becomes Mass Culture, 1940–1958," 53–94).

114. Both Tosches and Malone, for instance, fail to mention even the most popular female honky-tonk performer, Kitty Wells, in particular pieces focused on this genre of music. In fact, in his discographical essay on honky-tonk for the *Blackwell Guide to Recorded Country Music*, Tosches manages to mention Hank Thompson's "The Wild Side of Life" sans its much more famous "answer" song, Wells's "It Wasn't God Who Made Honky-Tonk Angels." Malone is guilty as charged in his essay "Honky Tonk" but does, of course, incorporate numerous women artists into his exhaustive history *Country Music, U.S.A.* As I suggest elsewhere in this chapter and book, Mary Bufwack and Robert Oermann's *Finding Her Voice* is a welcome departure from this practice.

115. *Billboard*, June 20, 1953, p. 1. Goldie Hill was dubbed the "Golden Hillbilly" and, as a member of the Opry as well as a featured performer on the *Louisiana Hayride*, seemed destined for stardom. However, her career turned out to be short-lived after she married Carl Smith in 1957; he preferred his wife to restrict her singing to her role "as a homemaker indulging in household hum-

ming" (statement in liner notes to Hill's first album, quoted in Bufwack and Oermann, *Finding Her Voice*, 155).

116. Oermann, "Honky-Tonk Angels," 224. Oermann also suggests that answer songs seem especially suitable to this genre due to country music's "predilection for telling a story; . . . the songs themselves often begged for sequels" (224).

117. Emily C. Neely makes this latter point in "Charline Arthur."

118. "Four Walls," written by Marvin Moore and George Campbell, 1957, Travis Music Company.

119. Written by Joe Maphis in 1952.

120. See Oermann's "Honky-Tonk Angels," whose inset piece, "Answer Songs: A Primer," argues that after Wells's first hit, "it became popular, almost common, for female singers to answer male artists' hits with the female perspective on the situation" (225). Jeffrey Lange also notes of Wells that she "explored the feminine side of the honky-tonk equation" (*Smile When You Call Me a Hillbilly*, 176). Nicholas Dawidoff writes, "By taking up the woman's point of view, Kitty Wells offered the first sustained feminine perspective in country music history" (*In the Country of Country*, 65). As will be explored later, female performers and their publicity materials also often subscribed to this notion.

121. K. Stewart, "Engendering Narratives," 223–24.

122. Butler, *Bodies That Matter*, 13–15.

123. K. Stewart, "Backtalking the Wilderness," 47. Stewart's work in this 1990 essay draws on key feminist theorists of the period—such as Luce Irigaray, Julia Kristeva, Teresa De Lauretis, and bell hooks—and also calls attention to the potential for agency in Butler's model of performativity. Influenced by Stewart's work, ethnomusicologist Aaron Fox takes a similar tack in his analysis of late-twentieth-century working-class Texan discourse, especially when performing songs of "gendered dialogue." He argues, for instance, that the "Honky-Tonk Angels" dyad of Thompson/Wells songs is frequently performed together in honky-tonk bars (the former by a male vocalist, the latter by a woman) so that they display both the traditional model of gender relations and its "feminist critique" (*Real Country*, 259).

124. K. Stewart, "Nostalgia," 232.

125. Her 1957 answer to Bobby Helms's big hit "Fraulein" essentially reinscribes its concoction of a faithful German girl still waiting for her American sweetheart.

126. Sanjek, "Can a Fujiyama Mama," 143. In this quote, Sanjek explicitly refers to Daphne Duval Harrison's theory of "talking smart" in female blues songs. He positions both African American blues "queens" and country's female honky-tonk singers as "foremothers" of rockabilly women performers (145).

127. K. Stewart, "Backtalking the Wilderness" 46. Stewart's exact quote is as follows: "Gender 'ways' are so conventionalized and so dramatically performed that they tend to be clearly externalized as discourses rather than internalized as identities."

128. Wells does emphasize, though, that Nashville in the 1930s was a "country town," with farmers bringing their vegetables to the downtown courthouse and wild animals afoot in the section called "Varmint Town" (interview in Dawidoff, *In the Country of Country,* 68).

129. The biographical information is drawn from several sources: Friskics-Warren, "Undisputed Queen"; Oermann, "Honky-Tonk Angels," 215–17; Bufwack and Oermann, *Finding Her Voice,* 150–52.

130. Oermann, "Honky-Tonk Angels," 216, 215. Dawidoff echoes the sentence's closing point by commenting, "Kitty Wells stayed jake with the good ol' boys and made it as a country singer in part because she seemed too placid to be much competition for anybody" (*In the Country of Country,* 66).

131. Her given name, Ellen Muriel Deason, was deemed too ordinary by Lowell Blanchard, program director at WKNOX, Knoxville. He convinced Wells's husband, then performing with his brother Jack, to find his new "girl" singer a "catchy name" (Dawidoff, *In the Country of Country,* 68).

132. "It Wasn't God Who Made Honky Tonk Angels," written by J. D. Miller, 1952; "The Wild Side of Life," written by William Warner and Arlie A. Carter, 1952.

133. William Warner relays, "She knew it was about her right off the bat, and a friend of mine overheard her say, 'I ought to go up there and pull that grey-headed son of a gun's hair all out'" (quoted in Horstman, *Sing Your Heart Out,* 210).

134. Clement quoted in Oermann, "Honky-Tonk Angels," 221; *Country Song Roundup,* no. 21 (Dec. 1952): 9. Ironically, the piece begins by noting, "It's rather odd when we stop to think about it that so few women ever break into that precious 'top ten'" on the country charts (9).

135. See photos of Wells and her "happy and content" family in *Rustic Rhythm* (July 1957, 50), and as "Country Music's First Family . . ." in *Country Music Life* (June 1966, 16). The latter photo's caption poses a distinct counter to Ernest Tubb's portrayal as the "king" of country on the front jacket of his album *The Daddy of 'Em All.* Peter La Chapelle's incisive work on country fan magazines during the 1950s has been useful to my research and will be explored in this chapter's final segment. See "'Spade Doesn't Look Exactly Starved.'"

136. Kitty Wells, *After Dark* (Decca, DL 8888, 1959).

137. Wells, quoted in Dawidoff, *In the Country of Country,* 65. The union-scale reference is in Friskics-Warren, "Undisputed Queen," 2.

138. Bufwack and Oermann, *Finding Her Voice,* 152. They also note that the song's very melody "had a nostalgic air" as it was borrowed from the Carters' "I'm Thinking Tonight of My Blue Eyes." Dorothy Horstman appears to agree, regretting that "Honky-Tonk Angels" depicts a sexual woman as "victim and thus perpetuates her subordinate role" (*Sing Your Heart Out,* 198).

139. Released in 1951 on MGM 11083.

140. Pearl quoted in Dawidoff, *In the Country of Country,* 66.

141. Friskics-Warren, "Undisputed Queen" 4, 7.

142. Dawidoff, *In the Country of Country,* 66–67.

143. Chap. 4, on country women performers' published autobiographies in later decades, discusses this kind of struggle for authenticity in much more detail.

144. "Paying for That Backstreet Affair" (Decca, 1953).

145. Written by Felice Bryant and Boudleaux Bryant, recorded in 1953.

146. "The Lonely Side of Town," written by Roy Botkin, originally recorded by Wells in 1955.

147. "Honky Tonk Waltz," written by Billy Wallace.

148. See Aaron Fox's essay "The Jukebox of History" for another reading of the jukebox trope. Fox concentrates on contemporary country music's representation of the jukebox "as a poetic 'operator' which introduces textual and melodic fragments of earlier country songs into an ongoing narrative" (62). I find his argument more useful to my next two chapters and will explore it more fully there.

149. Songwriting credit for this song includes Webb Pierce and Kitty Wells (my emphasis).

150. Elaine Tyler May, quoted in Sanjek, "Can a Fujiyama Mama," 165. Sanjek offers a compelling reading of Jackson's song in this context in order to examine how women in rockabilly "acted as . . . 'counter-irritants' to the social consensus of the 1950s" (140).

151. Patsy Montana's 1935 hit "I Want to Be a Cowboy's Sweetheart" can claim the important distinction of being the first record by a female country artist to sell a million records.

152. Friskics-Warren, "Undisputed Queen," 1.

153. *Billboard* reported that "the girls . . . rarely get on wax from 'out of the blue,'" citing the ex-wife of Floyd Tillman and Rose Maddox as two examples, though it also includes Cindy Walker, who attempted to parlay her position as a "prolific writer of country tunes" into a singing career with Columbia Records. See "Gals from the Hills," 27. Wells admitted as much when she told Nicholas Dawidoff, "I know a lot of women had a hard road to travel to make it on their own. I've never felt myself to be a feminist. I've always traveled with my husband. . . . I always had somebody to look after me" (*In the Country of Country*, 66).

154. Arthur was a dynamic vocalist, at home in both the honky-tonk and the rockabilly genres, yet her "feisty" personality and brazenly masculine performative persona proved controversial and, it is surmised, fatal to her career. See Bufwack and Oermann, who explicitly contrast Arthur to Wells (*Finding Her Voice*, 147–50); Bob Allen's liner notes to Arthur's *Welcome to the Club* (Bear Family Records, BCD 16279, 1998); and Emily C. Neely's essay "Charline Arthur."

155. Chris Skinker, liner notes to Jean Shepard, *The Melody Ranch Girl* (Bear Family Records BCD 15905, 1996), 6.

156. Nelson quoted in Skinker, liner notes, *Melody Ranch Girl*, 7–8.

157. Admittedly (and regrettably), any commentary on Shepard remains scant. Bill Friskics-Warren extols Shepard as "one of the finest honky-tonkers ever and a pioneering woman of country music" who "braved country's boys

club" by "open[ing] her own doors" ("Second to None"). Bufwack and Oermann call her the "tough little sparrow who braved the macho honky-tonk climate" and "the only early-1950s country music woman who made it on her own" (*Finding Her Voice*, 160). Skinker's 1990s biographical notes for the CD set *Melody Ranch Girl* remind us early on that "Jean managed to enter the dark, rough and tumble world of the honky-tonk scene without the benefit" of a family group or spouse (3).

158. The first three quotes are from "Program Patter on Jean Shepard," Capitol Records document, n.d.; the last quote is from "Jean Shepard," a publicity release produced by Hinton Bradbury in Hollywood (27 Oct. 1953). Both documents can be found in the Country Music Foundation Library's Jean Shepard File.

159. *Country Song Roundup*, no. 50 (June 1957): 10.

160. The quoted phrase is Skinker's (liner notes, *Melody Ranch Girl*, 3). When performing live, Shepard was often called "Jeannie" by male hosts, especially on the Opry, as noted in an interview with Bob Powel ("Jean Shepard," 30). Shepard also relayed that Nelson "wouldn't let me record a song where it showed me in a bad light" and specifically objected to her recording of "The Other Woman": "He says, 'Oh, no, no! We have to keep you the sweet little country girl!'" to which she replies, "'Ken, you don't know how mean I am!'" See Fulks, "Jean Shepard," 37.

161. Skinker, liner notes, *Melody Ranch Girl*, 9.

162. Songwriters credited as Lewis Talley, Fuzzy Owen, and Billy Barton (Capitol Records, F2502, 1953). Tubb later recorded a cover of the song with then–duet partner Loretta Lynn.

163. Statement made by DJ (and later songwriter) Slim Willet, who phoned Nelson to report his radio audience's immediate enthusiastic response to "A Dear John Letter" (Skinker, liner notes, *Melody Ranch Girl*, 10).

164. Skinker notes that the songwriting credits officially went to Shepard and Billy Barton but that Shepard confirmed that the songwriters were in fact the same as for the original "A Dear John Letter": Lewis Talley, Fuzzy Owen, and Barton (liner notes, *Melody Ranch Girl*, 11).

165. Written by Jack Rhodes.

166. Skinker, liner notes, *Melody Ranch Girl*, 11; Bufwack and Oermann, *Finding Her Voice*, 159.

167. Program videotape of episode 2, *Country Style USA*, accessed at Country Music Foundation Library, Nashville. While undated, this episode can be placed in the mid-1950s due to Shepard's song choices, as well as the appearance on her segment of Hawkshaw Hawkins, whom she married in 1960 but who here is referred to as simply her "old friend."

168. La Chapelle, "'Spade Doesn't Look Exactly Starved,'" 38.

169. Songwriting credit for this song formally goes to "Joe Franklin," but as noted above, this is one of Ferlin Husky's pseudonyms.

170. La Chapelle writes, "Although some contend that the song failed to hit the charts because it was too shocking for public tastes, . . . the most likely reason . . . was that disc jockeys, a group that was almost entirely male, were offended by

the unrepentant lyrics and failed to give it ample air time" ("'Spade Doesn't Look Exactly Starved,'" 39).

171. Sanjek, "Can a Fujiyama Mama," 146.

172. "Hello Old Broken Heart," written by Joe Allison and Audrey Allison, 1955. The album's jacket copy claims that the song served as "inspiration" for the entire project: "When Jean Shepard heard the song, it suggested to her an album dealing with the moods and experiences of a young girl in love. So Jean got busy collecting the rest of the special songs she needed to tell the story." However, Chris Skinker's brief description of the production process suggests that Shepard in fact had little to do with its conceptualization or with song choices (liner notes, *Melody Ranch Girl*, 12–13).

173. For wedding details, see Bufwack and Oermann, *Finding Her Voice*, 159; Skinker, liner notes, *Melody Ranch Girl*, 17, which also relays that the excessive wedding was Hawkins's idea, not Shepard's.

174. Martin, "Jean Shepard Enjoys."

175. "When Your House Is Not a Home," written by Roger Miller, released by Capitol Records. Even recent autobiographer Skinker frames the song this way (liner notes, *Melody Ranch Girl*, 23).

176. Written by Betty Amos, released by Capitol Records. Friskics-Warren uses the song as a commentary on Shepard's "second-fiddle" role to "female counterparts" such as Wells ("Second to None," 23). Its title, as many have noted, also came to name her back-up band, the Second Fiddles.

177. Shepard not only vehemently protested Olivia Newton-John's winning of the Country Music Association's Female Vocalist of the Year award in 1974, but she also demonstrated her class solidarity by fighting for a rise in local musicians' union scale. For the former, she suffered severe industry rejection by both her record label and radio DJs. See Friskics-Warren, "Second to None," 23; Bufwack and Oermann, *Finding Her Voice,* 160; "Jean Shepard," *Country Music People*, 32.

178. La Chapelle, "'Spade Doesn't Look Exactly Starved,'" 31 (two quotes).

179. See *Country Song Roundup*, no. 44 (1956), or no. 34 (1954). The latter issue's story "The Wright Way" covers Wells as just one part of the singing Wright family and casts Kitty and Johnnie's courtship as a romantic tale involving a "lovely young brunette" and "handsome young swain" (9). This publication also featured ads for piano-playing gimmicks targeting women readers that appealed to their desire for popularity with men as opposed to their interest in musicianship.

180. *Rustic Rhythm* 1:1, Apr. 1957, 8.

181. *Rustic Rhythm* 1:1, Apr. 1957, 8.

182. *Rustic Rhythm* 1:1, Apr. 1957, 9.

183. See Stephanie Coontz on how "cold war anxieties merged with concerns about the expanded sexuality of family life and the commercial world to create . . . the domestic version of George F. Kennan's containment policy toward the Soviet Union" (*Way We Never Were,* 33). Within the country music industry itself, the gendered conflict over commercialism is also reflected in the develop-

ment and eventual demise of fan clubs run almost entirely by working-class women. See Diane Pecknold's examination of such clubs, which emphasized members' status as "mature" homemakers dedicated to the music (as opposed to "erotically fixated teenage girls" [*Selling Sound*, 130]), yet by the end of the 1960s proved ill-matched to the industry's compulsive commercialism (124–32).

184. *Rustic Rhythm*, Sept. 1957, 4; *Rustic Rhythm*, Apr. 1957, 27 (two quotes) (my emphasis).

185. To wit: "The smiling lady manages to give full-time attention to the proper upbringing of a 12-year-old son, and a little daughter, 4 years of age. What could possibly keep this busy lady in such good spirits and so happy at the pace she's going? Perhaps it's because she and her family don't permit anything to interfere with their precious moments reserved only for themselves" ("Sunshine Sue," 39).

186. Rubin, "Sing Me Back Home," 93, 99 (two quotes), 101 (two quotes).

187. Rubin, "Sing Me Back Home," 99, 100.

188. Lynn found Wells an enormous inspiration. Upon hearing "Honky-Tonk Angels," she felt "it was such a treat to hear a woman sing. . . . With that song she touched in me what I was living and what I was going through and I knew there was a lot of women that lived like me. I thought, 'Here's a woman telling our point of view of everyday life'" (Dawidoff, *In the Country of Country,* 64). Decca producer Owen Bradley pointedly contrasted these two women artists, however, by arguing that Kitty "had no hardness to her" but that "Loretta Lynn had the opposite quality—'You don't straighten up, I'll beat the hell out of you'" (quoted in Dawidoff, *In the Country of Country,* 66).

Chapter 4

1. Lynn, *Coal Miner's Daughter,* 1, xii.

2. I am principally drawing on Richard Peterson's essay "The Dialectic of Hard-Core and Soft-Shell Country Music" for this claim, and any citations of his work come from this article. Other work touching on autobiography in country music includes Banes, "Mythology in Music," and "Dixie's Daughters"; Tharpe, "Homemade Soap"; Dunne, "Country Music"; Wilson, "Mountains of Contradictions."

Other larger studies that include discussion of country music autobiography or the autobiographical strain of country lyrics include: Malone, *Country Music, U.S.A.;* C. Ellison, *Country Music Culture;* Shank, *Dissonant Identities.*

3. Peterson, "Dialectic," 289.

4. A sampling of male memoirs includes: Willie Nelson, *Willie;* Johnny Cash, *Man in Black;* Merle Haggard, *Sing Me Back Home;* Hank Williams Jr., *Living Proof;* Roy Acuff, *Roy Acuff's Nashville;* Glen Campbell, *Rhinestone Cowboy;* Charley Pride, *Pride;* Hank Snow, *Hank Snow Story;* Travis Tritt, *Ten Feet Tall and Bulletproof;* George Jones, *I Lived to Tell It All;* Waylon Jennings, *Waylon.*

5. I use the term *literary* broadly but deliberately here. Clearly, the con-

temporary celebrity memoir as we know it scarcely pretends to pose as an aesthetic masterpiece, and I am aware that within the genre of autobiography itself, subcategories arguably exist that distinguish among "aesthetic," "confessional," and "popular" prose. (See, e.g., Rita Felski's discussion of feminist autobiographical confessional writing, which she claims often rejects explicitly "literary" devices in order to heighten its claims of "authenticity," in *Beyond Feminist Aesthetics*, 96–97.) But as I contend in the following pages, those who are marked (or market themselves) as "il-literate" can approach the publishing arena with a particular kind of trepidation, investing it with a cultural mystique whose "literary" conventions and trappings most assuredly do hold sway.

6. Brodzki and Schenck, *Life/Lines*, 1. For a glimpse of the foundational work in this area, see S. Smith, *Subjectivity, Identity, and the Body*; Gilmore, *Autobiographics*. Also see the anthologies Watson and Smith, *De/Colonizing the Subject*; Ashley, Gilmore, and Peters, *Autobiography and Postmodernism*; and Cosslett, Lury, and Summerfield, *Feminism and Autobiography*.

7. I am offering a necessarily reductive overview here to sketch out the basic lineaments of this position. Critics such as Felski, and certainly later scholars, complicate this gendered division. See Felski's chapter "On Confession" in *Beyond Feminist Aesthetics*, 86–121.

8. See Philippe Lejeune's *On Autobiography*, 185, along with the following work of feminist scholars: Davies, "Collaboration and the Ordering Imperative"; R. Carr, "Crossing the First World/Third World Divides."

9. Lejeune, *On Autobiography*, 186.

10. Lejeune, *On Autobiography*, 189 (two quotes), 194.

11. Dyer, *Stars*, 24–25.

12. Lejeune, *On Autobiography*, 197 (two quotes).

13. Lejeune, *On Autobiography*, 199. Lejeune explains, "The illustrious, or exemplary, person must be a full and complete subject. . . . As soon as he discloses his life in a book, the hero must be in control of the writing, or at least what represents it symbolically, the *signature*" (*On Autobiography*, 195).

14. Lejeune, *On Autobiography*, 196.

15. A. Fox, "Jukebox of History," 54.

16. A. Fox, "Jukebox of History," 55.

17. A. Fox, "Jukebox of History," 55–56.

18. The song/autobiography title "Stand By Your Man" is an especially interesting example, as Wynette's tortured personal and professional relationship with singer George Jones has in itself become a kind of country metanarrative. Reading *Stand By Your Man*, one senses that Wynette "knew" even as a young girl that women's conventional pathway to stardom in the country industry was to marry—and hence to live out the narrative expectations of—one of its greatest icons. Though defiantly proud of "making it" on her own, Wynette betrays an obsession with Jones throughout her text. From her early schoolgirl crush, to her dawning disappointment with and eventual fear of his violent alcoholic binges in her role as long-suffering wife, to her distant friendship with him after her own final remarriage, Wynette weaves Jones into nearly every chapter. Thus, though

many in the popular press have remarked on her multiple divorces when relishing the irony of "Stand By Your Man"'s refrain, the title certainly captures Jones's overarching presence in this memoir (and is, in this sense, an entirely appropriate title for the book as a whole).

19. For the record, male stars Johnny Cash, Merle Haggard, and Willie Nelson, each attaining rather mythic hard-core stature as much for their personal life histories as for their musical styles, produced autobiographies that similarly attempt to fuse literary text and song: Nelson's chapter headings are song titles, Haggard's book title borrows from one of his most celebrated tunes (*Sing Me Back Home*), and Cash's *Man in Black* sports both.

20. Jay, "Posing," 191.

21. Barthes, *Camera Lucida*, 12.

22. Judd, *Love Can Build a Bridge*, fourth page of photo insert.

23. Photo inserts in the male texts tend to use first-person captions as well, though they also deviate from this pattern with several intriguing formal additions: Nelson's *Willie* includes a "chorus" of other voices, provided by his family and friends, that comment on the author's version of events in the narrative. Haggard's *Sing Me Back Home* incorporates reproductions of actual documents pertaining to the singer-author's life—his police record, his pardon by then–California governor Ronald Reagan, etc. The former device has the potential to denaturalize identity, while the latter primarily works to reproduce claims of authenticity.

24. Quoted in Bob Allen's "What Hath Tom Carter Wrought?" 309.

25. Lynn, *Coal Miner's Daughter*, xiii–xiv.

26. Lynn, *Coal Miner's Daughter*, xiv (two quotes) (emphasis added), ix, xiii.

27. Allen, "What Hath Tom Carter Wrought?" 306 (two quotes).

28. Parton, *Dolly*, vii.

29. McEntire, *Reba*, ix.

30. Judd, *Love Can Build a Bridge*, ix–x.

31. Cannon, *Minnie Pearl*, acknowledgments page.

32. A. Fox, "Jukebox of History," 54, 60. Ruth A. Banes puts a more optimistic spin on this schema by arguing that country music has historically offered a "countermythology" of Southern womanhood ("neither belles nor trash") that honors "working-class women . . . as strong characters who celebrate the traditional virtues of southern culture: hard work, meaningful work, the importance of family and friends, marital fidelity, independence, honesty, simplicity, and inner strength" ("Dixie's Daughters," 83). Such a vision, however, seems to minimize if not neglect entirely the music's history of reproducing more conventional gender norms.

33. A. Fox, "Jukebox of History," 61.

34. A. Fox, "Jukebox of History," 58.

35. A. Fox, "Jukebox of History," 54.

36. Vestiges of this sentiment even emerge within relatively recent critical commentary on these women's autobiographical texts: Bob Allen, for instance, who was quoted earlier for his fetishization of *Coal Miner's Daughter* as "folk lit-

erature," objects to Reba McEntire's "voice," which, "despite all her accomplishments, lacks the color, unfettered vivacity, and startling insight" found in Lynn's memoir ("What Hath Tom Carter Wrought?" 310–11).

37. See Coltman, "Sweethearts of the Hills," 162–64; Oermann, "Mother, Sister, Sweetheart, Pal," 125–29; Bufwack and Oermann, *Finding Her Voice*, xiv and chaps. 3 and 4 (43–91); Banes, "Dixie's Daughters," 86–89; Malone, *Country Music, U.S.A.*, 119–20. Many recount the example of Rachel Veach, the banjo player and comedian, who after joining Roy Acuff's band was forced as late as 1940 to appear as the sister of fellow band member Beecher Kirby (subsequently billed as "Brother Oswald") to escape audience critique and concern.

38. To be sure, more current figures like body-baring performers Shania Twain and Sara Evans have produced a sea change in such expectations. Yet women artists must still arguably walk a fine line.

39. Judd, *Love Can Build a Bridge*, xiv.

40. Judd, *Love Can Build a Bridge*, xiii.

41. Wynette, *Stand By Your Man*, 10–11.

42. Wynette, *Stand By Your Man*, 320.

43. Judd, *Love Can Build a Bridge*, xiii.

44. McEntire, *Reba*, xii.

45. McEntire, *Reba*, xi, xii.

46. Tharpe, "Homemade Soap," 151.

47. Lynn, *Coal Miner's Daughter*, x.

48. Lynn, *Coal Miner's Daughter*, 19.

49. Lynn, *Coal Miner's Daughter*, 37. One memory strikingly captures this situation: when Doolittle first came courting, he brought Lynn a doll as a Christmas gift and informed her that they were going to be married so that "next Christmas we'd have a real live doll" (Lynn, *Coal Miner's Daughter*, 48).

50. Lynn, *Coal Miner's Daughter*, xii, 181, 183, 55.

51. Cannon, *Minnie Pearl*, 9.

52. Cannon, *Minnie Pearl*, 9, 118, 10.

53. Cannon, *Minnie Pearl*, 11, 21, 11.

54. Cannon, *Minnie Pearl*, 92–99, 120, 120–21, 129, 21.

55. Cannon, *Minnie Pearl*, 127, 168, 169.

56. Cannon, *Minnie Pearl*, 18, 43 (two quotes), 44, 44–45, 45.

57. Cannon, *Minnie Pearl*, 147, 154, 102 (two quotes).

58. Cannon, *Minnie Pearl*, 145, 203, 205, 154.

59. Most notably, Wilson, "Mountains of Contradictions."

60. Parton, *Dolly*, 194.

61. Parton, *Dolly*, 2, 58–59.

62. Parton, *Dolly*, 126, 61.

63. Parton, *Dolly*, 287.

64. Parton, *Dolly*, 278, 280–81.

65. Parton, *Dolly*, 69, 73, 76, 77, 78, 225–26.

66. Butler, *Bodies That Matter*, 244.

67. Lynn, *Still Woman Enough*, xx.

68. *Coal Miner's Daughter.*

69. Lynn, *Still Woman Enough,* xvi, xv, xii. The film similarly confused Lynn's young twin daughters, who at the time believed the screen version to be the "original" text. Lynn opens *Still Woman Enough* with their query, "Mommy, why do you try to talk like Sissy Spacek?" (ix).

70. This was true of Wynette even before her death in 1998. The three regained some visibility in 1993 by fittingly paying tribute to Kitty Wells in their cover of her song "Honky-Tonk Angels." (See the CD *Honky Tonk Angels,* released on Sony.)

71. Parton, for instance, has recorded at least two bluegrass albums with Sugarhill: 1999's *The Grass Is Blue* and 2001's *Little Sparrow.* Many recent top-selling women in the country field, like Martina McBride, Shania Twain, and Gretchen Wilson, have also gone on record to claim Wynette, Lynn, and others as important role models. Unfortunately, their testimonies have had little impact on country radio.

72. *Van Lear Rose* was released, however, on Los Angeles label Interscope Records.

Chapter 5

1. Scherman, "Country," 1, 14. Scherman tends to operate with an all-too-familiar masculinist bias when touting earlier heroes of authenticity, such as proclaiming "George Jones, Merle Haggard, Willie Nelson, and Waylon Jennings the last great infusion of country-music creativity" (14), but to his credit he singles out Emmylou Harris as one central precursor to the alt. phenomenon.

2. This appellation was chosen by *No Depression* magazine in the summer of 2007, replacing the previously noncommittal (and transmogrifying) tagline "Alt.Country (Whatever That Is)."

3. Until recently, this subgenre and growing subculture received scant attention from academics concerned with country music, popular music, or alternative cultures and was scrutinized primarily by music journalists and popular commentators, as well as a plethora of fan Web sites. For three overviews, see Goodman, *Modern Twang;* Alden and Blackstock, *No Depression;* Hinton, *South by Southwest;* and a collection of artist profiles by journalist Monte Dutton: *True to the Roots.*

For the first scholarly book devoted to alt.country, see P. Fox and Ching, *Old Roots, New Routes.* Three earlier essays by country music scholars particularly laid the foundation for such inquiry: Peterson and Beal, "'Alternative' Country," provides a sociological study focused specifically on the fans' use of an Internet listserv known as Postcard2 to develop an alt.country audience and discourse; Ching, "Going Back to the Old Mainstream," offers a valuable feminist critique of "macho nostalgia" (1) in *No Depression* magazine; and A. Fox, "Alternative to What?" interrogates the meaning of alt.country by examining the success of the alt. soundtrack to the Coen brothers' film *O Brother Where Art Thou?*, in the context of a post-9/11 United States.

4. See Ching and P. Fox, "Importance of Being Ironic."

5. R. Williams, *Marxism and Literature,* 116, 115, 122. My coedited volume with Ching is similarly informed by Williams's stance here.

6. Livingston, "Music Revivals," 66.

7. I am quoting Shocked's ad for her 2002 double album *Deep Natural/Dub Natural* (released on her own label Mighty Sound), which appeared in alt.country's premiere publication, *No Depression* (Spring 2002), 46.

8. See reviews of both *Southern Rock Opera* and *Decoration Day* in *Rolling Stone* (no. 888, 31 Jan. 2001, and no. 925, 26 June 2003) and the *Village Voice* (16 June 2003) (Robert Christgau, "Pick Hit").

9. Livingston, "Music Revivals," 66. See Neil Rosenberg's edited volume *Transforming Traditions.*

10. Mancini, "'Messin' with the Furniture Man," 226; Pecknold, *Selling Sound,* 61. Mancini is addressing the "anthologizing" impulse of pre– and post–World War II musicologists such as Harry Smith (*Anthology of American Folk Music*), Ruth Crawford Seeger (*American Folk Songs for Children*), and Alan Lomax (*Sounds of the South*) and explicitly links that trend to alt.country, noting that the 1997 reissuing of Smith's *Anthology* "appears to have launched yet another folk revival, exemplified by the hugely successful sound track to *O Brother, Where Art Thou?*" ("'Messin' with the Furniture Man," 222). Pecknold's quote references the recording criteria of Columbia Records' highbrow country music executive Art Satherly in the 1940s.

11. Livingston, "Music Revivals," 68.

12. Livingston, "Music Revivals," 77, 69.

13. While Williams is still considered a seminal figure in the British cultural studies tradition, his cultural materialist approach for a time fell out of favor, critiqued for naively clinging to certain humanist ideals as pure deconstruction took hold in the academy during the 1980s.

14. R. Williams, *Country and the City,* 7, 297.

15. R. Williams, *Marxism and Literature,* 114, 122.

16. Watkins, *Throwaways,* 7.

17. Watkins, *Throwaways,* 116 (emphasis added). See also Ching and P. Fox, "Importance of Being Ironic," 16–17. Williams uses the term *ratify* in *Marxism and Literature* (116).

18. Ching and P. Fox, "Importance of Being Ironic," 17–18.

19. Williams, *Marxism and Literature,* 112, 114 (two quotes).

20. Watkins, *Throwaways,* 40.

21. *No Depression* 38 (Mar.–Apr. 2002): 46.

22. F. Goodman, "Conversation with Michelle Shocked," 3.

23. Shocked, liner notes, *Arkansas Traveler,* 5.

24. Shocked, liner notes, *Arkansas Traveler,* 5 (two quotes). In the liner notes, Shocked also refers fans to an alternative treatise cowritten with her then-fiancé, music journalist Bart Bull. She calls the songbook, titled *Does This Road Go to Little Rock?,* an "illuminating booklet on Eurocentric High Culture's sordid little love affair with blackface minstrelsy" (5). When I contacted Shocked's Web site

about obtaining this text, she herself responded that Bull, whom she had since divorced, owned the rights to the booklet, which was thus no longer available.

25. Quoted in Dutch radio interview with host Hubert Van Hoof: "Michelle Shocked Song Explanations."

26. Her million-dollar lawsuit against Mercury took three years to settle. In the meantime, she released a record titled *Artists Make Lousy Slaves* (F. Goodman, "Conversation," 3).

27. F. Goodman, "Conversation," 12.

28. As quoted in Van Hoof, "Michelle Shocked Song Explanations."

29. During a 1995 performance in Sydney, Australia, Shocked explained that "pescado mojado me encontre" is "the Mexican equivalent of saying, 'I came in like a wet fish'" ("Michelle Shocked Song Explanations"). "33 R.P.M. Soul" serves as an even more appropriate departure point for the album, however, when one discovers that Shocked wrote and often performs an obscene version of the song, pronouncing certain words to intone "motherfucker," "shit-piss-fuck," "censorship," and "cocksucker" as a critique of the Federal Communications Commission. Such tactics were standard minstrel show fare, in which malapropism often served as a cover for both "blue" content and social protest.

30. The song's penultimate stanza declares, "You can't touch a tarbaby, everybody knows / Smiling all the while wit de bone in de nose / That's the way the story goes / That's the way my story goes."

31. Allen, "BR5-49," 45.

32. Founded in 1999, the AMA exists "to provide a forum for the advocacy of Americana music, promote public awareness of the genre, and to support the creative and economic viability of the professionals within this field." See its full mission statement at http://www.americanamusic.org. However, a kind of "counter"-organization appeared to challenge the AMA, called FARM: Friends of American Roots Music. It is, according to its founder, John Conquest, a "lampoon of the Americana Music Association, an unstructured, nonhierarchical, grassroots, anti-organization that would have none of the things the AMA has, but would offer what the AMA doesn't, practical reasons for people to belong. No dues, no rules, no officers, no mission, no special interests, *only* benefits." See http://austin78704.com/sites/FARM/ (accessed 10 Nov. 2003).

33. "Nashville Rash," written and recorded by Dale Watson, *Cheatin' Heart Attack* (Hightone Records, 1995); "Fuck This Town," written and recorded by Robbie Fulks, *South Mouth* (Bloodshot Records, 1997) (published by Songwriters Ink).

34. To wit: "I ain't sayin' that suburban moms ain't fun, but I don't think that's the way Hank wanted it done" (Dallas Wayne's 2000 cover of "If That Ain't Country" [a Robbie Fulks song]). Houston Marchman similarly charges Nashville with privileging the tastes of the "eighth-grade-level-divorced housewife" in his 1999 song "Viet Nashville." See P. Fox and Ching, "Importance of Being Ironic," 14.

35. See Bloodshot Records' Web site for other examples of its distinctive rhetoric: http://www.bloodshotrecords.com (accessed 14 March 1998).

36. As quoted in Remz, "Alternative Country."

37. Little Dog Records, http://www.littledogrecords.com/news.php (accessed 29 Jan. 2008).

38. Alden and Blackstock, *Best of No Depression,* 1.

39. P. Fox and Ching, "Importance of Being Ironic," 13; "true art": liner notes, *No Depression: What It Sounds Like,* vol. 1 (Dualtone Records, 1153, 2004).

40. See Peterson and Kern, "Changing Highbrow Taste," 904.

41. Fenster, "Buck Owens," 287.

42. The cited *Vanity Fair* issue was dubbed "The Country & Western Music Portfolio," Nov. 2006, 291. Also see John Schulian's "Country Music Crossbred with Country Literature," a *New York Times* article on "the stirring of a kinship between Southern literature and alt-country music" (August 19, 2001).

43. In 2002, Adams joined Willie Nelson in a Gap commercial, singing Hank Williams' "Move It On Over" (slogan: "For Every Generation"). In an interview, Adams insisted that "my ambition is strictly artistic" and, when asked about the ad, defensively replied, "who says no to $30,000 an hour? . . . I'm sorry if that's selling out, so be it. . . . I do Gap ads so that I don't have to work in a factory." See "Ryan Adams on 'Demolition.'"

44. Alt.country's mode of hero worship is catching on, however: witness Alan Jackson's championing—even rescuing—of George Jones, which certainly began earlier (see reference in 1991's "Don't Rock the Jukebox") but escalated over time to include duets such as "A Good Year for the Roses"; Toby Keith's strategic featuring of Willie Nelson in the song "Beer for My Horses" and its accompanying video; and Little Jimmie Dickens's cameo in Brad Paisley's "Celebrity" video. As noted at the end of chap. 4, only Jack White of the alternative garage rock band the White Stripes has ventured to identify with a female country icon, Loretta Lynn, offering to produce her album *Van Lear Rose* due to his unabashed respect for her music.

45. Quoted in Sacks, "Strange Motives."

46. Quoted in Clemmons, "Cow Punker Angry Johnny."

47. *Hell-Bent: Insurgent Country,* vol. 2 (Bloodshot, BS004, 1996).

48. P. Fox and Ching, "Importance of Being Ironic," 17–18.

49. *Country Love Songs* (Bloodshot Records, BS011, 1996); *BR5-49* (Arista, 0782218818-2, 1996).

50. "Drugstore Truck Drivin' Man," on *Clear Impetuous Morning* (Mammoth/Atlantic, 92730-2, 1996); *Sebastopol* (Artemis Records, 751 093-2, 2001); "Blue Devil," on *Lovesick, Broke & Driftin'* (Curb Records, D278728, 2002).

51. Phrase borrowed from Zehnbauer, "Twang Revolution Takes Off."

52. Clemmons, "Cow Punker Angry Johnny," 1.

53. Clemmons, "Cow Punker Angry Johnny," 2, 1 (two quotes).

54. See their Web site, http://www.getangry.com (accessed 15 Nov. 2002).

55. Sacks, "Strange Motives," 3.

56. "Risin' Outlaw" served as the title of Hank III's debut album on Curb Records; it is also the slogan tattooed on his arm. See http://www.curb.com/artists/artistbio_T1.cfm?ID=81 (accessed 10 Nov. 2003).

57. Bernstein, "Whatever Name He Goes By."

58. *No Depression* 6 (Winter 1996): 57. One wry take on this trend: the Dixie Chicks' "Goodbye Earl," a cheerful domestic-violence revenge narrative.

59. Words and music by Chuck Neese, Bob McDill, and Wayland Holyfield. Interestingly, the song can also be found on alt.country performer "Elmer"'s album *Songs of Sin and Retribution* as an arch example of "Punk Rock Hillbilly Silliness"—clearly upping the hipness quotient by satirizing even this blue-collar standard.

60. D. Cantwell, "Children of Detroit City."

61. Barbara Ching chooses another, equally damning model for Tosches's stature, noting that his book *Country: Living Legends and Dying Metaphors in America's Biggest Music* is "written with all the tedious bravado of a frat boy who knows what's in and what's out," (234). See "Acting Naturally."

62. Tosches, *Country: The Twisted Roots*, xiii, 66, 72–73.

63. The song appears on *Hell-Bent: Insurgent Country*, vol. 2.

64. Dawidoff, *In the Country of Country*, 15.

65. Copetas, "Bottle Rockets," 1.

66. Copetas, "Bottle Rockets," 1. The band reappeared in a *No Depression* cover story for the Winter 2003 issue, but writer Peter Blackstock chose to recast its class markers, converting economic and cultural marginality into a tendentious "socio-political sensibility" more evocative of Merle Haggard's noble migrant workers. See "Hell of a Spell," 94.

67. See One Riot One Ranger's Old Home Page at http://members.aol.com/oneriot/bandbio.html (accessed 26 June 1997).

68. Bloodshot Records catalog, unpaginated.

69. On *For Lovers Only* (Feedbag, 1992).

70. "Unknown Hinson," 33 (two quotes).

71. Alden, "Rocking Tall," 85.

72. Lyrics by Patterson Hood, music by the Drive-By Truckers, on *Southern Rock Opera* (Lost Highway Records, 088 170 308-2, 2002).

73. Alden, "Rocking Tall," 89.

74. Alden, "Rocking Tall," 86.

75. Lyrics by Mike Cooley, music by the Drive-By Truckers, on *Decoration Day* (New West Records, NW6047, 2003).

76. See, e.g., Benjamin DeMott's "Safe American Home," in which he calls *Southern Rock Opera* the "follow-up to Darkness [*Darkness on the Edge of Town*] that Springsteen himself never really managed to make. In part, because he couldn't quite cross over the color line" (4).

77. "Heathens,'" lyrics by Patterson Hood, music by Drive-By Truckers, on *Decoration Day*.

78. Lyrics by Mike Cooley, music by Drive-By Truckers.

79. *The Dirty South* (New West Records, 2004).

80. Patterson Hood, song "writeup" for "Puttin' People on the Moon," Drive-By Truckers Web site, http://www.drivebytruckers.com/writeup_tds.html (accessed 5 Feb. 2008).

81. Lyrics by Patterson Hood, published by Soul Dump Music.

82. "Cottonseed," lyrics by Mike Cooley, published by Wayward Johnson's

Music; "Boys from Alabama," lyrics by Patterson Hood, published by Soul Dump Music; "Goddamn Lonely Love," lyrics by Jason Isbell, published by House of Fame Music.

83. Patterson Hood, quoted in Alden, "Rocking Tall," 85.

84. "The Southern Thing," lyrics by Patterson Hood, published by Soul Dump Music. For what it's worth, a subsequent song on *Southern Rock Opera,* "Wallace," imagines a George Wallace sticker on the back of the devil's car.

85. Begrand, review of *Decoration Day.* For several other critical approaches to the Truckers' work, see S. Renee Dechert's review of *Southern Rock Opera* in *PopMatters* (2001), as well as her article coauthored with George H. Lewis: "Drive-By Truckers and the Redneck Underground"; and Barbara Ching's "Where Has the Free Bird Flown?"

86. Ridley, "No Depression, Any Country?" 41.

87. Cline, "No More Ms. Nice Guy," 1, 2.

88. Ching, "Going Back," 178.

89. Harrington, "Gillian Welch's Rural Delivery."

90. See Coltman, "Sweethearts of the Hills," 164–65; Oermann, "Mother, Sister, Sweetheart, Pal," 128–30; Peterson, *Creating Country Music,* 138–40.

91. Coltman, "Sweethearts of the Hills,"164; Peterson, *Creating Country Music,* 140; Tosches, *Country: The Twisted Roots,* 136.

92. Coltman, "Sweethearts of the Hills," 165, 164.

93. Peterson, *Creating Country Music,* 41, 35.

94. Bufwack and Oermann, *Finding Her Voice,* 49.

95. I borrow this phrase from the title of David Whisnant's incomparable study, *All That Is Native and Fine,* which provides a far more detailed overview of this phenomenon.

96. Quoted in Bufwack and Oermann, *Finding Her Voice,* 13–14, 14. Although the authors refrain from precisely documenting their quotations, it appears that this passage originally appeared in Sutton's "The Old English Ballads in North Carolina," *Charlotte Observer,* 23 Sept. 1928.

97. *Songcatcher.* The film soundtrack was released on Vanguard Records (79586-2, 2001).

98. Bufwack and Oermann, *Finding Her Voice,* 10.

99. The phrase is Whisnant's (*All That Is Native,* xiii).

100. R. Cantwell, *Bluegrass Breakdown,* 58. The subheading title is from Lomax, "Bluegrass Background," 108.

101. R. Cantwell, *Bluegrass Breakdown,* 210. Robert Cantwell's highly eroticized description of bluegrass performance underscores its status as an ostensibly male province: "It seems sometimes almost as if the powerfully expansive sound might blow the singer's head apart, and often the expressions on his face as he sings suggest that its release is harrowing or painful, like exorcism" (*Bluegrass Breakdown,* 210).

102. R. Cantwell, *Bluegrass Breakdown,* 61, 70, 33, 34, 18.

103. Alden, "Bring the Family," 60 (emphasis added).

104. R. Cantwell, *Bluegrass Breakdown,* 59.

105. Connor, "Roots Seller."

106. "I'll Fly Away" and "Didn't Leave Nobody but the Baby," on *O Brother, Where Art Thou?* (Universal, 2000).

107. Welch, "Biography."

108. Harrington, "Gillian Welch's Rural Delivery."

109. Welch, "Biography," 2.

110. Haiken, "Gillian Welch."

111. Welch, "Biography," 3.

112. "Revival," http://www.geffen.com/almo/gillian/revival.html (accessed 14 Apr. 1997).

113. Bernstein, "Gillian Welch."

114. Words and music for both songs by Gillian Welch, on *Revival* (Almo Records, AMSD-80006, 1996).

115. Words and music by Gillian Welch.

116. Both Johnson and Hurt recorded versions of the traditional gospel/blues song "John the Revelator," which narrates John the Apostle's writing of the Book of Revelations. Johnson's version is included in Smith's *Anthology of American Folk Music,* vol. 2.

117. "Revelator," words and music by Gillian Welch and David Rawlings, on *Time (the Revelator)* (Acony Records, ACNY-0103, 2001).

118. Welch appears to have particularly borrowed from several tunes about the *Titanic,* such as the African American folk song "The Titanic" (also known as "It Was Sad When That Great Ship Went Down"), first recorded in 1927 and covered by Leadbelly and Bessie Jones. Blind Willie Johnson also recorded the *Titanic* song "God Moves on the Water" in 1929.

119. "April the 14th—Part I," words and music by Gillian Welch and David Rawlings.

120. Words and music by Gillian Welch and David Rawlings.

121. Words and music by Gillian Welch and David Rawlings.

122. "Everything Is Free," words and music by Gillian Welch and David Rawlings.

123. Graham, *Graham Weekly Album Review.*

124. "I Dream A Highway," words and music by Gillian Welch and David Rawlings.

125. Mancini, "'Messin' with the Furniture Man," 223.

126. Friskics-Warren, "Gillian Welch," 37 (two quotes).

127. Connor, "Roots Seller," 1.

128. Schocket coined this term to refer to narratives produced by middle-class journalists, novelists, and social researchers in the United States between the 1890s and the 1910s (Stephen Crane being the most prominent) who "'dressed down' in order to traverse with their bodies what they saw as a growing gulf between the middle-class and the white working and lower classes" (110). See his "Undercover Explorations of the 'Other Half.'" While Welch cannot pretend to immerse herself *literally* in the experiences of her songs' characters, as

these earlier class "transvestites" did to attempt a more immediate knowledge of the poor, she does suggest a similar affiliation or connection.

129. Alt.country compilation or tribute projects include *Keep on the Sunny Side: A Tribute to the Carter Family* (Amoeba, 1991); *Insurgent Country Vol. 1: For a Life of Sin* (Bloodshot, 1994); and *Exposed Roots: The Best of Alt.Country* (K-Tel, 1998).

130. A. Stewart, "Spring Forward," 44.

131. Weisberger, "Foggy Mountain New Grass Breakdown," 1, 3.

132. MacIntosh, "Freakwater Doesn't Keep It on the Sunnyside of Life."

133. A. Stewart, "Spring Forward," 43.

134. A. Stewart, "Spring Forward," 43.

135. A. Stewart, "Spring Forward," 46.

136. Words and music by Freakwater.

137. Words and music by Sean Garrison.

138. Words and music by Freakwater.

139. After the release of *End Time* in 1999, Catherine Irwin and Janet Bean pursued independent music projects; in 2005, they recorded *Thinking of You* as a Freakwater release. I am focusing on *End Time* due to its explicit concern with time.

140. Words and music by Freakwater, on *End Time* (Thrilljockey, Thrill 066, 1999).

141. "Cloak of Frogs," words and music by Freakwater.

142. "My History," words and music by Freakwater.

143. "Written in Gold," words and music by Freakwater.

144. "Cheap Watch," words and music by Freakwater.

145. Friskics-Warren, "Freakwater."

146. Murray, "Freakwater at VZD's."

147. Friskics-Warren, "Freakwater."

148. deMause, "Louisville Lip."

149. J. Lewis, "Universal Soldiers."

150. D. Cantwell, "Homespun of the Brave," 44; Hoppenthaler, interview with Iris DeMent; Nichols, "American's Story."

151. Phillips, "'Poor Are Treated Like Enemies.'"

152. See Hoppenthaler's 1997 interview with DeMent.

153. Words and music by Iris DeMent, on *The Way I Should* (Warner Bros., 9461882, 1996).

154. Phillips, "'Poor Are Treated like Enemies,'" 2.

155. Words and music by Iris DeMent, on *Infamous Angel* (Warner Bros., 45238, 1993).

156. Nichols, "American's Story," 4.

157. Nichols, "American's Story," 1.

158. "Let the Mystery Be," words and music by Iris DeMent, on *Infamous Angel;* "The Shores of Jordan," words and music by Iris DeMent, on *My Life* (Warner Bros., 45493, 1994); "Keep Me God," words and music by Iris DeMent,

on *The Way I Should;* liner notes, *Lifeline* (Flariella Records, B0002ZUIJG, 2004).

159. "Mama's Opry" and "Higher Ground," both on *Infamous Angel.*

160. "Letter to Mom," words and music by Iris DeMent, on *The Way I Should;* "Easy's Gettin' Harder Every Day," words and music by Iris DeMent, on *My Life;* "You've Done Nothing Wrong," words and music by Iris DeMent, on *My Life;* "Quality Time," words and music by Iris DeMent, on *The Way I Should.*

161. Words and music by Iris DeMent, on *The Way I Should.*

162. Hoppenthaler, 1997 interview with DeMent, 2, 2–3.

163. Words and music by Iris DeMent, on *My Life.*

164. Words and music by Lefty Frizzell, on *My Life.*

165. Watkins, *Throwaways,* 40.

166. Watkins, *Throwaways,* 7; "We Can't Make it Here," words and music by James McMurtry, on *Childish Things* (Compadre Records, 6-16892-65842-9, 2005).

167. Peterson, *Creating Country Music,* 56.

168. Peterson, *Creating Country Music,* 57.

169. Bernstein, "Gillian Welch," 1.

170. See http://wwwcurb.com/artists/artistbio_T1.cfm?ID=81 (accessed 10 Nov. 2003).

171. See "Driving the Truckers."

Coda

1. Words and music by Rissi Palmer, on *Rissi Palmer* (1720 Entertainment, B000VZAV0I, 2007).

2. Her parents, however, were in fact Georgia natives who introduced her to the music of Patsy Cline, Johnny Cash, and Dolly Parton (E. Smith, "To Be Young, Gifted, and Country").

3. Released as an Erykah Badu single on Universal (B00000JYF7). Also recorded by Rahzel on *Make the Music 2000* (MCA, 2001).

4. See *Country Weekly,* 20 Nov. 2007.

5. "As Black Woman, Rissi Palmer Is Country Rarity."

6. Eddy, review of *Rissi Palmer.*

7. Elizabeth Cook certainly "channels" DeMent, however, in her neo-Appalachian voice and in songs such as "Mama's Prayers." See her 2007 album *Balls* (31 Tigers Records, TOT3101).

8. "Stealing Kisses," words and music by Lori McKenna, on *Bittertown* (Warner Brothers, 49869-2, 2004); "How to Survive," words and music by McKenna, on *Unglamorous* (Warner Brothers, B000RHRGF8, 2007).

9. Words and music by Lori McKenna, on *Bittertown.*

10. See, e.g., "Bible Song," words and music by Lori McKenna, on *Bittertown.*

11. I am referencing McKenna's song "Witness to your Life" on *Unglamorous.*

12. BMG Music, 1999. Following a comic portrait of everyday household chaos (screaming children, overdue bills, broken washing machine), Vassar's chorus declares, "well it's ok, it's so nice / it's just another day in paradise . . . / there's no place that I'd rather be."

13. One frustrated consumer, adding his informal "review" to Amazon.com, fumes about the album as a whole: "The pod people [McGraw and Hill] have helped Lori make an album of country glop. I guess once you make Oprah cry and have a feature made on you for Nightline, the uniqueness kind of goes away."

14. Lori McKenna Web site, video "Lori McKenna," http://www.wbrnash .com/lorimckenna/tv (accessed 2 June 2008).

15. Also see the concluding chapter to *Old Roots, New Routes* for an expanded discussion contrasting Wilson with Miranda Lambert, another young female artist brandishing a rebel attitude: Pamela Fox and Barbara Ching, "Conclusion: Top 40 Alternatives? Gretchen Wilson, Miranda Lambert, and the Dixie Chicks," 222–31.

REFERENCES

Acker, Joan. *Class Questions, Feminist Answers.* New York: Rowman and Littlefield Publishers, 2006.

Acuff, Roy, with William Neely. *Roy Acuff's Nashville: The Life and Good Times of Country Music.* New York: Putnam Publishing, 1983.

Albanese, Catherine. "Davy Crockett and the Wild Man; or, The Metaphysics of the *Longue Dur'ee.*" In Lofaro, *Davy Crockett,* 80–101.

Alden, Grant. "Bring the Family: Steve Earle and the Del McCoury Band Cultivate Bluegrass on Common Ground." *No Depression* 20 (March–April 1999): 56–65.

Alden, Grant. "Rocking Tall." *No Depression* 45 (July–August 2003): 76–91.

Alden, Grant. "The Wilds, The Innocent, and the Grand Ole Opry." *No Depression* 1 (Summer 1996): 48–55.

Alden, Grant, and Peter Blackstock, eds. *The Best of* No Depression: *Writing About American Music.* Austin: University of Texas Press, 2005.

Alden, Grant, and Peter Blackstock, eds. No Depression: *An Introduction to Alternative Country Music, Whatever That Is.* Nashville: Dowling, 1998.

Allen, Bob. "BR5-49: Searching for a Good Time." *Country Music* 186 (July–August 1997): 45–46.

Allen, Bob. Liner notes to Charline Arthur, *Welcome to the Club.* Bear Family Records, BCD 16279, 1998.

Allen, Bob. "What Hath Tom Carter Wrought?" In *The Country Reader: Twenty-Five Years of the* Journal of Country Music, ed. Paul Kingsbury, 306–12. Nashville: Country Music Foundation Press and Vanderbilt University Press, 1996.

"As Black Woman, Rissi Palmer Is Country Rarity." Associated Press. 19 October 2007. http://www.msnbc.msn.com/id/21307946/print/1/displaymode/1098/. Accessed 5 August 2008.

Ashley, Kathleen, Leigh Gilmore, and Gerald Peters, eds. *Autobiography and Postmodernism.* Amherst: University of Massachusetts Press, 1994.

Austin, Wade. "Hollywood Barn Dance: A Brief Survey of Country Music in Films." *Southern Quarterly* 22, no. 3 (1984): 111–23.

Banes, Ruth A. "Dixie's Daughters: The Country Music Female." In *You Wrote*

My Life: Lyrical Themes in Country Music, ed. Melton A. McLaurin and Richard A. Peterson, 81–112. Philadelphia: Gordon and Breach, 1992.

Banes, Ruth A. "Mythology in Music: The Ballad of Loretta Lynn." *Canadian Review of American Studies* 16, no. 3 (1985): 283–300.

Barthes, Roland. *Camera Lucida: Reflections on Photography.* Trans. Richard Howard. New York: Hill and Wang, 1981.

Begrand, Adrien. Review of Drive-By Truckers, *Decoration Day. PopMatters,* 25 June 2003. http://www.popmatters.com/music/reviews/d/drivebyturckers-decoration.shtml. Accessed 9 October 2003.

Berlant, Lauren. "National Brands/National Body: *Imitation of Life.*" In *Comparative American Identities: Race, Sex, and Nationality in the Modern Text,* ed. Hortense Spillers, 110–40. New York: Routledge, 1991.

Bernstein, Joel. "Gillian Welch: The Real Retro Artist." *Country Standard Time,* July–August 1998. http://www.countrystandardtime.com/d/article.asp?xid=860. Accessed 28 July 1998.

Bernstein, Joel. "The Insurgent Odyssey of Robbie Fylks," *Country Standard Time.* December 1996. http://www.countrystandardtime.com/d/article.asp?xid=441. Accessed 14 April 1997.

Bertrand, Michael. "I Don't Think Hank Done It That Way: Elvis, Country Music, and the Reconstruction of Southern Masculinity." In McCusker and Pecknold, *Boy Named Sue,* 59–85.

Biggar, George C. "Minstrels in the Hayloft." *Stand By!* 23 March 1935, 5.

Biggar, George C. "The WLS Barn Dance Story: The Early Years." *John Edwards Memorial Foundation Quarterly* 7, no. 23 (1971): 105–12.

Blackstock, Peter. "Hell of a Spell: What Hasn't Killed the Bottle Rockets Has Made Them Stronger." *No Depression* 48 (Winter 2003): 82–95.

Bourdieu, Pierre. "Habitus." In *Habitus: A Sense of Place,* 2nd ed., ed. Jean Hillier and Emma Rooksby, 43–49. Hampshire and Burlington: Ashgate Publishing Co., 2005.

Bourdieu, Pierre. *Outline of a Theory of Practice.* Cambridge: Cambridge University Press, 1977.

Bourdieu, Pierre, with Loic Wacquant. *An Invitation to Reflexive Sociology.* Cambridge: Polity Press, 1992.

Brodzki, Ella, and Celeste Schenck, eds. *Life/Lines: Theorizing Women's Autobiography.* Ithaca: Cornell University Press, 1988.

Bufwack, Mary A., and Robert K. Oermann. *Finding Her Voice: Women in Country Music, 1800–2000.* Nashville: Country Music Foundation Press and Vanderbilt University Press, 2003.

Butler, Judith. *Bodies That Matter: On the Discursive Limits of "Sex."* New York: Routledge, 1993.

Campbell, Glen, with Tom Carter. *Rhinestone Cowboy: An Autobiography.* New York: Villard Books, 1994.

Cannon, Sarah Ophelia Colley, with Joan Dew. *Minnie Pearl: An Autobiography.* New York: Simon and Schuster, 1980.

Cantwell, David. "The Children of Detroit City." *Twangin!* http://www.steam
iron.com/twangin/essay-detroit.html. Accessed 25 August 1997.

Cantwell, David. "Homespun of the Brave." *No Depression* 6 (Winter 1996): 44.

Cantwell, Robert. *Bluegrass Breakdown: The Making of the Old Southern Sound.* New York: Da Capo Press, 1992.

Cantwell, Robert. *Ethnomimesis: Folk Life and the Representation of Culture.* Chapel Hill: University of North Carolina Press, 1993.

Carr, Patrick. "Will the Circle Be Unbroken? Country's Changing Image." In *Country: The Music and the Musicians,* 2nd ed., Paul Kingsbury, Alan Axel-rod, and Susan Costello, 328–59. New York: Country Music Foundation and Abbeville Press, 1994.

Carr, Robert. "Crossing the First World/Third World Divides: Testimonial, Transnational Feminisms, and the Postmodern Condition." In *Scattered Hegemonies,* ed. Inderpal Grewal and Caren Kaplan, 153–72. Minneapolis: University of Minnesota Press, 1994.

Cash, Johnny. *Man in Black: His Own Story in His Own Words.* Grand Rapids: Zonderman Publishing House, 1975.

Ching, Barbara. "Acting Naturally: Cultural Distinction and Critiques of Pure Country." In Wray and Newitz, *White Trash,* 231–48.

Ching, Barbara. "Going Back to the Old Mainstream: *No Depression* and the Construction of Alt.Country." In McCusker and Pecknold, *Boy Named Sue,* 178–95.

Ching, Barbara. "Where Has the Free Bird Flown? Lynyrd Skynyrd and White Southern Manhood." In *White Masculinity in the Recent South,* ed. Trent Watts. Baton Rouge: Louisiana State University Press, 2008, 251–65.

Ching, Barbara. *Wrong's What I Do Best: Hard Country Music and Contempo-rary Culture.* New York: Oxford University Press, 2001.

Ching, Barbara, and Gerald W. Creed. "Recognizing Rusticity: Identity and the Power of Place." In *Knowing Your Place: Rural Identity and Cultural Hier-archy,* ed. Barbara Ching and Gerald W. Creed, 1–38. New York: Routledge, 1997.

Ching, Barbara, and Pamela Fox. "The Importance of Being Ironic: Toward a Theory and Critique of Alt.Country Music." In P. Fox and Ching, *Old Roots, New Routes,* 1–27.

Clemmons, Dallas. "Cow Punker Angry Johnny Explains His Anger." *Country Standard Time.* http://www.countrystandardtime.com/d/article.asp?xid=907. Accessed 4 April 1997.

Cline, Cheryl. "No More Ms. Nice Guy." http://www.steamiron.com/cgrrl/cgrrl-ed1.html. Accessed 10 August 2003.

Coal Miner's Daughter. Dir. Michael Apted. Perf. Sissy Spacek, Tommy Lee Jones. Universal Pictures, 1980.

Collins, Patricia Hill. *Black Feminist Thought.* Boston: Unwin Hyman, 1990.

Coltman, Robert. "Sweethearts of the Hills: Women in Early Country Music." *John Edwards Memorial Foundation Quarterly* 14 (Winter 1978): 161–80.

Connor, Mike. "Roots Seller: How Former Santa Cruz Songstress Gillian Welch

Beat the Odds to Become an Americana Sensation." http://www.metroac
tive.com/cruz/welch-0226.html. Accessed 9 September 2003.

Conway, Cecelia. *African Banjo Echoes in Appalachia.* Knoxville: University of
Tennessee Press, 1995.

Cook, Sylvia Jenkins. *From Tobacco Road to Route 66: The Southern Poor White
in Fiction.* Chapel Hill: University of North Carolina Press, 1996.

Coontz, Stephanie. *The Way We Never Were: American Families and the Nostalgia Trap.* New York: Basic Books, 1992.

Copetas, Jeff. "Bottle Rockets: Dirty White Boys Got the Red Wine Country
Blues." *No Depression On Line* 1 (Fall 1995). http://www.nodepression.net/
long/long-botrox.html. Accessed 5 July 1997.

Cosslett, Tess, Celia Lury, and Penny Summerfield, eds. *Feminism and Autobiography: Texts, Theories, Methods.* London and New York: Routledge, 2000.

Cott, Nancy F. *Public Vows: A History of Marriage and the Nation.* Cambridge:
Harvard University Press, 2000.

"The Country & Western Music Portfolio." *Vanity Fair,* November 2006, 291.

Covington, Dennis. *Salvation on Sand Mountain: Snake Handling and Redemp-
tion in Southern Appalachia.* New York: Penguin Books, 1995.

Crenshaw, Kimberlé Williams. "Mapping the Margins: Intersectionality, Identity
Politics, and Violence against Women of Color." In *Critical Race Theory: The
Key Writings That Formed the Movement,* ed. Kimberlé Crenshaw et al.,
357–83. New York: New Press, 1995.

Cusic, Don. "Comedy and Humor in Country Music." *Journal of American Culture* 16, no. 2 (1993): 45–50.

Davies, Carole Boyce. "Collaboration and the Ordering Imperative in Story Production." In *De/Colonizing the Subject: The Politics of Gender in Women's
Autobiography,* ed. Julia Watson and Sidonie Smith, 3–19. Minneapolis: University of Minnesota Press, 1992.

Dawidoff, Nicholas. *In the Country of Country: People and Places in American
Music.* New York: Pantheon Books, 1997.

Dechert, S. Renee, with George H. Lewis. "The Drive-By Truckers and the Redneck Underground: A Subcultural Analysis." In *Country Music Annual 2002,*
ed. Charles K. Wolfe and James E. Akenson, 130–50. Lexington: University
Press of Kentucky, 2002.

deMause, Neil. "Louisville Lip: An Interview with Catherine Irwin." *Here.*
http://www.heremagazine.com/irwin.html. Accessed 12 August 2003.

DeMott, Ben. "Safe American Home." *First of the Month* (2001–2).
http://www.firstofthemonth.org/archives/2002/06/safe_american_h.html. Accessed 9 October 2003.

Dorman, James. "Shaping the Popular Image of Post-Reconstruction American
Blacks: The 'Coon Song' Phenomenon of the Gilded Age." *American Quarterly* 40 (December 1988): 450–71.

"Driving the Truckers: Patterson Hood." *Jambase.* http://www.jambase.com/
headsup.asp?storyID=4139%20. Accessed 9 October 2003.

Dunne, Michael L. "Country Music: My Life Would Make a Damn Good Country Song." In *Metapop: Self-Referentiality in Contemporary American Popular Culture*, 124–44. Jackson: University Press of Mississippi, 1992.

Dutton, Monte. *True to the Roots: Americana Music Revealed.* Lincoln: University of Nebraska, 2006.

Dyer, Richard. *Stars.* London: BFI, 1979.

Eddy, Chuck. Review of *Rissi Palmer. Billboard,* 27 October 2007. http://bill board.com/bbcom/content_display/reviews/albums/e3i7b7f6bee78014d173 16043bb44228c7c. Accessed 5 August 2008.

Ellison, Curtis W. *Country Music Culture: From Hard Times to Heaven.* Jackson: University Press of Mississippi, 1995.

Ellison, Ralph. "Change the Joke and Slip the Yoke." In *Shadow and Act,* 45–59. New York: Random House, 1964. Originally published in *Partisan Review* (1958): 48.

Erbsen, Wayne. "Tommy Millard: Blackface Comedian and Bluegrass Boy." http://www.nativeground.com/tommymillard.asp. Accessed 1 August 2007.

Escott, Colin. *Hank Williams: The Biography.* Boston: Little, Brown and Company, 1995.

Felski, Rita. *Beyond Feminist Aesthetics: Feminist Literature and Social Change.* Cambridge: Harvard University Press, 1989.

Fenster, Mark. "Buck Owens, Country Music, and the Struggle for Discursive Control." *Popular Music* 9, no. 3 (1990): 275–90.

Flynt, J. Wayne. *Dixie's Forgotten People: The South's Poor Whites.* Bloomington: Indiana University Press, 1979.

Fox, Aaron. "'Alternative' to What? 'O Brother,' September 11, and the Politics of Country Music." In *There's a Star-Spangled Banner Waving Somewhere: Country Music Goes to War,* ed. Charles K. Wolfe and James E. Akenson, 164–91. Lexington: University of Kentucky Press, 2005.

Fox, Aaron. "Beyond Austin's City Limits: Justin Treviño and the Boundaries of 'Alternative' Country." In P. Fox and Ching, *Old Roots, New Routes,* 83–110.

Fox, Aaron. "The Jukebox of History: Narratives of Loss and Desire in the Discourse of Country Music." *Popular Music* 11, no. 1 (1992): 53–72.

Fox, Aaron. *Real Country: Music and Language in Working-Class Culture.* Durham: Duke University Press, 2004.

Fox, Pamela. *Class Fictions: Shame and Resistance in the British Working-Class Novel, 1890–1945.* Durham: Duke University Press, 1994.

Fox, Pamela. "Recycled 'Trash': Gender and Authenticity in Country Music Autobiography." *American Quarterly* 50, no. 2 (June 1998): 234–66.

Fox, Pamela, and Barbara Ching. "Conclusion: Top 40 Alternatives? Gretchen Wilson, Miranda Lambert, and the Dixie Chicks." In P. Fox and Ching, *Old Roots, New Routes,* 222–31.

Fox, Pamela, and Barbara Ching, eds. *Old Roots, New Routes: The Cultural Politics of Alt.Country Music.* Ann Arbor: University of Michigan Press, 2008.

Friskics-Warren, Bill. "Freakwater: Fundamental Things." *Puncture* 45 (1999). http://www.freakwater.net/readingroom.htm#ft. Accessed 12 August 2003.

Friskics-Warren, Bill. "Gillian Welch: Orphan Girl of the Hollywood Hills." *No Depression* 1 (Summer 1996): 37–38.

Friskics-Warren, Bill. "Second to None: Opry Veteran Jean Shepard Helped Pave the Way for Women in Country Music." *Nashville Scene,* 8 June 2000, 23.

Friskics-Warren, Bill. "The Undisputed Queen: Cause for Celebration." *Nashville Scene,* 26 August 1999, Accessed 19 September 2007. http://www.nashvillescene.com/Stories/News/1999/08/26/The_Undisputed_Queen/index.s.

Frith, Simon. *Performing Rites: On the Value of Popular Music.* Cambridge: Harvard University Press, 1996.

Fulks, Robbie. "Jean Shepard: The Woman in the Asbestos Suit." *Journal of Country Music* 22, no. 3 (2002): 34–39.

"Gals from the Hills: Kitty and Goldie Start Country-Girl Search." *Billboard,* 20 June 1953, 1.

Gilmore, Leigh. *Autobiographics: A Feminist Theory of Women's Self-Representation.* Ithaca: Cornell University Press, 1994.

Gluck, Sherna Louise. *Rosie the Riveter Revisited: Women, the War, and Social Change.* Boston: Twayne Publishers, 1987.

Goodman, David. *Modern Twang: An Alternative Country Guide and Directory.* 2nd ed. Nashville: Dowling, 1999.

Goodman, Frank. "A Conversation with Michelle Shocked." *Puremusic,* Accessed 10 May 2002. http://glimbo.tripod.com/marticles.htm.

Goodson, Steve. "Hillbilly Humanist: Hank Williams and the Southern White Working Class." *Alabama Review* 46, no. 2 (1993): 109–14.

Graham, George. *Graham Weekly Album Review,* no. 1251. http://georgegraham.com/reviews/welch3.html. Accessed 24 September 2003.

Green, Douglas. *Country Roots: The Origins of Country Music.* New York: Hawthorn Books, Inc., 1976.

Grundy, Pamela. "'We Always Tried to Be Good People': Respectability, Crazy Water Crystals, and Hillbilly Music on the Air, 1933–1935." *Journal of American History* 81 (March 1995): 1591–1620.

Gubar, Susan. *Racechanges: White Skin, Black Face in American Culture.* New York: Oxford University Press, 1997.

Guralnick, Peter. *Lost Highway: Journeys and Arrivals of American Musicians.* New York: Harper Perennial, 1979, 1989.

Hagan, Chet. *Grand Ole Opry.* New York: Henry Holt & Co., 1989.

Haggard, Merle, with Peggy Russell. *Sing Me Back Home: My Story.* New York: Time Books, 1981.

Haiken, Melanie. "Gillian Welch: The Orphan Girl Opens Up." *Paste* 5, 23 July 2003. http://www.pastemagazine.com/articles/2003/07/gillian-welch.html. Accessed 9 September 2003.

Hank Williams: The Honky-Tonk Blues. Dir. Morgan Neville. Nashville: Mercury Nashville, 2004.

Harkins, Anthony. *Hillbilly: A Cultural History of an American Icon.* New York: Oxford University Press, 2004.

Harrington, Richard. "Gillian Welch's Rural Delivery." *Washington Post,* 5 May 1997.

Hartigan, John, Jr. "Name Calling: Objectifying 'Poor White' and 'White Trash' in Detroit." In Wray and Newitz, *White Trash,* 41–56.

Hartmann, Heidi, ed. *The Unhappy Marriage of Marxism and Feminism.* London: Pluto Press, 1981.

Hay, George D. *Howdy Judge.* Nashville: McQuiddy Press, 1926.

Hay, George D. *A Story of the Grand Ole Opry.* Nashville: n.p., 1945, 1953.

Hennessy, Rosemary, and Chrys Ingraham, eds. *Materialist Feminism: A Reader in Class, Difference, and Women's Lives.* New York: Routledge, 1997.

"Hillbilly Nitery Makes Bow in Chicago July 1." *Billboard,* 26 April 1952, 17.

Hinton, Brian. *South by Southwest: A Road Map to Alternative Country.* London: Sanctuary Publishing Limited, 2003.

Hoppenthaler, John. Interview with Iris DeMent. March 1997. http://mem bers.aol.com/jarmode/irisInterview.html. Accessed 21 April 1998.

Horstman, Dorothy. *Sing Your Heart Out, Country Boy: Classic Country Songs and Their Inside Stories by the Men and Women Who Wrote Them.* 3rd ed. Nashville: Country Music Foundation and Vanderbilt University Press, 1996.

Huggins, Nathan. *Harlem Renaissance.* New York: Oxford University Press, 1971.

Jarman, Rufus. "Country Music Goes to Town." *Nation's Business* 41 (February 1953): 44–51.

Jay, Paul. "Posing: Autobiography and the Subject of Photography." In *Autobiography and Postmodernism,* ed. Kathleen Ashley, Leigh Gilmore, and Gerald Peters, 191–211. Amherst: University of Massachusetts Press, 1994.

"Jean Shepard." Publicity release, 27 October 1953.

Jennings, Waylon, with Lenny Kaye. *Waylon: An Autobiography.* New York: Time Warner, 2004.

Jensen, Joli. *The Nashville Sound: Authenticity, Commercialization, and Country Music.* Nashville: Country Music Foundation and Vanderbilt University Press, 1998.

Jones, George, with Tom Carter. *I Lived to Tell It All.* New York: Dell Publishing, 1997.

Joyner, Charles. "The Sounds of Southern Culture: Blues, Country, Jazz, and Rock." In *Shared Traditions: Southern History and Folk Culture,* 193–207. Urbana: University of Illinois Press, 1999.

Judd, Naomi, with Bud Schaetzle. *Love Can Build a Bridge.* New York: Villard Books, 1993.

Kaplan, Caren, and Inderpal Grewal, eds. *Scattered Hegemonies: Postmodernity and Transnational Feminist Practices.* Minneapolis: University of Minnesota Press, 1994.

Keillor, Garrison. "'Lovesick Blues': Long Gone Daddy." *New York Times,* 25 September 2005. http://www.nytimes.com/2005/09/25/books/review/25keil lor.html. Accessed 11 October 2007.

Kelley, Robin D. G. "Notes on Deconstructing the Folk." *American Historical Review* (December 1992): 1400–1408.

Kibler, M. Allison. *Rank Ladies: Gender and Cultural Hierarchy in American Vaudeville.* Chapel Hill: University of North Carolina Press, 1999.

La Chapelle, Peter. "'Spade Doesn't Look Exactly Starved': Country Music and the Negotiation of Women's Domesticity in Cold War Los Angeles." In McCusker and Pecknold, *Boy Named Sue,* 24–43.

Lair, John. "No Hillbillies in Radio." *Stand By!* 17 March 1935, 7.

Lange, Jeffrey. *Smile When You Call Me A Hillbilly: Country Music's Struggle for Respectability, 1939–1954.* Athens: University of Georgia Press, 2004.

Lejeune, Philippe. *On Autobiography.* Ed. Paul John Eakin. Trans. Katherine M. Leary. Minneapolis: University of Minnesota Press, 1989.

Leppert, Richard, and George Lipsitz. "Age, the Body, and Experience in the Music of Hank Williams." In G. Lewis, *All That Glitters,* 22–37.

Lewis, George H., ed. *All That Glitters: Country Music in America.* Bowling Green: Bowling Green State University Popular Press, 1993.

Lewis, John. "Universal Soldiers: Freakwater's Themes for Life." *Option* (1996). http://www.freakwater.net/readingroom.htm#us. Accessed 12 August 2003.

Lhamon, W. T., Jr. *Raising Cain: Blackface Performance from Jim Crow to Hip Hop.* Cambridge: Harvard University Press, 1998.

Lightfoot, William E. "Belle of the Barn Dance: Reminiscing with Lulu Belle Wiseman Stamey." *Journal of Country Music* 12, no. 1 (1987): 2–15.

Lipsitz, George. *Rainbow at Midnight: Labor and Culture in the 1940s.* Urbana and Chicago: University of Illinois Press, 1994.

Lipsitz, George. *Time Passages: Collective Memory and American Popular Culture.* Minneapolis: University of Minnesota Press, 1990.

Livingston, Tamara. "Music Revivals: Towards a General Theory." *Ethnomusicology* 43, no. 1 (1999): 66–85.

Lofaro, Michael, ed. *Davy Crockett: The Man, the Legend, the Legacy, 1786–1986.* Knoxville: University of Tennessee Press, 1985.

Lomax, Alan. "Bluegrass Background: Folk Music with Overdrive." *Esquire* 52 (October 1959): 108.

Lott, Eric. *Love and Theft: Blackface Minstrelsy and the American Working Class.* New York: Oxford University Press, 1993.

Lott, Eric. "White like Me: Racial Cross-Dressing and the Construction of American Whiteness." In *Cultures of U.S. Imperialism,* ed. Amy Kaplan and Donald E. Pease, 474–95. Durham: Duke University Press, 1993.

Lynn, Loretta, with Patsi Bale Cox. *Still Woman Enough: A Memoir.* New York: Hyperion, 2002.

Lynn, Loretta, with George Vecsey. *Coal Miner's Daughter.* Chicago: Henry Regnery Company, 1976.

MacIntosh, Dan. "Freakwater Doesn't Keep It on the Sunnyside of Life." *Country Standard Time.* http://www1.usa1.com/~cst.freakwaterCONCERT.html. Accessed 21 April 1998.

Mahar, William J. *Behind the Burnt Cork Mask: Early Blackface Minstrelsy and Antebellum American Popular Culture.* Urbana: University of Illinois Press, 1999.

Mahar, William J. "Ethiopian Skits and Sketches: Contents and Contexts of Blackface Minstrelsy, 1840–1890." *Prospects: An Annual Journal of American Cultural Studies* 16 (1991): 184–85.

Malone, Bill C. "Country Music and the Academy: A Thirty-Year Professional Odyssey." In *Sounds of the South,* ed. Daniel W. Patterson, 41–56. Chapel Hill: University of North Carolina Press, 1991.

Malone, Bill C. *Country Music, U.S.A.,* Rev. ed. Austin: University of Texas Press, 1985.

Malone, Bill C. "Honky-Tonk: The Music of the Southern Working Class." In *Folk Music and Modern Sound,* ed. William Ferris and Mary L. Hart, 119–28. Jackson: University Press of Mississippi, 1982.

"Man on the Cover." *Prairie Farmer's New WLS Weekly,* 2 March 1935, 15.

Mancini, J. M. "'Messin' with the Furniture Man': Early Country Music, Regional Culture, and the Search for an Anthological Modernism." *American Literary History* 16, no. 2 (2004): 208–37.

Mansfield, Brian. "Country Stars Find Their Way Back to Roots." USA Today.com. Accessed 24 June 2005.

Marcus, Greil. *Mystery Train: Images of America in Rock'n'Roll Music.* New York: E.P. Dutton & Co., 1982.

Martin, Harris. "Jean Shepard Enjoys Solid Carreer [*sic*] in Country Music." *Music City News* (October 1965): 32–33.

May, Elaine Tyler. *Homeward Bound: American Families in the Cold War Era.* New York: Basic Books, 1988.

McCusker, Kristine M. "'Bury Me Beneath the Willow': Linda Parker and Definitions of Tradition on the National Barn Dance, 1932–1935." In McCusker and Pecknold, *Boy Named Sue,* 3–23.

McCusker, Kristine M. *Lonesome Cowgirls and Honky-Tonk Angels: The Women of Barn Dance Radio.* Urbana and Chicago: University of Illinois Press, 2008.

McCusker, Kristine M. "Rose Lee Maphis and Working on Barn Dance Radio, 1930–1960." In Wolfe and Akenson, *Women of Country Music,* 61–74.

McCusker, Kristine M., and Diane Pecknold, eds. *A Boy Named Sue.* Jackson: University Press of Mississippi, 2004.

McCusker, Kristine M., and Diane Pecknold. "Introduction." In McCusker and Pecknold, *Boy Named Sue,* xix–xxiv.

McEntire, Reba, with Tom Carter. *Reba: My Story.* New York: Bantam, 1994.

"Meet the Mrs.: Mrs. Ernest Tubb." *Country Song Roundup,* no. 17 (April 1952): 13.

Meyerowitz, Joanne, ed. *Not June Cleaver: Women and Gender in Postwar America, 1945–1960.* Philadelphia: Temple University Press, 1994.

Morthland, John. "Honky Tonk Music: The Raw Sound of Hard Country." *Country Music* 5, no. 10 (1977): 42–43.

Murray, James. "Freakwater at VZD's in Oklahoma City, March 18, 1999." *100 Year War.* http://www.freakwater.net/readingroom.htm#vzd. Accessed 12 August 2003.

Neely, Emily C. "Charline Arthur: The (Un)Making of a Honky-Tonk Star." In McCusker and Pecknold, *Boy Named Sue,* 44–58.

Nelson, Willie, with Bud Shrake. *Willie: An Autobiography.* New York: Simon and Schuster, 1988.

Nichols, Lee. "An American's Story: Iris DeMent." *Progressive Populist,* April 1997. http://www.populist.com/4.97.dement.html. Accessed 21 April 1998.

No Depression: What It Sounds Like, Vol. 1. Liner notes. Dualtone Records, 1153, 2004.

Oermann, Robert K. "Honky-Tonk Angels: Kitty Wells and Patsy Cline." In *Country: The Music and the Musicians,* 213–33. New York: Country Music Foundation and Abbeville Press, 1994.

Oermann, Robert K. "Mother, Sister, Sweetheart, Pal: Women in Old-Time Country Music." *Southern Quarterly* 22:3 (Spring 1984): 125–34.

One Riot One Ranger. Old Home Page. http://members.aol.com/oneriot/band bio.html. Accessed 26 June 1997.

Ostendorf, Berndt. "Minstrelsy and Early Jazz." *Massachusetts Review* (Autumn 1979): 574–602.

"Over the Cracker Barrel." *Rural Radio* (March 1938): 19.

Parish, James R. *The Slapstick Queens.* New York: A. S. Barnes and Company, 1973.

Parton, Dolly. *Dolly: My Life and Other Unfinished Business.* New York: Harper Collins, 1994.

Pecknold, Diane. "'I Wanna Play House': Configurations of Masculinity in the Nashville Sound Era." In McCusker and Pecknold, *Boy Named Sue,* 88–95.

Pecknold, Diane. *The Selling Sound: The Rise of the Country Music Industry.* Durham: Duke University Press, 2007.

Peterson, Richard. *Creating Country Music: Fabricating Authenticity.* Chicago: University of Chicago Press, 1997.

Peterson, Richard. "The Dialectic of Hard-Core and Soft-Shell Country Music." *South Atlantic Quarterly* 94 (Winter 1995): 273–300.

Peterson, Richard, and Bruce Beal. "Alternative Country: Origins, Music, World-View, Fans, and Taste in Genre Formation." *Popular Music and Society* 25, nos. 1–2 (2001): 233–49.

Peterson, Richard, and Roger Kern. "Changing Highbrow Taste: From Snob to Omnivore." *American Sociological Review* 61, no. 5 (1996): 900–907.

Phillips, Richard. "'The Poor Are Treated like Enemies': An Interview with Iris DeMent." World Socialist Web Site. http://www.wsws.org/arts/1998/irs2-a18.shtml. Accessed 21 April 1998.

Porterfield, Bill. *The Greatest Honky-Tonks in Texas.* Dallas: Taylor Publishing Co., 1983.

Porterfield, Nolan. *Jimmie Rodgers: The Life and Times of America's Blue Yo-deler.* Urbana: University of Illinois, 1992.

Powel, Bob. "Jean Shepard: About Her Life and Music." *Country Music People* 18, no. 10 (1987): 30.

Pride, Charley, with Jim Henderson. *Pride: The Charley Pride Story.* New York: Morrow, 1994.

"Program Patter on Jean Shepard. " N.d. Country Music Foundation Library, Nashville.

Pugh, Ronnie. *Ernest Tubb: The Texas Troubadour.* Durham: Duke University Press, 1996.

"Real American Music." *Stand By!* 13 November 1937, 3.

Remz, Jeffrey B. "Alternative Country, Indy Scene Grows." *Country Standard Time.* http://www.countrystandardtime.com/d/article.asp?xid=250. Accessed 25 June 1997.

Ridley, Jim. "No Depression, Any Country?" *Journal of Country Music* 18, no. 2 (1996): 40–41.

Roediger, David. *The Wages of Whiteness: Race and the Making of the American Working Class.* London: Verso, 1991.

Rogin, Michael. "Blackface, White Noise: The Jewish Jazz Singer Finds His Voice." *Critical Inquiry* 18 (Spring 1992): 417–53.

Rosenberg, Neil, ed. *Transforming Traditions: Folk Music Revivals Examined.* Urbana: University of Illinois Press, 1993.

Rourke, Constance. *American Humor: A Study of the National Character.* Tallahassee: Florida State University Press, 1931, 1986.

Rubin, Rachel. "Sing Me Back Home: Nostalgia, Bakersfield, and Modern Country Music." In Rubin and Melnick, *American Popular Music,* 93–110.

Rubin, Rachel, and Jeffrey Melnick, eds. *American Popular Music: New Approaches to the Twentieth Century.* Amherst: University of Massachusetts Press, 2001.

"Ryan Adams on 'Demolition,' Writing, and Shopping at Gap." CNN.com, 25 October 2002. http://edition.cnn.com/2002/SHOWBIZ/Music/10/25/mroom.ryan.adams/index.html. Accessed 24 February 2008.

Sacks, Bill. "The Strange Motives and Skewed Romance behind the Waco Brothers." *Country Standard Time.* March 1997. http://www.countrystandard time.com/d/arti cle.asp?xid=839. Accessed 26 June 1997.

Sanjek, David. "Can a Fujiyama Mama Be the Female Elvis? The Wild, Wild Women of Rockabilly." In *Sexing the Groove: Popular Music and Gender,* ed. Sheila Whiteley, 137–67. New York: Routledge, 1997.

Saxton, Alexander. "Blackface Minstrelsy and Jacksonian Ideology." *American Quarterly* 27 (March 1975): 3–28.

Scherman, Tony. "Country." *American Heritage* 45, no. 7 (November 1994): 38–54.

Schlappi, Elizabeth. *Roy Acuff: The Smoky Mountain Boy.* Louisiana: Pelican Publishing Co., 1978, 1993.

Schocket, Eric. "Undercover Explorations of the 'Other Half'; or, The Writer as Class Transvestite." *Representations* 64 (Fall 1998): 109–33.

Schulian, John. "Country Music Crossbred with Country Literature." *New York Times,* 19 August 2001. http://query.nytimes.com/gst/fullpage.html?res=9C0

CE6DE163EF93AA2575BC0A9679C8B63&sec=&spon=&pagewa nted=print. Accessed 20 February 2008.

Shank, Barry. *Dissonant Identities: The Rock'n'Roll Scene in Austin, Texas.* Hanover and London: Wesleyan University Press, 1994.

Shocked, Michelle. Liner notes. *Arkansas Traveler.* Mercury/Polygram Records, 512 101–2, 1992.

Simon, Bill. "Hillbilly Center (54th St., NY) Not in Hills, But All Is Rosie." *Billboard,* 31 December 1949, 14.

Skeggs, Beverly. *Formations of Class and Gender.* London: Sage, 1997.

Skinker, Chris. Liner notes. *The Melody Ranch Girl.* Bear Family Records, BCD 15905, 1996.

Smethurst, James. "How I Got to Memphis: The Blues and the Study of American Culture." In Rubin and Melnick, *American Popular Music,* 47–64.

Smith, Ethan. "To Be Young, Gifted, and Country: Rissi Palmer Finds Her Place on the Country Music Charts." *Wall Street Journal Online,* 28 September 2007. http://online.wsj.com/public/article_print/SB119093704339641965 .html. Accessed 5 August 2008.

Smith, Sidonie. *Subjectivity, Identity, and the Body: Women's Autobiographical Practices in the Twentieth Century.* Bloomington: Indiana University Press, 1993.

Smith-Rosenberg, Carroll. "Davy Crockett as Trickster: Pornography, Liminality, and Symbolic Inversion in Victorian America." In *Disorderly Conduct: Visions of Gender in Victorian America,* 90–108. New York: Alfred A. Knopf, 1985.

Smyth, Willie J. "Early Knoxville Radio (1921–41): WNOX and the 'Midday Merry Go-Round.'" *John Edwards Memorial Foundation Quarterly* 18, no. 2 (1982): 109–15.

Snow, Hank, with Jack Ownbey. *The Hank Snow Story.* Urbana: University of Illinois Press, 1994.

Songcatcher. Dir. Maggie Greenwald. Perf. Janet McTeer, Aidan Quinn, Emmy Rossum. Lionsgate, 2001.

"Special Hank Williams Memorial Issue." *Country Song Roundup* 24 (June 1953).

Spigel, Lynn. *Make Room for TV: Television and the Family Ideal in Postwar America.* Chicago: University of Chicago Press, 1992.

Stewart, Allison. "Spring Forward, Fall Back: Freakwater Does the Two-Step around Fame and Fortune." *No Depression* 13 (Winter 1998).

Stewart, Kathleen. "Backtalking the Wilderness: 'Appalachian' Engenderings." In *Uncertain Terms: Negotiating Gender in American Culture,* ed. Faye Ginsburg and Anna Lowenhaupt Tsing, 43–56. Boston: Beacon Press, 1990.

Stewart, Kathleen. "Engendering Narratives of Lament in Country Music." In G. Lewis, *All That Glitters,* 221–25.

Stewart, Kathleen. "Nostalgia—A Polemic." *Cultural Anthropology* 3, no. 3 (1988): 227–41.

"Sunshine Sue, the Personality Queen." *Rustic Rhythm* 1, no. 1 (1957): 39.

Swihart, Kathryn. "From Near and Far: Folks Travel Hundreds of Miles to See the National Barn Dance." *Stand By!* 19 September 1936, 3.

Tharpe, Jac L. "Homemade Soap: The Sudsy Autobios of the Linsey Crowd." *Southern Quarterly* 22, no. 3 (1984): 145–57.

Thompson, Deborah J. "Searching for Silenced Voices in Appalachian Music." *GeoJournal* 65 (2006): 67–78.

Tichi, Cecelia. "Country Music, Seriously: An Interview with Bill C. Malone." In *Reading Country Music: Steel Guitars, Opry Stars, and Honky-Tonk Bars,* 296–306. Durham: Duke University Press, 1998.

Tosches, Nick. *Country: The Twisted Roots of Rock'N'Roll.* New York: Da Capo Press, 1977, 1996.

Tosches, Nick. "Emmett Miller: The Final Chapter." *Journal of Country Music* 18, no. 3 (1996): 27–37.

Tosches, Nick. "Honky Tonk." In *The Blackwell Guide to Recorded Country Music,* ed. Bob Allen, 42–69. Oxford: Blackwell Publishers, 1994.

Tosches, Nick. "Honky-Tonkin': Ernest Tubb, Hank Williams, and the Bartender's Muse." In *Country: The Music and the Musicians.* 2nd ed., Paul Kingsbury, Alan Axelrod, and Susan Costello, 152–75. New York: The Country Music Foundation and Abbeville Press, 1994.

Tosches, Nick. "The Strange and Hermetical Case of Emmett Miller." *Journal of Country Music* 17, no. 1 (1994), 39–47.

Tosches, Nick. *Where Dead Voices Gather.* Back Bay Books, 2002.

Traver, Jerome D., and Joel M. Maring. "*Stand By:* Journalistic Response to a Country Music Radio Audience." *John Edwards Memorial Foundation Quarterly* 19 (1983): 150–61.

Tritt, Travis, with Michael Bane. *Ten Feet Tall and Bulletproof: The Travis Tritt Story.* New York: Hal Leonard Corporation, 1995.

Tsuchiya, Hiroko. "'Let Them Be Amused': The Industrial Drama Movement, 1910–1929." In *Theatre for Working-Class Audiences in the United States, 1830–1980,* ed. Bruce A. McConachie and Daniel Friedman, 97–110. Westport, CT: Greenwood Press, 1985.

"Unknown Hinson: The Necks Are Red, the Trash Is White, the Collars Are Blue." *No Depression* 1 (Summer 1996): 33.

Vaillant, Derek W. "Sounds of Whiteness: Local Radio, Racial Formation, and Public Culture in Chicago, 1921–1935." *American Quarterly* 54 (March 2002): 25–66.

Van Hoof, Hubert. "Michelle Shocked Song Explanations." http://glimbo.tripod.com/derivations.htm#traveler. Accessed 10 May 2002.

Watkins, Evan. *Throwaways: Work Culture and Consumer Education.* Palo Alto: Stanford University Press, 1993.

Watson, Julia, and Sidonie Smith, eds. *De/Colonizing the Subject: The Politics of Gender in Women's Autobiography.* Minneapolis: University of Minnesota Press, 1992.

Weisberger, Jon. "Foggy Mountain New Grass Breakdown." *No Depression* 23 (Fall 1999).

Welch, Gillian. "Biography." http://www.geffen.com/almo/gillian/revival.html. Accessed 14 April 1997.

Whisnant, David. *All That Is Native and Fine: The Politics of Culture in an American Region.* Chapel Hill: University of North Carolina Press, 1983.

Whitburn, Joel. *Top Country Singles, 1944–1988.* Menomonee Falls, WI: Record Research Inc., 1989.

Williams, Hank, Jr. *Living Proof: An Autobiography.* New York: Putnam, 1979.

Williams, Michael Ann. "Home to Renfro Valley: John Lair and the Women of the Barn Dance." In Wolfe and Akenson, *Women of Country Music,* 88–108.

Williams, Raymond. *The Country and the City.* New York: Oxford University Press, 1973.

Williams, Raymond. *Marxism and Literature.* New York: Oxford University Press, 1977.

Williams, Roger M. "Hank Williams." In *Stars of Country Music: Uncle Dave Macon to Johnny Rodriguez,* ed. Bill C. Malone and Judith McCollough, 237–54. Urbana: University of Illinois Press, 1975.

Willis, Susan. "I Shop, Therefore I Am: Is There a Place for Afro-American Culture in Commodity Culture?" In *Changing Our Own Words: Essays on Criticism, Theory, and Writing by Black Women,* ed. Cheryl Wall, 173–95. New Brunswick: Rutgers University Press, 1989.

Wilson, Pamela. "Mountains of Contradictions: Gender, Class, and Region in the Star Image of Dolly Parton." *South Atlantic Quarterly* 94, no. 1 (1995): 109–34.

Wolfe, Charles K. "Clayton McMichen: Reluctant Hillbilly." *Bluegrass Unlimited* 13, no. 11 (1979): 56–61.

Wolfe, Charles K. "Davy Crockett Songs: Minstrels to Disney." In Lofaro, *Davy Crockett,* 159–90.

Wolfe, Charles K. *A Good-Natured Riot: The Birth of the Grand Ole Opry.* Nashville: Country Music Foundation and Vanderbilt University Press, 1999.

Wolfe, Charles K. *The Grand Ole Opry: The Early Years, 1925–35.* London: Old Time Music Booklet 2, 1975.

Wolfe, Charles K., and James E. Akenson, eds. *The Women of Country Music: A Reader.* Lexington: University Press of Kentucky, 2003.

Wray, Matt, and Annalee Newitz, eds. *White Trash: Race and Class in America.* New York: Routledge, 1997.

"The Wright Way." *Country Song Roundup* 34 (1954): 9.

Wynette, Tammy, with Joan Dew. *Stand By Your Man.* New York: Simon and Schuster, 1979.

Zandy, Janet. *Hands: Physical Labor, Class, and Cultural Work.* New Brunswick: Rutgers University Press, 2004.

Zandy, Janet, ed. *Liberating Memory: Our Work and Our Working-Class Consciousness.* New Brunswick: Rutgers University Press, 1994.

Zandy, Janet, ed. *What We Hold in Common: An Introduction to Working-Class Studies.* New York: Feminist Press, 2001.

Zehnbauer, Eric. "The Twang Revolution Takes Off." *Country Standard Time.* http://www1.usa1.com/~cst.twangfestCONCERT.html. Accessed 25 June 1997.

INDEX

220n47; Grand Ole Opry, 33–35, 39, 40, 43, 44, 47, 78, 81, 182; *Howdy Judge*, 213nn66–74; "Howdy, Judge" column, 35, 41, 50; minstrelsy, 52; Sam Blow character, 48; *A Story of the Grand Ole Opry*, 37, 38, 220n47; WLS, 45

Heath, Hy, 222n90

Hee Haw, 2, 169

Helms, Bobby, "Fraulein," 225n125

Hennessy, Rosemary, 208n20

Henry, John, 184, 185, 186

Hill, Faith, 203, 204, 243n13; *Fireflies*, 203; "Mississippi Girl," 2–3, 146, 200, 204; "Stealing Kisses," 203

Hill, Goldie, 217n7; Grand Ole Opry, 224n115; "Let the Stars Get in My Eyes," 91

Hill & Range Songs, Inc., 220n54

Hillbillies, "Mountaineers Love Song," 45

hillbilly/hillbillies: archetype, 7, 19, 20; comic team Lonzo and Oscar, 45; culture, 84; Decca's hillbilly series, 68; Ernest Tubb's aversion to/critique of the term *hillbilly*, 81–82, 220n57; image, and Loretta Lynn's autobiography, 124, 132; image, and Michelle Shocked, 154, 159–60; image, and mountaineer image, 19, 212n35; image, and Myrtle "Lulu Belle" Cooper, 60; masculinity, 89; masquerade, 16, 25, 30, 49, 152; performance/mode/representation and blackface performance/mode/representation, 18, 53, 154; use of term in *Billboard* into the early 1950s, 221n58; use of term as "self-mockery," 211n29; womanhood, 139

Holiday, Billie, 223n108; "Good Morning, Heartache," 106

Holyfield, Wayland, 238n59

Homer and Jethro, 12

honky-tonk: and alt.country, 15–16, 145, 146, 147, 148; angel, 5, 11; answer song, 14, 115; Bill C. Malone, 217n1; "Boys from Alabama," 238n82; and domesticity/home, 121–22, 126, 176; female artists, 225n120, 225n126; first-wave and second-wave, 13; "Heathens," 238n77; "Let There Be Rock," 169; loner, 7, 170; male artists, 13, 62; music's anxieties about its own respectability, 13; and Nashville sound, 14; and New Traditionalism, 114; persona, 5, 12; sincerity, 142; "The Southern Thing," 169, 172, 239n84; supposed autobiographical strain of, 14; and Texan "Outlaws" movement, 114; used to repre-

sent country "essence," 10. *See also* names of specific performers

hooks, bell, 225n123

Hoppenthaler, John, 193, 196, 241n150, 241n152

Horstman, Dorothy, 226n133, 226n138

Hurt, Mississippi John, 184; "John the Revelator," 240n116

Husky, Ferlin (pseud. Joe Franklin), 103, 104, 228n169; "Two Whoops and a Holler," 105

intersectionality, 5, 6, 29, 32, 201, 208n18

Irigaray, Luce, 225n123

Irwin, Catherine, 174, 188, 189, 190, 192; "Cheap Watch," 191; *End Time*, 187, 188, 189, 190, 191, 241n139; *Thinking of You*, 241n139–40. *See also* Freakwater

Jackson, Alan, 120, 145, 237n44

Jackson, Michael, 211n28

Jackson, Wanda, 105; "Fujiyama Mama," 101, 227n150

Jamup and Honey, 7, 12, 18, 38, 210n38, 234n1, 237n44; Grand Ole Opry, 1, 39–53, 65, 215n99, 217n5

Jason and the Scorchers: "Drugstore Truck Drivin' Man," 165; "Greetings from Nashville," 161

Jay, Paul, 121

Jayhawks, 166

Jennings, Shooter, 168; "Put the O Back in Country," 164

Jennings, Waylon, 114, 234n1; "Are You Sure Hank Done It This Way?," 14; *Waylon*, 230n4

Jensen, Joli, 5, 69, 70, 71, 73, 90, 218n25, 219n32, 224n112

Jim Crow, 24, 27, 28

Johnny, Angry, 160, 163, 165, 166

Johnson, Blind Willie, 184; "God Moves on the Water," 240n118; "John the Revelator," 240n116

Johnston, Max Konrad, 189

Jolsen, Al, 80

Jones, Bessie, 240n118

Jones, George, 14, 108, 127, 164, 167, 168, 209n31, 231n18; *I Lived to Tell It All*, 230n4

Journal of Country Music, 124, 212n44

Judd, Ashley, 125, 131

Judd, Naomi, 14, 123, 125, 126, 129, 130, 131, 132; *Love Can Build a Bridge*, 115, 120

Judd, Wynonna, 125, 131
Judds, 114, 120, 123, 125, 131

Kaplan, Caren, 208n18
Keillor, Garrison, 222n80
Kennan, George F., 229n183
Kern, Roger, 162
Kibler, M. Alison, 59, 216n116, 216n121
Killbillies, 160, 163; *Hankenstein,* 165
Kincaid, Bradley, 59, 61, 198, 214n91
"Knoxville Girl," 166
Krauss, Alison, 156
Kristeva, Julia, 225n123

La Chapelle, Peter, 109, 226n135, 228n170
Lair, John, 12, 59, 60, 61, 147, 216n120
Lambert, Miranda, 243n15; "Crazy Ex-Girl-friend," 146
Lange, Dorothea, 174
Lange, Jeffrey, 90, 220n47, 220n57, 224n111, 225n120
Langford, Jon, 163, 164, 165
Lejeune, Philippe, 116–17, 118, 231n8, 231n13
Lem and Martha, 54, 55
Leppert, Richard, 73, 84, 87, 88, 223n104, 223n106, 223n108
LeVan, Harold, 42
Lewis, George H., 239n85
Lewis, Jerry Lee, 166; "Great Balls of Fire," 167
Lhamon, W. T., Jr., 7, 8, 21, 28, 30, 154, 209n28, 210n9, 211n23; *Raising Cain: Blackface Performance from Jim Crow to Hip Hop,* 17, 24, 211n25
Lincoln, Abraham, 184
Lipsitz, George, 73, 84, 87, 88, 223n106, 223n108; "Rainbow at Midnight," 68
Little Dog Records, 162
Little Richard, 192
Livingston, Tamara, 148, 149
Lopez, Jennifer, *Jenny from the Block,* 207n7
loss, 126–29, 130, 132, 139, 140. *See also* desire
Lott, Eric, 7, 8, 18, 21, 23, 24, 27, 32, 39, 48, 154, 209n29; *Love and Theft,* 22
Louisiana Hayride, 68, 223n100, 224n115
Louris, Gary, 166
Louvin, Charlie, 167, 187
Louvin, Ira, 167, 187
"Lulu Belle," 60, 61, 62, 98, 114, 207n3, 213n60, 217n125
Lynn, Doolittle, 122, 124, 133, 233n49

Lynn, Loretta, 3, 15, 116, 118, 124, 125, 127, 128, 138, 143, 169, 228n162, 230n188, 233n36, 233n49, 234n71; 237n44; childhood, 129; *Coal Miner's Daughter,* 10, 112, 113, 115, 122, 123, 124, 126, 131, 132, 133, 140, 142, 232n36, 233n49; "Coal Miner's Daughter," 112, 114, 120; "Don't Come Home A'Drinkin' with Lovin' on Your Mind," 105, 112; "I'm a Honky-Tonk Girl," 112; songwriting, 112; *Still Woman Enough,* 142, 143, 234n69; "This Haunted House," 112; *Van Lear Rose,* 143, 234n72, 237n44

Macon, Uncle Dave, 45, 46, 53; "Grey Cat on a Tennessee Farm," 45
Macon Telegraph, 212n48
Maddox, Rose, 217n7, 227n153
Mahal, Taj, 157
Mahar, William, 21, 23, 24; *Behind the Burnt Cork Mask,* 209n28, 211n21
Malone, Bill, 65, 69–70, 72–73, 207n8, 214n94, 217n1, 219n30, 219n33, 224n110, 224n114, 230n2
Mancini, J. M., 212n50, 235n10
Maphis, Joe, 225n119; "Dim Lights, Thick Smoke (And Loud, Loud Music)," 92
Maphis, Rose Lee, 216n114; "Dim Lights, Thick Smoke (And Loud, Loud Music)," 92
Marchman, Houston, 236n34
masculinity, 5, 6, 7, 9, 11, 13, 15, 16, 20, 27, 32, 36, 47, 48, 59, 63–112, 115, 137, 144, 147, 151, 160–65, 166, 169, 170, 172, 173, 176, 178, 199, 205, 218n15, 219n38, 227n154, 234n1; loss, 126–29; postwar, 174
May, Elaine Tyler, 227n150; *Homeward Bound,* 218n11
McConnell, Ed, 35
McCusker, Kristine, 19, 20, 59, 60, 211n29, 214n96, 215n98, 216n114, 216n117, 216n120, 216n121, 216n123, 217n125
McDill, Bob, 238n59
McEntire, Reba, 15, 114, 120, 125, 128, 129, 131, 132, 232n36; *Reba: My Story,* 115, 131–32
McGraw, Tim, 202, 204, 243n13
McKenna, Lori, 200; "Bible Song," 242n10; *Bittertown,* 203, 204, 242n9–10; "Drinking Problem," 204; "How to Survive," 203, 204, 242n8; *The Kitchen Table Tapes,* 203; "One Man," 203; "Stealing Kisses," 203, 242n8; *Unglamorous,* 203, 204,

251; "Luke the Drifter," 89; "Move It On Over," 237n43; "My Heart Would Know," 87; "Take These Chains from My Heart," 87, 222n91; "Window Shopping," 88; "Your Cheatin' Heart," 87, 88, 99, 222n87, 222n91; "You're Gonna Change (or I'm Gonna Leave)," 88

Williams, Hank, Jr., 168; *Living Proof,* 230n4

Williams, Hank, III, 16, 160, 169, 198; "Blue Devil," 165; "Risin' Outlaw," 165, 237n56

Williams, Michael Ann, 60

Williams, Raymond, 16, 147, 151, 182, 198, 199; *The Country and the City,* 149, 150; *Marxism and Literature,* 235n17

Williams, Roger M., 222n80

Willis, Ginger, 221n68

Willis, Susan, 25, 160; "I Shop, Therefore I Am," 211n28

Wills, Roy, 18, 30

Wilson, Gretchen, 200, 205, 234n71, 243n15; "Redneck Woman," 3, 205

Wilson, Pamela, 230n2, 233n59

Wiseman, Myrtle Cooper. *See* "Lulu Belle"

Wiseman, "Scotty," 61

WLS, 20, 34, 35, 45, 59, 60, 61, 198, 207n3, 213n55, 213nn59–60

WMMN, *Family Album,* 58

WNOX, 44, 49, 215n102

Wolfe, Charles K., 18, 33, 34, 40, 209n33, 212n33

Woods, Tom, 42

working class, 3, 5, 11, 24, 32, 39, 48, 66, 68, 71, 72, 166, 171, 174, 225; audience, 12, 68, 69, 73, 198; blackface minstrelsy, 23; childhood, 94; community, 168, 194; culture, 9, 23, 60, 203; existence, 147; gender relations, 69; identity, 67; imagery, 6; listeners, 19, 53, 58; marriage, 171; men, 6, 11, 65, 71, 72, 73, 74, 76, 78, 81, 84, 86, 92, 172, 219n38; mother, 203, 204; musicians, 9; neighborhoods, 67; postwar, 82; rage, 197; social context, 118; Southern, 30, 70, 85, 87, 92; subjectivity, 162; theater, 39; urban, 27; white men, 7; whites, 32; women, 6, 44, 189, 229n183, 232n32; youth, 24

Works Progress Administration, 78

World War I, 33, 82, 223n94

World War II, 38, 44, 64, 80, 102, 123, 176, 210n5, 235n10

Wright, Johnnie, 94, 96, 229n179

WSM, 32, 33–38, 40, 41, 42, 58, 81. *See also* Grand Ole Opry; *Midnight Jamboree*

Wynette, Tammy, 15, 118, 127, 128, 129, 130, 131, 132, 133, 143, 234n70, 234n71; *Stand By Your Man,* 115, 125, 231n18; "Stand By Your Man," 120, 231n18

Yep Rock Records, 163

Yoakam, Dwight, 145

"You Are My Flower," 176

Zandy, Janet, 208n20